Peter
Francis
   oBrien, S.J.

March 27, 2001
Jersey City, N.J.

Bought
   Madison Ave.
Bookshop

Chester Himes
a life

Chester Himes

a life

James Sallis

WALKER & COMPANY NEW YORK

First published in the United States of America in 2001 by
Walker Publishing Company, Inc.;
first published in Great Britain in 2000 by
Payback Press, an imprint of Canongate Books Ltd.

Published simultaneously in Canada by Fitzhenry and Whiteside,
Markham, Ontario L3R 4T8

The chapter title on page 294, Black Ruins of My Life, is from
"The City" by C. P. Cavafy, *Collected Poems* (New Jersey:
Princeton University Press, 1992), p.28 ("Wherever I turn
I see black ruins of my life").

Library of Congress Cataloging-in-Publication Data
Sallis, James, 1944–
    Chester Himes : a life / James Sallis.
        p. cm.
    Includes index.
    ISBN 9-8027-1362-9 (hc)
        1. Himes, Chester B., 1909–84. 2. Novelists,
American—20th century—Biography. 3. Afro-
American novelists—Biography. I. Title

PS3515.I713 Z84 2000
813.'54—dc21   00-063328

Printed in the United States of America
2 4 6 8 10 9 7 5 3 1

To Lesley Himes
and in memory of Chester

Contents

Acknowledgments

I cannot, of course, thank everyone who has had a part in this book.

Like all who will come after, I owe an immense gratitude to those who, in first writing about Himes, have provided the floor we walk on: Stephen Milliken, James Lundquist, Gilbert Muller, Ed Margolies, Michel Fabre.

On a more personal level, I must thank Lesley Himes and Roslyn Targ, who have been close in spirit for many years now, and who have provided invaluable information, insight, and assistance.

Gratitude, too, to friends of Chester who took time to share with me their memories and impressions: John A. Williams, Joe Hunter, Jean Miotte, Herb Gentry, Melvin Van Peebles, and especially Constance and Ed Pearlstien.

Special appreciation is due my friend and fellow Himes enthusiast Bob Skinner, who throughout the project stood valiantly by ready to read, advise, even to ferret out the occasional recalcitrant fact. All biographers should have librarians as friends.

Similar thanks to Tish Crawford for many conversations face to face and via e-mail about Chester and his work, and to Patrick Millikin, draft reader, book finder, coffee mate, and friend extraordinaire.

Sincerest thanks to the staff of the Amistad Collection housed at my alma mater, Tulane, and to that of the Schomburg Center in Harlem.

Editorially, fond thanks to Robert Shapard, who many years ago as editor of *Western Humanities Review* published my first long essay on

Himes, and to Jamie Byng, whose encouragement and support quite literally brought this book into being.

Thanks, always, to agents Vicky Bijur and Stella Wilkins for taking care of business, running interference when necessary, and generally helping me maintain the illusion of professionalism.

Finally, thanks to Karyn, who has had to live with Chester and me, even when, as sometimes happened, Chester and I weren't getting along so well, for a year and a half of new chapters, endless revisions, self-interrogation, panic, sudden trips to New York or California, and not a little whining. Chester would have loved her.

Introduction

It is exceedingly strange to know so well a man one has never met. For a year and a half now my days have been spent in the company of Chester Himes. He had of course been with me, though not so intimately, far longer. I began reading Himes thirty years ago, first wrote of him some sixteen or seventeen years back. My own series of detective novels (one of them dedicated to his memory, in another of which Himes actually appears) began in part as homage.

I first came to Himes in the late sixties, in the wake of a newfound fascination with crime fiction. Introduced to Chandler and Hammett by Mike Moorcock while in London editing *New Worlds* magazine and having read their entire output in short order, upon returning to the States I looked about for more. On shelves at a friend's house I came across several paperbacks by Chester Himes. They were small books, wafer thin, with limp cardboard covers; a decade before, they had sold for thirty-five cents. I read them and went looking for others. As is my habit, I also tried to find out about the author of these strange, savagely comic novels, but no one seemed to know anything of him. A couple of years later the movie of *Cotton Comes to Harlem* arrived. I saw it while living in New York City, stepping over homeless folk asleep in the doorway as I came back at night to my downtown apartment.

For a time then, I didn't read Himes, and when again I felt the pull (for, perennially, his work collects me back to itself), his books had become difficult to find. Virtually all were—again—out of print. Haunting used bookstores, I unearthed ravaged copies of *For Love of Imabelle, The Crazy Kill, The Big Gold Dream*. I unearthed also, in time, *Pinktoes, If He Hollers Let Him Go*—and something titled *The Primitive*. This last, which I found and still find profoundly unsettling, certainly like nothing I had read before, I've since come to regard as one of America's great novels.

What I discovered was that Himes had a second or more accurately a first career as a "literary" writer, beginning with stories published in *Esquire* in the company of such as Hemingway, Fitzgerald, Ring Lardner, and Bertrand Russell. He had written those *Esquire* stories, moreover, while in prison. A much-acclaimed first novel was followed by two or three others. Then Chester Himes had fallen off the edge of the earth, sending back one last urgent message, *The Primitive*, a novel written not in fire, but in the glare and dead-white light of too many three o'clock mornings. No one I spoke to had ever read it.

Himes had not dropped off the face of the earth, of course, but had gone to Europe to write his detective stories, and as I read backward from them through the earlier books, then on into the two-volume autobiography, my picture of Himes changed radically. I'd begun seeing him simply as an extension of American crime fiction, one of the first great documenters of the inner city, but increasingly I came to perceive him as I do now: as America's central black writer. Himes stood squarely at the crossroad of tradition and innovation, shaking together in his mix remains of the Harlem Renaissance, the energies of newly developing genre fictions, African-American tropes, and arealist storytelling styles, the found life of the streets about him. Again and again he told his story of great promises forever gone unfulfilled, of men who perish from hunger in the shadow of statues of plenty and perish from lack of thought in the shade of great ideas, creating a literature in its absolute individuality, in its strange power and quirkiness, in its cruelty and cockeyed compassion, ineffably American.

Chester Himes was, or could be, a difficult man; he remains a difficult writer. Offering up little comfort or safe ground to the ideologue, he stood, sometimes by choice, always by inclination, at a hard right angle to the world. Nothing in *his* world is simple, nothing there can be taken for granted, ever. Neither he nor his characters fulfill our expectations. One moment likable, the next despicable, they refuse to behave as we wish them to; they are their own worst enemies as much as they are (and they are all) victims. The sources of their rage are deep, irrational, unquenchable. As readers we are, as Himes intended, forever off balance. The work gets to us. It's unsettling, disconcerting, upsetting—more *Do the Right Thing* than *The Color Purple*, as critic Gerald Houghton has put it, and as a quote from Himes's first novel, *If He Hollers Let Him Go*, demonstrates:

> Reactionaries hate the truth and the world's rulers fear it; but it embarrasses the liberals, perhaps because they can't do anything about it.

Biography at once can be, perhaps must be, an act of admiration and a betrayal. Certainly in some regard it violates its subject, distorting and simplifying, forcing complex events, thoughts, and actions into superficial patterns, seeking to sweep up thousands of shimmering, mobile, *living* moments in its nets. As biographers we take our brief from Goethe:

> For it seems to be the main object of biography—to exhibit the man in relation to the features of his time, and to show to what extent they have opposed or favored his progress; what view of mankind and the world he has formed from them, and how far he himself, if an artist, poet, or author, may externally reflect them.

Yet even Freud believed biographical truth unattainable. The biographer, he held, pledges himself to tell and to countenance lies, to become the hypocrite, to cover things up or paint them in glowing colors. "Remember that what you are told is really threefold," Nabokov warns us in *The Real Life of Sebastian Knight*, "shaped by the teller, reshaped by the listener, concealed from both by the dead man of the tale." Or as Stanislaw Lem considers in *His Master's Voice*: "With sufficient imagination one might easily write a dozen, three dozen, versions of any life, a union of sets in which the facts would be the only elements in common."

Finally, then, the biographer's brief, like that of the novelist or poet, is to construct not an imitation of the world but an alternate for it, a stand-in, an understudy, a *fictio*—from the Latin: a shaping. To do this he must not only select more or less arbitrarily from the vast array of data available but also invent structures that will hold those selections in place.

Properly speaking, biography is a subgenre of history, literary biography its bastard offspring in that it is precisely literature that forever seeks to *correct* history, to allay its indifference to the individual, its smothering generalities, what we would call in the human being its lack of affect.

"It is perhaps as difficult to write a good life as to lead one," Lytton Strachey declared. As writers we finish each book knowing we've failed yet again to bring down that vision of which we caught so many glimpses sitting alone in our rooms late at night or in the dull, repetitious purr of dawn. The whole time we biographers are at work, four years, or ten, or eighteen months, we wrestle with the angels of art and try to hold at bay the devils of history, waging war, as much as with the material given us, with "our own defenses and blocked memories and self-deceptions." That last is from Leon Edel, and it's the magnificent, sustaining example of his Henry James that I've tried to keep in mind through these months of absorption.

Time now to gather up this poor little thing from the filing cabinet atop which it's lived all these months, fattening daily, and send it out into the world.

Here, then, is my version of one man's reality, Chester Himes as I've come to know him. And yet, for all this, he remains a mystery, as we must, all of us, remain mysteries to one another. For it is in that very search, in trying to know the other, that all our art begins and ends.

It is exceedingly strange to know so little, finally, about a man with whom you have spent so much time.

Chester Himes
a life

1 Unnatural Histories

"That's my life—the third generation out of slavery,"[1] Chester Himes ended his 1976 autobiography, a book striking off in so many directions, encompassing so much, that it seems one life could never have contained all this.

Almost thirty years before, in a speech before a mixed audience at the University of Chicago on "The Dilemma of the Negro Writer in the United States," sounding remarkably like one of his models, Faulkner, Himes had written:

> There is an indomitable quality within the human spirit that cannot be destroyed; a face deep within the human personality that is impregnable to all assaults . . . we would be drooling idiots, dangerous maniacs, raving beasts—if it were not for that quality and force within all humans that cries "I will live."[2]

Himes knew a great deal about such assaults—about assaults of every sort. Champion Ishmael Reed[3] reminds us that by the time Himes reached the age of nineteen, he'd suffered more misfortune than most people experience in a lifetime. Already Himes had survived his parents' contempt and acrimony for one another, his father's slow slide into failure's home plate, his mother's crippling blend of pride and self-hatred, the childhood blinding of brother Joe for which he felt responsible, subterranean life among Cleveland's gamblers, hustlers, and high rollers, and, finally, a forty-foot plunge down an elevator shaft that crushed vertebrae, shattered bones, and, though he recovered, left him in a Procrustean brace for years and in pain for the remainder of his life. He'd go on to survive eight years in a state prison, early acclaim as a writer followed by attacks and, far worse, indifference, an ever-mounting sense of failure and frustration, tumultuous affairs leading in one case almost to murder, and, as Himes never lets us forget, a lifetime of pervasive, inescapable racial prejudice.

Hardly a representative life? Actually, "for all its inconsistencies, its contradictions, its humiliations, its triumphs, its failures, its tragedies, its hurts, its ecstasies and its absurdities,"[4] it is.

In prison Himes had come to believe that people will do anything, absolutely anything. "Why should I be surprised when white men cut out some poor black man's nuts, or when black men eat the tasty palms of white explorers?"[5] This belief, along with his own inner turmoil, accounts in large part for the level of violence and abrupt shifts of plot in his work, not to mention the absurd comedy, that so distinguish it. We grow to expect sudden desperate acts from characters who in fact often seem little more than a series of such acts strung together. Pianos and drunken preachers may fall from the sky, children may be fed from troughs like barnyard animals, stolen automobile wheels may roll on their own through most of Harlem, precipitating a chain of unrelated, calamitous events. In Himes's absurd world, Aristotelian logic holds no purchase; neither characters nor readers may rely on cause and effect. We can't anticipate the consequences of acts, have no way to predict what might be around the next corner, on the next page. It could be literally anything. So we're forever off balance, handholds having turned to razors, cups of wine to blood. We look out from eyes filled with a nebulous, free-floating fear that never leaves us. We can depend on nothing, expect anything. And nothing is safe.

Much like his work, Himes's life is filled with contradictions and uncertainties, sudden turns, stabs of violence, dark centers at the heart of light. In his time he was no easy man to know; time's filters haven't changed that. There is so *much* of the life, so many things done, so many places lived, so many apparent selves and so rich an internal life, that, every bit as much as his fiction, Himes's life seems always overblown, exaggerated, *too* vivid—as though all experience has been rendered down to one single dark, rich stock. One often feels that it is only the centripetal force of the tensions within him that keeps Himes's world from flying wholly apart. He seems a man who must always work everything out for himself and by himself, creating self and world anew with each effort at understanding, "remaining always (in critic Gilbert Muller's words) radical and unforgiving."[6]

Whatever they and their jacket notes claim, the majority of writers lead dull lives. They spend much of their lives alone in rooms staring at blank pages or half-filled screens. When not in those rooms, they wander half-lost about the house, quarrel with wives and lovers, drink, worry about their work going out of print or not finding a publisher, read new books to see who might be getting a leg up on them, share with other writers complaints over the horrible state of publishing.

Himes's life, on the other hand, is at least as fascinating as his fiction.

Autobiographical elements, of course, even appropriations of entire lives, are common in literature. Zuckerman is Roth in a funhouse mirror, Henry or Mr. Bones opens his mouth to let out John Berryman's words, Joyce cocoons his childhood in the guise of Stephen Daedalus: artful dodgers all. So one hesitates to insist too closely upon the link between writer and written. Perhaps especially in the case of Himes one hesitates. His late memoirs are rife with conflation and confabulation, highly suspect. Memory at best is an uncertain instrument, and the two volumes of autobiography Himes wrote when well past sixty resound with errors of fact, skewed sequences, even incorrect dates for central experiences. Nor does Himes ever back away from adorning fact, sending it out dressed in Sunday best or in rags according to his need, so that often the books are more documents of his emotions and reactions, of states of mind, than they are a record of the life lived. By selection and emphasis, then, the memoirs become as fictive in their own way as his novel *The Third Generation*, which in turn seems as much masked autobiography as fiction. And who is this writer, so much like Himes yet clearly invented, darting and skittering and peering out through the pages of *The Primitive*?

When Himes spoke of *The Third Generation* as his "most dishonest novel,"[7] it's just this manifest use of fact to which he may have been referring, this sense that he had failed in some elementary manner the mandates of fiction. Here Himes is writing so close to his own life that only crawl spaces remain.

Himes's life and fiction seem uniquely linked, then, if in complex ways, and his work, for all its apparent diversity, uniquely of a piece.

Chester Himes was no great thinker, never claiming a place among intellectuals. With a handful of exceptions, notably his 1948 speech at the University of Chicago, whenever he touched on ideas he spoke in commonplaces, and often as not what he shows in his work may subvert what he says. He *was*, however, a marvelous observer and prodigious inventor, working by instinct towards attainment of discoveries and a singular vision irreducible to mere ideas.

Himes could be shockingly *un*observant, even unmindful, of his own life and motives. Repeatedly, he let himself drift or be drawn into impossible situations. There was about him often a baffling passivity, a disengagement, that reminds us he spent formative adult years in prison and clashes oddly with the man's obvious passion. Again and again he voiced astonishment at actions or inactions that led (quite predictably, we should have thought) to disaster. Yet in his work he took close notice of the world from perspectives rarely encountered, convincing us with the sheer physicality of his writing, spinning out scenes we've never read before. When Himes writes of Harlem, you see the cars sunk like elephants onto tireless front wheels, cafés with hand-lettered signs and hustlers in tight bunches on corners; smell rotting garbage, sweat, bad grease, the sweet stench of pomades. When he shows Bob Jones and Kriss awakening in *If He Hollers Let Him Go* and *The Primitive,* respectively, *you* feel what they feel, all the fear, self-hatred, and confusion beating at the inner walls of selves.

Critic James Lundquist has called the opening chapter of *Blind Man with a Pistol,* with its hundred-year-old "black Mormon" advertising for a new wife to keep the number at twelve, with its stinking stewpot of chicken's feet and chitterlings and feeding troughs for children, "without exaggeration . . . one of the strangest in American literature."[8] The final scene of the same book, with Himes's once-powerful detectives Grave Digger Jones and Coffin Ed Johnson standing by helplessly shooting rats as full-scale riot breaks around them, is little less strange or memorable.

An hour later Lieutenant Anderson had Grave Digger on the radio-phone. "Can't you men stop that riot?" he demanded.

"It's out of hand, boss," Grave Digger said.

"All right, I'll call for reinforcements. What started it?"

"A blind man with a pistol."

"What's that?"

"You heard me, boss."

"That don't make any sense."

"Sure don't."[9]

In the second volume of his autobiography, *My Life of Absurdity*, Himes describes "a painting I had seen in my youth of black soldiers clad in Union Army uniforms down on their hands and knees viciously biting the dogs the Southern rebels had turned on them, their big white dangerous teeth sinking into the dogs' throats while the dogs yelped futilely."[10] That painting has always seemed profoundly emblematic of Himes's work. The terrible ambivalence of the black's place in society, Himes's own bitterness and rage, elements of graphic violence and *opéra bouffe*—this brief description of a painting seen fleetingly in youth describes as well four decades of work from one of America's most neglected and misunderstood major writers.

In *Cakes and Ale*, Somerset Maugham summarized the literary vocation thus:

I began to meditate on the writer's life. It is full of tribulation. First he must endure poverty and the world's indifference; then, having achieved a measure of success, he must submit with a good grace to its hazards. He depends upon a fickle public. He is at the mercy of journalists who want to interview him and photographers who want to take his picture, of editors who harry him for copy and tax gatherers who harry him for income tax . . . of agents, publishers, managers, bores, admirers, critics, and his own conscience. But he has one compensation. Whenever he has anything on his mind, whether it be a harassing reflection, grief at the death of a friend, unrequited love, wounded pride, anger at the treachery of someone to whom he has shown kindness, in short any emotion or any perplexing thought, he has only to put it down in black and white, using it as the theme of a story or the decoration of an essay, to forget all about it. He is the only free man.[11]

Chester Himes never forgot anything, least of all his pride and anger. At no time during his life did poverty and the world's indifference remove themselves far from his side. Chester Himes was never a free man.

Chester Bomar Himes was born in Jefferson City, Missouri, the state capital, on July 29, 1909, "across the street from the entrance to

Lincoln Institute, where my father, Professor Joseph Sandy Himes, taught blacksmithing and wheelwrighting as head of the Mechanical Department."[12] Chester was the youngest of three brothers: Eddie, eight years his senior; Joseph Jr., with whom Chester became in youth inseparable, but one. No original birth certificate survives; in April of 1942, offering as documentation a family record of birth (most likely a family bible) and WPA employment records, Himes applied for and received a "delayed or special" certificate.

Part of a network of land-grant Negro schools throughout the South, Lincoln Institute's curriculum was split into two parts, agricultural and mechanical; today's A&M colleges retain this nomenclature. Many of these colleges occupied campuses of formerly white schools. Alcorn College in Mississippi, for instance, where Joseph Sandy Himes later taught, moved onto a campus vacated by the state university's relocation to Oxford, where the latter became known as Ole Miss ("made famous by William Faulkner and James Meredith," Himes writes in a typical remark[13]). Other such facilities were ramshackle aggregations of buildings. Most were rurally located. Himes remembered his father quoting Booker T. Washington on the subject of these schools: "Let down your buckets where you are."

Lincoln Institute, founded in 1866 with $6,000 contributed by regiments of Negro volunteers from the Civil War, by 1914 had an enrollment of 435. Benjamin F. Allen's presidency from 1902 to 1918 brought marked physical improvement, including a central heating system and, in 1908, wiring of all campus buildings for electricity, as well as new emphasis on students' cultural development. A portrait of the 1912 faculty shows and lists "Joseph S. Himes, blacksmithing." His annual salary is given as $700. In the Jefferson City Directory this entry appears: "Himes, Joseph S (col Estella B) instructor Lincoln Inst, r 710 Lafayette."

Jefferson City at that time had a population of around 15,000 and covered an area just under four square miles, with twenty-three miles of paved streets. A 1904 ordinance set the city speed limit at nine miles an hour. The *Jefferson City Post* in 1908 wrote of an auto trip from Kansas City to Jefferson City in an astonishingly brief fourteen hours.

Himes, who was to become the chronicler of America's great dispossessed, began not in poverty, then, but in a black middle class that few Americans even suspect existed at the time. Joseph Sandy Himes was, by his own standards and those of the community at large, a man of substantial prospects.

Son of a slave, Joseph Sandy Himes never knew his father's first name, knew only that he had been bought off the slave block by a man named Heinz or Himes who trained him as a blacksmith. The end of the Civil War found Joseph's father in his mid-twenties and a father of four. With little real choice, he remained on his former master's plantation but after a quarrel with an overseer, whom he almost certainly attacked, perhaps killed, he fled, abandoning his first family.

Second wife Mary, herself an ex-slave from Georgia, bore him five children before dying of consumption. Joseph Sandy, Himes's father, was the middle child, born in North Carolina, fourteen at the time of Mary's death. Working at a variety of menial jobs, he put himself through South Carolina's Claflin College; he may also have attended Boston Mechanical Institute.

Now he taught metal trades, blacksmithing, and wheelwrighting and was called Professor Himes. At one college he also taught Negro history from texts that Chester wondered about but never saw again. There's something Hephaestian about descriptions of Joseph: short, broad-shouldered and muscular, barrel chest set squarely on bowed legs. He had dark blue eyes, an ellipsoidal skull, and a large hooked nose that both his wife and son Chester referred to as Arabic. Joseph Sandy seems to have been an artisan of great skill. From *The Third Generation*:

> He was a fine blacksmith and wheelwright. His students had built some of the best carriages and wagons seen in that city. He could make the most elaborate andirons and coal tongs and gates and lampposts imaginable. He had made jewelry and lamps and dishes from gold and silver. He was an artist at the forge and anvil. There was practically nothing he couldn't forge from metal.[14]

Almost certainly it was Joseph's ambition that attracted Estelle to him. In all other ways, physically, emotionally, in their background, they were markedly unalike. Himes spoke in later years of his father's slave mentality, "which accepts the premise that white people knew best," whereas mother Estelle "hated all manner of condescension from white people."[15] This contrast of attitudes was to establish in Himes networks of ambivalence extending to virtually every facet of his life. Initially, though, Estelle admired Joseph for the distance he had traveled; his by-the-bootstraps edification echoed her own family's self-elevation through hard work and determination. And, always, Estelle Bomar was a great seer not of what is but of what could be, a woman who, had she read Wallace Stevens, might have adopted "Let be be finale of seem" as her creed. In Joseph Sandy she saw not a simple teacher of practical skills. She saw a future dean, an administrator. Unfortunately Joseph had progressed as far as he was ever likely to go, and Estelle's relentless pushing for his advancement served only to cause him difficulties with superiors and to open marital rifts that with the years became unbreachable, till finally both he and the marriage broke on that wheel.

Estelle always felt she'd married beneath her, and in the last analysis believed the Negro colleges themselves demeaning. She was being held back by circumstance, by Joseph's lack of a resolve to match her own, and if she did not take steps, that same waywardness would claim her sons. Estelle pushed ever harder. "She could make allowances if he were a success."[16] She and Joseph quarreled bitterly again and again, endlessly, as young Chester and his brothers looked on "whimpering and trembling in terror."[17]

"I want my children to look like me," he muttered.

"So they can grow up handicapped and despised?"

"Despised!" His face took on a lowering look. "What do you mean, despised? I suppose you think I'm handicapped and despised?"

"Aren't you?" The question startled him. "Can't you see," she went on, "I want the children to have it better, not just be common pickaninnies."

"Pickaninnies!" Her thoughtless remark cut him to the quick. "That's better than being white men's leavings."

She whitened with fury. It was the second time he'd slurred her parents but this time was all the more hurting because they were dead, and she revered their memory. Striking back, she said witheringly, "You're nothing but a shanty nigger and never will be anything else. And you would love nothing better than to have my children turn out to be as low and common as yourself."[18]

With the years, giving up on high expectations she'd had for his father, Estelle seems to have transferred those expectations, and ultimately her profound disappointment as well, onto Chester.

In any account of Himes's life, it's at this point—in family recollections, biographical sketches, in Himes's novel *The Third Generation*—that Joseph begins to fade away. He moves from one job to another, each a retreat, each a notch or two down on the jack; he ends up doing manual labor, waiting tables, janitoring. Ghetto life in St. Louis and Cleveland completes the rift between parents. The children drift away. With Estelle very near madness, the parents are divorced.

It's difficult to assess to what degree Joseph's defeat arose internally, from lack of willfulness, some failure of will; which from his limited background and always tenuous position as a minimally educated black man in white society; and which from the pride and caprice of wife Estelle. More than once her refusal to mix with other blacks, her insistence upon being treated as though she were white, her confrontations with neighbors, college peers, and shopkeepers, led to a compromise in Joseph's position, even to loss of a job. Broader social factors were at work here as well. Increased segregation led to fewer opportunities for Negroes to improve their lot, as Estelle's parents had done, as merchants and in general service to whites. Meanwhile, increasing urbanization, industrialization, and rapidly advancing technology were well on the way to rendering trades such as those Joseph taught obsolete.

With ongoing, ever more outright marital discord, with the dominolike series of retreats, and finally with his inability to support his family by manual work, all he can attain to after the move North, Joseph's spirit falters and fails. He becomes the very image of the black man ground down, unable to care for his family. We know from his early history that Joseph once had great resolve. We know that he was a hard worker, a skilled artisan, a dedicated teacher. We know from Chester's descriptions that Joseph for many years possessed considerable personal dignity and a pride that if not on the gargantuan order of his wife's was equally manifest. ("Only his wife could make him feel inferior."[19]) And with what we know of family dynamics we recognize the emotional balance Joseph must have had, and the emotional expenditures he must have made, continually to counterbalance Estelle's excesses and bring the family back to an even keel. Finally Joseph seems to have exhausted his personal capital— seems to have been used up. To Estelle, this was proof of what she had suspected all along. God knows she'd done what *she* could to help this man make something more of himself. All to no avail.

An octoroon with hazel or gray eyes, aquiline nose, and straight auburn hair, Estelle Bomar looked "like a white woman who had suffered a long siege of illness."[20] Often Estelle seems, from accounts, a woman comprised entirely of adjectives: genteel, churchgoing, cultured, prideful, proper, driven, ambitious. She spoke constantly of their heritage and drilled her sons in the necessity of living up to it while squeezing the bridges of their noses to keep them from becoming flat. If Joseph's mind shaped itself around coals of accommodation and melioration, then Estelle's danced over flames of indignation and impatience. In some manner, hers was the ultimate Republican dream: to re-create what never existed. In another, or certainly it must have seemed so to her, she was doing what had to be done—at that time, given that history. Estelle, like her son Chester, possessed a talent for living as though events that had not yet occurred, but that should occur, already had. Chester often seemed to catch on to things twenty or thirty years before anyone else did. Speaking of the Watts riots in the sixties, he remarked how surprising it was that they'd waited so long to happen.

Look how far we've come with our superior blood and breeding, Estelle told her sons in a kind of litany. And it's true that all three went on to great achievements, even if Chester in later years wrote Carl Van Vechten: "As I look back now, I feel that much of my retardation as a writer has been due to a subconscious (and conscious and deliberate) desire to escape my past. All mixed up no doubt with the Negro's desire for respectability. It brought a lot of confusion to my mind."[21] This fundamental conflict within himself—of black versus white values, but just as importantly of patrician versus egalitarian— became perhaps the central theme in Himes's life.

Estelle's accounts of her background, of that heritage she held so important, changed with time, elaborated and edited in ways reminiscent of her son's later memoirs. Any narrative, after all, whether oral history, memoir, or fiction, takes shape from what, among countless possibilities, is chosen: what foregrounded, what passed over quickly. Memory, too, is a kind of storyteller, often more poet than reporter, selecting and rearranging details to correspond to some image we have of ourselves, or simply to make a better story.

Estelle's grandmother was born either to an Indian squaw or African princess, depending on when the story was told, and to an Irish overseer. Malinda, Estelle's mother, light-skinned like herself, grew up to become handservant to a Carolina doctor named Cleveland who traced his own heritage back through a Revolutionary War general to British aristocracy. Despite laws forbidding literacy to slaves, Malinda was taught to read, perhaps by her master's daughter. Malinda in turn gave birth to three children, two of them quite likely sired by Dr. Cleveland, the third by an Indian slave. Following the Civil War, Malinda married Chester Bomar, "a tall fair white-looking man with a long blond beard,"[22] himself the issue of an octoroon and master John Earl Bomar.

Chester, Malinda, and Malinda's three children lived in Spartanburg, South Carolina, on land ceded them by Chester's former master. Chester apprenticed as a brick mason while Malinda worked as a wet nurse and took in washing. Selling their land three years later, using money from the Freedman's Bureau for transportation, they moved to Dalton, Georgia, where Chester worked as a stonemason. Within two years they relocated again, this time to Atlanta, hoping for steadier work. Chester there fell ill, and upon his recovery the family returned to Spartanburg, bringing with them three new children, Estelle, the youngest, born in February 1874. Chester and son Tom set up as builders, counting among their achievements the region's first large cotton mills. They worked fiercely, every Bomar pitching in to do his part, pushing past setbacks, persevering, and by 1890 the family was well established in the local Negro bourgeoisie. Chester served his church as deacon, superintendent of the Sunday school and financial adviser.

This bourgeoisie was a new thing in the world, and like most new things, fragile. Years later Chester Himes would say of fellow black Americans that "The face may be the face of Africa, but the heart has the beat of Wall Street."[23] He would spend much of his life alternately courting and railing against middle-class white values, an exemplar of double consciousness as described by W. E. B. Du Bois,

> this sense of always looking at one's self through the eyes of others ... One ever feels his twoness,—an American, a Negro; two souls, two thoughts, two unreconciled strivings; two warring ideals in one dark body, whose dogged strength alone keeps it from being torn asunder.[24]

Blacks, Du Bois insists, are forced by reason of their African ancestry to see themselves as second-class citizens, inferior in every way: physically, intellectually, culturally. Having accepting that, then and only then are they allowed the privilege of seeing themselves as American citizens.

But it's at just such cultural crossroads, just such stress points, that cracks may reach down to our deepest wells of creativity. Jazz developed in New Orleans because of that city's uniquely rich cultural gumbo. Thus in *The African-American Novel* Bernard Bell points out that conflicts between black culture and white society led to crippling destructive tensions, as well as to intensely creative ones, in black people and their communities—as they did in Chester Himes himself. It's difficult, of course, to elicit one from the other, to assess how these opposing forces counterbalance; to say, for instance, to what degree the creative response to the destructive is that and only that. To some extent jazz developed as a continuation of banned African drums, but also as a subversion of the white society's music. Recent critics such as Houston Baker (*Blues, Ideology, and Afro-American Literature: A Vernacular Theory*) argue for the roots of African-American literature in blues, which wasn't a way of immersing yourself in your troubles, as Joe Williams once remarked, but a way of getting outside them. Others such as Henry Louis Gates (*The Signifying Monkey: A Theory of Afro-American Literary Criticism*) hold out for signifying, an African language art that foregrounds ironic and parodic rhetorical elements, dissembling's first cousin.

The creative thrust, then, may be simply a reflexive response to the destructive; it may be an attempt to distance oneself from that destructive element, to hold it at arm's length, as in dissembling and signifying; or it may strive to purge the destructive through catharsis. In Himes at various points, sometimes in the same work, even the same sentence, we see all three motives at work. He was a man of unresolvable tensions and contradictions, a man whose greatest strengths—as a writer—lay precisely where those conflicts remain manifest and unresolved.

Unlike her son, Estelle Bomar Himes kept well hidden any conflicts or second thoughts she may have entertained concerning the new bourgeoisie. Early piano lessons earned her a place at what was then the South's most elite school for young black women, Scotia Seminary in Concord, North Carolina. Following graduation "by virtue of her literary attainments and good moral behavior,"[25] she stayed on for two years as a teacher, though apparently taking time off for further study at the Philadelphia branch of the New England Conservatory of Music. Both her social status and religious upbringing fueled what was essentially a missionary zeal: she felt it her duty to spread the good word, to help in uplifting the more unfortunate of her race. Estelle pursued that duty in North and South Carolina public schools, the North Carolina School for the Deaf, Dumb and Blind, and at Tuskegee Institute in Alabama. In 1901, age twenty-seven, she married Joseph Sandy Himes.

Our sympathies flow to Estelle at the same moment we despise her elitism and (not to swallow the word) her racism. For her color, her sex, and her time, she was remarkably well educated. Few men of color and far fewer women had her education or advantages. Estelle had a dream: she saw what could be. Like Malcolm, she also saw what marshaling of will and personal sacrifice would be necessary to attain that dream. There were many like her, rarely heard from. Few black men or women at the time refused to say what was expected, to say *these* things instead. Negroes in America had in fact developed dissembling—saying one thing and meaning another—into an art; this was a primary mask of double consciousness. Estelle did not so much defy conventions as she steadfastly ignored them, believing that social status should be awarded not on the basis of race but of refinement and culture. It must have occurred to her at some point that this was but another guise of the very thing she fought against. But Estelle, remember, was a master at revision, forever cutting and pasting the paragraphs of her life.

Chester Himes rarely could bring himself to say what was expected. And he always refused to dissemble. For forty years we would hear Himes's voice, dead on, even when attacks contrived to silence him, when repeatedly his books fell out of print, when we stopped our ears and tried not to listen. Himes pointed unflinchingly at the situation of blacks in America, demanding response. And if his truthtelling often made blacks as uncomfortable as it made whites, well then: he was his mother's son in every way.

While Estelle sat learning the ways of noblesse oblige at Scotia Seminary, Southern legislators were passing laws that effectively fenced in and disenfranchised their Negro citizens.

In the period from Civil War's end to the first years of the new century, the U.S. elevated itself to a global power and bisected into the divided self—great wealth at one pole, great need at the other—still at the heart of its troubles. Robber barons like Morgan, Carnegie, and Rockefeller amassed obscene reservoirs of wealth while the populace at large fell ever deeper into poverty and thirst. Our founders' vision of an enlightened aristocracy of gentlemen rulers narrowed to a squint of wealthy privilege. Today, living in Hamilton's world, we go on espousing Jeffersonian ideals.

Though labor, beast of a million backs as it was, proved slow to organize, unions lumbered and stammered into being during this period, among them the Noble Order of Knights of Labor (1886), Samuel Gompers's American Federation of Labor (1889) and Eugene V. Debs's American Railway Union (1893). Crusading journalists like Ida Tarbell, Lincoln Steffens, and Jacob Riis, along with novels such as Stephen Crane's *Maggie, a Girl of the Streets*, Frank Norris's *The Octopus*, and Upton Sinclair's *The Jungle*, chronicled abuses of big business, government corruption, and worker exploitation. The tenor of the time shifted toward union and socialist ideals: that workers should control the means of production and profits be equitably distributed; that labor have fair representation; that any collective, properly united and with dynamic leadership, becomes a political force.

The most blatantly leftist of these new unions, in counterpoint to the conservative AFL (which excluded Negroes), was the Industrial Workers of the World, the Wobblies, whose founders included Eugene V. Debs, then head of the Socialist Party, miner "Big Bill' Haywood and Mary Harris "Mother" Jones, seventy-five-year-old organizer for United Mine Workers. Eventually wartime anti-Communist sentiments destroyed the IWW, but for the ten years of its life it served as a beacon for the workingman and suffered the full might of antiunion forces, including 1915's collusive execution of the now-legendary Joe Hill.

The Negro agenda overlapped labor's at select points while remaining discrete, as with Venn diagrams. The dominant black voice of the time was that of accommodation as represented by Booker T. Washington:

> To those of my race who depend on bettering their condition in a foreign land or who underestimate the importance of cultivating friendly relation with the Southern white man, who is their next door neighbor, I would say, "Cast down your bucket where you are . . ."
>
> The wisest among my race understand that the agitation of questions of social equality is the extremest of folly.[26]

Washington, born a slave and educated in the wake of Reconstruction reforms, bespoke a transliteration of middle-class values: hard work, deference to social forms, elevation through manners, education, and restraint; a doctrine that not only accepted but in fact, with its emphasis on doing one's best in a time of limited options, advocated the status quo, acknowledging individual and collective weakness. The accommodationists' advocacy of craft and agriculture, too, was sadly out of step with economic realities in this age of rapid industrialization and urbanization—as we witness in Joseph Sandy's life.

W. E. B. Du Bois stood in direct opposition to Washington's voice of accommodation. Northern-born, an undergraduate at Fisk University in the South where, encountering uninured the daily insults of racial discrimination, he grew ever angrier, Du Bois received his Ph.D. from Harvard in 1895. In 1905 he helped organize the Niagara Movement, committed to wresting leadership of the Negro community from accommodationists such as Washington and to denouncing persistently at every turn and opportunity the specter of white prejudice.

The growth of racism in the early years of the century, this move toward untying the promises of Reconstruction, encouraged development of Negro institutions and revived white interest, as during abolitionist times, in joining the fight for racial justice. In the century's first decade, 754 Negro lynchings occurred.

Plessy v. Ferguson proved the watershed. Arrested for sitting in an all-white railroad coach, a seven-eighths-Caucasian Negro appealed to a Supreme Court whose earlier ruling held that companies controlling 98 percent of the sugar business did not constitute a monopoly, and who had jailed striking workers for restraint of trade, thereby corrupting the Fourteenth Amendment, originally meant to protect the rights of slaves, to protect business interests. If separation of races stamps the colored race with a badge of inferiority, this court ruled, then it is "solely because the colored race chooses to put that construction upon it," introducing not only the pernicious principle "separate but equal" but also the far more deadly sanction of doublethink: if those *others* are poor/sick/deprived, then surely it's because they somehow *choose* to be. It's *their* problem. So with a blow are all Reconstruction's gains upended, thus is divisiveness given not only local habitation and name, but a pedigree our nation will overcome legally only sixty years later.

With this imprimatur, every former Confederate state rushed to enact "separate but equal" laws, sending Jim Crow to dance in gay abandon in the streets. Separate railroad cars became separate waiting rooms, then separate entrances, even separate windows. Shadowy fears of black men having sex with white women were everywhere exploited by those who had or desired power. Populist efforts to unite poor white with poor black, particularly in the South, were undermined by land and business owners driving in the chock of fear of black usurpation of jobs, locustlike hordes of black children, black economic power. Restrictive registration laws such as poll taxes and literacy requirements kept blacks away from ballot boxes. Beatings and lynchings were another great, time-honored discourager.

James Weldon Johnson held the great divide in African-American history to be that of the conflict between integration into a biracial society and withdrawal into separatism. Coopting white impulses toward racial justice spurred on by the time's flagrant racism, and believing with Johnson that isolationism denied an inevitable economic interdependence, the Niagara Movement shaped itself into the NAACP. In 1909, the year Chester Himes was born, W. E. B. Du Bois joined in founding this biracial organization, for whose journal *The Crisis* (in which Chester would later publish) he served as editor for a quarter century.

One result of racial unrest and Jim Crow was a mass exodus of poor blacks north and west trying desperately for better circumstances. All too often these better circumstances took the form of overcrowded ghettos with ramshackle housing, menial work when there was work at all, enmity from immigrant groups and other poor whites who feared their ever-tenuous footholds might be arrogated, the beginnings of inner-city despair. Race riots erupted north and south; the cities seethed.

One of the worst of the riots took place in East St. Louis in the summer of 1917, five years before Himes's family moved there, primarily because of white fear of a massive influx of Negroes from the South. Both the Democrats, courting poor whites, and unions, anticipating that Negroes might be brought in as strike breakers, played on this basic fear. For several days, as police and National Guardsmen stood by—and, some said, participated—fires were set, freight cars overturned, people beaten or shot down in the street. Whites set black homes ablaze and shot those who fled, throwing some back into the burning shacks, others into the river. "The bodies of the dead negroes," one eyewitness testified, "were thrown into a morgue like so many dead hogs."[27] At least a hundred were killed, perhaps 750 seriously wounded, three hundred buildings and forty-four railroad cars destroyed.

The riots had begun when on the night of July 1, an automobile (some said two) raced through the Negro section of East St. Louis firing indiscriminately into homes. Negroes rallied at the prearranged signal of the church bell at midnight and marched armed into the streets where they were met by a carload of policemen. An argument broke out, with a volley of shots fired into the car before it sped away, one officer killed immediately, another dying shortly thereafter. Soon mobs of whites and blacks clashed everywhere.

The report of a special committee convened by Congress to investigate the riots offers a glossary of exploitation, lawlessness, and subhuman conditions in the Negro ghettos.

During the year 1917 between 10,000 and 12,000 negroes came from the Southern States to seek work at promised high wages in the industries of St. Clair County. They swarmed into the railroad stations on every train, to be met by their friends who formed reception committees and welcomed them to the financial, political and social liberty which they had been led to believe Illinois guaranteed. They seldom had more than enough money to exactly defray their transportation, and they arrived dirty and hungry. They stood around the street corners in homesick bundles, seeking shelter and hunting work.[28]

Responsibility, the committee held, rested on the railroads and manufacturers who had lured the workers here with unrealistic promises, and on corrupt politicians, unscrupulous real estate agents, and landlords who took advantage of them once they arrived. The Negroes gravitated of necessity to "unsanitary sections" where they existed in "the squalor of filthy cabins" and fell inevitably into drunkenness and crime.

Notice of many kinds was being served by the riots in East St. Louis, soon to be echoed in cities all about. Underscoring the appalling conditions of Negro life in the ghettos, these riots gave troth to the volatile anger growing in those communities. No longer would violence against Negroes be met docilely. From now on Negroes, many having served their country in the war and returned home with new experiences, new attitudes, and a new sense of self, would fight back. As Harlem Renaissance poet Claude McKay wrote of the later riots:

> If we must die, let it not be like hogs
> Hunted and penned in an inglorious spot,
> While round us bark the mad and hungry dogs,
> Making their mock at our accursed lot.
>
> If we must die, o let us nobly die,
> So that our precious blood may not be shed
> In vain . . .[29]

1901: Joseph and Estelle join the faculty at Georgia State College, Savannah. Joseph teaches blacksmithing, wheelwrighting, occasionally a history course. Estelle teaches English composition and music. Here their first son, Edward, is born. Apparently Estelle lobbies among the light-skinned black elite for an administrative position for her husband. This fails, and they move again to Greensboro.

1906: Joseph moves up to teaching his usual trades at the Lincoln Institute, Jefferson City, Missouri. It's a more prestigious position but, losing her social contacts, Estelle feels isolated. Here, two years later, the couple's second son, Joseph, Jr., is born, and on July 29 the following year, Chester. Estelle had wanted a daughter, and until he was six or more dressed Chester, as did Rilke's mother, in girl's clothing. Estelle, with only her children to occupy her, plunges into whatever cultural activities are available and spurs on her husband's ambitions. Complaining of their poor speech, Estelle keeps the boys apart from neighbors' children.

1913: Joseph Sandy resigns his post. Reasons are problematic. Joseph's ambition, along with his wife's superior attitude and constant canvassing for position, may have alienated colleagues. Perhaps Joseph began to see his limits. In Himes's *The Third Generation* the protagonist's father resigns upon learning that a younger man who specializes in automobile mechanics is about to be made dean.

Whatever the reasons, the world is catching up with Joseph Sandy.

Now after a brief relocation to Cleveland, the family moved, south again, to Alcorn College in Mississippi. The site had been occupied originally by Oakland College, a school for whites established in 1830 by the Presbyterian Church and shut down at the beginning of the Civil War. (The first degree issued by any Mississippi college was conferred there in 1831.) After the war the facility was sold to the state and renamed in honor of the state's governor; in 1878, in accordance with 1862's Morril Act, it became a land-grant college, Alcorn Agricultural and Mechanical. Himes gives in *The Third Generation* a fine account of the family's Mississippi arrival.

They moved like a boat down a shallow river of darkness beneath a narrow roof of fading twilight. As the road deepened, roots of huge trees sprang naked from the banks like horrible reptilian monsters. Now high overhead the narrow strip of purple sky turned slowly black . . .

The mules moved down the tunnel of darkness with surefooted confidence as if they had eyes for the night. They knew the road home. Professor Taylor tied the reins to the dashboard and gave them their head. It was so dark he couldn't see his hand before his eyes. The black sky was starless. As they moved along the old sunken road the dense odor of earth and stagnation and rotting underbrush and age reached out from the banks and smothered them. It was a lush, clogging odor compounded of rotten vegetation, horse manure, poisonous nightshades and unchanged years. Soldiers of the Confederacy had walked this road on such a night following the fall of Vicksburg, heading for the nearby canebrakes.

The college provided a spacious house for which Joseph built much of the furniture; Estelle even had a servant for cooking and cleaning. As at Lincoln she kept the children apart from neighbors. She gave music lessons in her home and, since there was no elementary school for blacks, taught the children herself. Nonetheless, she grew restive. Alcorn College was set deep in the rural South, far from any city or town of appreciable size, accessible by gravel roads cutting through farms and sharecropper fields, and there simply *was* no cultural life. The boys, on the other hand, seem to have been quite happy at Alcorn, and Chester always remembered the period fondly. They were enthralled when, in 1917, Joseph bought an old Studebaker. They loved to sit in it pretending to drive. From time to time, taking the boys to his workshop, Joseph would teach them basic carpentry. A rare outing with him to the all-black town of Mound Bayou, with its wealthy black merchants and farm owners and its shiny automobiles, introduced the boys to a new face of Southern Negro life. They were fascinated.

Here Himes inserts a detail straight out of his own later fiction, the gun-toting neighbor lady of his story "A Nigger," or any of a number of substantial women tugging a half yard of blue steel from among feminine attire in the Harlem novels.

My mother used to take us for rides in the country with a student driving, but we got into so many controversies with the cracker farmers of the county by frightening their mule teams that my father was dismissed from the school and driven from the state . . . Of course part of that was due to my mother's attitude; she always carried a pistol on our car rides through the country, and whenever a cracker mule driver reached for his rabbit gun she beat him to the draw and made him drop it.[30]

Estelle's disquiet, while in truth not going so far as to express itself in gunplay, was palpable. She remained in distress at the lack of cultural life and intellectual stimulation, coupling it now to her growing concern over the boys' education. Tensions also appear to have been accumulating between Joseph and Estelle. When she received an offer to teach in South Carolina, she accepted, taking Joseph Jr. and Chester with her. Cheraw, South Carolina, quickly proved worse than Alcorn. Within weeks Estelle withdrew to Augusta, Georgia, where two of her nieces taught at the Haines Normal and Industrial School. Estelle obtained a temporary position as music teacher and the boys were admitted to eighth grade. Many of their classmates were Geechies, descendants of African slaves from the Georgia Sea Islands, whose dialect Chester loved. For the first time Chester and Joe were among other black children.

The family reunited in early summer, and the following year both boys entered Alcorn College. Edward meanwhile departed home to attend Atlanta University. Never close to parents or siblings, he broke with the family, eventually making his way to New York to become an official in the waiters' union.

At the end of the school year, rather mysteriously, Joseph again resigned and removed the family to St. Louis, where he had earlier bought a house as (he had believed) an investment. Joe suggested that Professor Himes angered farmers by driving his Studebaker along country roads, frightening wagon teams and livestock. Edward and Chester agreed that the reason was Estelle. From *The Third Generation*:

> In the end, Mrs. Taylor got them out. She went to Vicksburg and registered in a white hotel. When she came down next morning the manager confronted her.
>
> "You gave a college for your address. What college is this, Madam?"
>
> "The state college."
>
> "The state college? But that's in—"
>
> "The state college for Negroes."
>
> Again the governor had to intervene. He telephoned Professor Taylor at the college.
>
> "Willie, Ah'll give you forty-eight hours to get that woman out of Mississippi."[31]

By September, however, Joseph had received an offer from the Branch Normal School in Pine Bluff, Arkansas, thirty-eight miles south of Little Rock and 142 miles southwest of Memphis, where they soon resettled.

Branch Normal (now UAPB) was established in 1875, ten years after passage of the Thirteenth Amendment abolishing slavery, under guidance of Professor J. C. Corbin, who labored as its only teacher until 1882, and with seven students. Black voters had been enrolled in Arkansas, some 21,000 of them, for the first time in 1868. During Reconstruction, Negroes served as justices of the peace, sheriffs, county clerks, and tax assessors; more than forty-five held seats in the state legislature. By the 1890s, however, black Arkansans, like blacks throughout the South, found themselves under siege. In 1891 Arkansas's General Assembly passed a bill requiring separate railroad coaches. By 1900 Negroes were largely denied access to public facilities and excluded from voting.

The school, as one might expect, was shabby and half derelict, the entire area severely depressed economically. It was here that, in addition to mechanical arts, Joseph taught black history. Family tensions remained high. Estelle busied herself with church affairs and with public-school teaching. Further clashes with administration resulted from Estelle's demeanor.

Chester, struggling with internal conflicts, during this period seems to have become introverted. Joe remembered him as all but living in Poe's stories. Enrolled in freshman classes with students eight years older, the boys could not have felt other than isolated and alone; they clung to one another. And while Chester with his smooth talk and excellent manners could easily be gracious and charming, his fierce temper could flare at any moment. He did well in studies, however, and under the influence of an English teacher who communicated her own deep love of the language and of literature, first may have been turned toward writing.

Everything changed on graduation day in June of 1923. Demonstrating before the assembly how gunpowder was made, Joe was blinded when the ingredients spontaneously ignited. This moment traumatized Chester. He felt responsibility, even guilt: he was supposed to be with Joe for the demonstration but because of an argument with his mother had been forbidden by his father to participate.

Joe was rushed to the nearest hospital, where white doctors refused to treat him. At the hospital for blacks his eyes were bathed and bandaged and he was put to bed; doctors told Estelle there was nothing more they could do. Five days later, Estelle took Joe to a St. Louis hospital specializing in eye injuries. Getting decent treatment and training for Joe would dominate all their lives over the next years, as the family came fully apart. Chester stayed on in Pine Bluff with his father until September, then the family again moved into the house in St. Louis, "within walking distance of the one black high school, Wendell Phillips, and the Overton beauty products company known as Poro College, which made hair straighteners and skin lighteners and creams and scents for Negro women."[32] There the family lived in close quarters, letting out the rest of the house to tenants. Estelle took Joe to Barnes Hospital every day for treatment—doctors were scraping scar tissue from his eyes—then returned him to the Missouri State School for the Blind, where he learned braille and music. He spent weekends at home. Joseph Sandy worked at odd jobs, and for a time as a waiter in a speakeasy. All in all, these were terrible years.

St. Louis became a city of frustration for the Taylor family. Though they'd gotten back their house, it never became a home. Within it they became prisoners of their despair.[33]

Now completely alone, having lost even his beloved Joe, Chester was more than ever a man of contradictions, "lonely, shy, and insufferably belligerent."[34] His guilt enlarged itself as though to fill the growing spaces between members of his family, to the point that he believed himself responsible not only for Joe's blinding, but for the family's dissolution as well. He cut classes, made certain to become unpopular with other students, threw himself into sports with "suicidal intensity."[35] Such self-destructive activity took its toll: a broken shoulder blade that healed poorly, chipped teeth, one ear torn half off.

Only Eddie, long flown, and Joe, in part protected by his residency at the school, escaped damage in the marital storms.

Professor Taylor had no ability at all for city life. At heart he was a missionary. He'd lived his life in southern Negro colleges. There, a professor was somebody. He counted in the neighborhood. His family counted too. But in St. Louis he didn't count . . .

It was in his home that he'd been defeated. He was a pathetic figure coming home from work; a small black man hunched over and frowning, shambling in a tired-footed walk, crushed old cap pulled down over his tired, glazed eyes, a cigarette dangling from loose lips.[36]

Estelle in turn, at least by evidence of *The Third Generation*, seems to have come perilously close to madness. At one point she sent Joe out into the streets to peddle copies of a poem she'd written, "The Blind Boy's Appeal." Suffering bouts of acute paranoia, she would flee the house for white restaurants and compulsively engage strangers in conversation, telling them, "I destroyed my life by marrying a Negro."[37]

All their lives had lost mooring. Nothing connected anymore, there were no patterns or certainties to grasp, the family seemed to Chester as sundered from its past and as devoid of future as had been slaves torn from their African homeland. They merely endured, pushing through one day after another, moving between temporary shelters. The situation improved slightly when Joseph sold the house and the family moved into larger quarters in a better part of town. Their stay there was brief, however. Medical treatment at Barnes Hospital had done all it could for Joe, who now was able to distinguish dark from light, even to perceive movement and large nearby objects. Nothing bound them to St. Louis any longer. Within months the family decamped once again, moving to Cleveland, where in 1913, after leaving Jefferson City, wife and sons had lived with Joseph's sisters while he settled into the Alcorn College job. Joseph himself had worked in Cleveland years back, before Chester was born, and been happy there. Also, the public school system included programs for the blind.

The Third Generation suggests that relocation once again was at Estelle's urging:

Professor Taylor lost his will. He lost his grip on ordinary things. Caught out in the backyard, halfway to the shed, with a hammer in his hand, he'd forget where he was going, what he'd intended to do.

Only the mother's indomitable will saved them. Now that she had overcome the attack of paranoia, she was stronger than before. She wouldn't admit defeat.

"We'll go to Cleveland," she told her husband. "They have a famous clinic there. And we can live with your relatives until we get settled."[38]

Joseph blamed himself, obliquely, for Joe's blinding and for his own incapacity to do much to make things better for Joe afterward. He never forgot that he had forbidden Chester to take part in the demonstration; what might have been, what might not have been, weighed heavily on him.

The family soon discovered that, as with most of the others, this move had failed to improve its lot by any good measure. Though there was no formal, legal segregation, blacks were largely ghettoized. Laborers from Poland and other European countries claimed the abundant unskilled jobs in factories and steel mills. The family moved in with Joseph's sister Fanny Wiggins and husband Wade, who lived on East 69th Street in a racially mixed neighborhood near the Cleveland Indians' ballpark. Estelle got along no better with her in-laws than she had with college administrators and faculty. Dark-skinned like Joseph, they neglected to show appreciation, Estelle thought, for Joseph's initially having helped set them up here on his salary as a professor, and instead patronized him for now being unemployed. Certainly their ordinariness and their country ways put them beneath her own family socially.

The little house was always crowded and the air was charged with flaring tempers and the clash of personalities.

"You don't like black people but soon's you get down and out you come running to us."

"I married a black man who happens to be your brother."

"Yes, you just married him 'cause you thought he was gonna make you a great lady."

"I'll not discuss it."

"You're in no position to say what you'll discuss, sister. This is my house. I pay taxes on it."

"If Mr. Taylor hadn't spent all of his money sending you and your sister here from the South he'd have something of his own now."

"You dragged him down yourself, don't you go blaming it on us. If you'd made him a good wife instead of always nagging at him, he'd be president of a college today."

"Mr. Taylor would never have been president of my foot. He hasn't got it in him."

"Then why did you marry him?"

"Only God knows. I certainly don't."[39]

Chester and Joe enrolled in Cleveland's chiefly white East High School, commuting by trolley, while Joseph did piecework, carpentry, and construction, and continued to seek full-time employment. Tensions between Estelle and Joseph weren't much better than those between Estelle and her in-laws. At one point, Estelle gathered up Joe and fled to a rented room far across town. "I don't think my father ever forgave her for that," Chester wrote.[40]

Presumably with money from the sale of the St. Louis property, Joseph and Estelle bought a house on Everton Avenue in the Glenville section of Cleveland, at that time a middle-class Jewish neighborhood, and the family once again reunited. Among the Himes's new neighbors in Glenville were Joseph's older sister, Leah, and husband Rodney Moon, a federal meat inspector and part-time real estate agent. The couple had two children, Henry Lee and Ella. Henry Lee graduated from Howard University (it's been suggested that Joseph may have contributed to his college expenses, outraging Estelle) and taught for a time in Alabama before settling in as editor of Harlem's *Amsterdam News*. Later he served on the national executive board of the NAACP and as editor of *The Crisis*. Years along, he would provide introductions for Chester to New York's literati, wife Molly Moon providing the model for Harlem hostess Mamie Mason in Himes's satire of those very intellectuals in *Pinktoes*.

Himes's counterpart in *The Third Generation* delights in the new quarters: "The house did something wonderful for Charles. He was home again. He'd never realized how much he'd missed a home."[41] The family's history of rootlessness deeply affected Himes. Most of his life, until he settled in Spain in 1968, Himes would wander, Cleveland to

L.A. to New York to Paris and back again, moving in and out of successions of hotel rooms, apartments, loaned houses, and cabins. And he would write of characters with no home, or whose homes had been taken away, or who had forcibly removed themselves from homes: the uprooted, the dispossessed, the torn away—material ghosts.

Chester was now one term short of graduation, which took place in January 1926. His grades were not the best, and that final semester became a struggle. He actually failed his Latin exam, but a clerical error, 86 getting entered instead of 56, saved him. Still, any graduate of a public high school in the state was eligible to attend Ohio State University, and Chester planned to do so the following September. Meanwhile he intended to find work and stockpile as much money as possible.

He was in rough waters, just coming to his sexuality, confused and driven. "I was sixteen years old and still a virgin," he wrote in *The Quality of Hurt.* "I remember standing behind the curtains of the parlor windows and masturbating at the sight of the big-tittied Jewish girls when they came out of school."[42] He still felt guilt over Joe's accident and his family's dissolution. His relationship with his mother was particularly exasperating for a young man in search of separate identity: all in the same breath he loved her, desperately wanted free of her, reviled himself because of his desperate need for her. "Tender and turbulent," Edward Margolies[43] says of their relationship—a phrase describing many of Chester's relations with women. For his father he could feel sorrow, along with rage at his failures ("that room that stank of my father's fear and defeat"[44]); and, always, new guilt for feeling such things.

Joe's account of this period differed markedly from that of Chester in both memoirs and novel. Where Chester presented himself as overly sensitive, rejected and misunderstood at every turn, rather a Byronic figure, Joe recalled him as being immensely popular among black and white alike, a handsome young man who charmed everyone he saw, an enthusiastic dancer and a favorite of the girls. Adolescence, of course, is a stage in which we try on various personalities, swinging wildly from emotion to emotion, and quite likely both Chesters existed at different times. For that matter, both Chesters, the socially adept and the reclusive brooder, coexisted in the adult as well.

Chester's uncle Andrew helped him find work as a busboy in chic Wade Park Manor Hotel in east Cleveland, where at his first job Chester felt simultaneously superior and hopelessly intimidated.

> He felt like an intruder, a tourist who has wandered upon the ceremonial rites of a primitive tribe. He didn't know it was his manner that set him apart. At one glance they knew he was not of them. He had none of the extroversion the occupation requires. Inside he was taut with timidity. Outwardly he strove to show a hard indifference.[45]

His job was to retrieve room service trays and roll them two or three at a time into the service elevator for return to the kitchen. Two young women sat in a glass booth facing the elevators to check the trays before waiters took them upstairs. These women were white and good-looking, and immediately took to Chester. In *The Third Generation*'s account, a supervisor jokes with Charles:

> "These young ladies cause more havoc on my station than a four-alarm fire," Mr. Jackson warned. "You must inure yourself against their charms, son. You won't be able to find the elevators."[46]

In fact the women got Chester so worked up that he sallied off to the ghetto slums on Scoville Avenue and lost his virginity to "an old fat ugly whore sitting on a stool outside her hovel."[47] Himes's description of Scoville Avenue, with its poverty, its aimless men living off whores, drinking raw alcohol and cutting one another up, reads like a sketch for the Harlem of his detective novels.

One morning two weeks after he started the job, feeling less at odds, Chester stopped by the girls in their booth planning to ask for a date. Sensing this, the checkers quickly steered the conversation elsewhere. Chester, crestfallen, pulled open the elevator doors, stepped in—and fell forty feet.

> I remember the sensation of falling through space and landing on a solid platform with the feeling of my body spattering open like a ripe watermelon.

I remember calling for help in a tiny voice. My mouth felt as though it were filled with gravel. Later I discovered that it was only my teeth.

My chin had hit something that cut the flesh to the bone, broke my lower jaw, and shattered all my teeth. My left arm hit something and both bones broke just above the wrist so that they came out through the skin, dead white with drops of blood in the bone fractures. My spine hit something and the last three vertebrae were fractured.[48]

Finding the hotel responsible for the accident—it should not have been possible to open the outer doors when the elevator was on another floor—the Ohio State Industrial Commission paid all hospital bills and awarded Chester a disability payment of $75 a month. The hotel offered to continue his salary of $50 a month. This led to further bitterness between his parents. Joseph had urged Chester to sign waivers to all rights for additional claims; Estelle believed that he should have rejected pension and waivers alike and sued Wade Manor. She went so far as to confront the hotel's management, accusing them of taking advantage of her son. The hotel responded by withdrawing its offer to maintain Chester on salary. Joseph and Estelle quarreled horribly, he insisting that she was only making a fool of herself and antagonizing everyone who might help them, she accusing him of inertia and Uncle Tomism.

At this point in *The Third Generation* there's a moment of great feeling for both parents.

Mrs. Taylor's long and bitter fight was to save herself as much as anything. She didn't realize this. She thought of herself as doing what a mother should. And yet, in the end, she lost herself. Both lost themselves. She became mean and petty. And although Professor Taylor had been without a teaching post for four long years, he had still felt he belonged. Deep down he had still considered himself a teacher. Now he didn't. It broke him inside where it counted. He gave up. He lost his will to try. In many ways, the effect on this little black man born in a Georgia cabin, who'd tried so hard to be someone of consequence in this world, to live a respectable life, rear his children to be good, and teach his backward people, was the greatest tragedy of all. Mrs.

Taylor never gave up as he did. But she had to feel the world was turned against her to justify herself.[49]

After four months in hospital, Chester returned home wearing a complicated back brace of leather and stainless steel that made him feel "like a trussed fowl."[50] His teeth were repaired by Industrial Commission dentists in a long series of visits. Chester was happy to return home, but tensions ran high there. He looked forward to September more than ever before.

Arriving in Columbus, Himes took a room in a boarding house several blocks off campus. Ohio State at that time had a student population of 12,296, of which some 600 were black. Cost of a year's schooling, with room and board, books, deposits, and other fees, came to approximately $658. Black students were not admitted to the dormitories, student union, or dining halls.

"I bought a coonskin coat for three hundred dollars, a knickerbocker suit, a long-stemmed pipe, and a Model T Ford roadster, and I became a collegian,"[51] Himes wrote years later. He even pledged one of the two black fraternities. "The white students didn't know exactly what to make of me . . . I rarely spoke to white people, and never unless I was addressed first by them, and yet I would find them always looking at me."[52] Himes struck quite a figure tooling about campus in his raccoon coat, cruising town in his roadster, taking in movies like *Flesh and the Devil* and black road shows with young artists such as Josephine Baker and Ethel Waters. He seems to have been popular with college women. Classes were a different matter. Here Himes found himself far behind the other students. He quarreled openly with a chemistry teacher, was utterly at sea in German, couldn't fathom the math needed for physics. Himes's account of this period is a curious mixture of braggadocio (that he scored fourth highest on the IQ test, that he could have had his pick of college women) and self-sorrow (that he was always on the outside, that he didn't belong and never would).

Charles was in conflict with the university from the day of his arrival. He was at once inspired by the thought of being a student, and dispirited by the knowledge this thought inspired. On the one hand he began to run, not outwardly, but in his emotions, like a dog freed from its leash; while on the other he was fettered by every circumstance of the university life which relegated him to insignificance. He dreaded the classes where no one spoke to him, he hated the clubs he couldn't join, he scorned the restaurants in which he couldn't eat.[53]

Though like alter ego Charles he contrived many excuses for essentially not even trying—he hadn't the academic background for the pre-med courses he'd chosen; the studies were too difficult, the classes too formal; his hit-or-miss schooling, from Georgia to Mississippi to Arkansas to Missouri, had left him unprepared for the discipline of university study—Himes knew deep down that he was rebelling. He'd always been like that: if he couldn't take part in everything, then he wouldn't take part in anything. And without his mother to push him on through this inertia, he succumbed to it. He had started off doing his best to become a kind of pastiche of the white collegiate. The rigidity and hypocrisy of Northern segregation gnawed away at him, though, and turning against that, he turned against himself as well.

Himes began to withdraw, taking refuge in the brothels and clubs of the sprawling Negro slums. He seems to have had a steady companion there, from whom he may have contracted venereal disease. Fully expecting dismissal, he was shocked to learn that he'd passed all his courses and, following Christmas vacation at home, would have to return to the university.

But by then I was tired of Ohio State University and its policy of discrimination and segregation, fed up with the condescension, which I could never bear, and disgusted with myself for my whoremongering and my inability to play games, my instinctive withdrawal from intimacy, and my schizophrenic impulses to be inconspicuous and conspicuous at the same time. It was much later in life that I came to understand I simply hadn't accepted my status as a "nigger."[54]

Following a disastrous Christmastime at home, where father and mother engaged in what now seemed one endless argument, head of one dispute eating the tail of the last, Himes returned to campus more disenchanted than ever. Toward the end of the second quarter his fraternity sponsored a formal dance. Himes attended with tux and a young woman he hardly knew: "I was bored and my teeth were set on edge by the very proper behavior of these very proper young black people who were trying so hard to ape white people."[55] He decided to introduce these sheltered, privileged young people to the real world, and took them to the brothel he frequented. Here they sat drinking home brew and listening to recordings until Himes's steady came upon them and exploded in fury. This self-immolative pattern would repeat itself often in his life, Himes sailing blithely into mined waters, professing surprise when the ship went down.

Called before the dean the following morning, Himes was allowed to withdraw for reasons of ill health and failing grades. In gentlemanly fashion, the previous evening's incident was never mentioned.

> For a long time he stood on the stone steps of University Hall, looking across the snow-covered oval. He was saying good-bye again, this time to many things, to all of his mother's hopes and prayers, to so many of his own golden dreams, to the kind of future he'd been brought up to expect, and to a kind of life . . . But at the time he didn't realize it. He felt trapped again, pushed into something against his will.[56]

Chester Himes, the wizard of leave-taking, in his life stood on many such shores.

Back in Cleveland, though his parents argued fiercely over how he was to be disciplined, Himes escaped any reckoning, their arguments between themselves deflecting anger from him. Joseph Sandy, now working as a janitor, refused to take responsibility or action, however loudly Estelle railed. Chester fell ill, perhaps reacting to the tensions about him: "My back froze up . . . The atmosphere in our house was depressing. Thoughts of myself were depressing. I didn't think. I passed the spring in a daze."[57] But when summer came, he was up and about, making rounds of the brothels, bars, and gambling clubs. His favorite was Bunch Boy's on Cedar Avenue near Ninety-fifth Street. He and a young man he'd worked with at Wade Park Manor, Ramsey, hung out there so much that the owner started calling them "the Katzi Kids" after the Katzenjammer Kids cartoon strip, and eventually put Himes to work at the blackjack table.

To cover, Himes told his mother he'd taken a night job at the Gilsy Hotel on Ninth Street. He'd leave home early afternoon and return at three or four the next morning. He actually did work at the Gilsy for about a month, filling in for an acquaintance, running prostitutes up to the rooms and providing whiskey brewed by the bell captain. Himes never made less than fifty dollars a night, but the money went fast, on clothes and gambling. "I bought very expensive suits," Himes recalled, "shirts, ties, shoes, and coats—stylish, but not outlandish . . . I liked tweeds, Cheviots, and worsteds. I remember my most daring venture was a pair of square-toed yellow pigskin bluchers by Florsheim, which today in Paris would be the height of fashion. I got to know the expensive men's stores where blacks rarely ventured."[58] In the spring he bought a secondhand Nash, parking it several blocks from his home so his parents wouldn't know.

> I seemed to be in a trance. I think it was the result of so many emotional shocks. My parents' quarreling had entered its final stage; sometimes my father would strike my mother and she struck back. I would separate them when I was home . . . I ran my car into a concrete stanchion underneath the railroad bridge over Cedar Avenue and wrecked it.[59]

Joe won honors at East High and a scholarship to Oberlin College. Bunch Boy left the gambling club to devote his attentions to a policy house. Ramsey stopped coming around. Bunch Boy had been something of a father figure to Himes, certainly a stabilizing influence, and with him gone, solitary once again, Himes was at loose ends. Eventually he fell in with a sneak thief named Benny, "a big-framed, light-brown-skinned, simpleminded boy who elected me as his hero."[60] To live up to Benny's adulation, Himes later wrote, he did a lot of things he'd otherwise not have done, including learning to smoke opium and stealing cars. It was at a party in Benny's basement apartment just off Cedar Avenue in the Eighties that Himes first met his future wife Jean Johnson.

Soon Himes and Jean were working together at a whiskey joint in the alley behind Bunch Boy's. They lived there, too; that way, the owner, a woman named Margaret, said, when times got bad, Chester could put Jean to tricking for him. Times got bad pretty quickly. Chester had bought the twenties equivalent of a Saturday night special, a little Owlshead .32, and developed the habit of shooting at people who pressed for Jean's favors. Luckily he always missed, but that was enough for Margaret to put them out.

Himes proved hardly the gentleman his appearance and manner might first suggest. Seventeen at the time, Jean was

> the most beautiful brownskin girl I had ever seen ... Her skin was the warm reddish brown of a perfectly roasted turkey breast the moment it comes from the oven. She had a heart-shaped face, thick hot lips, and brown eyes. What there was about me that attracted her so I never knew, but she fell desperately in love with my immortal soul ... Eight years later I was to marry her and live with her for fourteen years, but at that time I treated her in the most casual manner; sometimes I would leave her standing on a corner waiting for me hours on end; and other times I would leave her in rooms we had rented for the night, in lieu of room rent, which I didn't have, and wouldn't see her again until several days later.[61]

Himes was desperate for money. There is also considerable evidence, from his clothes and flashy gambling, his performances for Benny, and treatment of Jean, that he was to some degree striking postures, trying on the mask of a hardened criminal. So when Benny asked him to come on a burglary, that fit right in. Through a friend who worked for the Ohio National Guard, Benny had learned that arms and ammunition were stored in the Negro branch of the YMCA on Cedar and Seventy-sixth. He planned to steal a case of Colt automatics and sell them to blacks who worked in the steel mills in nearby Warren and Youngstown. His friend would drive, he and Chester would break into the Y and get the guns.

The actual robbery went well. Everything else went wrong. On the way to Warren both back tires blew, forcing the Himes gang to hike into the nearest village and catch a bus to Warren. Himes remained there, knocking at doors in the ghetto asking after rooms to let, while the others left to find a tow truck. Finally they moved the guns into a hotel room and went off seeking buyers. As he made the rounds of dice games and drinking parties, Himes ran into a woman he'd seen earlier that afternoon and came within a breath of a shooting match with her man. At three o'clock that morning police broke into the hotel room to arrest Benny and Himes. They were taken back to Cleveland.

> The judge was a woman. My mother testified that I had been led astray by bad influence because my father didn't exercise the proper influence. The judge questioned my mother about my father's position and background and learned about my brother's accident and my father giving up his job as a Southern "professor" to bring his son North for treatment. She learned about my own accident and my withdrawal from college and was extraordinarily moved by the predicament of our family. Because the guns had been recovered and no harm had come from the theft she gave me a suspended sentence, over the vehement protest of the prosecuting attorney.[62]

Estelle tried first to gain control of Chester's pension, then, failing that, to have him placed in an institution for delinquents. For this, however, she needed Joseph's permission, which he refused to give. Chester always claimed there was a tacit agreement between him and his father; that since his disciplining Chester had resulted in Joe's blindness, he would never do it again. Furious and at wit's end, Estelle sued for divorce. Not long after, Joseph packed up and left. Benny meanwhile had returned from serving thirty days in jail; Chester moved in with Jean to occupy one of his two rooms. A week later he and Benny stole a car and drove back to Columbus.

Chester was exhilarated at being back on campus, driving a grand new car, looking every bit the great man. Benny, though, felt ill at ease, insisting they should steer clear of the school, find rooms in the ghetto, and sell the car as soon as possible. The next day he left and returned to Cleveland. On impulse Himes stole a student's ID card and doctored it to show his own signature. Then he went from store to store in downtown Columbus buying small items and paying for them by check. The checks were from a pad of blanks he'd picked up at the local bank; he wrote them on a fictitious Cleveland account, each time for fifteen or twenty dollars over purchase cost. Finally at a chic men's store a clerk questioned the check he offered and, when Himes protested that none of the other stores had refused him, demanded to know *which* stores. The one across the street, he told her. Shortly the clerk from that store showed up with Himes's check. The police showed up not long after.

This time it was Joseph who came for the trial, at which Chester pled guilty and drew a two-year suspended sentence plus a five-year bench parole. Himes returned with his father to Cleveland, to a rented room on Eighty-Ninth off Cedar Avenue stinking "of my father's fear and defeat."[63] Chester stayed away as much as possible, over at Jean's or hanging around Bunch's old place and the brothels on Scoville and Central, packing his little Owlshead.

> I discovered that I had become very violent. I saw a glimmer of fear and caution in the eyes of most people I encountered: squares, hustlers, gamblers, pimps, even whores. I had heard that people were saying, "Little Katzi will kill you." I can't say what I might have done.[64]

Himes traded his .32 for a huge .44 Colt that "looked like a hand cannon and would shoot hard enough to kill a stone."[65] When one restaurant refused him service, he boasted—we're again in Himesland—that he leapt onto the counter, kicked everything off it, and beat the restaurant's owner about the head with his new pistol.

Himes had appeared in court in Columbus, on the check charge, in early November. By month's end he was arrested in Chicago for armed robbery.

One night at Bunch Boy's he'd heard a chauffeur bragging about how rich his boss was, about his platinum watch and two Cadillacs and how he always had loads of money at the house: "Like many blacks still possessed of a slave mentality, he boasted of his employer's possessions as though they were his own, or as though he had a vested interest in them."[66] Himes also heard the chauffeur say that he had Thanksgiving Eve off. On that night Himes drove out to Fairmount Boulevard in Cleveland Heights. He intended to ring the doorbell and, when the maid answered, force his way in at gunpoint, but the maid, suspicious, refused to open the door, instead calling the police. Himes hid in shrubbery until the police were gone and the owners returned home. Then, breaking a garage window, he let himself into the house and confronted the elderly couple. He took the cache of money, as well as jewelry, and fled in one of the Cadillacs. Pursued briefly by police, he eluded them, eventually miring the car in mud and continuing on foot.

In *The Quality of Hurt* Himes asserts that he relieved the elderly couple of "five or six stacks of hundred and twenty dollar bills still wrapped in the bank bands," plus "necklaces, bracelets, rings . . . platinum pocket watch and diamond-studded watch chain,"[67] some $20,000 in cash, plus jewelry insured at just over $28,000. Biographers Fabre and Margolies put the take at $300 cash, $5,000 in jewelry. Court records list only a single ring valued at $1,500 and $200 cash. As so often, details of Himes's life are multiple choice.

In an early short story, "Prison Mass," convict and would-be writer Brightlights thinks how "He could still experience a thrill as he recalled that midnight ride."[68] Himes recalled it this way in *The Quality of Hurt*:

So I just stepped on the gas and drove the Cadillac in a straight line down the snow-covered street. I remember it being exceedingly pleasant in the softly purring car moving swiftly through the virgin blanket of snow and the white translucent falling curtain. Soon the sound of shooting died away and the sight of the pursuing car disappeared in the snowscape in the rear-view mirror, and I was moving swiftly through the completely deserted, almost silent night. There was not a sign of life in sight. Falling snow refracted the headlights and shortened the perimeter of visibility and I had the illusion of hurtling silently through an endless cloud.[69]

Back downtown, Himes headed straight for Union Station and bought a ticket to Chicago. He'd heard Bunch Boy and others talk about a fence named Jew Sam; the next morning he dropped by his pawnshop near the Loop to sell the jewelry. Next stop, Tijuana. Sam took one of the rings and said he had to check it out. He went into a back room. Soon after, police arrived.

I suspected he was calling the police. I should have let him keep the ring and escaped. But I couldn't run; never could run. I have always been afraid that that one stupid mental block is going to get me killed.[70]

Critic Stephen F. Milliken says of this incident: "The inability to run that can affect a threatened man, the absolute refusal to collaborate in any way, to acknowledge the existence of the threat even in avoiding it, was to remain one of his distinctive literary themes."[71] This was another manifestation of Himes's psychic inertia, his refusal-by-inaction to choose and so to be carried along, the Bartlebyan "I would prefer not to." Himes himself wondered if his novel *Run Man Run* had its origin in this incident.

Finding the rest of the jewelry, the detectives took Himes downtown. He was interrogated. Then detectives handcuffed his hands behind his back, handcuffed his feet together, and hung him upside-down on a door. They wrapped their pistols in felt hats and beat him on the ribs and testicles. Just as he used elements of the robbery in various stories such as "Prison Mass," Himes used the beating and general background in his prison novel, first published in truncated form as *Cast the First Stone* and recently, in its original version, as *Yesterday Will Make You Cry*. New convict Jim Monroe is trying to get to sleep.

All that stuff that happened in Chicago kept coming back. I could see myself asking that sonofabitching pawnbroker for five hundred dollars for the ring, and him saying just a minute and slipping out in the back room. I'd known he was calling the police. Even if he did have that one ring I had a lot of other stuff. But I couldn't run. I never could run.

I could feel the cops hitting me in the mouth, hanging me by my handcuffed feet upside down over a door, beating my ribs with their gun butts. I could feel the blood running down my legs from where the handcuffs pinched them on the anklebone.

I had stood it as long as I could, I thought, looking at the ceiling. I might have stood it longer if I'd lost consciousness. But there had been too much pain and not enough hurt to lose consciousness. I had confessed.[72]

*   *   *

There's a very absurdist, very Himesian touch here, in that the detectives actually were working on a robbery that occurred at the Blackstone Hotel the night before. The victim had already been in to identify the jewelry as hers, a captain of detectives told Himes, and was only awaiting his confession before she claimed her jewelry. When Himes said he could prove he'd been at his hotel room all night, the captain said "You better not try" and left, telling his men to get a signed confession. Himes suspected that he and the woman were accomplices.

The squad were startled, then displeased, when Himes confessed to a burglary in Cleveland Heights, Ohio, instead of the hotel robbery, but there was little they could do. Accompanied by an insurance agent to identify the jewelry, a detective came out from Cleveland to retrieve Himes.

Estelle visited him at Cuyahoga County jail, crying "My poor boy, you were so brilliant"—already speaking in the past tense, Himes notes. His father secured a lawyer for him and on one visit, touchingly, brought along the back brace Chester had stopped wearing long ago. On December 18, 1928, Judge Walter McMahon handed down the sentence: twenty to twenty-five years of hard labor. Himes was remanded to the Ohio State Penitentiary in Columbus nine days after sentencing, on December 27, and remained there until September 21, 1934. At that time he was transferred to the London Prison Farm before being paroled to his mother's custody on April 1st, 1936. Chester would later say that he grew to manhood in prison.

2 59623

One year before the gates clanged shut behind Himes, in 1927, Al Jolson peered out from blackface and the screen of the first talkie, *The Jazz Singer*, to tell the audience "You ain't heard nothing yet."

The twenties were an economic house of cards, borne up by hopefulness at the end of the war and about to collapse into the Great Depression. Fitzgerald gave us, in Gatsby, the era's representative character. Mencken and Sinclair Lewis pilloried middle-class complacency and the oxymoron of received wisdom. Dos Passos and Hemingway wrote of the great dislocations and disillusionments of wartime. W. E. B. Du Bois had *his* say about Negroes and the war in 1919:

> We return.
> We return from fighting.
> We return fighting.[1]

Meanwhile America managed to scare itself half to death over the boogeyman of Communism, paving the way for demagogues like J. Edgar Hoover and Joseph McCarthy. With mainstream society pitched full tilt against foreign influences, perhaps also as aftermath to the race riots that occurred in many major American cities in 1917–19, the Ku Klux Klan revived, claiming five million members by 1924.

Unemployment reached 50 percent, turning the highways and ditches, as John Steinbeck wrote, into swarms of migrants looking for work. Henry Ford remarked what a great education those young folks were going to get from all this traveling about.

FDR jacked up the wreck our economy had become and started hammering out dents, establishing the relief programs and federal projects his predecessor the ever-patrician Herbert Hoover categorically rejected. FDR also took himself directly to the American people with his fireside chats. In conservative, well-to-do households he became reviled as "that man." In poorer ones he was the closest thing they'd seen to a savior outside church. Blacks in vast numbers deserted the Republican Party, their home since Reconstruction, for FDR's Democrats.

"I grew to manhood in the Ohio State Penitentiary,"[2] Himes wrote. He was nineteen when he went through the gate, twenty-six when he came back out. He learned what he had to do to survive, he said, or he wouldn't have, even if at the time he didn't realize he was learning. "On occasion, it must have seemed to others that I was bent on self-destruction."[3]

Here we come to a major enigma of Himes's memoirs. In two books totalling 743 pages, only six pages are devoted to Himes's years in prison. Of these almost a full page is given to disclaimers of homosexuality, most of another to gambling, two to his writing. If prison was the chief turning point of his life, and it must have been, why then do we have so little information here about it? This, again, is the overarching problem with the memoirs: throughout, Himes skips lightly over central issues, barely touching down, while lingering on peripheral matters. Little is shown of the inner life and a great deal of the outer: clothing, pets, cars, visitors, apartments, quarrels. It's a curious lens through which to watch. Rarely have candor and reticence so cohabited. Himes makes a very odd kind of hero of himself, picking open wounds one moment, telling us nothing can touch him the next.

There's little doubt that prison was the first major pivot point of Himes's life. H. Bruce Franklin writes in *Prison Literature in America*:

> Himes's achievement as a writer of fiction, indeed his very existence as an author, came directly from his experience in prison, which shaped his creative imagination and determined much of his outlook on American society.[4]

Franklin goes on to say that looking back at those early stories of the 1930s one finds, along with overwhelming evidence both of his power and internal contradictions, the very matrix of Himes's vision: the stamp of characteristic images and symbols that would occupy him for his forty years as a writer.

Himes's voiced feelings about prison remained deeply ambivalent. "Nothing happened in prison that I had not already encountered in outside life,"[5] he wrote at one point. At another: "It is nonsense, even falsehood, to say that serving seven and a half years in one of the most violent prisons on earth will have no effect on a human being. But as far as I could determine at the time, and for a long time afterwards, the only effect it had on me was to convince me that people will do anything—white people, black people, all people. Why should I be surprised when white men cut out some poor black man's nuts, or when black men eat the tasty palms of white explorers?"[6] Beginning the memoirs by speaking of his reasons for moving to Europe, Himes wrote:

> I don't remember them clearly. It was like the many impressions my seven and a half prison years had made on me: I knew that my long prison term had left its scars, I knew that many aspects of prison life had made deep impressions on my subconscious, but now I cannot distinctly recall what they are or should have been. I find it necessary to read what I have written in the past about my prison experiences to recall any part of them . . . And I think it has partly convinced me . . . that I can never again be hurt as much as I have already been hurt, even though I should live one hundred thousand years.[7]

In addition, imprisonment largely severed any remaining intimate connections with his family (a fact that Himes, subconsciously at least, may have welcomed), so that we have no secondary sources concerning this period. Eddie had vanished. Joseph Sandy was working at menial jobs when he could find them, living in a squalid apartment. Joe concentrated on school work while Estelle kept house for him. Only future wife Jean Johnson could have told us; sadly, she never did.

Because Himes wrote so little about the experience in his memoirs, then, and given this utter lack of alternative sources, most of our information (as in the passage above he said of his own) must come obliquely from reading what he wrote elsewhere. We proceed, wobbling and trying to make them ours, on legs of conjecture and extrapolation. The short stories are of some use in catching up the moods of prison life, more so in documenting Himes's development as a writer. And whatever land mines it may contain, the best plot of ground we have on which to build remains his prison novel, first published as *Cast the First Stone*. (A recent restoration of the original version, published as *Yesterday Will Make You Cry*, will be discussed in Chapter 10.)

At the end of that book's first chapter, new inmate Jimmy Monroe lies abed at night recalling his disgrace at the Chicago police station, thinking how strange everything is, and remembering his fear upon arrival. The fear has not vanished; it's still there, will always be there in the background; but now a kind of acceptance builds as well.

> I turned my head and looked out the window that was just a little above the level of my eyes. I saw the moon in a deep blue sky and a guard-turret with spotlights down the walls. I saw the guard silhouetted against the sky, a rifle cradled in his arm, the intermittent glow of the cigarette in his mouth. I saw the long black sweep of the walls . . . When you looked at the walls your vision stopped. Everything stopped at the walls. The walls were about fifty feet from the dormitory building. Just fifty feet away was freedom, I thought. Fifty feet—and twenty years.[8]

No one who has forfeited freedom for whatever reason, even briefly, ever forgets what it was like the moment those doors swung shut behind. Absolutely no part of your life belongs to you anymore; you're utterly at the mercy of others. The very thought of prison was terrible, of course, to Himes as to character Jimmy Monroe. There were strange, wholly irrational rules at work here. Yet prison life was unspeakably mundane. "It was all anticlimax," Himes wrote. "All seven and a half years of it."[9]

Time no longer exists. There is only the monotonous procession of days, each of them as featureless as every other, until finally you find yourself longing for eruptions of violence, an attempted escape, rioting—*anything* that will break the dull chain, make you feel alive again, even if only for a moment. Each identical morning you get up and put on your gray stained underwear and sweat-stiffened socks and the bagged stinking trousers you wear week after week and stand in line to wash your face in water so cold that the rock-hard lye soap won't lather, then try to dry your face on a greasy towel that only smears the water and dirt around. You stand up on command from your breakfast of bread, watery oatmeal with powdered milk and sausages cold-welded to aluminum plates by congealed grease, go across one or another of crisscrossing brick sidewalks to the tin shop, or the mill, or back to the dormitory with its rows of double-decked bunks.

Tuesdays and Thursdays are barbershop days. Friday everyone gets a three-minute bath. There's sick call Monday, Wednesday, and Friday but you learn that if you complain of cramps they'll take you to the hospital right away. At night the bugs swarm. They fall onto your pillow and face, drop to the floor too bloated with blood to move. Once, trying to smoke them out, you set your mattress afire and your bunkmate puts it out with the bucket of stale urine you both use as a toilet.

Joseph Sandy visited Chester only once in those years. Chester claimed that it wasn't so much visit as forage; that his father came to him for money and walked off with most of Chester's earnings from gambling. Estelle visited regularly at first, but in 1932 moved with Joe Jr. to Arkansas, where he had a teaching position. When Joe returned to Columbus and graduate school at Ohio State two years later, Estelle resumed regular visits. Jean Johnson was a stalwart visitor.

Just as he mines *The Third Generation* for information about Himes's early life with caution, the critic approaches *Cast the First Stone* as documentation of Himes's prison experience at his own peril—and if the critic is at peril, the biographer is doubly so. Multiple problems present themselves.

First, of course, there's the general question as to what proportion and portions of the novel are directly autobiographical, what recon-structed or reimagined autobiography, and what fully fictive. This is a difficult enough question in its pure form, but to complicate things still further, the novel existed in several avatars as Himes rewrote it over the decade it took to get published. Its black protagonist somewhere along the way became white; Himes's original title was *Black Sheep*. Also, in the published version, probably at the behest of Himes's editor, the story gets updated to the years just after World War II, the occasional anachronism flashing like a Victorian ankle from beneath the skirt of this transformation.

In *The Quality of Hurt* Himes wrote: "I had made the protagonist of my prison story a Mississippi white boy; that ought to tell me something but I don't know what—but obviously it was the story of my own prison experiences."[10] By 1976 and the second volume of the memoirs, however, he'd changed his mind: "My publishers wished to imply that the story in *Cast the First Stone* was the story of my life and problems and I wanted to state outright that it had nothing to do with me."[11] Much quite patently is from Himes's own experience: the background on "all that stuff that happened in Chicago,"[12] the general outline of the prison term, Jimmy's awakening interest in writing, the pervasive sense of fear wrapped in deadly tedium.

Writing of prison creates, of course, a society in microcosm, abstracting social forms and strains to bold strokes, throwing them into high relief. The novel's prison yard is described as though it were, say, a frontier town, workshop here, barber there, sidewalks, bath house, dining hall; *Cast the First Stone* easily might be read as an account of Jimmy Monroe's socialization. On the one hand, deleting racial considerations falsifies the field. On the other—perhaps this is what Himes or his editor had in mind; we are, after all, by definition dealing with an artificial society—considerations of racism might draw attention away from other, primary issues.

A third major question here is that of homosexuality. *The Quality of Hurt* contains a 245-word disquisition on "wolves," "wolverines," "boy-girls," "pussy without bone," and Chester's exemption from rape by dint of intimidating intelligence and an air of violence. In *All Shot Up*, Caspar Holmes's closet homosexuality serves as symbol of the evil nature concealed beneath his outward goodness. John Babson in *Blind Man with a Pistol*, cooperating with Grave Digger and Coffin Ed because he is attracted to them, is treated by them with contempt and needless cruelty. *The Primitive* likewise voices disdain and disgust in such portrayals. Homosexuals in Himes, if they are not killers, are effeminate and ineffectual, moral weaklings, prostitutes—people to be used. Yet *Cast the First Stone*, particularly in its second half, is beyond question a love story, and while in prison Himes had relationships with at least two fellow convicts. Of course, it's not at all unusual that men finding themselves in prison adapt to same-sex practices and continue so for years without ever considering themselves other than heterosexual.

Critic Stephen Milliken sums up the basic problem here vis-à-vis the memoirs, novels, and life lived.

> Unfortunately, Himes did not choose, in his autobiography *The Quality of Hurt* (1972), to clarify in any detail the exact relation of fiction to fact in his three autobiographical novels of the early 1950s—*Cast the First Stone* (1952), *The Third Generation* (1954), and *The Primitive* (1955). The sections of his life that he explored so exhaustively in the novels are hastily sketched in *The Quality of Hurt* . . . The love affair that furnished the central theme for *The Primitive* is given only three pages. It is firmly established that almost all of the basic events that make up the plot structures of the three novels are factual, but no light at all is shed on the validity of the characterizations and patterns of motivation developed in the novels.[13]

As it turned out, Himes arrived at prison with survival kit well packed. Gambling was a major occupation in the closed prison society, and Himes soon discovered that his years hanging around Bunch Boy's had prepared him well: "I survived, I suppose, because I knew how to gamble."[14] Soon he was gambling boss among black convicts. He kept it clean, headed off fights, stopped the cheating, did what he could to protect the chumps. His pension made him a rich man among poor. All in all, though, it was intelligence that proved his greatest advantage. His education and ability to negotiate payments with guards and disputes among prisoners became invaluable. Most fellow inmates were dull-witted, practically illiterate, and Himes found that he could talk them into almost anything.

Despite a relatively small stature at 5 feet 9 inches and 165 pounds, his violent air also gave him some measure of protection. He broke into such explosive rage that men twice his size would back away: "In my fits of insensate fury I would have smashed the world, crushed it in my hands, kicked down the universe."[15] But that violent air could just as easily back up on him. He wrote that he lost his temper constantly while gambling, and that it was a wonder he was still alive. Explosive episodes, along with his refusal of work assignments and disobedience of orders, led again and again to beatings, reduced rations, even solitary confinement. Once he was on starvation wages so long that his hair began falling out. He bore all his life the scars of head whippings.

> They punished me in many more subtle ways which I have discovered to be peculiar to the white race. During my last year, when I was at the farm, the deputy warden, a sick man with a paralyzed arm, used to stand beside the dining-room door when we went to meals and wait for me so he could lean forward and grit his teeth at me.[16]

Intelligence and gambling acumen were two reasons Himes survived. He also survived, not only in prison, but ultimately, for another reason: he became a writer. Prison would turn Chester Himes into a writer and simultaneously deliver to him a lifetime of subject matter.

Writing, Stephen Milliken suggests, gave Himes a foothold on treacherous ground, offering him some degree of mastery over the most painful, even all but unendurable, experiences. Certainly it helped him, if not to control, then at least to channel, his rage. We don't really know what triggered this transformation. In the story "Prison Mass" Brightlights muses on his need for adulation, vowing no longer to seek that adulation as gambler, but as writer.

> "I shall pass beneath this earth no common shade." That was his motto now—I shall be no *forgotten man.* What was important in life? From his burning thoughts came the answer—ambition, achievement, fame.[17]

Himes himself gave several reasons for taking up writing. Not the least was the protection it afforded him. Fellow prisoners respected and superstitiously feared those who wrote. Guards thought twice before killing or too severely beating a prisoner known outside the walls, "or else convicts like Malcolm X and Eldridge Cleaver would never have gotten out of prison alive."[18] Filling the train of endless empty days and years doubtless played some part as well. In *Cast the First Stone* a murderer who's befriended him tells Jimmy Monroe about a writing course he's taking. When Jimmy questions this, saying that he understood writing to require talent, the man responds: "Oh, I don't ever expect to really write any stories . . . I'm just studying this for something to do. You know a fellow has to do something."[19] When in the sixties Melvin Van Peebles, interviewing Himes in Paris, asked how it was that he became a writer, Chester responded: "I had a lot of free time."[20]

Brother Joe believed that upon finding himself imprisoned, looking up the long, empty tunnel of his future, Himes "took himself in hand and decided that he had to do something with his life."[21] Estelle supported Chester in his ambition. She provided a typewriter, paper, and pencils, helped persuade prison officials to let him work, encouraged him in every way.

Himes says, starkly, "I began writing in prison,"[22] and goes on to catalog his publications. His first story was published in a black-owned magazine, *The Bronzeman*, sometime in 1931, but neither a copy of the story nor files of the magazine exist. Other early stories appeared in black newspapers and magazines such as *Abbott's*, the *Atlanta Daily World*, the *Pittsburgh Courier*, and the *Afro-American*. In 1934 he sold two stories to *Esquire*. "Crazy in the Stir" was published with only his prison number, 59623, as byline. "To What Red Hell," a fictionalized version of the 1930 prison fire that claimed over 300 lives, which Himes would depict again in *Cast the First Stone*, soon followed. "After that," Himes wrote, "until I was released in May 1936, I was published only by *Esquire*."[23]

Himes's two stories for the magazine had been accepted simultaneously. "Crazy" appeared in August ("a long-term prisoner in a state penitentiary tells an authentic story about life on the 'inside'"), "To What Red Hell" in October. Editor Arnold Gingrich would buy five more from Himes in the period 1934 to 1942; they'd appear alongside contributions from Hemingway, Dos Passos, Fitzgerald, Ring Lardner, Ben Hecht, Conrad Aiken, Bertrand Russell, Theodore Dreiser, and Langston Hughes. Exhilarating company for a young convict in an Ohio prison, Stephen Milliken points out. "He was at last, beyond all question, a writer."[24]

Interestingly enough, Himes's first stories for *Esquire* were not about blacks. (Himes was not identified as black until 1936, when a sketch appeared on the contributor's page.) They *were* about what Himes just then knew best, crime and the people who committed it. As critic Robert Skinner remarks, characters in these stories with titles like "The Visiting Hour," "Crazy in the Stir" and "The Night's for

Cryin'" often resemble Himes, "men with violence deeply imbedded in them,"[25] men already in prison or half a step away. But, influenced as much by popular "slick" magazine fiction of the day as by anything else—and despite Himes's admiration of Dashiell Hammett—they were quite different beasts from the sort of crime stories one encountered in pulps such as *Black Mask* and *Detective Story*. They exhibit little of the trademark headlong narratives and violence of those magazines, or, for that matter, of Himes's own later work. And while often strong on character and plot development, they remain, the earliest of them at any rate, essentially apprentice work. Swayback syntax peeps out from the corners of uncertain sentences, the clichés and commonplaces of received wisdom float to the top, a scab of sentimentality forms over them. Himes may have realized this in 1971 when, assembling his anthology *Black on Black*, he passed over all but one of these stories, 1937's "The Night's for Cryin'."

Yet even as he postured, writing (one assumes) the sort of things he imagined readers (and editors) wanted, Himes, ever intuitive, had begun groping his way toward what would become his real work; the engines are there. He was stretching muscles, trying out this new, deeper voice, finding out just how large a container he might fill. The stories are a kind of laboratory, then. Himes quickly eliminated his more obvious mistakes, Milliken notes, and just as quickly began showing considerable control over his medium; the stories "represent an amazingly rapid progress towards professional competence."[26] If early stories are manifestly didactic, if others court clichés of film and romance fiction, if moments of spare brilliance alternate with doldrums of troweled-in autobiography, soon all this starts cooking down in the stew. The leap from the overwrought and overwritten thickets of "His Last Day" (published November 1932) to "Prison Mass" (March, April, May 1933) with its control, clarity, and complexity is truly impressive.

For all its faults, however (and they are peculiarly Himesian faults), "His Last Day" demonstrates the kind of evocation of fear at its basest, physical level, the reek and swelter of it, that Himes does better than anyone else, calling to mind those nightmarish waking scenes of *If He Hollers Let Him Go* and *The Primitive*. In "Prison Mass" we encounter early examples of the cadenced, poetic writing we grow to expect from Himes:

A tiny flake of vagrant snow fluttered in through an open window, appearing eerily from the translucent gray of the early morning like a frightened ghost seeking the brilliant cheer of the lighted chapel, and quickly melted on the back of a convict's hand.[27]

Similarly, while chapters 14 and 21 of *Cast the First Stone* closely parallel the first two *Esquire* stories "Crazy in the Stir" and "To What Red Hell," even to the point of retaining phrases and sentences, Himes has not only fully rewritten but also fully *reimagined* the material. These chapters are as structured and precise as the stories are simplistic and wayward. Nothing better illustrates Himes's growing skill.

Not only does Himes learn to write in these stories but, as Franklin suggests, all his major themes, all the engines of his art, surface in them.

There is, for instance, the fascination with grotesques that came to fruition in the Harlem cycle: ogrelike Pork Chop Smith of "Pork Chop Paradise," half frog, half ape; or the monstrous Black Boy of "The Night's For Cryin'" with his thick red lips, plate-shaped face, and perpetual popeyed expression.

There is, too, this weird, duple integrity Himes's characters so often have. His hustlers and hard cases may represent themselves outwardly as unbreachable and unyielding, and may in fact be so, but the front doesn't carry over to their inner lives. There they become, like all of us, simple Boolean equations of fear and desire. Himes's monsters don't rationalize or dissemble: they know themselves for what they are.

In the account of his Chicago arrest Himes cited his inability to run. That same inability, to flee when flight is the only sane choice, or to act when action is imperative, turns up repeatedly in Himes's characters, as far back as Signifier in "Prison Mass." The protagonist of "Crazy in the Stir," driven mad by loss of privacy and the prison's constant din, is forever pulled back from the brink of violence by conditioning, "that queer docility common to prisoners."[28] Prison conditioning has so diminished the protagonist of "To What Red Hell" that during the fire he finds himself wholly incapable of functioning.

He heard a voice say: "Get a blanket and give a hand here." His lips twitched slightly as a nausea swept over him. He said: "No can do," in a low choky whisper . . . He really wanted to go up in that smoking inferno . . . But he couldn't, just couldn't, that's all.[29]

Similarly unmanned, Jimmy Monroe in *Cast the First Stone* climbs atop a wall to jump to his death but, when lights flash signaling bedtime, docilely climbs down and into bed, boiling with helplessness, frustration, and rage.

Most important perhaps, in the *Esquire* stories Himes developed his genius for observing and then recording a scene in such physical detail as to completely overtake the reader. These stories also demonstrate a technique Himes would perfect with *Cast the First Stone* and use ever thereafter, a kind of jacking up of reality, amassing physical detail and impressions with such rapidity and to such degree that they collapse into one another, become distorted, almost surreal.

I swung at his shiny face. I missed him and went sprawling over a corpse. The soft, mushy form gave beneath me. I jumped up, shook my hands as if I had fallen into a puddle of filth. Then the centipede began crawling about in my head. It was mashed in the middle and it crawled slowly through my brain just underneath the skull, dragging its mashed middle. I could feel its legs all gooey with the slimy green stuff that had been mashed out of it.

And then I was running again. I was running blindly over the stiffs, stepping in their guts, their faces. I could feel the soft squashy give of their bellies, the roll of muscles over bones. I put my face down behind my left hand, bowed my head and plowed forward.

A moment later I found myself standing in front of the entrance to the Catholic chapel. I felt a queer desire to laugh.[30]

Finally, then, the place of violence in Himes's work.

Nathanael West remarked that he was able to write such short yet intense books because in the United States we don't have to prepare for violence. Violence is our birthright, the very air we breathe. In prison Himes watched fellow prisoners cut, cripple, or kill one another for nonsensical reasons, or for no reason at all. Himes cites two convicts killing one another over their argument as to whether Paris was in

France or France in Paris. (In *The Crazy Kill* Grave Digger tells this same story to an Irish police lieutenant who then tops him, in what musicians would call a cutting contest, with his own absurdist tale of two Irishmen.) Another was murdered for not passing the bread. Once Himes awoke to the sound of a gurgling scream and the sight of blood spurting from a cut throat onto the mattress below. The experience taught him, he said, that people will do anything. And he carried that sense of pervasive, absurdist violence into his mature work, where it became that work's major theme: the violence society lowers against its members, the violence blacks level against blacks, the violence we do against those we love and against ourselves.

For Himes, violence is at the same time matter-of-fact and so intense as to be almost cartoonlike: an inescapable, mundane part of black life as well as a metaphor for the absurdity of that life. When after treading across that carpet of corpses Jimmy Monroe feels "a queer desire to laugh" he points up a fundamental element in Himesian violence. Violence is always edged with humor in Himes. Boundaries dissolve; often we're unable to say where one leaves off and the other begins. We laugh at the woman fused to the wall by a hit-and-run driver and arctic temperatures, clothes falling away to reveal her as a transvestite—laugh, then are horrified at ourselves for doing so.

Or this scene from well along in *Blind Man with a Pistol*:

> The black man walked forward down a urine-stinking hallway beneath the feet of a gigantic black plaster of paris image of Jesus Christ, hanging by his neck from the rotting white ceiling of a large square room. There was an expression of teeth-bared rage on Christ's black face. His arms were spread, his fists balled, his toes curled. Black blood dripped from red nail holes. The legend underneath read:
> THEY LYNCHED ME.[31]

One of many subplots in *Pinktoes* is that of black journalist Moe Miller, fighting a perpetual war against a giant rat in his home in Brooklyn. The rat even moves traps that Moe sets for it, placing them strategically where they break Moe's toes. When at one point Moe throws his hunting knife at it, the rat clasps the knife in its teeth and rushes him. Moe flees the apartment, telegraphing his wife: FOR

GOD SAKE DO NOT COME STOP RAT HAS GOT KNIFE STOP IN POSSESSION OF HOUSE STOP I AM DROPPING THE NEGRO PROBLEM UNTIL RAT IS CAUGHT STOP.[32]

It's in *The Primitive* that this fusion of comedy and violence reaches its apotheosis, moving from there into the Harlem cycle.

Others of the early stories introduce what will become typically Himesian themes.

"Every Opportunity" with its portrait of a prisoner released into a world where he has no way of getting by recalls Himes's contention that America's racial problems truly began with emancipation, when whites "gave Negroes their freedom" without providing any way for them to meet their basic needs: "Well, this whole problem in America, as I see it, developed from the fact that the slaves were freed and that there was no legislation of any sort to make it possible for them to live."[33]

"A Nigger" introduces the theme of the black's silent collaboration in the damage done him. A conservative white businessman regularly visits his mistress Fay in the Harlem apartment he maintains for her. Fay also has a black lover, Joe, "some kind of writer or poet or something," who one day when Sugar Daddy arrives unexpectedly has to hide in the closet and listen to his harangues about "the lower classes" and FDR's welfare and social programs. Just before the white man leaves, he opens the closet door and, pretending that he's not seen Joe, immediately closes it—failing even to acknowledge Joe's existence.

> The fact was he had kept standing there, taking it, even after he could no longer tell himself that it was a joke, a trim on a sucker, just so he could keep on eating off the bitch . . . Uncle Tomism, acceptance, toadying—all there in its most rugged form. One way to be a nigger. Other Negroes did it other ways—he did it the hard way. The same result—*a nigger*.[34]

Joe takes his fury and frustration out on Fay, stopped only by the arrival of a neighbor brandishing a long-barreled .38.

"The Night's for Cryin'" moves from one closed society into another, from prison to Cleveland's black ghetto, to document the monstrous inhumanities spawned there. In the same interview quoted above, that with old friend and fellow novelist John A. Williams in

1970, Himes held that a major motivation in his writing was to force white Americans to confront the horror and violence-making of the black ghettos. Himes was working the claim of *Do the Right Thing* and *Boyz N the Hood* forty or fifty years before the rush.

> White people in America, it seems to me, are titillated by the problem of the black people, more than taking it seriously. I want to see them take it seriously, good and goddamn seriously, and the only way that I think of to make them take it seriously is with violence.[35]

"Headwaiter" depicts a man (patterned after Himes's uncle) willfully following the rules in what he knows nevertheless to be an absurd world. In so doing the story prefigures Grave Digger's and Coffin Ed's knowledge of the futility of their efforts to effect real change, or, finally, even to keep the Harlem chaos in check. They're prefigured more directly in the detective team of "He Knew," a story prefiguring, as well, Himes's theme of black-on-black violence and growing sense of absurdity.

Detectives John Jones and Henry Walls tramp their weary beat, "heads pulled down into the upturned collars of their overcoats like the heads of startled turtles, hats slanted forward against the cold December drizzle," investigating a series of robberies in the waterfront district of "dismal warehouses and squalid tenements."[36] Their white precinct captain, sounding very much like the Harlem Cycle's Lieutenant Anderson, tells them: "I'm putting you two men on this job because it's a Negro neighborhood and I believe that it's Negroes who are pulling these jobs. You fellows are plodders and it's plodders we need." The story's climactic shoot-out in pitch dark is something Himes will use again in the first Harlem novel, *For Love of Imabelle*. Like Grave Digger and Coffin Ed, the detectives are plain men doing an unpleasant, thankless job, in the final analysis little more than beards for the white power structure, just another form, even if a tacitly sanctioned form, of black-on-black violence.

Himes first was assigned to the so-called coal company, carting shavings from the lumber mill for use in heating. One frozen morning he refused to dig out shavings from under snow and ice and was thrown in the hole with two others, with only scraps of blankets for warmth and the bite of bedbugs to keep their minds occupied. Pointing out that he continued to receive disability payments from the state, Himes was moved to lighter duties. He swept floors and swept away wheelbarrow tracks, taught briefly at the prison school, worked in the soup company, was in and out of the hospital with pneumonia, flu, sprained back, a broken arm or leg. Eventually he signed up for a correspondence course in law. He began writing petitions for parole and, finally, stories.

We assume that many of Jimmy Monroe's fellow convicts are modeled on those Himes knew. Redheaded runt Starlight, claiming Mafia connections and saying he was MacArthur's orderly in the war. Blackie, a mob gunman, serving two life terms for multiple murders. Male tramp Bobby Guy. Metz the ex-jeweler and wife killer who introduces Monroe to writing. Short Britches, Froggy, Donald Duck, Jumpy Stone, Dew Baby, Signifier, St. Louis Slick.

> What a convict has been on the outside means very little in prison, no matter what they tell you. The convicts who were gangsters outside usually turn into finks inside, or they acquire t.b. and die, or they have money to buy their way and then they are still big shots. The toughies who had nothing but their outside reps got their throats cut by hickville punks who had never heard of them. Money talked as loud there as it does anywhere—if not louder.
>
> And the days passed. Square and angular, with hardbeaten surfaces; confining, restricting, congesting. But down in the heart of these precise, square blocks of days there was love and hate; ambition and regret; there was hope, too, shining eternally through the long gray years; and perhaps there was even a little happiness.[37]

At heart, *Cast the First Stone* is a coming-of-age novel. Gradually, in part from a network of preceptors, in part from observation (and he is, like Himes, a fine observer), Jimmy Monroe (again like Himes, we presume) learns the bounds and mores of this world *bouleversé*. He understands the way in which prison forms and institutions are distorted versions of those in the larger society outside. He understands, too, that he must come to terms with—learn to control, or at very least rechannel—his anger. In this he is not always successful, as his creator was not, then or in later life. The outward story documents down-and-out prison life; the inner story records Jimmy Monroe's wrestle with the angel of his own self-destructive impulses, a match he wins, but just barely.

We struggle, in part by our sufferings, in part by our identification through art and relationships with others, in part by those relationships themselves, toward redemption, Jimmy Monroe and Chester Himes no less than the rest of us. Monroe-Himes enters prison a man closed off, a man who will *not* be hurt again. There he relearns to open himself, learns not so much to make connections with others as to let them form spontaneously. As Robert Creeley says: It's only in the relationships we manage, that we live at all.

Cast the First Stone is structured around four relationships, each marking a period of Jimmy's development. Mal shows up early in the book to appoint himself Jimmy's tutor-protector. Adamantly against "degeneracy," he steers Jimmy clear of those "filthy sons of bitches" and instructs him in the small ways a man can maintain dignity in prison surroundings. The friendship comes to an end with the fire, when Jimmy, at the edge of hysteria, tells Mal "I want you for my woman." Next is Blocker, after Jimmy gets transferred into the cripple company. Presented in more or less idealistic terms, this is the most uncomplicated relationship, as Jimmy learns to fit in; he and Blocker become central to prison society, buddies who might easily stride off together into the film's closing moments. With Blocker's parole Jimmy befriends Metz, who offers something new: "His conversation was a relief from the stale, monotonous babble of the prison. I'd get away from that when we talked . . . Metz was the first really decent fellow whom I had met in prison, although Blocker was my only true friend."[38]

The final, all-important relationship, coming after Jimmy drifts to the very rim of madness then solidly back, is with Duke Dido. They're of an age, and Jimmy must see in Dido something of himself as newcomer five years before. Jimmy's commitment is instant, total. The two become inseparable, denounced, and persecuted by other convicts for whom same-sex acts are the norm but who can't accept such passionate engagement. When Dido is transferred to the girl-boy company, Jimmy insists upon going along, but the warden transfers him to the prison farm instead. Dido, a naif who unlike Jimmy never was able to adapt to prison life, hangs himself.

> I knew, beyond all doubt, that he had done it for me. He had done it to give me a perfect ending. It was so much like him to do this one irrevocable thing to let me know for always that I was the only one. Along with the terrible hurt I could not help but feel a great gladness and exaltation.[39]

Letters, drafts, and anecdotal evidence validate the Dido story in both broad outline and detail. Duke Dido was in real life Prince Rico. Whereas Himes's previous relationship, with a Catholic called Lively in one early draft of *Cast the First Stone*, was never consummated (despite Himes's devotion being such that he enrolled in catechism classes and probably converted), Rico and Himes quickly became lovers. They read to one another, wrote plays and an opera called *Bars and Stripes Forever* together, talked endlessly about movies they'd seen, called one another by pet names. Early drafts of the novel contain letters and instances of more frank romance between the lovers. Upon publication of *Cast the First Stone* in 1952, Himes wrote to Carl Van Vechten that the most fulfilling relationship he had ever had was with the character he'd called Dido in that novel.

One bond between Himes and Prince Rico was their strong need for fantasy. Like Luis and Valentin in Manuel Puig's *Kiss of the Spider Woman*, they talked endlessly of movies and their stars, pored over movie magazines. Himes felt a similar draw to stories in the slick popular magazines, experiencing as he read them "all the soft, mushy emotions"[40] forbidden him by the prison experience and by his own obdurate nature. Subsequent shame over his sentimentality, he wrote, would lead him to become "invariably more vulgar, obscene, callous,"[41] as though two men coexisted (and in many ways they did) inside Chester's skull. Himes's early plots, too, career from familiar hard-boiled attitudes to frank sentimentality.

That same double consciousness emerged in somewhat different form in correspondence with Van Vechten:

> As I look back now I feel that much of my retardation as a writer has been due to a subconscious (and conscious and deliberate)

desire to escape my past. All mixed up no doubt with the Negro's desire for respectability and such. It brought a lot of confusion to my own mind, added to which was a great deal of pressure of a thousand kinds being exerted by friends and relatives and loved ones who were half ashamed of what I wrote, forgetting that it was what I wrote that made me what I was, until I was caught in a bag which I didn't begin to break out of until I wrote *If He Hollers*. I wrote that defiantly, more or less, at the time without thought of it being published.[42]

Indeed, Stephen Milliken finds in this biform nature, this constant tug to discrete ends, the central critical problem presented by Himes's work. The work has obvious power, he asserts. It rarely fails to claim and move the reader.

Yet at all points in every part of Himes's work weaknesses of the most obvious kind are evident. The author seems continually to be choosing, for example, the more striking effect for its impact value alone, or to be choosing the most tired cliché available in full and triumphant knowledge of its falsity and tawdriness. He can in fact be embarrassingly bad, and yet the apparent weaknesses in Himes's work seem somehow to be essential to the strengths.[43]

Cast the First Stone ends with Jimmy looking back at the prison on his way to the farm: "You big tough son of a bitch, you tried to kill me but I've got you beat now, I thought."[44] So does Himes's first-written novel become, finally, a story of redemption, for its author as much as its protagonist. In prison, in his stories, and especially in this novel, Chester Himes learned how our lives can be ransomed, if forever imperfectly, by the relationships we manage and by literature. Chester Himes, always "the hardbitten old pro"[45] *Life* magazine made him out to be, never one to take advice, never one to do things the right or expected or easy way. He'd create his books the same way he steered his life, by impulse and instinct, and if the life boiled over into chaos, then it would be a very *personal* kind of chaos, and the work that lanced out from it, those messages and novels, would be just as personal—like no light ever seen before.

In that idiosyncrasy, Himes's work seems peculiarly, unmistakably American. As a nation, as individuals, our strengths often rise directly from our weaknesses. We've a particular genius for quirkiness, for getting the job done despite ourselves. As has been suggested already, Himes's greatest strength as a writer lay precisely in his ability to confront the unresolvable tensions and contradictions within himself, to draw them out in all their untowardness and give them temporizing shape.

In the wake of the Easter morning fire and subsequent disclosure of prison conditions—beginning with 4,000 inmates housed in a facility built for 1,800—special review boards had been set up and many prisoners' sentences commuted to the statutory minimum. Following six months at the prison farm, having now served seven and a half years of his twenty to twenty-five-year sentence, on April 1, 1936, Himes was paroled to his mother's custody. He stepped back out from that small world whose hard rules he had learned into a confusing, larger, somehow forever *soft* world, a world you could never quite get a hold on—and into the arms of the Depression.

3 "One Way to Be a Nigger"

In his story "On Dreams and Reality" Himes tells of a young man returning home from prison with high hopes of a new life, only to find his family living in one squalid room, hanging on by the barest of threads. The story is a miniature, perfect tragedy, paralleling the failures of the prisoner unable to make his way in the outside world with the general failures of the Depression.

"In the stagnant isolation of prison, dreams grow as tall as redwood trees,"[1] that story begins as James "Happy" Trent awaits release. Reentry with all its joys and terrors must have been much on Himes's mind, before and after his own. "Every Opportunity" presents another ex-con's inability to break old habits despite best intentions, and, in the kind of abrupt, revelatory ending Himes favored for a time (a kind of shattering of the text), his return to prison. Other stories deal with memory and dreams that let prisoners go on—to them, there is little difference between memory and dream—and with irruptions of reality. Nailed awake by his sense of loss in "Face in the Moonlight," a prisoner half dreams, half remembers the life that brought him here. "I Don't Want to Die" gives us the reveries of a prisoner with a terminal disease, "His Last Day" the experience of a man pacing down his final hours to execution. Both these last stories evidence the evocation of physical detail and the sensual surface, simultaneously lush and spare, that become a Himes trademark.

"The Meanest Cop in the World" drops us with great immediacy into a poor college student's wondrous fortune at meeting the beautiful Violet, then tears us from the dream, as he himself is torn from it, when for absolutely no reason a policeman shows up in the dream to attack him.

And then suddenly Jack realized that he wasn't a freshman in a nice old college, and he wasn't in love with a pretty girl called Violet, that he didn't even know such a girl, that he was just convict number 10012 in a dark, chilly cell, and he had eaten too many beans at supper. But for hours afterward he lay there silently cursing the huge policeman who had made him realize this.[2]

Again and again, rents are torn in the sky, in walls thought solid, and unwanted truths push their way into his characters' worlds.

Amorphous fear, occult oppression, were by then signature Himes. Yet another story ends: "All that day, copying records down at the city hall, half blind with a hangover and trembling visibly, he kept cursing something. He didn't know exactly what it was and he thought it was a hell of a thing when a man had to curse something without knowing what it was."[3]

Whereas the stories of the thirties deal mostly with prison and criminals, in the forties Himes began to extend his reach. He had become, inasmuch as he would ever align himself with any movement, a social activist, publishing fiction and articles in the National Urban League's *Opportunity* and the NAACP's *Crisis*. In part this was typical Himes role-playing, in part the usual writerly trying on of new masks, in part simply the result of new opportunities for publication. But stories such as "Black Laughter" and "All He Needs Is Feet" reflect Himes's deeper awareness of the great American inequation; many of them edge toward attitudes and preoccupations we closely associate with the mature writer.

And although he tried to get outside this teaching of America, it was inside of him, making him scared . . . Not of being lynched; this was Cleveland, Ohio. They don't hang Negroes in the north; they have other and more subtle ways of killing them.[4]

Or this from the same story, "All God's Chillun Got Pride," published nine years before Himes's expatriation:

Having been educated in America, he had learned of course that living and breathing unaccompanied by certain other inalienable rights, such as liberty, and the pursuit of happiness, were of small consequence; but he had learned, also, that this ideology did not apply to him. He never really sat down and thought about it for any length of time; because he knew that if he ever did, living in America would become impossible.[5]

Subsequently incorporated in *Lonely Crusade*, this story seems a landmark on several fronts. It offers what amounts to a prototype of the emerging Himes protagonist: a well-educated, articulate personality disintegrating under pressures of circumstance, pervasive fear, and his own self-destructive patterns. Compulsively he analyzes himself, picking at the scab, but he can never get at the wound. The story exhibits, moreover, an adroit use of reimagined autobiography prefiguring Himes's first novels and, most importantly, *The Primitive*.

In much the same way that the free-floating fear of "All God's Chillun Got Pride" transports us to *If He Hollers* territory ("I felt torn all loose inside, shrivelled, paralyzed, as if after a while I'd have to get up and die"[6]), stories like "A Night of New Roses" underline Himes's castings-about with hypotheses on their way to becoming axioms, here an equation of racial pain with personal. By the time we reach "Daydream," we're deep into Himesland. A wild and woolly tale of wreaking vengeance on white Southern peckerwoods fades to a black man sitting alone in his New York hotel room: "'You are sick, son,' I said to my smiling reflection. After a moment I added, 'But that isn't anything to worry about. We are all sick. Sicker than we know.'"[7]

In these stories Himes, as always, worked by instinct, blindly feeling his way through rooms of unaccustomed furniture, eccentric doorways, sudden walls. From all accounts he wrote in a state of fervid excitement, flailing away at the material with both hands. Chips of logic and emotion fell where they might. Yet his face begins recognizably to emerge.

Reimagined autobiography, along with a new sense of structure and with an intensity deriving more from that structure, from interiority and from the language itself than from incident, all come together in "Da-Da-Dee," a remarkably mature story from 1948 whose protagonist shares his author's alcoholic blackouts, dalliance with radicalism in L.A., and residence at an artist's colony (here called Skiddoo). Written in the wake of hostile criticism for his early novels and amidst the wreckage of his marriage to Jean, the story is a virtual sketch for *The Primitive*; its protagonist even plans a story titled *I Was Looking for a Street*, a title Himes will attribute to alter ego Jesse in that novel. Here Jethro Adams, genius kid turned writer turned drunk, lies abed thinking over the course of his life. *When they started talking about how things could be you believed them, didn't you?* he tells himself.

> He felt as if nothing would ever matter again one way or another. He thought it was something Congress Street did to him . . . It was like going back to Central Avenue, a street of dives and whores of which he had been a part at seventeen and nothing mattered but the night. It was like putting behind him everything that he had learned and experienced since and going back to that year of vice and indifference. He was never meant to be anything but a cheap, smiling gambler with a flashy front, he told himself. He was a simple man.[8]

The Chester Himes who stepped to freedom from the Ohio State Penitentiary on April 1, 1936, was anything but a simple man. He had survived. Learned what he had to, done what he had to, to survive. He had seen the worst in man and, in rare instances, as when inmates labored to save others during the Easter fire, he had seen the best as well. He had found friendship and, briefly, love. And if he had been to some degree unmanned (as he must have been) by the prison experience, as by racism and by his own self-destructive urges, prison had also given him, in his writing, a means of redirecting pain and anger, a field phone he had only to crank and spark to discharge those emotions, to *use* them.

The state of Ohio ended Himes's disability payments just weeks prior to his release. What money he'd had in prison was gone, some of it put toward Joe's college expenses. "Broke and without income for the first time in my adult life,"[9] Himes must have felt himself shipwrecked on the Depression's shores. Back in Columbus Joe was completing his doctorate in sociology; soon he'd begin working as an administrator for the Columbus Urban League. Estelle kept house for Joe, and herself would soon return to South Carolina. Theirs was an orderly, directed life. They must have awaited Chester's return with profoundly mixed feelings.

Chester, of course, had profoundly mixed feelings of his own. He emerged into a changed world. Now twenty-six years old, having survived and come to his manhood in one of the toughest prisons in America, suddenly, from lack of money and from parole stipulations, he found himself in a state of almost childlike dependency. Still, he resolved that, despite the marks against him, despite the Depression, he would make his way by sheer force of will and innate talent. He would be, *was*, a writer.

First, though, he'd take time out: after all those years locked away, he deserved the chance to savor his freedom. One wonders, too, if rebelliousness against his dependency on Estelle and Joe may have been as much a factor in his behavior as simple recidivism. At any rate, soon he was back among whores in the city's black slums. He was also back among gamblers, pimps, and other ex-convicts. This, we assume, he kept from Estelle, as he had earlier kept secret his work at Bunch Boy's. But she smelled the women on him when he came home in the early hours, leading to "such dreadful rows that Joe had to intervene."[10]

Characteristically, Himes boasted in his memoirs that the Columbus whores serviced him free, presumably for his general attractiveness, charm, and educated manner as much as for his prodigious sexual appetite.

> I didn't have any money so I had to look for whores I could have for free. There were numerous white whores in the black ghettos of Columbus at the time, and I had success because I took them out, so long as they paid. Of course I had to keep out of the way of their pimps. Several times landlords had to intervene to keep me from being shot.[11]

He also tells of being persuaded by a group of ex-cons to go along with them to "Georgia," a teenage black whore, that is, to use her then not pay her, and, touched by her tears as she realized what was going on, of refusing to take part. That split-hair moral stance within what was from any perspective a contemptible situation seems typically Himes, as does his derisory final word on the matter: "I learned afterwards that all the others had caught gonorrhea from her."[12]

Another instance of easy acquiescence finally pushed Estelle to action. One Sunday, telling Estelle he had to go see about a job, Chester instead joined a young man he knew slightly to smoke marijuana and returned to the house so high that he thought he was having a heart attack. (His description of his response to the drug takes up two full pages and recalls more than anything else "psychedelic" sequences from sixties movies.) Chester admitted marijuana use to the doctor, who passed the admission on to his mother, who immediately dressed and left for a long tête-à-tête with Chester's parole officer. The following week, parole was reassigned to his father.

Chester arrived in Cleveland in July. Joseph at that time was working for the WPA as a mechanics teacher. He lived in a two-room flat off Cedar Avenue on Ninety-third Street and spent much of his free time with a woman friend. Mostly he left Chester alone and to his own devices, as he'd always done. So while Chester's economic prospects remained grim, at least he had escaped his mother's oppressive witness and the resentment he felt at forced dependence on her. He no longer like a bad conjurer had to obscure his every move with misdirection and quick patter. Any man that long shut away under the supervision of others must hunger to be his own man. Add in Chester's age and obstinacy, and the hunger becomes volatile.

Though he found temporary part-time work as a waiter and bellhop, this did little to improve his finances in any substantial way. He turned again to fiction, trying unsuccessfully to write for the slick magazines. He did manage to sell again to *Esquire*, stories that Fabre and Margolies characterize as expressing "a mix of melancholy and unrelenting fury."[13] "The Visiting Hour" appeared in September 1936, "The Night's For Cryin'" the following January. "Headwaiter," also from this period and first published in the National Urban League's *Opportunity* as "Salute to the Passing," memorializes Himes's boss at his first job out of prison, when uncle Andrew arranged for Chester to wait tables part-time at Wade Park Manor Hotel, the very place Chester had met his accident in the elevator.

Himes continued to work at his writing, squeezing out stories and recasting several as plays, among them a homoerotic tale of two prisoners titled "Idle Hours." During this period he also continued writing and rewriting his prison novel. At least three distinct drafts of it exist, along with fragments. And if writing never quite turned the corner from avocation, nor seemed likely to do so anytime soon, Himes did begin to find supporters and sponsors. One was his cousin Henry

Lee Moon, then working as a federal housing official in Washington and later to become publicity director for the NAACP, who read Chester's work, told him what he thought, even suggested possible venues for publication. Through Joe he met editors and writers for magazines like *Opportunity* and *The Crisis*, for which he himself began writing stories and strident editorials. Sidney Williams, director of the Cleveland Urban League, and politician-minister Grant Reynolds also offered Himes advice and support.

Editor N. R. Howard of the Cleveland *Daily News*, who had read Chester's work in *Esquire*, supposedly took him under wing as well; they'd sit talking for hours about writing and books, Richard Wright's *Uncle Tom's Children* among others. While local newspapers at the time didn't employ blacks (one editor telling Chester that he couldn't hire him if he was Jesus Christ reincarnated), Himes always maintained that he wrote fifty pieces titled "This Cleveland" for Howard, who paid him out of pocket, a dollar apiece. A typically hyperbolic 1946 letter to Carl Van Vechten ups the ante on all this: "I wrote by-line articles for the CIO weekly organ, the *Union Leader*, and then the daily vignettes for the editorial page of the *Cleveland News* which were very popular (one or two were reprinted in the *New Yorker*). I wrote for two or three Cleveland magazines."[14] No such columns or evidence of same exist in the newspaper's files; a single draft for what may have been intended as such a piece is among Himes's papers at Yale.

Sometime in August Himes made his most important new contact. When Oberlin graduates Russell and Rowena Jelliffe opened the Karamu House as a neighborhood arts center in 1927, one of their most faithful patrons was high-school student Langston Hughes. Now Hughes had become well known, and Karamu House stood alone in regularly producing plays written and performed by Negroes; they remained loosely associated. Hughes was impressed enough by two plays Himes submitted, reworkings of "To What Red Hell?" and "Day After Day," that, while the plays were passed over, the two became friends of a sort. Hughes would later champion Himes's first novel, recommending it to his own publisher, Blanche Knopf. He would also provide introductions for Himes in New York and Los Angeles.

The year before, Karamu House had staged Hughes's *Little Ham*, a slapstick comedy set in the Harlem of the twenties, whose lead character, shoeshine boy and ladies' man Hamlet Hitchcock Jones, seems in direct contradiction to its author's manifestoes for a new Negro literature.

The movement in which Hughes had become a major figure, the Harlem Renaissance, reflecting monumental changes in American society and within the Negro intelligentsia, attained its zenith about the time Himes entered prison.

In the period from 1890 to 1920 with the breakneck transition of their social base from peasantry to urban proletariat, blacks suffered a dislocation second only to slavery. Doubling its population, Harlem became a discrete metropolis within the greater metropolis of New York City; it became, also, a kind of racial capital. The times were a rare cocktail of postwar catharsis, Jazz Age liberties, defiance of authority, sexual revolution, and spiritual alienation. White society romanced the Negro, setting him up as a symbol of freedom from restraint—the innocent at his pleasure, unbound by strictures of civilization: the primitive. Blacks themselves, reversing assimilationist trends, entered into a period of self-discovery, searching for alternative values within their own tradition. In part this was fueled by waves of black nationalism taking forms as diverse as Marcus Garvey's Back to Africa movement and alignment with the Communist Party whose official gloss held that Negroes comprised an internal oppressed nation. Black self-realization had worked its way from the Niagara Movement, through Negro defense groups such as the NAACP and National Urban League, particularly by way of their house organs *The Crisis* and *Opportunity*, to this New Negro movement of the twenties.

As LeRoi Jones pointed out in *Blues People*, the earliest black art ignored African-American culture, striving instead to join the mainstream. Only with the Harlem Renaissance's New Negro did black writers and artists embrace their folk culture. The shift was from social mimicry to individuality, from a sense of the marginal (marginal both, as Negroes, to that mainstream culture and, as a cultured elite, to their own) to a sense of their own centrality. Not until the militant spirit of the sixties will we see again such concerted motive. The Harlem Renaissance dead-ended in the economic crash; reflecting the cynicism, disillusion, and dashed hopes of the time, that later movement shattered into pieces.

Whatever was distinctly Negro, by Harlem School creed, was of folk or slave origin. Its practitioners recognized that Negro literature came of different roots than those of the dominant, white literature, roots based in the folktale, in exaggeration and in specific language arts. Such a distinctive literature required distinctive language; it would co-opt rhythms of jazz, inflections of the street, jive. And it would be more interested in interpreting Negro culture than in pleading the cause of racial justice. With Santayana, members of the Harlem School might have said that a culture could be judged only by the excellence, or example, of the individual life.

Writing in *The Nation* in 1926, Langston Hughes proclaimed: "We younger Negro artists who create now intend to express our individual dark-skinned selves without fear or shame. If white people are pleased, we are glad. If they are not, it doesn't matter . . . If colored people are pleased, we are glad. If they are not, their displeasure doesn't matter either."[15]

The Depression broke the back of the Harlem Renaissance movement as it broke so many others. Primacies of survival reasserted themselves. Any black culture apart from the mainstream American culture seemed sheerest fantasy now. James Weldon Johnson had been correct: separate black institutions were contingent. Increasingly the black intelligentsia turned toward leftist movements, curling and tucking and holding their breaths to fit into the Procrustean bed of identification with the masses, with workers black and white alike moving together toward Bartolomeo Vanzetti's "serene white light of a reasonable world."

Hughes's sponsorship of Himes was not unreserved. In one 1946 essay, citing *If He Hollers Let Him Go* and Richard Wright's *Black Boy* and sounding a bit Old Guard, Hughes called for "a good novel about *good* Negroes who do not come to a bad end," pointing out that there were millions of Negroes "who never murder anyone, or rape or get raped or want to rape, who never lust after white bodies, or cringe before white stupidity, or Uncle Tom, or go crazy with race, or off-balance with frustration."[16] Asked to provide a blurb for *Lonely Crusade*, Hughes declined, writing to Blanche Knopf that "Most of the people in it just do not seem to me to have good sense or be in their right minds, they behave so badly, which makes it difficult to care very much what happens to any of them."[17]

With his first published novels, Himes had tried his level best to go with the times, writing stories of educated Negroes (sons of the rising black middle class, like those of the Harlem Renaissance) who (like the adaptive intellectuals they were) now pledged their talents to the great work of unionism. Himes never had much luck fitting his work to others' standards, though. He'd aim his ship for India and hit America every time. He'd start out with this simple enough notion, a story for the slicks, a proletariat novel, a detective story, then intuition and improvisation would take over and the notion started squirming and changing and whipping about in his hand. As often as not, he wouldn't even notice how it had changed fundamentally: that it had become something else. That he'd created, yet again, something profoundly against the tide and profoundly (the very word) unfashionable. In work as in life, for all his efforts and resolve, somehow Chester generally wound up going about things the hard way, standing ashore looking at the wreckage in the water about him, thinking *Hell of a swim!*

The same month he met Hughes, on August 13, Himes made another important move: with the consent of his parole officer, he married Jean Johnson. Immediately the couple went off "to live by ourselves in a series of shabby rented rooms" and begin "slowly starving together."[18] Thin ice everywhere, the situation further complicated by Chester's not wanting Jean to work. He felt it incumbent upon him to be provider, even if providings were slim. "She didn't seem to mind too much, she was loyal and loving and she believed in me. But I began to feel cornered in a black world."[19] Uncle Roddy and Aunt Leah had the newlyweds over for dinner whenever they could, and sent them home with extra food. The marriage was strong in the face of all adversity. Jean and Chester loved one another deeply. She knew his background, had been with or beside him for years, knew at first hand his moodiness and explosive temper. Chester found new identity in the role of married man and provider, new sources of strength in his wife's steady initiative. He was no longer alone.

Several descriptions exist of the young couple during this period. Pearl Moody, Chester's supervisor at the Cleveland Public Library, where he soon found work, spoke of him as a remarkably attractive, capable young man, but "nervous, restless, not at all settled in his ways."[20] Co-worker Ruth Seid (who then had published a couple of stories and later wrote novels under the name Jo Sinclair) talked endlessly about books with Chester and often joined the couple for cheap evenings out. Chester was a charmer, she said, handsome and articulate.[21] Jean was his perfect counterpart: every bit as intelligent and articulate as Chester, every bit as attractive, and crazy about him into the bargain.

Dan Levin got to know them when he put word out for writers for his new magazine *Crossroad*. He'd later serve as model for *Lonely Crusade*'s Abe Rosenberg. Chester struck him from the first as "hurt, high strung and brilliant,"[22] Jean as rather reserved but possessed of great dignity and poise. Levin described standing at the window watching Himes stride away forcefully from their initial meeting with Jean walking "calmly beside him as if steadying him to keep him from blazing away like an angry comet."[23]

A brief stint as WPA laborer precipitated a flurry of letters to local and state officials pointing out his status as a writer, whereupon Chester was reassigned to the library. He began as a research assistant writing vocational bulletins and earning ninety-five dollars a month; within the year, promoted to writer, he was engaged in writing a 75,000-word history of Ohio and, by 1940, a Cleveland Guide. Neither saw print.

Quite aside from providing employment to hundreds of writers during the Depression, the Federal Writers' Project became important on other counts. Within its closed society, Negroes were accepted on a basis of social equality—this in a period when black and white musicians could record together only surreptitiously. Through the government workers' union the Project also brought writers into position with the American labor movement, an association that was to have far-reaching effect. This would also provide settings for Himes's first published novels.

Here, too, Himes managed to make a bed he had trouble lying in. Demoted to research assistant for an irreverent piece he wrote concerning struggles between nineteenth-century Shakers and Mennonites, he was restored only after another burst of letters to state and national directors and, finally, FDR himself. Possibly his cousin Henry Lee Moon intervened as well.

The stories published during this period are odd ones. As in Himes's early stories, race recedes in order to foreground other concerns, there prison experience, here abject need. Humiliation and despair are everywhere in these stories. "A Modern Fable" deals with the shooting of Harold A. McDull, who "oozes" Americanism and wants to end the WPA because it costs too much, by citizen and onetime "true believer"

Henry Slaughter. "Looking Down the Street" finds a man in utter extremis, starved and freezing, hoping for "the biggest Goddam war that was ever fought" to save him. "With Malice Toward None" ends with a passage previously quoted: "All that day . . . half blind with a hangover and trembling visibly, he kept cursing something. He didn't know exactly what it was and he thought it was a hell of a thing when a man had to curse something without knowing what it was."[24] Interestingly, Himes's characters now have acquired wives whom they cannot support.

Himes himself, meanwhile, was well on his way to being unmanned as never before, not even by prison, by his failure to provide for Jean.

His parents' troubled marriage still much in his mind, Himes must have equated his father's failures to provide with his own failure, and remembered Joseph's crumbling manhood. Often he would react to inner turmoil with promiscuous behavior and with drinking, both of which served only to compound his self-contempt, then turn his bloated fury against Jean. Later he would put names to the serpents uncoiling then in his chest. He would come to understand poverty as the source of despair, a kind of bottomless well. He would perceive poverty as both origin and reflection of the racism he saw all about him, in every aspect and mien of American life. And he would wonder again and again at poverty's social, psychological, and sexual consequences.

Of that time he wrote: "While on the Writers' Project I did not feel the racial hurt so much . . . My domestic life was happy and we were all, black and white alike, bound together into the human family by our desperate struggle for bread."[25]

Years later, long after Jean had disappeared from his life, he would write of the marriage's decline: ". . . I had convinced myself I was a failure as a writer, and poverty and loneliness and our enforced separation had convinced me I was a failure as a husband. After fourteen years of love and marriage we had lost each other."[26]

4 The Things a Writing Man Will Do

Particulars of a life accumulate, thickets of incident and action we look back on later, try to see through.

In fall of 1941, Jean and Chester Himes joined the waves of hopefuls breaking on California's beach: poor whites trying to get out from under Depression hard times, blacks fleeing Jim Crow laws to seek work in shipyards and munitions plants, soldiers and sailors gearing up for the gathering war. Chester came hoping for work in the studios, the dream of living by his writing reborn. He carried his *Esquire* stories and a draft of *Black Sheep* from studio to studio but was turned down everywhere. Later he claimed that he stalked out of one story conference because of the racial attitudes of other writers. This may be true but sounds suspiciously like Himes self-reinvention. It's far more likely from what we know that he would have been on his best behavior as he made the rounds and that whatever stalking out there was took place afterward, verbally, before Jean. Jack Warner's simple interdiction "I don't want no niggers on this lot," Himes said, reversed his employment as a script reader. He was also considered, but finally passed over, as publicity writer for *Cabin in the Sky* starring Ethel Waters, Bill "Bojangles" Robinson, and Lena Horne, none of whom, he liked to point out, could be served in the MGM commissary.

Mounting a Greyhound in Columbus, Chester and Jean rode it to the continent's edge in Los Angeles, half expecting (as one perennially does with each relocation, each new quest, each rebirth or reinvention of self) to disembark in a different world. Back in heartland Ohio, Chester had joined the queues of the bedraggled seeking work at Cuyahoga Valley's thriving private industries, American Wire & Steel, Warner & Swasey, the Aluminum Company of America, only to be turned down day after day, week after week. Helplessness, frustration, and rage rose in him like sap. He thought his subsequent withdrawal to Malabar Farm might assuage these feelings but finally decided that he was only hiding out there.

Himes's citizenship had been fully restored the previous March when he petitioned the governor for termination of parole. In July that year, Chester and Jean visited cousin Henry Lee Moon in New York. Moon, now working as a writer and editor for the NAACP, had married Molly Lewis, herself a well-known intellectual, who became Chester's model for *Pinktoes'* Harlem hostess Mamie Mason. The trip didn't pan out as Himes had intended, many of the people he had wanted to meet proving unavailable, though he enjoyed the time spent with Moon, toward whom he was surprisingly deferential. The trip also provided Himes with his first glimpse of the city that would prove so important to his work—a city he always loved, widow Lesley Himes says, even after he'd grown to feel that he could no longer possibly live there.

Early that year also, Himes became involved with the Council of Industrial Organizations, purportedly writing articles on CIO history for the Cleveland Industrial Council's yearbook and the Cleveland *Union Leader*. With many others, Himes believed that the fledgling organization, which unlike the American Federation of Labor neither catered to skilled laborers nor excluded Negroes, offered blacks a rare chance for advancement. Experiences here, his early enthusiasm and eventual disillusion, his belief that organized labor never understood Negro psychology and Negro needs but instead merely exploited them to its own ends, would become central to *If He Hollers* and *Lonely Crusade*.

Chester's term with the WPA Writers' Project ended in March 1941. After working briefly for a coffee and tea importer whom he left for unknown reasons, he was unable to find further employment. At one point he and Jean were forced to sell their furniture to provide a few more days' food and shelter. Outside personnel offices at industries newly revived by war efforts—just as his character wished in "Looking Down the Street," war had indeed brought an end to the Depression—he was turned away in favor of white applicants.

Then there was that one final stopover before taking off for the promised land.

In Lucas, just southwest of Cleveland, set among rolling hills in an area called Pleasant Valley, best-selling novelist Louis Bromfield had reclaimed acres of arid land and now practiced new agrarianism on Malabar Farm, as described by E. B. White in a book review for the *New Yorker.*

> Malabar Farm is the farm for me,
> It's got what it takes, to a large degree:
> Beauty, alfalfa, constant movement,
> And a terrible rash of soil improvement.
> Far from orthodox in its tillage,
> Populous as many a village,
> Stuff being planted and stuff being written,
> Fields growing lush that were once unfitten . . .
>
> From far and wide folks came to view
> The things that a writing man will do.[1]

Bromfield, winner of the 1926 Pulitzer Prize for *Early Autumn,* also worked extensively in Hollywood, on screenplays for *Brigham Young* and *For Whom the Bell Tolls* among others. The farm became a magnet for the talented and famous. Humphrey Bogart and Lauren Bacall were married there in 1945.

Years later John A. Williams asked Himes if he had had any idea at the time that his own work would long outlive Bromfield's.

> No, it never occurred to me at all. But I didn't think that Bromfield's work was substantial enough to last. It didn't occur to me that Bromfield had been very successful then with *The Rains Came.* He was making quite a bit of money at that time. This was in the late thirties or 1940, and writers like Bromfield were getting that large money from the serialization in magazines. They were not so much concerned with things like book clubs or reprints and so forth. But the magazine serializations: *Cosmopolitan* was paying Bromfield seventy-five thousand dollars for the serialization of the book.[2]

Through the intercession of the Jelliffes from Karamu House, Jean and Chester spent part of 1941 working as butler and cook for

Bromfield, at a combined salary of $120 a month. It's very difficult to picture Himes, that blazing, proud, angry being described by Dan Levin, in the role of domestic servant, but the two men seem to have gotten along well. Bromfield read Chester's prison novel and offered help in getting it published. When he left for Hollywood that fall, he took a copy of the manuscript along with him.

Chester and Jean soon followed, fetching up against racial barriers at every turn. Blacks in L.A. were treated the same way they were in Southern industrial towns, Himes said; the only difference was hypocrisy. In L.A. they turned you away thinking "Nigger, ain't we good to you?"[3]

It wasn't being refused employment in the plants so much . . . It was the look on the people's faces when you asked them about a job. Most of 'em didn't say right out they wouldn't hire me. They just looked so goddamned startled that I'd even asked. As if some friendly dog had come in through the door and said, "I can talk." It shook me.[4]

Himes's dreams of studio work soon evaporated. Folks out there loved to have black faces around, Himes said; any meeting you went to, there'd always be one—for decor.

One time Marc Connelly, who wrote *Green Pastures*, had a number of screenwriters, so-called intellectuals, and various others whom he had invited to a conference to discuss a film on George Washington Carver—along with two black faces for color, me and Arna Bontemps, I think . . . Marc Connelly was sitting at the head of the table with about twenty people sitting around, and he said, "Well, now I know how we're going to start this film; I know that much about it, and then we can go on from there. Well, you see, Dr. Carver was a very humble man and he always ironed his own shirts. So when we start this film on Dr. Carver, he goes into the kitchen and irons his shirt." So at that point I left.[5]

Earlier, Himes thought he had a good chance of getting on as publicity writer for *Cabin in the Sky*, for which Hall Johnson, fellow traveler in the West Coast communist circles to which Himes had been admitted by referral from Langston Hughes, served as technical adviser. Himes resigned his shipyard job in San Francisco to return to Los Angeles, only to find that the position had already been given to a young black man named Phil Carter, now shut away in an ancient tiny dressing room safely distant from the public relations offices.

Finally Himes tried out as a reader with the young man who ran that department at Warner Brothers.

> It was a job of no consequence. They were only offering some-thing like forty-seven dollars a week to start, whereas you could make eighty-seven a week as a laborer. Anyway, he offered me the job and I was going to take it. I wrote the synopsis for *The Magic Bow*, a well-known book about Paganini, and submitted it. He said it was a good job and that they would employ me. And then—this is what *he* said: he was walking across the lot one day and he ran into Jack Warner and told him, "I have a new man, Mr. Warner, and I think he's going to work out very well indeed." Warner said, "That's fine, boy," and so forth. "Who is he?" And he said, "He's a young black man." And Warner said, "I don't want no niggers on this lot."[6]

By his count Himes held twenty-three jobs in the three years before, with *If He Hollers* accepted by Doubleday, Doran, and Company, he left California for New York. Despite his intelligence and background, and despite the fact that he'd picked up valuable skills from his father—he could read blueprints, knew basic carpentry and construction, and was able to operate any number of machine tools—only two of those jobs, as apprentice shipfitter in Kaiser's Shipyard No. 1 and as shipwright's helper in the L.A. shipyard at San Pedro Harbor, were skilled. For the most part he worked at common labor, rebuilding tires and labeling cans, shoveling rock and sand for the California Rock Company, casting pipe for the Crane Company, carting about two-ton rolls of paper for the California Towel-Saver Company, warehousing for the Hughes Aircraft Company. Totin' barges, liftin' bales.

Just as selectively he would remember other times and places (college and the Chicago police station among them) as those in which awareness of racism overcame him like tumblers falling in a lock, Himes spoke of his three years in L.A. as such in a Paris interview twenty years later.

There, racism became an inescapable fact of life for me. I'd been able to ignore segregation up until then, but now I couldn't. I felt I could "see" racism, and it seemed to stick to me. It contaminated everything. It was like a disease I couldn't shake.[7]

Los Angeles hurt him, he insisted, terribly. His own plight having sensitized him to others' difficulties, he perceived the effects of racism everywhere he looked: in the armed forces, where Jean's brothers confirmed a thoroughgoing racial prejudice; toward Japanese-Americans, many of whose families had lived for generations in California, then being torn from their lives like paper figures and relocated to detention camps; among Mexican- and Filipino-American communities. In a 1943 article for *The Crisis*, Himes described riots in which uniformed white servicemen mounted a savage attack on zoot-suited Hispanics on L.A. streets while (echoing the 1917 St. Louis riots) police remained conspicuously absent.

This we know: That during the first two nights of the rioting, no policemen were in evidence until the gangs of sailors, outnumbering the pachucos two-three-four to one, had sapped up on the pachucos with belt buckles and knotted ropes. When the sailors departed in their cars, trucks, and taxi-cabs, furnished them no doubt by the nazi-minded citizenry, the police appeared as if they had been waiting around the corner and arrested the Mexican youths who had been knocked out, stunned, or too frightened to run.[8]

Himes's writing during this period generally became more political and more focused on race, in part, no doubt, due to personal experience but also due to valuable contacts through brother Joe and cousin Henry Lee Moon with activist publications where Himes knew his contributions would be welcome. In addition, close upon introductions from Langston Hughes, Himes was being courted by the Communist Party. So for a while he danced with the ones who brought him. At least a dozen pieces appeared in *The Crisis* alone, others in *Opportunity* and *Common Ground*; several were reprinted in 1975's *Black on Black*.

"Democracy Is for the Unafraid" (*Common Ground*) entreats white America once and for all to join the struggle for equality.

"Now Is the Time! Here Is the Place!" (*Opportunity*) is a kind of rhetorical conjuring act calling for Negroes to invest the war effort with the energies of their own age-long battle for justice, to accept the folded lie that (in Milliken's words) "the nation's fight to preserve the *status quo* and their own fight to end the *status quo* were in fact the same fight."[9]

"Negro Martyrs Are Needed" (*The Crisis*) urged the black middle class to help bring about a peaceful revolution by giving up its silent complicity, by exposing injustice in all its sundry daily forms and influencing the Negro lower classes to follow. With this article Himes came under scrutiny by the FBI, which on June 12, 1944, opened file number 105–2502 on his suspected seditious activities.

The names that Langston Hughes had given as contacts to help him find work led Himes in a straight line to the Communist Party. Wilford Wilson, working for the U.S. Employment Service at the time, routinely and pointedly sent Himes to businesses and plants that everyone knew did not employ Negroes. The Party was providing useful contacts, though, and while Himes may have resented being used as a chess piece, he went along, attending cell meetings and lectures and mixing with veterans of the Spanish Civil War and radical Hollywood writers such as John Howard Lawson and Dalton Trumbo.

> Anyway, I went out to Hollywood—Los Angeles—where I met Hall Johnson and a number of other black people on the fringes of the movie industry ... Most of them were connected with the Communist Party. I saw these people and then I got involved also with the Communists out there.[10]

One Party project involved collecting used clothing from wealthy Hollywood patrons. Proceeds from sale of these donations supposedly went to refugee camps for those uprooted by the Spanish Civil War, but the collectors (perhaps more in touch with Communist reality than theory) as often as not wound up appropriating the finery for themselves. "I had more expensive clothes then than I've ever had since,"[11] Himes remarked in a letter to Williams. Chester and a companion made the pickups at huge Hollywood estates where well-wishers would set them up with a few drinks in the kitchen. Sure, it was all for one and one for all, Himes said, laughing—but that didn't mean they got out of the kitchen!

> I swear to God, my material for writing *Lonely Crusade* came from these experiences. I met these people. And the CIO union there was beginning to print a newspaper. At the same time I had been considered for a place on the staff. But, you see, the communists were also playing a game. They wanted people like me to help break the color line. I was a tool: they wanted to send me to thousands of places that had no intention of employing blacks at that time because Los Angeles was a very prejudiced place and the only jobs black people had were in the kitchens in Hollywood and Beverly Hills.[12]

Believing it to be as exploitative in its own way as capitalism, if in a somewhat different manner, Himes grew increasingly cynical toward the Communist Party, and his final connections shattered with the Party's condemnation of *Lonely Crusade*, published in 1947.

Milliken contends that the articles Himes published between 1942 and 1945 "leave no doubt at all as to the completeness of his own commitment at that time to a social philosophy that was frankly idealistic and totally optimistic."[13] The important words here, the ones that go by so fast you hardly notice them, are *at that time*. For there's much in the stridency of these articles, as there is in the very structure of *Lonely Crusade*, to suggest a man talking himself into something. Himes may have been reacting like the rest of the country, of course, to wartime camaraderie and factitious optimism, though neither his letters and memories of the time nor the self-questioning themes of *If He Hollers* or *Lonely Crusade* support that idea. The sense once again is more that of the fitting of a new, if temporary, self. Himes always wrote like some manic actor preparing for a part, spurring himself to the task, forever raising the stakes, as though he knows that in order to maintain momentum and intensity he has to jack reality up several notches and keep it there.

"He was, as always," Milliken reminds us, "a creature of extremes, and one set of preoccupations or one particular orientation never seemed to exclude another, even the most apparently incompatible."[14] Himes liked a new suit of clothes as much as the next man, so for a time he could be seen in public wearing political tracts and mawkish stories. Making sure, just as in his college days, that he was turned out well.

Some apprehension of knife's-edge truth may have attracted him to this work as well. In all of Himes's writing there is a sense of gospel—of truth-telling, *word* in current slang—held in delicate balance with despair, one hauling furniture downstairs on its back as the other hauls it up. Specific gospel, word, or writ would change; would be abandoned, turned in for some new model. The despair and disillusionment remained the same. They'd come back onstage in patched old clothes, telling the same crusty jokes ("Then we must hang ourselves immediately"), and what else could you do but listen, laugh and, afterward, cry?

As Himes's articles grew more strident and posturing in this period, so too did the stories. In "All He Needs Is Feet" (1943) a black man, because he will not step off the sidewalk to let a white couple pass, has his feet doused with gasoline and set afire and consequently loses them. At the end of the story another white man becomes enraged when the man fails to stand for the playing of the national anthem at a movie theater, even though it is pointed out that he has no feet. In "Christmas Gift" (1944) a father and husband returning decorated from the war is senselessly beaten to death by two white sheriff's deputies who refer to him only as "the Stevens nigger."

With stories like these, and with the far more accomplished "All God's Chillun Got Pride" (also 1944), Himes began to edge toward his belief that racism is so endemic to American society, so much at its heart, that nothing short of programmed violence could ever erase it. This Himes is very close to the Himes of the Harlem novels, to the fulminating culmination of *Blind Man with a Pistol* and the apocalyptic "final" Harlem novel *Plan B*. Pitting Grave Digger and Coffin Ed against one another, *Plan B* tells the story of that necessary programmed violence: America's second revolution. Left unfinished at Himes's death, it has been ably completed by novelist and Himes scholar Robert Skinner.

Soon with *If He Hollers*, all these strains, Himes's own experiences in the L.A. shipyards and unions, his growing concern with racism as crippling and ubiquitous, the slow, inevitable failure of his marriage, would come together. Scooping up all of the promised land's iciness, Himes threw it in America's face, a snowball with the hard, hard rock of racism at its core.

Not to put too keen an edge of romance on the thing, most writers by virtual definition are social if not metaphysical outlaws. They don't make much money, they keep peculiar hours and habits; their very choice of profession makes for a lifestyle and a way of relating to the world that are rather outside the norm. This person living in a cheap room somewhere, burrowed in and obsessively trying to do what he does best, is necessarily at odds with much of the culture around him. As Frederic Exley, a man who knew better than most, pointed out, not only the act of writing but the enterprise itself sets one apart: "The malaise of writing—and it is of no consequence whether the writer is talented or otherwise—is that after a time a man writing arrives at a point outside human relationships, becomes, as it were, ahuman."[15]

Writers, then, like many artists, choose to stand sideways to mainstream culture. All too often hardship and poverty, along with solitude, become part of the fallout they accept. Perhaps, too, they instinctively recognize that often the best work is done by outsiders, by those such as Tocqueville who move between cultures, by self-exiles such as Joyce and Beckett, or by those who stand so apart from their culture by temperament and perspective that effectively they become outsiders within it.

In contemporary American culture where the writer becomes ever more marginal, it's important to recall just *how* marginal a writer like Himes, a black ex-convict writing novels on themes and in manners no one seemed prepared to confront, was. Himes stood apart from America's bounty long before he departed from America itself. For much of his life he lived on air, shuttling between cheap rooms or apartments and houses lent him by others, a chronic borrower (Ruth Seid recalls) as early as his Federal Writers' Project days. Even Joe spoke of Chester's habit of using people, especially women, without the least embarrassment or remorse. His early books earned little by way of advances; *Cast the First Stone* went begging for years; *The*

Primitive knocked on door after door; most of the Harlem books appeared solely as cheap paperback originals in the States. Only late in life, with *Pinktoes*, movie sales and a steady income from foreign editions—even while his works were out of print in his own country —did Himes achieve some measure of comfort.

"Dirty deals were Himes' lot," Calvin Hernton wrote in his introduction to the *Collected Stories*, "and he was consistently robbed. Broke most of his career, he was easy prey for the exploitative advance. Such was the situation with several of his nine Harlem novels . . . He wrote these novels quickly and sold them (practically gave them away) just as quickly, because he badly needed whatever money he could get."[16] In rhetoric reminiscent of his principal, Ishmael Reed remembers "the piddling advances, the racist distribution and promotional policies, the sleazy covers, and dumb jacket copy" that dogged Himes's career that "make the promotional abilities of his publishers seem a step below those of the man who hawks hot dogs at the football game."[17]

Claiming to be the lowest-paid writer on the face of the earth ("It's pitiful, you know, it's really pitiful, pitiful"), in a 1970 interview Himes told John A. Williams that again and again publishers had paid him a thousand-dollar flat fee, then turned around and sold rights for ten times that.

Typical of many others, this interview is a *corrida*, an invitation to perform. Anyone often interviewed knows the tedium of repeating the same things yet again. Responses become reflex, formulaic, harden into icons. At the same time there's an innate hyperbole to the whole process. Rooms become ever larger, situations more intense, moments of personal adventure more pointed. Himes approached interviews as opportunities for aggrandizement, as well he should— but also as another kind of fiction. He used interviews, as he used his work, for purposes of self-definition, to push shadows out of the circle, to hold the forces of self together. He is signifying, yes, but signifying around that hard knot of truth at the heart of the thing.

> Williams: Now wait a minute, Chester, people have known you since the forties. They know everything that you produced and they offered you a thousand-dollar advance for each of these three books?

Himes: Oh, yes, that's what they paid, a thousand-dollar advance.

Williams: Goddamn!

Himes: You talk about double standards. I find this quite annoying. Y'know, I have been in desperate circumstances financially, which everybody has known and they've just taken advantage of this—friends and enemies and everybody alike.[18]

Back home, Williams tells him, young black writers always say Chester Himes has given away more books than most people have written.

Himes: Now, I couldn't find a publisher for *The Primitive*. I was very broke and desperate for some money, and I finally thought that I would send it to Weybright because they had begun to publish originals. So I sent it to Weybright, and Weybright wrote me this long letter about how we'll pay you a thousand-dollar advance on this because we feel it's best for the author to have a small advance and have substantial accruals [laughter]. I'll never forget that phrase. I never got any accruals, substantial or otherwise, from that book [laughter].[19]

Moving from job to job, writing when he could, Himes, a man who had difficulty keeping his balance at the best of times, tottered at the edge there at the edge of the continent, playing off his charge as husband and breadwinner against a compulsion to make his way and earn fame as a writer. Working in California for low wages at a succession of jobs he hated among people he considered bigots, Himes must have felt he was in training for a lifetime of mere subsistence. Whatever feelings of inadequacy or impending failure he harbored were intensified when Jean became employed, at much higher wages, as codirector of women's activities for the eighteen Los Angeles area USOs, and Himes's frustrations, for all the new ease of their life together, mounted. They lived in a comfortable house on a hill in the City Terrace area. Himes worked at the San Pedro shipyard and, after hours, at the writing of *If He Hollers*. His always vulnerable pride had taken a big hit, and thirty years later, when he wrote of it briefly in *The Quality of Hurt*, this still stung.

It hurt me for my wife to have a better job than I did and be respected and included by her white co-workers, besides rubbing elbows with many well-to-do blacks of the Los Angeles middle class who wouldn't touch me with a ten-foot pole. That was the beginning of the dissolution of our marriage. I found that I was no longer a husband to my wife; I was her pimp. She didn't mind, and that hurt all the more.[20]

Himes's feelings toward women were deeply ambivalent. On the one hand, reared as he was to middle-class values, he believed it was the man's place to provide for and protect his woman. There loomed, however, the foundering, confounding example of his father. Built into that responsibility, too, was the desire to have women dependent upon him. On the other hand, for much of his life, in order to continue writing he used women, living off them (as Joe emphasized) just as he lived off and used others. Himes always claimed that his and Jean's separation, when it came in 1952, arose from his inability to bear being supported by his wife. In reality it was another manifest of what we see often in Himes's life, some long-smoldering ember suddenly bursting into flame—like people consumed by spontaneous combustion in Charles Brockden Brown novels.

Chester did what writers too often must do, staying home to tend his small garden, becoming ever more inward in his self-obsession and ever more misanthropic, while Jean, flourishing, sallied out into the world. In his first novel Chester would lampoon the very people, those liberal whites and middle-class blacks, among whom she now made her life. Later still, with a slight dramatic pause before the word, a kind of catch, he would hint at the "friends" who had made all this possible for her, and of what *she* had made possible for them.

In 1944 Molly Moon pulled strings to see that Himes received a fellowship from the Julius Rosenwald Foundation, and Chester traveled to New York for publication of *If He Hollers* by Doubleday, Doran, and Company. He had written his bitter novel, he said, out of the accumulation of racial pain. He would make good use of his time among New York's black intelligentsia years later in the satirical *Pinktoes*.

Up to the age of thirty-one I had been hurt emotionally, spiritually, and physically as much as thirty-one years can bear: I had been kicked out of college, I had served seven and a half years in prison, I had survived the humiliating last five years of the Depression in Cleveland; and still I was entire, complete, functional; my mind was sharp, my reflexes were good, and I was not bitter. But under the mental corrosion of race prejudice in Los Angeles I had become bitter and saturated with hate. And finding myself unable to support my black wife, whom I loved desperately, I had become afraid. My wife deserved the support of her man. She was as beautiful and as feminine as a woman can be. I was thirty-one and whole when I went to Los Angeles and thirty-five and shattered when I left to go to New York.[21]

I had become afraid.

Fear is a part of what begins to surface now: Bob Jones comes awake in his room from yet another dream, fear carving its way along his spine; Kriss Cummings unfolds from the night in blind panic at finding herself alone; Jesse Robinson glances up expecting to see God's piano hurtling down towards him. Fear comes up, in Himes's life and the lives of his characters, like images swimming into being in a developing tray.

5 Round Us Bark the Mad and Hungry Dogs

Stations rush by.

Early in 1944 Doubleday accepted *If He Hollers Let Him Go*. Henry Moon, working as a reader for the publisher, may have influenced its decision. Doubleday wanted revisions, at any rate, and in May, presumably to talk these over, Himes visited New York.

On the way back to L.A. he stopped in Chicago to meet Vandi Haygood, now administering the Rosenwald Foundation in her husband's absence. Like many other young men of the time William Haygood was serving in the armed forces, and his wife had stepped in, in best Rosie-the-Riveter fashion (Rosie having come to life the year before as a Norman Rockwell cover for *The Saturday Evening Post*), to do his work. But the marriage, Vandi told Himes, was adrift. The ship had gone down. She and Bill were left together without provisions or sight of land on the life raft. Beginning a mutually destructive relationship that would continue sporadically over the next nine years, flaring up, coming under control, then breaking out again, a relationship that bore them to the border-crossing of madness and, in heart and mind if not in actuality, to murder—almost to the very comma and conversation as recounted in *The Primitive* (Chester later would say that of it all, only the murder was not true)—she and Chester passed the weekend together at her apartment.

By September he was back in New York, alone metaphorically if not in fact. "I lost myself in sex and drunkenness,"[1] he wrote. He was staying with the Moons, who now lived in central Harlem and whose parties gave ample opportunity to meet not only the intelligentsia he'd missed on his earlier junket, people such as labor leader Lester Granger of the Urban League, the NAACP's Walter White and Congressman Adam Clayton Powell, but also a seemingly endless chorus line of available white women. Henry worked for both the NAACP and the CIO; Molly had recently been named director of the New York chapter of the Urban League; both were staunch supporters of a fourth term of office for Roosevelt, pursuit of which had become the North Star of liberal causes. Himes held, and so represented them in *Pinktoes*, that these parties existed not so much for political reasons as for the forging of interracial liaisons. Many of the white women whose bodies he accepted, Himes thought, tacitly identified dispensation of sexual favors with social reparation, throwing their bodies dramatically, Raleigh-like, over the gulf: just as foolishly. Water roared dark beneath these pale bridges. Chester Himes as man, as writer, was not being courted. Rather, with obeisance paid to some courtly image of his black, intelligent face, some icon of it, was he being patronized.

One of those Himes met that fall in the whirl and dive of affairs was Ralph Ellison, intellectual, Communist, future author of *Invisible Man*, published in 1952, the same year as Himes's *Cast the First Stone*.

I am an invisible man. No, I am not a spook like those who haunted Edgar Allan Poe; nor am I one of your Hollywood-movie ectoplasms. I am a man of substance, of flesh and bone, fiber and liquids—and I might even be said to possess a mind. I am invisible, understand, simply because people refuse to see me. Like the bodiless heads you sometimes see in circus sideshows, it is as though I have been surrounded by mirrors of hard, distorting glass. When they approach me they see only my surroundings, themselves, or figments of their imagination—indeed, everything and anything except me.[2]

New York, far too eager to turn its mirrors on him, hurt him, Chester said. "I knew that, as much as I had been hurt by then, I was sick. But New York accepted me as normal, and that made me sicker."[3]

This was in *The Quality of Hurt*, 1976, thirty years after the fact. Four years before, for CBS, he recalled the descent to New York rather differently: how as he looked out on thrilling views from his bedroom window at the Moon's apartment in Sugar Hill and strolled through fluttering Harlem streets, past Fat Man's Bar at 155th or Eddie's Chicken Shack, past barber shops and beauty parlors, the old Theresa

Hotel at Seventh and 125th, he was the happiest man on earth, connected, electric, alive.

One can easily imagine these two Chesters sitting across a table, some morning TV "cultural" talk show, debating one another.

They so often did.

Stations rush by. In our determination to understand—to invest the plod of our lives with substance, heft, form, at very least the appearance of same—metaphors accumulate, streets we can understand. Desire consumes our lives from within, silently, while out along the edge of the light, darkness waits its cue.

Himes's first arrival in New York, in May 1944, came one month before D day; his second, one month after Paris was retaken. Times fold easily at this seam, like an old letter. Impatient to get started, the fifties fired up in essence if not in fact late that year or early the next. Uncle Ike and Aunt Mamie, bland as pudding, were everywhere. Perry Como held sway. Four million TVs found their way into homes in 1950. Within the decade, paper-doll housing first developed by William J. Levitt as Levittown, Long Island, spread like mold. Thirteen million new homes came up in clumps and clusters and were called suburbs, communities cobbled together out of nothing, spun from white sugar and air, *ex nihilo*, wholly invented, more so than most novels, most fiction.

As his November 1945 publication date approached, Himes grew ever more hopeful. The book might be chosen as a Book of the Month Club selection, he was told. Unquestionably it would win Doubleday's George Washington Carver award, given to the best book of the year on Negro life. Advance orders of 10,000 copies were guaranteed. Chester always held that it could have been, would have been—sometimes, in later years, that it *was*—a best-seller.

Lifelong friend Constance Webb Pearlstien, later Richard Wright's biographer, recalls first meeting Himes at that time.

I met Chester in 1945 at the home of Richard (Dick) Wright. His book, *If He Hollers*, was about to be published and, as I recall, Chester was hoping that it would be chosen as a Book of the Month Club selection. Wright had read the book and was enthusiastic. My impression of Chester was that he was tall and slim, extraordinarily handsome, and utterly charming. He seemed very gentle, but had a penetrating gaze. He had a humorous cast to his mouth, as if he saw something amusing, not in us, but in the world in which he lived. This of course he brought out later when he talked about the life of absurdity. His eyes also seemed to reflect this view; they seemed to sparkle with laughter. After Himes left, Wright put on a half gleeful, half supposedly mysterious expression and said that Himes had been in prison and was a killer. That he wouldn't think twice about murdering someone. Wright loved to spin tales, sometimes to the point of believing them and half frightening himself.[4]

"*If He Hollers Let Him Go* has most of the qualities that assure wide popular appeal," Milliken writes: "an exciting backdrop, a fast pace, a tight plot, a smoothly fluid and readable style, and a hero who is easy to identify with."[5] On the other hand, he reasons, it is an angry and "bitterly indignant" book, qualities uncommonly associated with broad sales. Henry Moon, reading the novel in typescript, took objection to its frankness in a way that sums up the double bind affecting Himes: "Everything you say here is true, but these aren't things that white people want to hear about. Things like this need to be kept quiet, between colored people."[6]

It is just at this point that variations on the word *bitter* (bitterness, bitterly) begin pushing themselves forward in all accounts of Himes's life.

The appearance of Himes's first book, which should have marked a time of great joy in his life, Robert Skinner says, held more than its share of bitterness for him.[7]

The whole episode left me bitter, Himes writes. And elsewhere: I had become so bitter I wished to change publishers.[8]

The publication of his novel was only briefly a triumph, then a source of new and deeper bitterness, Milliken writes.[9]

Bitterness welled up, it seemed, from the earth itself, touching everything. Beginning bad, 1945 ended worse. Journal of the siege year. Relations with the Moons had grown strained, perhaps because the cousins got into dispute over an employee of Henry's whom Chester was dating, perhaps simply because Chester went on living off the Moons' bounty. Chester and Jean made their way precariously through the year, often prevailing upon friends for a place to stay.

When Estelle died, at seventy-one, they were too strapped to attend the funeral. Chester finally borrowed money from Van Vechten to get to Columbus. Jean remained behind.

Himes says little of his mother's death, as, typically, he says little of Jean's supposed suicide attempt upon rejoining him in New York at the end of 1944 and finding him involved with other women.

> I lost myself in sex and drunkenness . . . I almost lost my wife, too. She came to New York and found me deeply involved in so many affairs that she tried to take her life. I was shocked back to normalcy, what was normalcy to me, and when I came to, *If He Hollers Let Him Go* had been published and well received.[10]

Scant pages after sailing past Jean's purported suicide attempt in half a sentence, he is describing at length the plumbing, repairs, neighbors, nests of rats and rattlesnakes at the California ranch to which they soon relocated, and the rifle he took along. Supposedly Jean suffered another crisis at the ranch after reading a draft of *Lonely Crusade* and believing herself the model for staid, color-conscious Ruth, fleeing into the desert afoot, stumbling along aimless and half-blind with shame, weeping.

Chester would remember those days on the ranch as the best of his life, and write of them as pastoral.

> Despite the rattlesnakes and other minor nuisances, it had been a calm and creative period, and we had enjoyed making love in complete isolation, at any hour of day or night, to the constant sound of the wind in the leaves of the huge overhanging oak.[11]

He was also buoyed by the fact that he'd again become the breadwinner, "something we both recognized and accepted as just and right."[12] But under new tile the floorboards of the marriage rotted. Discord introduced in Los Angeles, both the impersonal racial lacerations he suffered there and his diminishment by Jean's employment, fed on Chester's self-destructive behavior in New York, his drinking, his indiscriminate sex. Chester's absolutism and self-doubt put him at double peril. This man called upon to withstand so much in life (never mind how much of it was of his own devising) finally could not withstand the failure of his novels, nor could his marriage.

Curious that a man whose work at its best could float so free of prevailing wisdoms and become transgressive of genre and of ordinary categories of thought, could be at the same time in his life so rigid, everything black and white, adamantly right, starkly wrong. The central contradiction, perhaps, out of which all others spin? Absolutism dwells in Estelle's stubborn avowals and hovers over Joseph's shadowy passage; shrouds itself in Chester's assumption that his position as breadwinner (with which Jean agrees, of course) is "just and right"; slouches up again in the all-or-nothing black-power sentiments of later years, which pushed him through multiple miscarried drafts of *Plan B* into silence.

"I have been a Puritan all my life," he wrote.[13]

An absolutist, then. A man who carried within his deeper self some implicit template of what is right against which not only the hard fact of the world but his own actions and inactions must be measured always: a shield that shatters at its approach every charitable perception of the world, every action made in good faith, every intention. At the same time, in living contradiction, Himes as meliorist. He writes to, expects to, change the world. Yet he has little faith in mankind or its institutions. Like Voltaire at Ferney, his night is still filled with wrong, earthquakes, and executions. Things must change. Of course they must. But he will have that change, you understand, only on *his* terms.

When the dominoes fell, they fell askew.

It could just as easily, mind you, have gone well. That book might have been first stop on a line, might have become foundation for the very thing Himes was never to achieve: a career. Again and again circumstances in Himes's life seemed to line up for a major strike, only to founder. And when the spills came, Chester was quick to see, not coincidence, not the common vagaries of publishing or of the marketplace, but all manner of machinations; conspiracies to censor and silence him as black, as writer and as individual.

The first blow came with the resignation of his editor, Bucklin Moon, who left to concentrate on his own novels, orphaning Himes at Doubleday.

Next Himes heard that the publisher planned to cut thirty pages from the manuscript. This comprised a scene between Bob Jones and white temptress Madge in a hotel room, mild indeed by today's standards and little less so by contemporary ones, but firmly transgressive of racial barriers. Rushing back to New York from a California visit, Himes objected so strenuously that the proposed cuts were restored. But he was growing ever more restive.

Then he learned that the George Washington Carver Memorial Award was going not to him but to a white woman, Fanny Cook, for a novel titled *Mrs. Palmer's Honey*. Chester held, moreover, that the ads for this book, referring to another Doubleday book on the black problem as a "series of epithets punctuated by spit," referred in fact to *If He Hollers*, and that Doubleday had gone about methodically undercutting his novel's success. He told John A. Williams:

What actually happened to *If He Hollers* was that this woman editor—Doubleday was printing their own books in Garden City—had telephoned to their printing department in Garden City and ordered them to stop the printing. So they just arbitrarily stopped the printing of *If He Hollers* for a couple of weeks or so during the time when it would have been a solid best-seller.[14]

From a strong start, sales rapidly fell off. Friends wrote complaining to Himes that they'd been unable to purchase or to order copies of *If He Hollers* at bookstores.

Himes's disappointment deepened with the book's critical reception, generally favorable though lacking the hoped-for encomiums. Reviewers largely echoed what Himes believed to be Doubleday's attitude, approaching the novel in aliterary fashion and dwelling on its social implications as a manifesto of racial anger—treating it as a kind of cultural artifact—with little notice of the author's literary ambitions and accomplishments, overlooking completely the many pleasures of the book's rich wit and humor.

Other factors tempered Himes's disappointment. Meeting at Estelle's funeral, Chester and Joe had reestablished their relationship after years apart and were getting on beautifully; that holiday season, Joe and wife (also named Estelle) came for a visit. With time, Joe's vision had improved considerably. This may have mitigated somewhat Chester's old feelings of guilt. That year and the next, further stories were published in *Esquire* and in *The Crisis;* five appeared in a new publication, *Negro Story.* Most importantly, whatever his novel's ultimate reception, its publication did much, after what must have seemed a long, broken-field run, finally to validate Chester as an artist. It also brought two thousand dollars in royalties, which along with another two thousand as advance for a second novel, did much to repair, at least temporarily, Chester's financial situation. More than anything else, the friendships he was forging with Carl Van Vechten, Ralph Ellison, and Richard Wright at this time, their interest in and encouragement of his work, sustained Himes.

Van Vechten he met late in 1945 upon accompanying Richard Wright to a photo session at Van Vechten's studio, a session in which Wright behaved so pompously, Chester said, that he collapsed in laughter. Aside from his work as critic and as novelist (notably *Nigger Heaven*), Van Vechten was a great champion of emergent Negro art; his photos of jazzmen, writers, artists, and other Harlem denizens form an invaluable document of the period. Soon Himes sat for his own portrait in that studio, and soon the two began seeing one another, and corresponding, regularly. Chester's first letter is dated March 22, 1946. Another written three months later from California refers to photos Van Vechten has sent.

> Thanks for your letter and the photographs which were very fine indeed. However, there is a smoothness in the facial lines which I do not quite like. I would like for all the blemishes, marks, scars and lines of the face to show, even at the risk of appearing like a thug.[15]

Chester called Van Vechten Carlo, borrowed money from him, wrote to him about current projects, sent work-in-progress for advice and appraisal. It was Van Vechten who interceded when Chester, furious over what he believed Doubleday's bad faith, made the decision to leave. After protracted negotiations, Van Vechten's own publisher, Blanche Knopf, bought out Doubleday's interest, Himes's agent Lurton Blassingame appending to the contract an advance of two thousand dollars for his next novel. Over the years at Van Vechten's request

Chester would donate manuscripts and assorted papers to Yale's James Weldon Johnson Collection.

Ralph Ellison at the time lived in a basement apartment that would serve as model for one in *Invisible Man*, much of the substance of that novel, its ideas and themes, gestating in his conversation and in what he was then writing, much of that in turn the basis of conversation between him and Himes. Ellison and wife Fanny periodically had Chester and Jean for dinner; the two men saw one another, casually, more often. Like many of Himes's friendships theirs became a curiously on-again-off-again one that eventually faded away entirely; again like many, a curious mixture of admiration, self- and common interest, envy, disregard. They shared the apartness of the outsider who, having apartness thrust upon him, makes that apartness his choice.

Quite a fine book might be written around Himes's relationship with Richard Wright alone. The two met in July 1945 at a party given for W. E. B. Du Bois by Langston Hughes. From the first, as never between Wright and the more reserved Ellison, who had known him already for seven years, the connection between Wright and Himes was intense. Of that first meeting, witnessing self as much as other, Chester wrote:

Du Bois was reigning in the place of honor in the middle of the settee, surrounded by admirers, when Dick arrived with an African writer. By then Dick had published both *Native Son* and *Black Boy*. But he was practically ignored by that gathering of intellectuals and middle class matrons, and he was antagonistic and resentful.[16]

Later Wright wrote the first major review of *If He Hollers*; he also provided an introduction for the French edition of *Lonely Crusade*. And when in 1953, the same year Wright published *The Outsider*, Himes moved to Paris, they became again close friends. As John A. Williams in *The Most Native of Sons* recalls:

Richard and Chester Himes would come together and talk about their work, the problems back in America, and their future . . . Himes was far, far more bitter than Richard about the racial situation, not only in America, but around the world, but Himes, when most of Richard's friends began to slip away for one reason or another, remained his chief ally and confidant, his friend and brother.[17]

The three writers were a fascinating study in like and contrast. Formally educated, Ellison came of a "talented-tenth" middle-class mentality and lived ensconced among books and ideas in the self-exile of his basement apartment. Wright in turn was a self-educated Southerner, raised by the bootstraps of his talent from hardscrabble Mississippi life to a life of the mind. As with most autodidacts, his learning was ragged, shot through with potholes, lacunae: on certain subjects he might have the most obscure facts at hand while otherwise remaining totally ignorant of whole areas of knowledge. Lack of sophistication flashed forth, too, sometimes in his comportment. He could be awkward in social situations, ungainly in intellectual ones. He could be pedantic, even (as Chester pointed out) pompous.

Himes hovered somewhere between. His middle-class upbringing and mother's influence drew him to Ellison's patrician ways, his own self-education, prison, and street life to Wright's ruder, egalitarian manner. Whatever their differences, both Himes and Ellison looked to Wright as spiritual father, someone who had given them moral permission to be writers, who in fact had cleared a space in American culture to make that possible. Other links quickly suggest themselves. Wright's extensive work with and for the Communist Party, Ellison's investigation in *Invisible Man* of the American left and of black participation, Himes's own survey of labor movements in *If He Hollers* and *Lonely Crusade*—they're all remarkably of a piece.

The arc of Wright's career and Himes's in many ways, save the former's success, paralleled one another. *If He Hollers* might be read as a response or reaction, a counterbalance, to *Native Son*. Of *The Outsider* Wright wrote: "I well know that the attitude of mind evinced in *The Outsider* is one that will incite frustrated Communists to brand me a Fascist and will prod many hysterical Americans to pin on me the label of a crypto-Communist."[18] This was much the same reception Himes's own *Lonely Crusade* received, impelling him to flee America.

It was Himes who encouraged Wright in what many, including wife Ellen, thought recidivist work, his novel *The Long Dream*. Richard had become too important a writer now to go back to all that, Ellen felt. Others believed that, too long away from America, Wright had fallen out of touch with urgent changes in relationships between blacks and whites and, more importantly, in the lives of blacks themselves; that his concerns in the novel had become irrelevant to today's world. Himes championed his friend's return to literary origins, though, and in this book, in Tyree's entreaty to the son who has just discovered his father to be crime czar of the black community, Himesian logic rings out. This easily could be one of Grave Digger's speeches to Lieutenant Anderson.

"And don't call me corrupt when I live the only way I can live. Sure, I did wrong. But my kind of wrong is right; when you have to do wrong to live, wrong is right."[19]

Himes was on vacation in the south of France in November 1960 when an innkeeper asked if he knew the black American writer Richard Wright. Himes said he did, and was told of Wright's death. He jumped into his car and drove all night, back to Paris, where in turn Tyree's son Fishbelly, Wright, and Himes himself had all fled.

Fishbelly surfaced again as Wright's counterpart in his last work, the 1958 story "Island of Hallucinations" with its satirical use of figures from Richard's actual life on the Left Bank, among them William Gardner Smith, James Baldwin, Ollie Harrington, and Himes. Himes's own *roman à clef*, *A Case of Rape* (1963), same cast of characters, same setting, may have been, at least in part, a response. Wright biographer Margaret Walker deems the novella "a retort or angry answer"[20] to Richard's story, adding that Wright was outraged upon hearing of Chester's book.

Rarely willing to accept criticism as other than personal assault, in February 1946 Himes reacted to frustration at his novel's reception in a contribution to the *Saturday Review of Literature*, "The Author Talks Back." This was one of two great explosions, the other being his address at the University of Chicago two years later.

Himes wrote this piece, he said, to flay "the carping white critics," but it is, like the Chicago speech, a jeremiad to America whole. He responds briefly to those objecting to his novel's forthrightness and language: they remind him of the prostitute who after passing the night at every sort of oily trade complains of the fly in her rice. He then takes exception to the generally aliterary reception of his book, to all those who would insist upon his novel not as art, presenting a situation in all its reality and resonance, but instead as some sort of social tract that should sum up what had to be done. It is not a part of his manifesto to solve the world's problems, only to re-create as fully as he can his particular vision of that world.

And to those who complained that I had offered no solution for the problem my book presented, I wrote that I belonged to a nation which, coming from a severe depression, had had its fleet sunk at Pearl Harbor and had been caught in a war totally unprepared, without army or weaponry, but which had mustered its will and its energy and its ability and in five short years had amassed the greatest Navy and the greatest Army in the history of the world and had learned to split the atom as a weapon more powerful than could then be conceived by the average intelligence, and to ask me, an incidental black writer with a limited education and no status whatsoever, to solve its internal racial problem, was preposterous.[21]

He ends his polemic "Let the white people solve it their own goddamn selves"—pure Himes.

Stations rush by, as though we've somehow gotten aboard the wrong train. Every station we come to is the wrong one. So the wrong stops go on, year after year: choices, work, homes, countries, women. And still we cannot bring ourselves to turn, to invest what we have of self into another life, to plow it under, break the crust of our solitude, the pull of the past, the gravity of our pride: to risk that. Only in art, only in the stories we tell ourselves and others, can we reinvent ourselves. Never in life.

6 "I'm Still Here"

It's not by coincidence that the American detective novel developed in the late thirties, at the very point this country changed virtually overnight from a rural to urban, agricultural to industrial, society. After the Industrial Revolution, Robert Bly writes, all things happen at once. And now of a sudden there were these cities, these towered, sprawling climes into which we were all tossed, where the old rules, and the old values, no longer applied.

Our frontier myth of the loner, the good man who stands apart (deriving as much from European romances as from the frontier itself), easily became that of the private eye. He, later she, would traverse the city from high to low, wealthy suburb to shabby bar, giving up everything in his search for truth and justice. He would be our eyes and ears, the very voice, the soul, of the city itself.

From this initial impulse, from the attempt to make sense of the urban environment, to forge new maps and codes of conduct, stems our ongoing identification of detective and city: Matt Scudder with New York, Spenser with Boston, Marlowe inextricably with L.A. The impulse abides, and crime fiction remains today *the* urban fiction.

Not so surprisingly in light of his short stories and what eventually became *Cast the First Stone*, the original design of Himes's first published novel had it a mystery in which whites were being killed apparently at random all about L.A. Transformed to airier stuff, something of that original intent lives on in Bob Jones's pervasive fear, in his near-murderous rages, and in his railings against "peckerwood" white workers holding him back, the self-satisfied black bourgeoisie endlessly rationalizing its own caste system, and dronelike ghetto dwellers.

Then I turned over and dreamed on the other side.

I was working in a war plant where a white fellow named Frankie Childs had been killed and the police were there trying to find out who did it.

The police lieutenant said, "We got to find a big tall man with strong arms, big hands, and a crippled leg."

So they started calling in the colored fellows.[1]

Soon enough Bob Jones wakes from his dreams, where events *seem* at least to have meaning, to a reality where they have none. Leaderman at a shipyard, owner of a shiny fast car he adores, engaged to a beautiful, professional, light-skinned woman, Bob Jones has a life most others might envy. In elemental ways he remains a simple, ordinary man, wanting nothing more than to be resolutely that: to go about his life unnoticed, to be left alone.

Anyone who wanted to could be nigger-rich, nigger-important, have their Jim Crow religion, and go to nigger heaven.

I'd settle for a leaderman job at Atlas Shipyard—if I could be a man, defined by Webster as a male human being. That's all I'd ever wanted—just to be accepted as a man—without ambition, without distinction, either of race, creed, or color; just a simple Joe walking down an American street, going my simple way, without any other identifying characteristic but weight, height and gender.[2]

Such simplicity will not be allowed him, however. Fear has inhabited him like a parasite and slowly devours him. And before his story ends, his nightmares of impotence and injury will become real.

The alarm went off again; I knew that it had been the alarm that had awakened me. I groped for it blindly, shut it off; I kept my eyes shut tight. But I began feeling scared in spite of hiding from the day. It came along with consciousness. It came into my head first, somewhere back of my closed eyes, moved slowly underneath my skull to the base of my brain, cold and hollow. It seeped down my spine, into my arms, spread through my groin with an almost sexual torture, settled in my stomach like butterfly wings. For a moment I felt torn all loose inside, shrivelled, paralysed, as if after a while I'd have to get up and die.[3]

For critic Edward Margolies *If He Hollers* is a kind of halfway house, fusing the protest and hard-boiled genres, focusing on characters in states of constant threat. Graham Hodges in an introduction to the Thunder's Mouth reissue of *If He Hollers* agrees, emphasizing not only Himes's stylistic indebtedness, the muscular prose and pervasive violence, but also that air of existential despair so much at the heart of hard-boiled writing. Further, Hodges remarks, the novel affords a capsule history of black workers during an important transitional period. Escalating demand for labor in a war economy having opened new doors to employment for Afro-Americans, they migrated by the hundreds to Los Angeles and San Diego, to the munitions factories and shipyards there. It's a little-known chapter in American history, one to which Himes's novel uniquely bears witness: "Through Jones' eyes, we are given a street tour of L.A.'s bars, restaurants, fast-food joints, and party scenes in nearly photographic detail. The novel is a Baedeker of high and low, white and black Angeleno life during the 1940's."[4]

H. Bruce Franklin first pointed out that Himes's novels form a concise social history of the United States from World War II through the black urban rebellions of the 1960s.[5] *Cotton Comes to Harlem* was published on the eve of those rebellions, in 1964.

Five years would pass before the appearance of the next and the final complete novel in the Harlem detective series, *Blind Man with a Pistol.* Himes published no novel at all during this period of the rebellions, as though waiting to see how they would turn out. In 1965 Himes met another convict, Malcolm X, and found that he thoroughly agreed with all his politics (but not with his religion). Two weeks later, Malcolm X was assassinated. Then in 1965–66, an America in upheaval began to discover Chester Himes. In 1968 Martin Luther King was assassinated. The following year appeared *Blind Man with a Pistol,* whose subject is explicitly the black rebellions, the political and religious leadership of the black community, the disintegration of the power Coffin Ed and Grave Digger are supposed to enforce, and the beginnings of an apocalypse.[6]

In a 1964 interview, recalling cousin Henry Moon's contention upon reading *If He Hollers* that "these aren't things that white people want to hear about," things that should be kept quiet, between colored people, Himes remarked:

My novel, which Malcolm X read when he was twenty, is a violent, angry story. I meant for it to be a shock treatment, the same kind of treatment that Malcolm X wanted to inflict on the American public. *If He Hollers Let Him Go* expressed feelings that black people had always known, things that were always kept quiet, but are today exploding into the American consciousness. My novel is being reprinted, in some measure because of today's racial climate. But when it was written, even black people were shocked by what I wrote.[7]

Violent and angry it is indeed. Bob Jones lives at the very border of double consciousness, out there on the edge of violence, one moment conforming, the next poised for open rebellion, "battered from emotional pillar to post by external pressures which he can't control."[8] Anger flares at the slightest provocation: the borrowing of a tool, the impossible position he's been put in as leaderman whose crew will not take his orders, his girlfriend's accommodationist parents and good advice. Meeting the trampy, white Madge, he recognizes that she will prove the instrument of his destruction yet cannot stay away from her. For all his anger, all his fear, for all the times he goes out into the world with gun or club, Bob Jones will destroy himself before he destroys anyone else. This is the most pervasive criticism Himes makes of American society, Lundquist writes: that the black's anger is turned back on himself, that his life is "wired for destruction."[9]

Halfway through the novel, Wednesday in a narrative running from Monday through Friday of a single week, Bob Jones admits that "I never knew before how good a job the white folks had done on me"[10] and, earlier, that

I was even scared to tell anybody. If I'd gone to a psychiatrist he'd have had me put away. Living everyday scared, walled in, locked up, I didn't feel like fighting any more . . . I had to fight hard enough each day just to keep on living.[11]

But of course Bob Jones *has* been put away—defined, reduced, and shelved, rendered ineffective—his life whittled down to mere existence: "I'm still here," as he says at the end of a narrative in which he loses everything.

Calling the former "a vicious and bitter commentary on American involvement in World War II," Lundquist approaches both *If He Hollers* and *Lonely Crusade* as war novels. *If He Hollers*, he says, is "a nightmarish vision of American society as an enormous war factory" within which is going on a racial war not unlike those being waged without in the Pacific or at Auschwitz, one "fueled by racial hatred as much as it is by love of freedom or a commitment to the preservation of democracy."[12]

Propaganda said: America's war against Hitler was in large part a war against Hitler's racism, therefore by extension against the entire notion of white supremacy. Propaganda said: Surely this was the theater in which mankind's new conscience would be forged. Surely, inevitably, a new era in race relations was now at hand.

Truth, as so often, was something apart.

"Every time a colored man gets in the Army he's fighting against himself. Of course there's nothing else he can do. If he refuses to go they send him to the pen. But if he does go and take what they put on him, and then fight so he can keep on taking it, he's a cowardly son of a bitch."

Smitty had stopped his work to listen. "I wouldn't say that," he argued. "You can't call colored soldiers cowards, man. They can't keep the Army from being like what it is, but hell, they ain't no cowards."

"Any man's a coward who won't die for what he believes . . . As long as the Army is Jim Crowed a Negro who fights in it is fighting against himself . . . You'll never get anything from these goddamn white people unless you fight them . . . Isn't that right, Bob?"

"That's right," I said.[13]

Early in the novel, trying to recall just when he became so terrified, Bob Jones thinks of his arrival in Los Angeles and his first applications for jobs. It wasn't being refused employment that bothered him so much as the attitude. They wouldn't tell him outright they wouldn't hire him, but instead looked startled that he'd even ask—as though some friendly dog had come through the door and said "I can talk."

Maybe it had started then, I'm not sure, or maybe it wasn't until I'd seen them send the Japanese away that I'd noticed it. Little Riki Oyana singing "God Bless America" and going to Santa Anita with his parents next day. It was taking a man up by the roots and locking him up without a chance. Without a trial. Without a charge. Without even giving him a chance to say one word. It was thinking about if they ever did that to me, Robert Jones, Mrs. Jones's dark son, that started me to getting scared.

After that it was everything. It was the look in the white people's faces when I walked down the streets. It was that crazy, wild-eyed, unleashed hatred that the first Jap bomb on Pearl Harbor let loose in a flood. All that tight, crazy feeling of race as thick in the street as gas fumes. Every time I stepped outside I saw a challenge I had to accept or ignore. Every day I had to make one decision a thousand times: *Is it now? Is now the time?*[14]

For Bob Jones carries in his heart like a serpent, and cannot set it loose, those very ideals America so constantly espouses. Steadfastly, for reasons he himself but partly understands, he refuses to acknowledge the tacit agreements of discrimination. He is the most intransigent of idealists, saying no to the folded lies, vocably preferring *not to*, insisting that the world be as it seems. And consuming himself in the process.

In one key scene, giving Bob an ultimatum, accede to his inferior station with grace or she will end their engagement, fiancée Alice offers one reading of the book's title. Blacks exist in the white world only by dint of sufferance, she says, ever dependent on the support and shelter of white patrons. They must never disturb those patrons, never trouble the waters. For if they do so, if they break the code—if they holler—they'll be let go, to fall back into nothingness.

On the textual level, *If He Hollers* demonstrates that jacking up of reality we've seen already in the stories, "magnifying normal emotions to pathological intensity,"[15] in critic Robert Bone's words. Every gleam of light on a surface is a blade, every glancing regard a blow, each rejection a measured apocalypse. Gilbert Muller adds:

> Filtered through Jones's hard-boiled comic imagination, all people seem to be portrayed in absurd one-dimensional postures. This is not a naturalistic or realistic style but rather the style of the grotesque.[16]

The narrative proceeds in the foreground by thematic repetition of key words and phrases—"beyond my control," "I didn't have a chance," "I don't have anything at all to say about what's happening to me," "the white folks sitting on my brain, controlling my every day and night," various forms of *to die* as metaphor—and overall, similarly, by accrual of incidents which are basically variations on a theme. Though marvelous scenes abound, there's little true narrative thrust, and the novel comes to a stop finally as much from the exhaustion of its effort—as though worn down, like Bob Jones, by the sheer weight of events—as from dramatic necessity.

The whole of the story is a chain of ironies. In one incarnation of a principal Himes theme, that of demanding from a man what he is simultaneously barred from doing (remember the man with no feet, think of the detectives in *Blind Man with a Pistol*), Bob Jones is made leaderman with full knowledge that no one will follow his lead. In the course of the book Bob discovers that he cannot kill a white man and cannot rape a white woman, yet at book's end he is jailed for attempted murder and rape. On the book's last night Bob dreams of a sergeant who brags "I done killed all kinda sonabitches, raped all kinda women" and has been highly decorated for it, while Bob is about to be lynched for crimes which he did not commit.

Its surface narrative a series of confrontations, understory a series of dreams, *If He Hollers* is, with *The Primitive*, Himes's best structured work. Each morning of the book's five days, Bob Jones wakes from dreaming. Not only do these dreams give local habitation and name to Bob's fears of death, powerlessness, injury, and rejection, they also, like *The Primitive*'s newscasts, foreshadow actual events.

On Monday, Bob dreams that someone gives him a sad-eyed black dog on a wire leash that no one wants. He is interrogated about the killing of a white man and humiliated when, upon asking two other white men for work, they begin to laugh because he doesn't have tools for the job.

Late for work, Bob experiences even the drive there in his '42 Buick Roadster as an exercise in survival. He and his all-black crew need help and since none of the white tackers will work with his crew, Bob is forced to keep asking. Finally a woman, Madge, is assigned but refuses to work for a nigger. Bob calls her a cracker bitch and winds up in the superintendent's office, where he is lectured to by his boss and told that as of next week he'll be demoted back to mechanic, losing his deferment. He finds a crap game to ease his mind and gets knocked out by Johnny Stoddart in a dispute. Bob grabs a knife and goes after Stoddart but at the last moment backs off, deciding he'll wait for a better time.

> I wanted to kill him so he'd know I was killing him and in such a way that he'd know he didn't have a chance. I wanted him to feel as scared and powerless and unprotected as I felt every goddamned morning I woke up. I wanted him to know how it felt to die without a chance; how it felt to look death in the face and know it was coming and know there wasn't anything he could do but sit there and take it like I had to take it from Kelly and Hank and Mac and the cracker bitch because nobody was going to help him or stop it or do anything about it at all.[17]

That afternoon he threatens Stoddart with a gun but again pulls back. Just knowing that someday he will kill Stoddart somehow makes everything all right.

> I was going to kill him if they hung me for it, I thought pleasantly. A white man, a supreme being. Just the thought of it did something for me; just contemplating it. All the tightness that had been in my body . . . left me and I felt relaxed, confident, strong. I felt just like I thought a white boy oughta feel; I had never felt so strong in all my life.[18]

Bob reserves a table that night at the best hotel in town for himself and Alice. When the check comes, a note clipped to it reads: *We served you this time but we do not want your patronage in the future.* As they leave, Alice, embarrassed by the scene at the hotel restaurant and furious with Bob, takes the wheel. They're stopped for speeding by two motorcycle cops and have to post cash as bail. Alice then drives them to a house of homosexuals. Bob gets drunk, slaps Alice, hits one of the homosexuals, barely avoids wrecking his car on the way home.

On Tuesday, Bob dreams that he is being beaten by two white peckerwoods while the shipyard president stands by, dressed as an army general, supervising. Bob struggles to wake up but can't. Two older black couples come by and agree that, yes, some boys do get "out of their place" and into trouble.

Hungover, Bob skips work, has a few drinks at a bar in Little Tokyo where a young white girl comes in with two soldiers and starts eyeballing the bar's black patrons. Bob thinks how Madge is just like her, and about heroes from the movies sinking German ships single-handed, going out in glory.

> Just a simple nigger bastard, that was me. Never would be a hero. Had a thousand chances every day; a thousand coming up tomorrow. If I could just hang on to one and say, "This is it!" And go out blowing up the white folks like that cat did the Nazis.[19]

Bob decides to go see Alice, with whom he had words earlier. Several of her friends are there and ask Bob what's to be done about conditions in Little Tokyo. He answers in three stages. Initially he suggests that they should simply kill the colored residents of Little Tokyo and eat them, thereby not only solving the race problem but alleviating the meat shortage as well. Next he admits that if he knew any solution for the race problem he'd use it on himself first of all. Finally he claims that "the only solution to the Negro problem is a revolution." Once they're alone, Alice lectures to Bob, then gives her ultimatum.[20]

On Wednesday, Bob dreams that Alice is menaced by a herd of wild pigs in the city park and that he rushes to her aid, pistol in hand. Killed by the pigs, Alice shrinks to doll size as Bob looks on, watched over, himself, by "millions of white women."

I woke up overcome with a feeling of absolute impotence; I laid there remembering the dream in every detail. Memory of my fight with Alice came back, and then I saw Madge's kidney-shaped mouth, brutal at the edges, spitting out the word "nigger"; and something took a heavy hammer and nailed me to the bed.[21]

Bob returns to work, where he finds little support among fellow blacks, much celebration among whites at his failure. Foreman Kelly, against Bob all along, tells a baldly racist joke in his presence. Bob tries to confront Madge but winds up withdrawing, tongue-tied. To compensate, he terrifies Johnny Stoddart again.

The white boy came out of it and color came back into his face and it got beet-red. White came back into his soul; I could see it coming back, rage at seeing a nigger threatening him. Now he was ready to die for his race like a patriot, a true believer . . . And then he lost his nerve.

I smiled at him. "I don't want to fight you," I told him. "I want to kill you. But right now I'm saving you up."[22]

That night, in a scene parodying *Native Son* and involving the racial taboo that so intrigued Himes in work and in life, Bob goes to Madge's hotel room and pushes her down on the bed but, as she chatters on about this getting him lynched in Texas and begs him to rape her, he loses nerve and flees. Madge runs after him and tries to get in his car. He speeds away.

On Thursday, Bob dreams that a young white man and a young black man are fighting. The black has a long knife. At first the white seems to be empty-handed, but then Bob sees that he has a penknife. With it he is slashing at the black, opening wound after wound, laughing.

Bob wakes again to a sense of hopelessness, telling himself: *Bob, there never was a nigger who could beat it.*

Negro people had always lived on sufferance, ever since Lincoln gave them their freedom without any bread. I thought of a line I'd read in one of Tolstoy's stories once—"There never had been enough bread and freedom to go around." When it came to us, we didn't get either one of them. Although Negro people such as

Alice and her class had got enough bread—they'd prospered from it. No matter what had happened to them inside, they hadn't allowed it to destroy them outwardly . . . They hadn't stopped trying, I gave them that much; they'd kept on trying, always would; but they had recognized their limit—a nigger limit.[23]

He thinks how he learned the same stuff whites learned, all that stuff about liberty, equality, justice, how he'd heard that all his life. "That was the hell of it: the white folks had drummed more into me than they'd been able to scare out."[24]

He decides that Alice is right: hers is the only way. He sets a marriage date with her, vows to return to school, become a lawyer. Back at the plant, he finds himself alone with Madge, who first tries to seduce him, then, hearing others approach, screams that she is being raped. Bob is beaten, hit in the head with a ball-peen hammer, and wakes in the shipyard infirmary to learn that the police are coming for him. He flees in his car but there's no way out. He decides now is the time to kill Stoddart and give them something to hang him for. When he stops at a red light in a white neighborhood, police pull alongside. Finding the pistol in his glove compartment, they arrest him.

On Friday, Bob dreams that he kills Johnny Stoddart but that a Marine sergeant then chases him, bragging how many people he's killed, how many women he's raped, and saying that all his life he's wanted, more than anything else, to kill a black man.

Waking, Bob is taken to judge's chambers where he is lectured to by the shipyard president, then offered a break by the judge: if he joins the armed services and promises to stay away from white women and out of trouble, charges will be dropped. Two Mexicans waiting with him at the police desk asks how he's doing. "I'm still here," Bob responds. The three of them go up the hill toward the induction center together.

Contemporary reviews of the novel that Himes later said brought him his "only honest audience reactions"[25] were largely complimentary, most of them praising the vividness of Himes's style, many directly addressing the book's strengths and shortcomings.

Herbert Kupferberg in the *New York Herald Tribune* took exception to what he considered Bob Jones's (and, he assumed, the author's) pugnacious racial attitudes while admitting that

Nevertheless, Chester Himes gets across his main point, which is that in a different sort of world the Bob Joneses would be able to lead wholesome and happy lives.[26]

"How warping an influence can bitterness and hatred toward white folks be for a Negro?" Henry Tracy asked in *Common Ground*, going on to characterize the novel as "a ruthless analysis of an emotionally unstable Negro whose finer qualities are so quickly blacked out by ungovernable compulsions that no high motive outlasts the contact that evoked it."[27]

Roy Wilkins in *The Crisis* remarked Himes's often brilliant style and offered this summary of the book's intent:

It is a tale of confusion over the race problem and of blind revolt, a revolt that thrashes out against every incident, every idea, every unuttered whisper that would separate, humiliate, and shackle American Negroes on the basis of color.[28]

The *American Mercury* also praised the novelist's style, if with a caveat:

Himes's style, though too faithful to that of James M. Cain, is nonetheless effective in defining sharply the inner turmoil of an intelligent Negro [whose] violent mental conflict drives him to the verge of rape and murder . . . He is left bitter, almost broken.[29]

Surprisingly often, in fact, reviews mirrored the novel's own divided heart, which in turn mirrors protagonist Bob Jones's deeply conflicted nature. He wants both to run over whites with his car and to gain their acceptance. He hates everything Madge stands for, even finds her sexually repulsive, yet cannot leave her alone. For Bob Jones, as for Chester Himes, neither rebellion nor measured success, revenge nor accommodation, is satisfactory. As one critic put it, "the book is at war with itself, as is Jones, as is Himes, as is the American Negro."[30]

Calling *If He Hollers* "an impressive failure—with accent on the adjective,"[31] Robert Bone agrees, also accenting what he believes a basic structural flaw. The entire book, he notes, proceeds from a presumption that sanity and stability for Bob Jones will require some form of accommodation; that *this* is what the novel, with its plumbings of psychological depth, its confrontations and drama, will educe. Starting out from bleakness, shut in a cave of racial oppression, Bob Jones climbs through the novel's events, learns, chooses, and seems latterly to have found a clearing for himself—at which point we're confronted with a denouement that seems directly out of his original view of reality, a note from the cave. Having followed Bob's inner conflicts all this way, thinking they mattered, Bone contends, we're now shown they were meaningless, that the world will have its way with Bob Jones irrespective of his striving. In some ways the ending recalls borderline plays opting at their climax for "good theatre"—a flashy visual or dramatic flourish—rather than consistency.

Probably Bone overstates the case here, and what Himes had in mind was more along the line of classical tragedy, tragic flaw, hubris and all, with Bob Jones's dreams serving as chorus. In this respect *If He Hollers* closely resembles *The Primitive* with its tight structure and the relentless fall of its characters; that novel's morning TV newscasts serve the same choruslike purpose as Bob's dreams.

Critic Gerald Houghton has observed that, though set in the city with a nominally free man as protagonist, *If He Hollers* in its dynamics—the pervasiveness of threat, arbitrary authority, pointless violence—shares much with prison novels, giving it an enclosed, shut-down, airless feel.[32] Interestingly in this regard, Himes himself at one point wrote to Richard Wright of *Cast the First Stone* that "The book is a simple story about life in prison; maybe the boys can stand the truth about life in a state prison better than they can stand the truth about life in the prison of being a Negro in America."[33]

The novel's bifold nature may result in part from a division in Himes's own mind. At times he appears to intend Bob Jones to be a "normal" or representative black man, other times as someone special. Himes himself felt special all his life, and here as elsewhere, notably in *The Primitive*, directly autobiographical elements inform the narrative. Bob works in a shipyard, as did Himes. His girlfriend has superior work as a social worker, as for a time did Jean. Himes subordinates these elements, though, using them primarily for verisimilitude and for whatever emotional resonance they may lend his telling; he is not yet using these elements, as he will in *The Primitive*, explosively, forcing them onto and into his story like so many depth charges. Asked in 1985 whether *If He Hollers* was autobiographical, Himes replied:

> It isn't really autobiographical, although I always strive to develop a story within an environment I can recreate from my own personal experience. These are the reasons, I believe, why a novel such as *If He Hollers Let Him Go* has such a ring of truth.[34]

It's useful in this light to compare *If He Hollers* with Richard Wright's *Native Son*. A sentence from that book might almost serve as epigraph for Himes's novel: "He knew that the moment he allowed what his life meant to enter fully into his consciousness, he would either kill himself or someone else."[35] But Himes's novel is more a reaction or response to Wright's than it is a reverberation. Both depict the shattering effects of racism on the individual. But Bob Jones, educated, superficially at ease in his society, is quite a different man from Bigger Thomas. At one point in the novel, conversation turns to Negro literature.

> "*Native Son* turned my stomach," Arline said. "It just proved what the white Southerner has always said about us; that our men are rapists and murderers."
> "Well, I will agree that the selection of Bigger Thomas to prove the point of Negro oppression was an unfortunate choice," Leighton said.
> "What do you think, Mr. Jones?" Cleo asked.
> I said, "Well, you couldn't pick a better person than Bigger Thomas to prove the point. But after you prove it, then what? Most white people I know are quite proud of having made Negroes into Bigger Thomases."[36]

Implicit is his determination *not* to be made into one, of course.

In his 1948 speech at the University of Chicago Himes responded to criticism that his characters were *too* special: too angry, too confused, too rebellious, to the point of being pathological. Negro life *is* pathological, Himes insisted—shaped, controlled, and defined by fear.

> There can be no understanding of Negro life, of Negroes' compulsions, reactions, and actions; there can be no understanding of

the sexual impulses, of Negro crime, of Negro marital relations, of our spiritual entreaties, our ambitions and our defeats, until this fear has been revealed at work behind the false-fronted facades of our ghettoes; until others have experienced with us to the same extent the impact of fear upon our personalities. It is no longer enough to say the Negro is a victim of a stupid myth. We must know the truth and what it does to us.

If this plumbing for the truth reveals within the Negro personality, homicidal mania, lust for white women, a pathetic sense of inferiority, paradoxical anti-Semitism, arrogance, uncle-tomism, hate and fear of self-hate, this then is the effect of oppression on the human personality. These are the daily horrors, the daily realities, the daily experiences of an oppressed minority.[37]

Especially in the early novels it often seems as though Himes's characters earn their keep by energetically competing, as individuals, with their role as representations. There is a curious struggle going on between fiction's very specific intent—to portray one man's life in society—and a broader, almost salvational intent. This is part of the latticework of internal contradictions that serves to give Himes's work its singular power. It may also be in part what reviewers at the time reacted to, and what readers still do: reading Himes can be unsettling in ways that have little to do with mere subject matter, theme, or style. Beginning with *The Primitive* and culminating with the Harlem cycle, Himes learns to exploit and turn this to his advantage, introducing characters *as* icons and playing a double-edged game, his own brand of dirty dozens, off our preconceptions and presumptions.

7 A Street He Could Understand

The first atomic bomb went off at Alamogordo, New Mexico, on July 16, 1945; Truman learned of the trial's success while meeting with Churchill and Stalin at Potsdam. Three weeks later the real show, no mere test pattern this time, tore open the sky above Hiroshima.

Time now (in this country with its particular genius for building on the ruins of others, generations of black slaves, the whole of an indigenous population, exploited immigrants, proud fallen Europe) for "the American century." Time for Uncle Miltie, the *Today* show, *Peyton Place* and Perry Como, Ike alounge in his golf shirts and *The Power of Positive Thinking*. This country that would carry so many burdens (its own double vision of self perhaps the greatest of all) became responsible (again, in its own view) for the world.

The shift to creature comfort and consumerism initiated with thirties urbanization and interrupted by the war now in postwar prosperity came to full bloom. Conformity—homogeneity—became America's *vade mecum*.

Popular literature, as ever, provided a shibboleth, pressure relief valves, safe enclosed spaces where society could say what it was about without seeming to do so. Original paperback novels flourished, their garish covers speaking of "the ignoble corners of life beyond the glow of Jane Powell, *Father Knows Best*, and the healthy, smiling faces in magazines advertising milk or frozen dinners or trips to California,"[1] writing the subtext of a nation.

The boogeyman of World Communism was coming for us, you see, and if a movie such as *Invasion of the Body Snatchers* suggested that the danger lay not without, but within, that we brewed, bottled, and bonded our own boogeymen—well then, that was only a cheap science fiction movie, after all. Loyalty boards came into being in

1947, paranoia peaking two years later with accusations against Alger Hiss. Small-minded men with smaller spirits, all those Nixons and McCarthys, floated to the top grinning.

In July 1950, segregated black troops of the 24th Infantry Regiment scored our first victory of the Korean War with recapture of Yechon. Months later Pfc. William Thompson received the Medal of Honor for heroism, the first black so honored since the Spanish-American War. In September 1950, Gwendolyn Brooks became the first black to win the Pulitzer; that same month Ralph J. Bunche received the Nobel Peace Prize for his mediation of the Palestine conflict.

Fifteen million blacks lived in America in an invisible, borderless compound, lives rigorously delimited, illiteracy all but guaranteed by "separate but equal" school systems. Finally in 1954, 1896's *Plessy v. Ferguson* was overturned. Sounding not a little like Himes in his Chicago speech six years before, Chief Justice Earl Warren held that separating children "from others of similar age and qualifications solely because of their race generates a feeling of inferiority as to their status in the community that may affect their hearts and minds in a way unlikely ever to be undone."

Coming when it did, the court's decision reaffirmed that, at some point within its conflicted, confused, often errant and chaotic heart, the United States still stood for something beyond chickens in pots, material comfort, endless passive amusements.

The mad and hungry dogs were leashed. The gleam that's always there, always there even when the eye itself wanders, the gleam of this impossible created place and union, the hopeless ideals we've broken ourselves upon again and again, this gleam expressing something more than mere humanism, something more like the essence of humanity itself—shone again in America's eye.

Some of the bases and bus stops:

All the King's Men (1946), *The Naked and the Dead* (1948), *The Catcher in the Rye* (1951), *On the Road* (1955).

Casablanca (1942), *The Lost Weekend* (1945), *The Big Sleep* (1946), *Sunset Boulevard* (1950).

Meanwhile books such as David Reisman's *The Lonely Crowd* (1950) and William Whyte's *The Organization Man* (1956) explored that peculiar American need to conform noted by Tocqueville a hundred years before. And therein perhaps lies America's most profound schism, the great divide at its heart: on the one hand, our need to conform, on the other, this eternal fascination we have with the outlaw, the loner, the mountain man, cowboy, private eye, gangsta.

The celebrated author completes a new novel, caps his elegant pen, and immediately takes himself off for several weeks' well-earned relaxation at beach or mountain retreat, lounging about his lavish rooms in dressing gown and pajamas fresh from the laundry, sipping at fine wines, dipping in and out of conversation with friends old and new. Soon, in a month, or three, but not now, not now, it will be time to begin another book.

Truth is, most times he must get right along to the next book, or back to the real work, teaching, journalism, carpentry, that supports his literary avocation. He ends this book beset by doubt, as he has ended each of the others, uncertain if anyone out there is still listening, uncertain if anyone *ever* was, or why they should be, finding it harder each time to marshal the arguments to persuade himself to go on, that it's worth the effort, the dedication, the many renunciations.

Maybe he takes an afternoon off to go bowling, or watches three movies back to back in a suburban cineplex close by, or does a little reading. Or maybe he spends a few nights pounding down Scotch. Then it's back to work. With the fox, that knows many things, farther out ahead than ever now.

Himes mined memory hard to make an idyll of the time between first and second books, some weeks of it spent in splendid isolation in the desert near Milford, California, in a shack belonging to Jean's brother Hugo.

> I remember that summer as one of the most pleasant of our life. Despite the rattlesnakes and other minor nuisances, it had been a calm and creative period, and we had enjoyed making love in complete isolation, at any hour of day or night, to the constant sound of the wind in the leaves of the huge overhanging oak.[2]

Withdrawal becomes a subterranean river, its presence, its draw, never far off: withdrawal from society, first to this Western frontier, then to various shadowlands; from the company of peers during his

1948 stay at Yaddo; from marriage; from writing; finally in 1952 from America itself.

The brief California idyll ended with return to the east that fall, where Chester signed on as caretaker for the summer home of New York physician Frank Safford in Wading River, Long Island. There he continued working on *Lonely Crusade*. There, too, began a transmutation of his anger. Previously directed socially toward whites and middle-class blacks, now it began to embody also, even primarily, his growing rage at the failure of his books to achieve the readership or notice they deserved. That rage burrowed more deeply inward with every catapult, every cannon volley, let go over the walls. Soon Himes would plunge into terrifying drinking bouts, debilitating, arbitrary affairs, horrendous lapses. The idyll had lasted three months, the marriage fourteen years. Both were over. So too, for a time it seemed, was his career. This is, after prison, the second great turning point in Himes's life. Once again we're left to question to what degree the transformation was chosen, to what degree ordained.

Cornerstone here is the story "Da-Da-Dee," written in 1948 shortly after Himes's aborted stay at the Yaddo artists' colony, called Skidoo in the story. He'd applied at the urging of Langston Hughes and Carl Van Vechten, one of a number of stopgap measures that included a fresh appeal to the Rosenwald Foundation, a new advance from Knopf engineered by agent Lurton Blassingame, and a loan from the Authors' League arranged by Richard Wright. Pointing one long finger down the road toward *The Primitive*, which it closely resembles both in substance and in its manner of reconstructed autobiography, the story sums up, with painful verisimilitude, this desperate period in Himes's life.

Like *The Primitive*'s Jesse Robinson (both have works in progress titled *I Was Looking for a Street*), Jethro Adams is a failed black novelist, "famous author of two race novels" and "something a little inhuman," out of his element, out of inspiration, out of tricks, out of bounds. The story follows Jethro's drunken retreat from a bar in town to his berth at Skidoo, trying all the while to sing a song he can't quite remember, scatting his way shakily through this relentless hour of an unredeemed life.

His skin was greasy; his eyes deep-sunk and haggard. There were harsh, deep lines pulling down the edges of his mouth. His age was showing in his face. At such times he looked a great deal like his father, a small, black man who had faded to a parchment-colored mummy in his old age.

. . . .

He was humming and he could feel the sharp vibrations of the sounds in his nostrils. It filled his head with a great melancholy. He felt as if nothing would ever matter again one way or another . . . He was never meant to be anything but a cheap, smiling gambler with a flashy front, he told himself.[3]

When you're in the last bloody ditch, Beckett wrote, there's nothing left but to sing. Jethro's procession "home" is that song, "a melodic wailing of pain as if he were being beaten to some rhythmic beat . . . as if the loud wailing notes, themselves, relieved the pain."[4] He becomes ship and sea in one: reader or listener seeking in art a conduit, a container, for his own pain, and artist forever grasping after a thing he has glimpsed yet knows he will not, cannot, ever quite get; he is his own pain, and Chester Himes's pain, and at the same time something larger, something curiously beyond pain, something crudely transcendent.

Westward again, then.

Jean's brother Hugo had offered use of his California ranch on Honey Lake along U.S. Highway 395, about seventy-five miles north of Reno. Chester hoped that there he'd be able to write with few distractions. That May of 1946 he bought a six-year-old Mercury and (because he'd heard the Ku Klux Klan was active in northern California) a rifle, and he and Jean set out across the continent, rolling past Joliet, Des Moines, Davenport, Omaha, Salt Lake City, Reno. They passed through towns too small to have self-supporting ghettoes where they might find food and shelter, Himes wrote, and literally none of the whites operating hotels, motels and restaurants along the way wanted to serve the "clean, respectably dressed black couple."[5]

They stopped in Cleveland to visit Chester's father and his old friend from WPA days, Ruth Seid, then called in at Malabar Farm to say hello to Louis Bromfield. Unwelcome there, Himes said, they were kept waiting, shown into the kitchen, introduced to the servants, and shown the door. Not too surprising, perhaps, that Bromfield should shortly emerge as *Lonely Crusade*'s misanthropic archconservative and capitalist Foster.

In Columbus the couple stayed overnight with Joe and Estelle. Joe had accepted a position at North Carolina State College (later North Carolina Central University) in Durham, where he would remain as professor of sociology from 1946 to '49 before moving up to the university at Greensboro. Meanwhile he planned on spending the summer seeing new parts of the country, and promised to visit his brother at the ranch.

Following a brief stop in San Francisco to visit friends of Jean's from L.A. days, Chester and Jean picked up Hugo in Oakland and rode back through Reno to his property seventy-five miles to the north between Susanville and Milford, just across the California line. Hugo was an impressive figure, "a heavy-set man with the blunt brown face of a Filipino and a cauliflower ear from the time he had been middleweight champion of the Navy, in his neat blue chief's uniform with six gold hash stripes down the sleeve." He commanded respect of everyone, Himes wrote, "from brothel keepers to the proprietors on Oakland's famous Seventh Street, one of the gaudiest, most violent, treacherous, and dangerous main streets of any black ghetto nation."[6]

The ranch comprised several hundred acres of arable land bordering the lake and, across the highway, hundreds of acres more, this larger portion mostly arid mountain land. The land had lain dormant for years, unfarmed and untended. The three-room shack into which Chester and Jean settled was heavily populated with lizards and with field rats that chewed away in the walls at night; rattlesnakes often came for visits. There was a main house as well, whose longtime occupants, a Portuguese couple, had moved out upon learning they were to have black neighbors. Another couple, an ancient Texan and his forty-year-old, sluttish woman "Fertile Myrtle," had replaced them. Myrtle was said to have had eleven children, each by a different father; she and the Texan lived in incredible squalor.

Immediately Chester set to work, putting up a new door and screens, patching the cabin's many holes with sheet metal, rigging a hammock made from rope and a set of iron bedsprings in the patch of sand that passed for backyard. Himes's Savage rifle went up, cocked and loaded at all times, on an improvised rack of tenpenny nails at the head of their bed. He'd pull it down to blast away at rattlesnakes. These were so bad that whenever he returned to the shack, even if he'd only been away on a brief shopping trip to Susanville, he searched thoroughly, poking at every conceivable hiding place with the gun barrel. Once as Jean sat on the porch a snake emerged from beneath the shack and crawled under her legs. The resulting *mano a mano* between snake and writer led to Chester's 1955 story "The Snake" for *Esquire.* Far worse than the rattlesnakes, though, were the rats. Hundreds of them had been living in and around the shack for years. When Himes put out poison, the smell got so awful so quickly that he had to rake their swollen, rotting bodies into piles and burn them.

Amid riding out for provisions to Susanville, defending the homestead from vermin, and his poor man's version of *Better Homes and Gardens,* Himes the gentleman rancher, planting his typewriter on a table in the front room, got down to his real work. Chester wrote, as always, steadily, compulsively. Even when Joe and Estelle came in July as planned, Chester went on working as the others tiptoed past him in the front room. The brothers hiked and hunted in the mountains, reminisced about their childhood and talked about their father's illness, shared Joe's concerns as a sociologist with Negro crime and delinquency and labor movements in Ohio, and Chester's with the legacy of subjection, the character traits of an oppressed people.

On one of Hugo's visits he and Chester painted the main house and shack. On another they took a friend of Hugo's, a young, seemingly retarded man, deer hunting, Himes's account of which in *The Quality of Hurt* becomes pure Faulknerian comedy.

All this time as he plodded along at the new book Himes felt at his ankles familiar nibbles and snaps of self-doubt. Was it all too automatic, too obvious? Too much a rehash of *If He Hollers?* Some would think the sex excessively graphic, he knew—and be outraged in the first place at the very recognition of interracial sex. And the Communists would hate it, of course, no question of that. Ever ready in his letters to throw on the buskins, ever the masterful complainer, Himes in those of this period to Van Vechten spoke of exhaustion, despair, of his feelings (like those of Jethro in "Da-Da-Dee") that nothing would ever matter again. While Van Vechten tried to reassure him, his letters upon reading the book in manuscript confirmed at least some of Chester's own misgivings.

In typical fashion Himes responded that he was going to take Van Vechten's advice to heart, then promptly ignored it.

Chester's concerns about the novel's possible reception were underscored in an incident bespeaking his and Jean's rapidly deteriorating relationship. Chester had gone with Hugo to Susanville to see about repairs on Chester's car, damaged, irreparably as it turned out, in an accident. Returning after dark, they found the house empty and, panicked by thoughts of the ranch's isolation, deadly snakes, and rumors of Klan activity, they searched barns, outbuildings, fields, and hills before starting out for nearby Janesville around midnight, hoping to organize a search party.

> About three miles down the highway we found her stumbling aimlessly along, sobbing to herself. We thought at first she had been attacked. My first emotion was a violent rage: if I discovered who attacked her, I would blow off his head, I wouldn't give a damn who it was.
>
> But she threw herself into her brother's arms and denied that anyone had approached her, but begged him to take her away. We were both flabbergasted. She said she didn't want to live with me. Finally Hugo persuaded her to return to the house, chiefly perhaps by explaining that he couldn't take her away that night if he wanted to because the next bus to Reno wouldn't pass until nine-thirty the next morning and we didn't have any other means of transportation.
>
> We eventually discovered the reason for her sudden animosity. She had been reading some of my manuscript, which I had advised her not to do. The black wife of the black protagonist in my book *Lonely Crusade* is named Ruth; and I think the relation between her and Lee (the protagonist) is one of the most beautiful love stories in American fiction; but both characters have pronounced race and color complexes. I did not intend to portray myself or anyone I knew. But Jean thought that I had patterned the character Ruth after herself, and she was chagrined and hurt to learn I had had this opinion of her after all the years of our marriage.[7]

Himes of course routinely used characters drawn from life: his family, Molly Moon, Vandi Haygood. And he could be (or feign to be) blissfully oblivious of people's reactions to this piracy. The Moons broke off all relations after *Pinktoes*; one has to wonder what Vandi may have made of her transformation into *The Primitive*'s Kriss. Himes did like to play the innocent set upon by the misunderstandings of others: it was a favorite role. Later in the passage concerning Jean he admits that he often wonders if in his analysis of a marriage in *Lonely Crusade* he had not "drawn a true picture of which I was not consciously aware."[8]

In a 1994 conversation with Gwendoline Lewis Roget, Joe Himes spoke at length of Chester's use of people—in both senses.

Himes: There were so many times when he was using some woman to pay his bills and keep him while he wrote his books and lived the good life. If you look at the people who have been the basis for the characters in his stories . . . You remember, in *The Quality of Hurt*, he talks about this white woman in Chicago who worked with the Rosenwald Foundation?

Roget: Yes, you are referring to Vandi Haygood. In speaking about his affair with Vandi, Chester spares neither the intimate nor graphic details of their relationship, which he portrays as tempestuous and destructive, filled with lust and brutality, with obsessive jealousy on both sides.

Himes: Vicious. I wouldn't do that to my enemy. But it made a good episode for his stories. So he didn't hesitate to use her [in his fiction], to call her by name [in his autobiography]. That's why I hope he never uses me in his books, because every time he mentions me, he uses me. One of the ways he uses me, one of his great themes, is, "Joe is blind because I didn't help him that day. If I had been there to help him in that experiment, he wouldn't be blind. I am to blame." It's a wonderful cross to carry for a whole generation, publicly . . . It was not his fault, but he did not ask me what I thought about it. He didn't pay a bit of attention to me. It's a good gimmick for the image of Chester Himes, so he did it.[9]

While Chester had managed to complete a first draft of *Lonely Crusade* at the ranch, he and Jean couldn't go on living there without a car; he'd finish the novel back east. Late that fall they traveled by bus to

Reno, then by train to New York. By mid-October, probably through an introduction from Richard Wright, they had settled in "a tiny flat over a one-car clapboard garage"[10] in Wading River, Long Island, on the estate of neurologist Dr. Frank Safford. Aside from the garage apartment and the big house in which Safford's family stayed during the summer and on weekends, the estate consisted of four or five picturesque cottages. Summers, the grounds became an impromptu artist's colony as writers swarmed from the city to occupy the cottages. During winter the estate's isolation was all but complete, residents of Wading River seldom about or visible, the Himeses' only company a stone-deaf, stone-drunk caretaker.

Their flat consisted of four tiny rooms of which only one, heated by a Franklin stove, was habitable. Chester's chief duty seems to have been feeding and looking after Safford's pregnant English setter Susie. Putting the finishing touches on *Lonely Crusade,* he again took up work on his prison novel, now called *Yesterday Will Make You Cry.* He and Jean took long walks in the woods, gathering dead branches for firewood. The Saffords came out during Christmas; Susie, sleeping so soundly by the Franklin stove that she didn't budge even when sparks flew out and singed her fur, kept them constant company; and at least one weekend Ralph and Fanny Ellison came to visit. A brief passage from *The Quality of Hurt* concerning his host demonstrates how closely descriptions of people in Himes's life resemble those of characters in his fiction: that materials are fed through the same filter.

The Saffords brought their family down and occupied the big house during the Christmas holidays. He had two children by a former marriage: a daughter who was a jazz buff, and caused her father a good deal of concern by sitting about small nightclubs until the early hours of the morning, mesmerized by black jazz musicians; and a big-framed, silent teenage son with corn-colored hair who spent most of his holiday chopping logs for their big fireplace. And from his second marriage, he had a precocious girl-child of about four when we were there, who used to dance at her mother's instigation when they were entertaining grownups and would brook no distraction when she was performing her ballet. Once she banged me in the face with a sofa pillow for not paying attention.[11]

Another demonstrates his growing disillusionment with America.

There was a cauliflower plot on the other side of the woods from which most of the edible cauliflowers had been picked. By January, when the sun shone, it smelled to high heaven. And farther on there was a section of the long pile of Long Island potatoes, reaching almost from one end of the island to the other, which had been sprayed with kerosene to render them unfit for human consumption as part of the federal price control program. In that year, 1947, with all the starving people in the world, we wondered why these millions of tons of potatoes couldn't be shipped abroad. But I read that the cost of shipping would be prohibitive. Just like America, I thought; lots of money for the war-ravaged governments of the world but nothing for the hungry people to eat.[12]

Jean and Chester remained in Wading River until the second week of January, moving at that time to Harlem's Theresa Hotel, the famous stopover at Seventh Avenue and 125th Street where Himes and Jean had stayed on an earlier trip to visit the Moons, and which Chester would recall lovingly (if contradictorily) in his 1972 talk for CBS. Jean found work as recreational director for a Welfare Island facility where delinquent girls were detained pending trial in youth court and, if committed for psychiatric treatment, held. Chester meanwhile was in a familiar holding pattern, suspended in anticipation as he circled the field of *Lonely Crusade*'s publication, banking all his bets on one more throw of the dice.

To get past the shoals of what he felt sure would prove a temporary shortage, what he *always* felt sure would prove a temporary shortage, book after book and year after year, Himes appealed again to the Rosenwald Foundation, where he was rejected; to Knopf, where agent Lurton Blassingame levered a second advance of two thousand dollars; to Richard Wright, who arranged a loan from the Authors' League; and, at Hughes's and Van Vechten's urging, to Yaddo.

Soon Jean and Chester were forced to relocate again, this time to a dismal, shabbily furnished room on West 147th before moving on in mid-June to quarters on Welfare Island where Jean worked. Some respite from the dreariness of existence in that dismal room came in trips out to Vermont to see Bill Smith, a writer Himes knew from L.A. days. Married to a white woman, Smith had moved to Vermont to escape L.A.'s pervasive racism. Richard Wright, also married to a white woman and encountering similar racism in Greenwich Village, considered a move to Vermont before deciding on expatriation.

Himes himself daydreamed of householding in Vermont. Because someday, you see, once this book was published, or the next one, and its brilliance became recognized—once the dice rolled and fell into place, they'd create, like the sweep of a magician's cape or a screen wipe in movies, an utterly new world. One in which he had choices. One in which he did more than simply react, pushed about on the board by exigencies of need, weakness, retreat. A world that *fit*.

Chester Himes could never accept the world as it was. Some would suggest that it may be this very quality, this combination of repudiation and willfulness, that goes to form the artistic temperament. The artist sets out to change the world and, if he is fortunate, ends up changing himself. Should he be not so fortunate, he may succeed only in bending world and self toward new intolerances, blurring and burring the borders till they slip and grind and cut ever deeper.

Awaiting publication, as he seemed always to be waiting for something, Chester felt himself diminished, worn down by possibilities, by his sense of what could be, as much as by the scramble of day-to-day life. Like Auden's striver,

> looking down,
> He saw the shadow of an Average Man
> Attempting the Exceptional, and ran.[13]

Letters to Van Vechten and others speak of Himes's uncertainties and confusion, express the dialogue he was carrying on with himself. He doesn't mind, he says, working at insignificant jobs (all that are available to him), but fears that doing so could derail him "into a lot of personal protests and humiliations which might stop the objective flow of my thoughts."[14] In part this is the tread of noblesse oblige, sentiments Himes's mother would have understood. But it's also the typical artist's self-rationalization. Because he *can* do a thing, he feels somehow ordained to do it; devoting so much time to the activity, he reassures himself that it must be important; and finally, since he is ordained, and since the activity is so important, he must protect and nurture it at all costs. He has to guard his talent, must not allow himself to be captured by the mundane.

Once this syllogism is in place, its heartbeat resounds everywhere. Knowing that family and friends react with consternation and embarrassment both to the vulgarity of his subject matter and to his exploitation of them in his fiction—most recently Jean's response to his portrait of Ruth in *Lonely Crusade*—and anticipating the reactions of readers to the general subject matter and homosexual love story of his prison novel, or of Communist Party affiliates to the discursions of *Lonely Crusade*, Himes again invokes the sanctity of his art. To pull back, to avoid this material, would be to belie his vision, to fail the all-important demands of his talent.

> As I look back now I find that much of my retardation as a writer has been due to a subconscious (and conscious and deliberate) drive to escape my past. All mixed up no doubt with the Negro's desire for respectability . . . It brought a lot of confusion to my own mind added to which was a great deal of pressure of a thousand kinds being exerted by friends and relatives and loved ones who were half ashamed of what I wrote, forgetting that it was what I wrote that made me what I was.[15]

Or what he was that made what he wrote? And are these, in fact, discrete questions?

Over the years it is possible, perhaps even inevitable, for a man to shape himself by the language he uses; possibly there was never a writer who better demonstrates this.

Those same markers of exemption came up even at Van Vechten's and Hughes's urging Himes to apply at Yaddo. He feared, he wrote to Van Vechten, that others' viewpoints might influence or distract him—doing much to reaffirm his outlaw status. He needed to hold himself apart, felt that he had to: "I become confused and lose my point around other writers."[16]

One might also perceive in Himes's secretiveness and stealth the stamp of alcoholism, an identification that seems borne out by "Da-Da-Dee" with its limning of themes to be explored (all but exhausted) in *The Primitive*. The addicted personality, having one great secret, invests all else with secrecy: shrouds or continuously reinvents its past; speaking of the same events, relates quite different accounts; makes its way through each moment, relationship, and day in a series of feints and misdirections. Ever evasive, fluid, it must not, cannot, be held.

That withdrawal initiated by Himes's retreat to the counterfeit frontier of Hugo's ranch continues into withdrawal from peers, marriage, and America itself. It's a renunciation, an apostasy, as definitive in its own way as that of castrati, and we watch as it takes form, moving from Chester's life to his art, from instinctive practice to articulate principle (though to what degree rationalized we will never know), echoing the great theme seemingly at the heart of so much fine American writing: the dialogue between solitude and community.

Perhaps Himes would have taken to Robert Frost's "The Fear of God":

> Beware of coming too much to the surface,
> And using for apparel what was meant
> To be the curtain of the inmost soul.[17]

As publication drew near, Knopf's publicity engines appeared to be pumping away. Interviews, appearances, and signings were arranged for Himes. Lawyers expressed concern at the possibility of libel action, believing that the novel's aircraft company president (actually patterned on Louis Bromfield) too closely resembled a real industrialist, but eventually cleared the novel. Richard Wright, now in Paris, was approached for a blurb; though he later wrote an introduction for the French edition, he seems to have declined at this time. Agent Lurton Blassingame used the honeymoon period to pry loose a new advance from Blanche Knopf, seemingly for a book, *Immortal Mammy*, to be based on Chester's Hollywood experiences.

In August, Chester and Jean left for a ten-day visit to Vermont. On September 7 Chester's father arrived from Cleveland to share the great day. Chester's balloon was up, winds favorable. Days tipping their bright yellow hats.

Then the crash.

His several personal reversals and rejections on publication day, Himes wrote, set the pattern for his novel's reception. They were staying at the time in Jean's supervisor's flat on Welfare Island, and Himes got up early that morning to catch a ferry across to Manhattan, where he was to appear at Macy's at 8:30. The bookstore manager met him at the employee entrance, took him for coffee, and told him that the store had made the decision to stop sponsoring authors' appearances, believing it rang of favoritism and caused ill will. He was sorry the decision had come now, the manager told him, because he liked the book a great deal, believed that Himes had important things to say.

> I had heard the exact phrases uttered by various editors so many times before that I understood. They had canceled my appearance. I shook hands warmly to show him there were no hard feelings—although if he believed that, he was an idiot—and hastened over to Bloomingdale's, on Fifty-ninth Street.[18]

There the first clerk he encountered didn't know who he was and had never heard of his book. Again his appearance had been canceled with no notice.

He had planned to return to the island to pick up Jean and his father before his next booking, on Mary Margaret McBride's radio show, but now hadn't sufficient time. When he called Jean to ask her to meet him at the studio, she said she'd tried to reach him by phone at both Macy's and Bloomingdale's. The studio had called to cancel his interview. Crestfallen, Chester withdrew home (i.e., to their borrowed flat), then to Vermont to await reviews.

"After the publication of *Lonely Crusade*," James Lundquist writes, "Himes found himself in a position that few other American novelists have occupied. He was being assaulted by communists, fascists, white racists, black racists, and practically every reviewer within those extremes."[19]

Attacks from the Communist press were voluble, as expected. *Mainstream*, the *Daily Worker* and *People's Voice* all ran negative reviews. Perhaps the most outspoken was Lloyd Brown's in *New Masses*: "I cannot recall ever having read a worse book on the Negro theme."[20] One ran a cartoon depicting Himes marching, white flag in hand, across the page. Not only had Himes abjured the party line of internal secession holding that blacks within the United States were a separate nation, he had satirized with characterizations drawn directly from life the self-serving attentions of the party toward Negroes, and had called into question the whole notion of a progressive society.

Other publications closely associated with the labor movement took similar exception. The Jewish magazine *Commentary* in particular objected to anti-Semitic elements. In *The New Leader* a young James Baldwin, clumsily comparing Himes's novel to *Uncle Tom's Cabin*, held that while the novel was poorly written, it gave an accurate portrayal of how black Americans viewed their lives. Here Baldwin hit upon what, behind all the smoke, remains most important about *Lonely Crusade*. Like its predecessor, it aired black sentiments largely unspoken in public, any public, at the time.

Stoyan Christowe in *Atlantic Monthly* echoed Baldwin's observation, relating contemporary Negro literature to the previous generation's novels of immigrants fighting to escape prejudice and establish their place in society. At the same time he acknowledged Himes's dissection of deeper, more insidious rifts:

> Chester Himes' new novel is a study of the American Negro, a brave and courageous probing into the Negro psyche. His diagnosis reveals a racial malady for which there is no immediate remedy.[21]

Himes will quote brilliantly from Christowe in his impending speech at the University of Chicago, taking the reviewer's words and making them forever his own.

The *New York Times Book Review*'s Nash K. Burger spoke well of Himes's abilities as a serious writer in both his novels. *Lonely Crusade* is a novel of fear, he wrote, of the fear ever present in the mind of a Negro living in a white man's America, yet because of the novel's complexity and Himes's skill,

> Lee Gordon's lonely crusade to put down his feeling of fear and isolation becomes only an exaggeration of every man's struggle to find himself and his place in the world.

While also noting its anti-Semitism, Burger warned that the novel, like its protagonist's life, might be too tough for some readers, its incidents "presented as bluntly as they happened."[22]

Arthur Burke's review for *The Crisis* lauded Himes's gift for characterization with favorable comparisons to Dickens and his talent for psychological analysis with mention of George Eliot, and perceived his theme as essentially a pathology of race.

The New Yorker wrote that "Mr. Himes considers this problem intelligently and convincingly; regrettably, though, he seems to think that an ugly narrative is necessarily a powerful one."[23]

The *New Republic's* John Farrelly found the story "much too extended and repetitious" and its protagonist "not so much . . . an individual as a catalogue of the Negro's emotional distortions."[24]

Eric L. McKitrick in *Saturday Review of Literature*, while generally praising the novel, identified its chief weakness as a lack of focus resulting from the novel's attempt, in its analysis of the racial question from every conceivable angle, to be too many things at once. He also felt the protagonist's instability and lack of mooring made him unsympathetic.[25]

Fellow novelist Arna Bontemps reviewed the novel for the *New York Herald Tribune*, stating that Himes had produced "an even more provocative book this time." He celebrated Himes's engagement with depicting "the struggles of individuals who find themselves occupying newly won ground and trying to make the personal adjustments the task requires," but took exception, in true socially progressive, proletariat fashion, to Himes's emphasis on pathology.

> Certainly this is not exactly the mood in which to work for any kind of progress, and those who look to *Lonely Crusade* for a chart are likely to turn away sour.[26]

Earlier we've seen Langston Hughes's similar charge in a letter to Blanche Knopf declining to provide a blurb:

> Most of the people in it just do not seem to me to have good sense or be in their right minds, they behave so badly, which makes it difficult to care very much what happens to any of them.[27]

In short, many of the criticisms were familiar ones—Himes's reliance on melodrama and violence, for instance, or his failure to provide any proper racial model—and some of them new, such as censure of the book's confused thematic structure and extended philosophical dialogues, or complaints that the author's outlook was, on the one hand, too limited, and on the other, too encompassing.

Just as he overstated the unfavorableness of reviews (some in fact were quite good), Himes ever afterward simplified these criticisms, rendering the whole experience down to a conspiracy marshaled by Communists and complicity supported, in a kind of collaborationist Vichy of the mind, by Negro peers and the literary establishment. Thirty years later he'd still be arguing with reviewers.

His "improbable" characters were drawn from life, he said: Luther based on a criminal he had known in prison, the monstrous industrialist Foster on Louis Bromfield, party members on those he'd known in California.

> I think that many of the critics on the big weekly reviews disliked most the characterization of the industrialist Foster, who in my book called President Roosevelt "a cripple bastard, with a cripple bastard's sense of spite." I had heard those words spoken in a Cleveland, Ohio, country club. Maybe the critics had heard them too—maybe that was what they most disliked, my audacity in repeating them . . . I think that what the great body of Americans most disliked was the fact I came too close to the truth. Reactionaries hate the truth and the world's rulers fear it; but it embarrasses the liberals, perhaps because they can't do anything about it.[28]

Or as Marlon Brando shortly (1954) will respond in *The Wild One* to the question What are you rebelling against: "What have you got?"

In addition to its airing of social identity ("issues and attitudes that hitherto had been left to smolder unrecognized by the public at large," as Fabre and Margolies have it[29]) and its introduction of the theme of black anti-Semitism so much with us today, *Lonely Crusade*'s importance lies in its limning of Negro resentment over their exploitation by Communist "champions," and in its insistence on black America as pathological.

This theme of psychopathology, implicit in *If He Hollers*, central to *The Primitive*, ontological in the Harlem cycle, will be picked up most explicitly in Himes's address at Chicago that summer. An important aspect emerges in *Lonely Crusade* with Lee Gordon's argument that, kept down so long (one recalls Jack London's vision of fascism as a boot heel stamping on a human face—forever), the Negro is unable to envision anything else, unable to take advantage of what opportunities do exist for him—and so must be given, at the outset, special consideration. This principle, which in recent years we've come to call affirmative action (and which as this book is written has begun disappearing), is another form of Himes's complaint that slaves were "given their freedom" without also being given the means to support themselves. Ideally an affront to democracy, in reality it's bent all too facilely to justification for continuance of mechanisms of oppression—and it flew in the face of the Negro elite's principles of self-elevation.

Himes returned to this point in his 1970 interview with John Williams:

> But I know why the black people disliked the book—because they're doing the same thing now that I said at that time was necessary. I had the black protagonist, Lee Gordon, a CIO organizer, say that the black man in America needed more than just a superficial state of equality; he needed special consideration because he was so far behind. That you can't just throw him out there and say, "Give Negroes rights," because it wouldn't work that way. And so this is what most of the black writers had against it; in saying that, of course, by pleading for special privileges for the black people I was calling them inferior.[30]

Beneath the bluster, though, predictably, typically, Himes was wounded. His pain is ever the egotist's pain: all or nothing. And so a verbal formula we come to know well clicks into place in his discussion in *The Quality of Hurt* of his second novel's reception.

> Of all the hurts which I had suffered before—my brother's accident, my own accident, being kicked out of college, my parents' divorce, my term in prison, and my racial hell on the West Coast—and which I have suffered since, the rejection of *Lonely Crusade* hurt me most.[31]

From this rejection arises another familiar lamentation as well, hinging on a single word. He had poured his heart and mind into this book, Himes said—

I had attempted to be completely fair. I had written what I thought was a story of the fear that inhabits the minds of all blacks who live in America, and the various impacts on this fear precipitated by communism, industrialism, unionism, the war, white women, and marriage within the race.[32]

—but people did not want to know the truth. *Truth* becomes a rosary he fingers while speaking. Often in professionally difficult times (and Chester had few other) he took refuge in asserting that, whatever his failings as a writer, he was engaged in something more substantial than mere storytelling, these games of literature; he perceived himself to be in the purest sense witnessing, to be setting down truth, gospel, *word*.

Certainly Himes exaggerated both reviewers' hostility to his second novel and his own response to their criticisms. Finally, though, he wasn't far off the mark. The book sold poorly, perhaps four thousand copies. "For the next five years I couldn't write," he'd later announce.[33] Again hyperbole: he'd continue to work on his prison novel, and would write *The Third Generation*. But he was drifting ever further from any mainstream of literary activity. Never again would he be able to envision for himself, as he had done heretofore, any authentic position in American letters: the breakthrough book, recognition, induction by acclaim. Henceforth he'd remain ever the outsider, half proud of his alienation, half galled at it.

8 Going Too Far and Too Far Gone

At midpoint in *Lonely Crusade*, union organizer Lee Gordon sits with the newspaper on the bus to work, reading of growing racial tensions within the city.

> A Negro had cut a white worker's throat in a dice game at another of the aircraft companies and was being held without bail; and a white woman in a shipyard had accused a Negro worker of raping her.[1]

Not only does this directly echo Bob Jones's predicament in *If He Hollers*, it's also a deliberate recapitulation of Chapter 9 of *this* book in which Lee sits on a bus reading the transcript of a rape case, one of a number of parallels laid into the book, brick on brick. The transcript in turn prefigures *A Case of Rape*. Even the strain of racial murders initially meant to be central to *If He Hollers* and there abandoned reemerges here in Lester McKinley's scheming to kill exploitative capitalist Foster, and in Luther McGregor's murder of a corrupt deputy sheriff. Throughout his career Chester would go back again and again to the same wells, carrying different buckets.

These echoes of *If He Hollers* point up the diptych nature of the novels. Though *Lonely Crusade* is twice the length of *If He Hollers*, the novels in many respects are alike in purpose and scope, both exploring the social milieu of wartime Los Angeles. Twins, we're told, often complete sentences for one another. *If He Hollers* gives voice to one twin's bald, unreasoning fear and fury; *Crusade* is the other twin's struggle to argue their case calmly, logically.

Lonely Crusade was published on October 8, 1947, twenty-three months after publication of *If He Hollers*. Set in the spring of 1943 in wartime Los Angeles and spanning fifty days, it is Himes's most ambitious and outward-directed novel, judged by Fabre and Margolies a "rich, complex, yet ultimately unsuccessful book."[2] Gilbert Muller thinks it "one of the most radical novels about the structures of American domination and about California life as a symptom of the corrupt power of both capitalism and communism."[3] Stephen Milliken has this estimation:

> The prose style of *Lonely Crusade* is, in many passages, much more brilliant, containing some of Himes's most successful efforts at "fine writing," and in its ultimate effects this long novel is a much more deeply disturbing book, but in immediate impact it is distinctly less powerful than *If He Hollers Let Him Go*. It is, of all of Himes's books, the one that comes closest to failure, due to the sheer abundance of things packed into it . . . But it is also Himes's supreme effort as novelist, thinker, propagandist, and crusader[.][4]

Milliken's final catalog of nouns speaks strongly to the novel's fundamental problems. For not only is it a programmed work, malleable fiction patted into shape about rigid forms of discourse, it's also, in all-things-to-all-men manner, heroically inclusive. Swept into its purview are unionism and labor relations, the Communist Party, a panoply of wartime sentiments, black rage and impotence, the sprawl of the new urban landscape, black-white sexuality, the social role of media, the nature and abuse of political power, black anti-Semitism, and much else. Milliken underscores the burden of information carried by the novel in noting its resemblance to historical fiction, passages in which Himes, though writing what is ostensibly a contemporary novel, takes advantage of set pieces to unload baskets of background data. Abandoning the limited scope and classically tragic structure of *If He Hollers* with its choruslike dreams, Himes forsakes as well that novel's simple power and intensity. The new novel is a sprawl—a sprawl as problem-ridden as those new, burgeoning cities, and just as filled with energy and fascination.

The primary problem lies with the novel's schematic, contrived structure, one providing (Milliken again) "a platform for extensive editorializing, none of it entirely gratuitous, though much is seemingly contradictory."[5] Throughout we hear machinery grinding and occasionally groaning backstage as Himes bends the story toward scenes and confrontations having more to do with exigencies of his various arguments than with considerations of similitude or internal consistency. Feet hitting marks blocked by the play's director, characters are drained of life. They become flat; simple counters of meaning, signifiers, allegorical, costumes too long at arm and leg, too stiff, inappropriate to their station or role, colors poorly matched.

Nor does Lee Gordon himself, as protagonist, escape such manipulation. Passive throughout—so passive, in fact, that he comes perilously close to losing the reader's sympathy—Lee undergoes in the book's final pages what is effectively a metempsychosis and emerges as savior, communal soul, carrier of the universal banner. For all Himes's push-and-pull, the reader is hard put to accept this miraculous transformation. Eminently convincing as failed lover and as victim, Milliken remarks, Lee Gordon proves an unsatisfactory crusader; we never latch on to any core of faith that might sustain him, and little foundation is laid for character traits counter to his prevailing negativism.[6] Bernard W. Bell in *The Afro-American Novel and its Tradition* agrees:

> Unfortunately, Himes's handling of Lee Gordon's deep-seated conviction of the basic inferiority of black people and the abrupt, spiritual transformation that results in his redemptive heroic death for the cause of unionism at the end of the novel violate the formal integrity of the narrative, and are more melodramatic than naturalistic.[7]

Gilbert Muller takes exception to this reading, insisting that, while some critics find Lee's shift from reaction to action too sudden,

> It is more appropriate to assert that Gordon, as a thinking being, has been attempting to comprehend his behavior through the fifty days of narrative constituting *Lonely Crusade* and that, with Abe Rosenberg's help (and also Smitty's allegiance), he is now prepared to act. The conversion of Meursault in Camus's *The Stranger* to a posture of existential rebellion is also abrupt but based on an unfolding recognition of the oppressive essence of

his condition. Like Meursault, Lee Gordon seizes his existence and embraces the gestures and actions of rebellion on the day of the union rally.[8]

James Lundquist in turn calls attention to several structural problems. Lester McKinley's elaborate plot to murder Foster, so carefully set up, simply evaporates. Ruth, though given such seeming importance, never comes fully to life. There are too many characters and too many points of view to develop any of them fully. This is nonetheless a powerful novel, Lundquist concludes, reminding us that sudden turns of plot and character, as well as melodramatic developments, are signature Himes. Other of Himes's strengths, among them his realistic reproduction of speech patterns and creation of intensely physical settings, redeem the flow of ideas and keep them from becoming mere abstract chatter, Lundquist feels. The novel has, too, rare value as social history, shot through with images of a city in transition, evoking the physical presence and atmosphere of the war plants, documenting the mood of workers making good wages for the first time in their lives and worrying what will become of them at war's end, offering insights into the relationship between unionization and communist activities: all stations in that peculiar mix of purpose and apocalypse in the air at the time.

> The Avalon streetcar was crowded with servicemen and workers, all in the uniform of their participation—the navy's blue woolen and the workers' blue denim, the army's khaki and the workers' tan.
> Soldiers for democracy, for an eighty-dollar check or death on some distant isle; the home front and the battle-front; relief clients of yesterday and of tomorrow too—who knows? Lee Gordon asked himself as he shouldered down the aisle. But soldiers today—important, necessary, expendable.[9]

Protagonist Lee Gordon is as deeply conflicted, as *cloven*, as Bob Jones. Both fill "Negro first" jobs in wartime industry, Bob as leadman worker, Lee as union organizer. Both are educated, racially preoccupied, inhabited at one and the same time by deep feelings of inferiority and a profound sense of outrage. Where Bob simply reacts, responding emotionally to slights and demeaning situations, Lee has learned (at least on one level, the outward) to distance himself from his instincts, to stand apart from them by means of intellectualization, rationalization, analysis. Like Bob, Lee in the course of the novel is manipulated and used by everyone: white union officials, Communists, white women, workers with their own agendas, his bosses, what Pynchon called the whole sick crew. Bob is a victim; Lee begins as "the happiest man in the world"[10] and, after spending most of the novel learning to be a victim, chooses to become a special *kind* of victim, a martyr. Until this moment of existential choice, Lee's character remains labile, tenuous, transitional. By turns he appears passive, fearful, insecure, headstrong, honest with others, deeply dishonest with self and wife, his insubstantiality perhaps best symbolized in the habitual response he makes to challenge or revelation: "Well—yes." "No one man could be as contradictory as Lee Gordon seems," Smitty thinks at one point.[11]

The story surrounding Lee Gordon is altogether a grim one. Lee, presumably, is destroyed, as are six others with whom he crosses paths. Yet *Lonely Crusade*, dark as it is, "ends on a high note of pure affirmation—without parallel in the rest of Himes's fiction."[12] As in Wallace Stevens:

> After the final no there comes a yes
> And on that yes the future world depends.[13]

In the Harlem novels soon to come, Himes largely rejected plot, adopting the simplest gimmicks (what mystery folk call a MacGuffin)—cotton bales stuffed with money, mysterious packages passing from hand to hand, a man in a red fez moving through Harlem—as frameworks upon which to hang vivid scenes and confrontations among outlandish characters. Similarly, what plot there is to *Lonely Crusade* you could put (as guitarist Eddie Lang did the cues for the entire Whiteman Orchestra repertoire) on the back of a business card.

Lee Gordon, a college-educated Negro who has always felt himself to be special and who has consistently refused to accept the low-end work available to him, lands a "Negro first" job as union organizer in wartime industry. His once deeply romantic marriage to Ruth is failing, reeling beneath the blows of social sanction, personal failure, and Lee's ever-increasing insecurity. Going about his work, Lee becomes involved with various others: Smitty, the union secretary, and, though white, Lee's staunchest supporter; battle-scarred organizer Joe Ptak from national headquarters; the monstrous Luther McGregor, who "knows how to be a nigger and make it pay"[14]; soft-spoken former Latin professor Lester McKinley with his white wife and lifelong compulsion to kill white men; Jackie Fork, who becomes Lee's lover, like himself used by others to their own ends; black Communist leader Bart whose puritanical rearing clashes with Party ruthlessness; Abe Rosenberg, the Communist whose pragmatic progressive philosophy provokes Lee's spiritual rebirth.

Confronted by these factions and forced to face similar divisions within himself, Lee takes up with Jackie, leaves Ruth, is swept up in Machiavellian industrialist Louis Foster's maneuverings, becomes in the company of Luther party to bribery then murder, seems defeated both personally and professionally at every turn, a scooped-out, hollowed man, then in a fleabag hotel of a Damascus undergoes conversion. Next morning he attends the union demonstration toward which the novel has been unwinding. Deputy sheriffs block the street and drive back union marchers. All but Joe Ptak are repulsed, and when Joe, carrying the union banner, himself falls, in a perfect existential moment Lee rushes in to take up the banner and advance toward the deputies.

That's about it. Though Himes provides many dramatic and melodramatic flourishes to keep us moving through the story, it's from the rich interplay of characters, the play of conflicting ideas, and the manner in which Lee's personal deficits, fears, and failures unfold into the overall concerns of the narrative, that the novel's power comes. As Gilbert Muller points out:

> Lee Gordon's quest for an authentic identity is cast in several dimensions—economic, racial, sexual, existential—but it is ultimately his political identity that gives him unique substance as a character and *Lonely Crusade* its special force as a novel of ideas.[15]

Central to that play of ideas is an ongoing dialogue, both express and implicit, concerning Communism. In the thirties and forties the Communist Party actively courted and seemed to offer rare hope of true equality to Negroes. The Party had helped in defending the Scottsboro boys; through agencies such as the American Writers' Congress and the League of American Writers, through journals such as *New Masses*, it spread its influence. Richard Wright, longtime stalwart worker for the Party, explained its attraction in providing him with an intellectual framework for understanding his life as a Negro. He felt the Party's message was not that you must be one of us, and like us, but, instead, that "If you possess enough courage to speak out what you are, you will find that you are not alone."[16] By the early forties, however, the Party's failure to stand against fascism and its wartime suspension of support of civil rights in favor of national unity disillusioned many Negroes, who felt themselves betrayed. Communists in turn felt threatened by the unions they ostensibly supported, the two of them vying for power even as the bosses and owners worked to play one off against the other, just as they conspired to set black against white. Against this background *Lonely Crusade* unfurls. Unionism, Communism, morality, race relations—these and other such topics are explored in set-piece, debatelike dialogues between Lee and fellow travelers: Smitty, Joe Ptak, Luther, Jackie, Foster, Abe Rosenberg.

The central character conflict, meanwhile, is that between Lee and wife Ruth, whose marriage, like all else in Lee's life, has gone from bright promise to despair.

His love for her was so intense he could feel it like a separate life throughout his body.[17]

Before had been nothing but a bewildering sense of deficiency and a vague fear of momentarily being overtaken by disaster.[18]

He thought that with Ruth he would never be afraid again. But it merely changed the pattern of his fear. Now it was the fear of being unable to support and protect his wife.[19]

Despair, like all else in the dialectics of this book, has two sides. Battered and bruised, Lee takes "the hurt of all these things"[20] home to Ruth, finding release into her through "sex and censure and rage."[21] He has debased his marriage, his wife, and his own best feelings. And yet he has never told her how afraid he is of going out into the white world in search of what he feels is rightly his—"sowing in the fields where the harvest was nothing but hurt."[22] Here is Ruth's despair:

> She had been absorbing Lee's brutality for six long years. At first, she had been convinced of his essential need for it. Hers had been a confidence in his ability to eventually come through and in some way find the verification of manhood he seemed eternally to be seeking . . .
>
> But now her faith in him was gone. Now she did not believe that anything would ever help Lee Gordon. And she herself was through trying.[23]

She sees her husband as a man who "failed, as if failure was his destiny,"[24] yet when Lee leaves her, Ruth's world dissolves. In a striking scene, she stands at the mirror painting her face sickly white.

Lee's despair is just as palpable:

> She did not reply, and in the silence his loneliness returned. Eight years before, when they had been married, he had thought that she would be the answer to his loneliness . . . It had seemed like something burnished—almost silver, almost gold. Really, it had been tin foil.
>
> . . .
>
> Well—yes, Lee Gordon thought. When you were a Negro, so many things could happen to keep you from fulfilling the promise of yourself. No doubt he had been some sort of promise to her that he too had never fulfilled.
>
> Yet now he was of a mind to blame her for all of it. He had acquired the habit of blaming her for most of the things that happened to him, knowing as he did that she was not to blame.
>
> . . .
>
> Because he knew what was wrong with them was only what was wrong with himself.[25]

Fulcrum for Lee's mountebank efforts both to understand his world and to lay blame, the Ruth-Lee relationship in its mirroring of Chester's and Jean's own dissolving marriage adds considerable autobiographical tension. Reading *Lonely Crusade* with knowledge of Himes's biography, one finds it extremely difficult to refrain from wondering to what degree in this novel, consciously or unconsciously, Chester might be preparing his farewell to Jean. Other, frank use of autobiographical elements gives some weight to such reading. Lee's remembered drunken, libertine flight to New York is Chester's own; the cabin occupied briefly by Lee and Ruth as newlyweds, with its lizards, rats gnawing away in the walls and snake beneath the porch, is clearly the desert cabin they borrowed from Hugo, to whom the novel is dedicated.

Lee's affair with Jackie Forks, on the surface as simple as the relationship with Ruth is complicated, proves, beneath that, every bit as fraught. Blatant and unguarded in her sexuality, Jackie is a naif, undeveloped mentally and emotionally, a slate others write on. Lee, who with her rediscovers his capacity for tenderness, who becomes able again to live briefly on "the ladder to the way it might have been," is only one among many exploiting the young woman's artless good feelings: "He pitied her, and to be able to pity this white girl gave him equality in this white world."[26] Circumstances of the novel grind away at all the best that is in Jackie until finally, emptied by the needs of others, she becomes filled instead with the same pain, fear, and impotent rage as Lee, another example of Himes's identification of the Negro's and woman's plight.

In its *Bildungsroman* aspect, the novel depicts Lee's learning (even as the gulf between him and Ruth widens) to leave aside his apartness and join himself to others: to others of his race, to other workers, finally to all mankind. He has always sensed his apartness, we are told. That sense of being special, so like Chester's own by way of mother Estelle, has kept him from accepting work as a domestic following his college graduation even when nothing else was available. He is reserving himself for better things—and simultaneously excepting himself from the hell that is other people.

> He did not like people that much, anyway—neither Negro people nor any people. He did not feel that much involved in humanity or in the struggle of humanity.
>
> And to try to convince against their wills a bunch of ignorant Negro migrants of the value of a union, which he doubted as much as they, was a task he found personally repellent. He was

no medicine man, no Marcus Garvey, no Black Messiah. Let people go to hell in their own particular way was one thing America had taught him.[27]

He is embarrassed by Negroes who attend the first union meeting ("Lee felt a shame for them, ashamed of being one of them"[28]), and at one point proclaims: "I'm not trying to solve the Negro problem, Jackie. I'm trying to solve my own problem."[29]

Fear becomes the mind's native land. Fear comes up as it does in Himes's memory of the break with Jean (*I had become afraid*), as it does in Bob Jones's dreams, Kriss Cummings's despair, Jesse Robinson's damn-the-torpedos self-destruction: images swim into being in a developing tray, step into frame in the mirror. For try as Lee might to disallow the knowledge, those other faces return a vision of his own. Words like *terror, danger, hazard* and *disaster* leave their spore across pages describing Lee's childhood.

And what Lee learned . . . was disheartening, discouraging, and depressing. First of all, he learned that not only did he know very little concerning the Negroes of America, but that he knew very few of them. As he gained in knowledge concerning them he also gained in fear. For the knowledge of them was like looking into a mirror and seeing his own fear, suspicion, resentments, frustrations, inadequacies, and the insidious anguish of his days reflected on the faces of other Negroes . . . What life held for them, it also held for him—there was no escaping.[30]

As Milliken points out, Lee has been unable to discriminate between his rejection of the penalties imposed upon blackness and rejection of blackness itself. So thoroughly indoctrinated that "he accepted implicitly the defamation of his own character and was more firmly convinced of his own inferiority than were those who had charged him thus,"[31] the American Negro is an absence, a wanting, a lack. Lee himself has come "to believe that something was lacking in Negroes that made them less than other people."[32]

Nor does alienation from fellow Negroes bring in abreaction any identification with the white world; here, Lee is even more fully, and forever, excluded. He is a man without country, a man without brief, people, or prospect, with only the sigh of history's unbearable weight settling on him.

> He could not understand what he had done that called for so great a penalty . . . He came to feel that the guilt or innocence of anything he might do would be subject wholly to the whim of white people. It stained his whole existence with a sense of sudden disaster hanging just above his head, and never afterwards could he feel at ease in the company of white people.[33]

Even his speech changes in the presence of whites, as in his first meeting with Smitty: "Now, addressing a white person, there was a difference in his speech, something of a falter, a brief, open-mouthed hesitancy before sound, the painful groping, not quite a stammer, for the exact word."[34]

One extended passage early in the novel (while also prefiguring *The Primitive*) pulls together many of Lee's confounded thoughts and feelings. He's been out celebrating his new job and returns to the stone steps outside his home.

> He sat brooding over that crazy, depressed period he had spent in New York trying to escape from himself. In the dull, aching reality of his beginning hangover, it seemed dreamlike.
>
> Nights end to end there of whoring around. Up and down St. Nicholas Avenue. In and out the joints of Harlem. Drunk every night. Never seeing the light of day. Unable to remember any morning the name of the one who had been his bedmate the night before.
>
> There had been that deep fascination, that tongueless call of suicide, offering not the anodyne of death, but the decadent, rotten sense of freedom that comes from being absolved of the responsibility of trying any longer to be a man in a world that will not accept you as such.
>
> You could not be a man in a war plant, so you were a man in a bed. Everything you could not be in a war plant you were in a bed. So to the women in the war plant where you could not work you became the promise of what you were in bed. But always you had the depressing knowledge that it was not so

much your masculine superiority as your enthusiasm to prove you were that which in the war plant they said you were not, that fed the legend of what you were in bed. The difference between you the denied and those who denied you lay in the objective— theirs being to re-create themselves, and yours being to find creation of yourself. And when you had learned hurtingly and sufficiently that it never would, you came home to where at least it might have been.

"Well—yes," Lee Gordon thought. He stood up and went into the house and went to bed, where he was nothing.[35]

Lee's ultimate alienation, of course, is from himself. Like Ellison's invisible man, he feels overtaken, co-opted, not so much dispossessed as possessed. "I had the feeling that I had . . . used words and expressed attitudes not my own, that I was in the grip of some alien personality lodged deep within me,"[36] Ellison's protagonist says at one point, sentiments Lee would well understand. With no central sense of self, the world won't hold together around one; the molecule, the solar-system model, collapses. Even to give oneself, in marriage, in love, in service to mankind, one must first have a self to give. Lee's failure to embrace the identity of others finally reflects his impotence to become himself, to run the risk of humanity. This time, Lee realizes, "he could not excuse his predicament on grounds of race. This time he alone was to blame—Lee Gordon, a human being, one of the cheap, weak people of the world."[37]

As previously suggested, Lee's sense of being special, even in its coexistence with feelings of inferiority, echoes Himes's own. An argument might be made that Lee's quitclaim on self in favor of union with humanity prepares the ground for the demotics of the Harlem novels; in this light *The Third Generation* could be read as a search for communality with his race, *The Primitive* as Himes's dirge for personal exemption, his good-bye to all that.

All too often, young artists strive most urgently to set themselves apart, to make of themselves special cases—such is the nature of introspection, and one result of all this time spent alone—when the real task, the actual charge given us, is to demonstrate how much alike we all are.

* * *

Speaking of Joyce's *A Portrait of the Artist as a Young Man*, Ralph Ellison remarked that "Stephen's problem, like ours, was not actually one of creating the uncreated conscience of his race, but of creating the uncreated features of his face; our task is that of making ourselves individuals."[38]

What one carries away from *Lonely Crusade* and *If He Hollers* as from Richard Wright's work, the final residue, is a firm recognition of the manner in which every moment of their black protagonists' lives is a solitary, violent struggle to attain ideals of American manhood denied them by the very society that defines and continually impels them toward those ideals.

It makes them, shall we say, just a little crazy—a madness Himes will describe with clinical precision in his University of Chicago speech.

Writing of Richard Wright in the summer 1945 issue of *The Antioch Review*, Ellison discussed the Negro's options in confronting his American destiny. He may accept social invisibility and the role created for him by white society, with religion as bulwark; in so doing he becomes an accomplice to the white man in oppressing others. *Or he can reject the role urged upon him and become a criminal, a revolutionary* in continuous battle against the white world. Ellison's own *Invisible Man* surveys through its protagonist's varied roles as teacher, Party member, and cellar-dwelling acolyte, the strategies available between those poles of submission and rebellion. Himes in *Lonely Crusade* does much the same with his choice of characters and with the ongoing dialogues.

Himes has called the American Negro the most complex human being on this earth. Lester McKinley, upon first meeting Lee, thinks: "Insanity? Of course it was insanity, McKinley told himself, looking at the tired, dull hurt in Lee Gordon's eyes. This thin, too intense, tightly hurting boy across from him was also insane, but did not know it yet, as were all Negroes, he told himself."[39] Obsessed with hatred for whites and driven to kill them, McKinley has gone to great length—psychoanalysis, marrying a white woman and fathering her child, making himself intellectually superior—to cure himself of that for which, in American society, there is no cure; to recover from centuries of oppression that "had completely destroyed the moral fiber of an entire people, abuses to the innate structure and character and spirit so brutal that their effect was inheritable like syphilis."[40]

The novel's real monster, though, is Luther McGregor, who seems cobbled together out of racial stereotypes, every boogeyman story and irrational fear, the man "who knows how to be a Negro and make it pay."[41] His comments in a final dialogue with Lee, after Lee has seen him cut a man's throat for no good reason, sound—like much of Himes's later work—frighteningly contemporary.

"Look, man, goddamn, for all your education, they's a lot of things that you don't seem to know. In this goddamn world they's all kind of wars always going on and people is getting kilt in all of them. They's the races fighting 'gainst each other. And they's the classes cutting each other's throats. And they's every mother's son fighting for hisself, just to keep on living. And they's the nigger at the bottom of it all, being fit by everybody and kilt by everybody. And they's me down there at the bottom of the bottom. I gotta fight everybody—the white folks and the black folks, the capitalists and the Communists, too. And now I even gotta fight you. 'Cause everybody's looking out for theyself. Trying to get what they want. And cutting everybody else's throat. So I cuts me some throat, too."[42]

It's this specific indictment of the psychotic Negro, and by extension Himes's vision of black America as pathological, that *Lonely Crusade* brings into focus. He'll define this concept at length in his address the following summer at the University of Chicago. And it will hereafter prove a constant theme.

Much as with the failure of *Lonely Crusade*, he abandoned expectations of earning a place in American letters, Himes also gave up pretense of combining the two worlds, black and white, in *any* sort of motley. Henceforth the two worlds would be sharply divided. With that change, another change occurred: his brief as a naturalist writer relaxed to embrace elements progressively less mimetic, more mannered, more fantastic. His city becomes a stark, lightning-struck place of dark folds where anything might happen, where violence is as common and meaningless as trash cans or hunger, where children are fed from troughs, deadly nuns roam the streets, and a black Christ hangs with a sign on his neck saying They Lynched Me. In this fabulist, surrealist manner Himes has found his way, unknowingly, toward the Harlem cycle.

Remarkable also for its depiction of sex and love as weapons in a race war pitched between blacks as much as between blacks and whites (thus looking ahead to *Pinktoes*), *Lonely Crusade* is an altogether grim portrait of the city as a primal stage upon which Communists, unions and employers alike fight to bind the souls of men they nonetheless go on insisting are free.

Lonely Crusade has not done much better in ensuing years than at time of publication. It is Himes's least popular work, mined by critics for its ideas and attitudes while its fictional values remain largely ignored. The novel is as well written, however, as any of its time, and though mostly of historical interest now, Himes's discussions of Communism, unionism, and other social issues are balanced, informed, and well thought out, giving his novel a firm intellectual substructure. As often with Himes, one must draw a distinction between European and American reception: Yves Malartic's translation of *La Croisade de Lee Gordon* helped firmly establish Himes's reputation as a serious novelist in France.

Milliken perceives in the clash between too-good, iconic characters like Smitty, Joe, or Rosie and naturalist characters like Luther, Jackie, or Lee himself, a fundamental structural schism, fault lines spreading out from contradictory inclinations. He regards this as a conflict between naturalism and traditional storytelling values, while others read it as indicative of Himes's pull between realistic despair and headstrong optimism, or between mimetic and more figurative writing. All perceive the disjuncture, whatever name they give it, and all locate within it strength and weakness alike. Elsewhere Milliken remarks that

> The label "naturalistic" is a particularly attractive one, suggesting as it does the extraordinary fidelity of Himes's fiction to his actual experience, but this label too needs to be challenged. Himes is preeminently a writer who is fully aware of the gap that separates art from life, of the permanent incapacity of art to capture fully the complexity of life itself. His style can veer sharply from soberly conventional naturalism to the most radical extremes of sur-

realism. He is forever seeking the form that will fit, and he never denies to his characters the full range of contradictions that he finds in himself.[43]

So the disparity does indeed put a strain on the system, but it's a strain producing at least as much energy and momentum as it consumes; it is also, as suggested, a misalignment whose contradictions Himes subsequently will tap into and exploit.

One writes expecting change; if not in mankind (if one's ego is not quite that oversize) then at least in one's immediate environment, next month's rent taken care of, a trip paid for; change, perhaps, in oneself.

When Gertrude Stein said that in America every new generation is a new people, she was addressing the covetous lie of perfectibility so close to the heart of our nation. Tolstoy is said to have scratched out on the sheets of his deathbed: Keep . . . striving. And so we do, our task forever the same task undertaken here by Lee Gordon: generation after generation, against all odds, adversity and distraction, constantly and continuously to relearn what it is that makes us human.

9 "I Don't Have That Much Imagination"

Where is Chester Himes in all this?

He was a man who always defined himself as a writer, a man who sifted the materials of his life, working and squeezing away at them, mining them, assaying them, in his writing. Alter ego Jesse Robinson in *The Primitive* finds solace even in the detritus of his trade.

> Inside the cabinet, behind the closed doors, were his stacks of unpublished manuscripts, carbon copies, old papers and letters which he always kept nearby, carting them from place to place, hanging on to them year after year, to remind himself that—no matter what he did for a living—he was a writer by profession.[1]

Those stacks of paper are Jesse's history, are in quite an actual sense his life. They're what remains of the best part of him, of Jesse's talent and aspirations; for Jesse has become a ghost, a roomer in his own life. Himes, however, is that version of Jesse who went on to write *The Primitive* and in doing so saved himself. His connection to their trade is a more vital one.

> No matter what I did, or where I was, or how I lived, I had considered myself a writer ever since I'd published my first story in *Esquire* when I was still in prison in 1934. Foremost a writer. Above all else a writer. It was my salvation, and is. The world can deny me all other employment, and stone me as an ex-convict, as a nigger, as a disagreeable and unpleasant person. But as long as I write, whether it is published or not, I'm a writer, and no one can take that away.[2]

Without that work, then, largely unable to write, what does he become? What is he? Antonin Artaud said that very little is needed to destroy a man; one has only to convince him that his work is useless. So it often must have seemed to Himes in this bleak period: that his work was useless, and he himself careening toward destruction.

> For the next five years I couldn't write. I reworked my prison novel, *Black Sheep*, cutting it down to half its original size, and I tried to write a stage play from *If He Hollers Let Him Go*, but these were just reflex motions. Jean got a job as recreational director for the Federal Housing Projects for New York City, which necessitated her visiting all the various boroughs, and I worked at anything I could get—dishwasher, janitor's helper, snow shoveler . . .[3]

So complete was his sense of rejection, Himes said—assailed as he was by Communists, scorned by reactionaries, spurned by white and black alike, abandoned by the literary community—that he felt like a man without a country. "It was then that I decided to leave the United States forever if I got the chance."[4]

The chance would present itself at the end of those five despairing years. Meanwhile, in February 1948 Himes applied to the artists' colony Yaddo in Saratoga Springs and was offered residence for May and June of that year. There were also in attendance two other writers, two artists, and a composer. Himes had a room in the West House just across the hall from Patricia Highsmith, whose *Strangers on a Train*, when filmed by Hitchcock in 1951, would bring her fame, and whose unique creation of the amoral character Ripley later set her apart from other mystery writers of the time and, one suspects, many readers. It was that first novel upon which Highsmith, age twenty, was working while at the colony; when she died in 1998, she left her $3 million estate to Yaddo.

Himes had little idea what he might work on while at Yaddo. He had proposed a novel titled *Immortal Mammy*, which at one time he described as being about an exceptional Negro woman living in the white world, though this well may have been the Hollywood novel he'd been talking up for some time. Eventually he settled to work on "Stool Pigeon," the story of a prisoner who informs on others planning an escape. As a result they are thwarted, but only after a diversionary fire destroys much of the prison, and in anger over the damage done his standing as much as that done the prison, the warden divulges the informer's name. Himes wavered between making his characters black or white. He must have been going through the same self-interrogation in his revisions of *Black Sheep*, which codified his own prison experience through the guise of a white man; may have been paralyzed to some degree by criticisms of his depiction of the racial divide in *Lonely Crusade*; and, as previously suggested, from this time began to reject what he'd come to believe an optimistic, unrealistic representation of racial commingling in favor of black and white America as discrete, parallel worlds.

"Stool Pigeon" had become a novel-in-progress (he claims to have written fifty pages of it at Yaddo) when Himes applied for a Guggenheim that fall and was passed over. The Rosenwald Foundation, to which he had also applied, shut down that year.

Himes was quite taken by Yaddo's gorgeously landscaped grounds, rose gardens, and buildings, but his experience there was otherwise wholly negative. *The way your life is ruined here in this one small corner of the world*, poet Constantine Cavafy wrote, *is the way it's ruined everywhere.*[5] Chester carried his own climate with him, nestled among shirts, neckties, toiletries, and undernourished manuscripts in his luggage. Alone in his room he sat poring over such assured mood elevators as Rimbaud's *A Season in Hell* (Louise Varèse's translation had appeared in 1945 from New Directions) and Faulkner's *Light in August*, which pivots on the racial ambiguity of its central character, Joe Christmas. Isolation, meant to give him time to work undistracted, served only to send Himes crashing further into himself, intensifying his fear and self-doubt, underscoring his sense of failure and throwing into sharp relief his alienation. Like his doppelgänger in the story "Da-Da-Dee," Himes held himself apart from others, did little or no work, and spent much of his time drinking, sinking ever more deeply into despair and self-despite, becoming "something a little inhuman."[6] All is gravity, pulling him relentlessly down, back to the earth:

His face was twisted to one side and down-pulled with weariness. His skin was greasy; his eyes deep-sunk and haggard. There were harsh, deep lines pulling down the edges of his mouth.[7]

Meanwhile, the song at which he hums on his drunken way back from town bars to the colony Skidoo—for the song, like so much in his life, eludes him—never becomes the liberation through art that he hopes for, but remains only a loud wail of pain, filling his head with melancholy: "He felt as if nothing would ever matter again one way or another."[8]

Perhaps he was already sick when he went there, Himes wrote, and Yaddo just brought it out; he didn't know. "But I do know I was sick when I left."[9] The sickness, or perhaps some lucidity wrought from it ("with an ice-cold clarity derived from two Benzedrine tablets and a half bottle of champagne"[10]), found voice that summer in the speech Himes delivered at the University of Chicago. He came at the invitation of the Chicago South Side Community Center, where his old friend Horace Cayton was director, and must have felt himself uniquely qualified to speak on "The Dilemma of the Negro Novelist in the United States." His speech met with dead silence from the largely white audience. Himes was thirty-nine, again a failure.

When I finished reading that paper nobody moved, nobody applauded, nobody ever said anything else to me. I was shocked. I stayed in Chicago a few days drinking, and then I was half-drunk all the rest of the time I was in Yaddo. That was the time I started getting blackouts, I was drinking so much. I would get up in the morning and go into town, which you weren't supposed to do, and by eleven o'clock, I was dead drunk.[11]

That this speech manages to be at once masterful self-analysis, uncompromising manifesto, and cry of despair is full measure of its strength.

The writer, Himes said there in Chicago, seeks an interpretation of the meaning of life from the sum of his experiences. That is what urges him, and allows him, to go on. When, as with the American Negro, his experiences have been brutal and relentlessly oppressive, he cannot avoid bitterness, fear and hatred. His inclination will be to draw dwarfish, misshapen characters in a life without apparent form or purpose. But he must not accept that.

Rejecting it, immediately he will be set upon by a host of personal, social and professional conflicts.

First he must struggle with himself, because telling the truth about his degradation will open old wounds *and* bring new agonies.

And when he manages against all odds to win through and tell the truth, his reward will be to be reviled by whites and blacks alike. There will be great temptation to submit to patterns set by centuries of oppression: to retrench, equivocate, compromise. He will be driven to rationalize that he must shed his racial consciousness and become merely a man among other men. But his instinct for truth will finally determine that he cannot free himself of racial consciousness simply because he cannot free himself of race.

This conflict resolved, he will next discover the many factors working in concert to stay his pen. The American public does not want to know: truthful novels by honest Negro writers aren't good business. And if by some chance this writer does find a publisher, he'll find also new swarms of preconception and prejudice. White liberals, who have mingled exclusively with financially successful, materially secure, educated blacks (these darker versions of white), are likely to regard anything outside the pale of their limited personal experience and comforting illusions as aberrant, deranged, even psychotic.

Should the writer through pain and perseverance manage to get his book written and into print, new struggles await him, perhaps the most disheartening and bitter of all. For he cannot expect the patronage and support of the Negro middle class. Rather must he be prepared for displays of hatred and antagonism from black leaders, black clergy, and the black press, from all those who wish in shame to hide their own battered, scarred souls. They do not want it known that they have been so badly injured for fear they will be taken out of the game.

To white America those same scars are not only reminders, but affronts as well. It is his guilt that keeps the oppressor outraged and unrelenting; he will go to any length to keep from confronting that guilt and the contradictions within himself.

Of course American Negroes hate American whites, Himes said that warm day in Chicago; hating white people is one of the first reflexes black Americans develop as they begin to learn their place in

American society. They would not be human if they did not despise their oppressors.

It could not, he said, be otherwise. But the real question lies in asking how much a man must sacrifice of himself to this necessity of hate. The American Negro experiences hate doubly: he hates first his oppressor, and then, because he lives in constant fear of this hatred being discovered, hates himself because of this fear.

There can be no understanding of Negro experience, of Negro behavior or compulsion, of Negro sexual impulses, of Negro marital relations, of Negro crimes or Negro thought, until the impact of this fear upon the Negro personality is understood.

And if one divines in that personality elements of homicidal mania, lust for whites, paradoxical anti-Semitism, a pathetic sense of inferiority, arrogance, Uncle Tomism, hatred and fear and self-contempt, then these are the effects of oppression on the human spirit, the daily horrors and daily realities of the American Negro.

Yet, Himes said in conclusion, there is an indomitable quality within the human spirit that cannot be destroyed; a quality, a force, impregnable to all assault. Prejudice, oppression, even three hundred years of submission, cannot corrode or destroy it. Were it not for this quality the whole fiber and personality of Negroes would have been utterly destroyed, their white oppressors become drooling idiots, savage maniacs, raving beasts. It is the quality within all humans that cries out "I will live!"

By mid-June Himes was back in New York, living in a furnished room in the Bronx belonging to a black orchestra leader named Bonelli and borrowing money from Van Vechten and his old friend Dan Levin, for whose magazine *Crossroads* he'd written back in his WPA days. He was still trying to hum the song from "Da-Da-Dee," and remembered Jean going with him to low-end bars and dives and taking him home when he became too drunk to make it on his own: "I suppose that was all anyone could have done."[12] Then Jean's job, upon which they were wholly dependent, was eliminated.

A rare glimmer of good news came through from France, where a translation of *If He Hollers Let Him Go* was to come out in October. Himes himself during this period recast *Hollers* as a two-act play, sending it to Van Vechten for comment.

In October, having advertised himself in newspapers as an experienced caretaker, Himes took on duties as overseer at a dormant lakefront resort in Newton, New Jersey. He and Jean occupied a three-room apartment over a tavern; Chester was to look after the cottages, grounds, and the owner's three dogs while attending to such repairs as were needed. Otherwise he spent his time writing, drafting the dramatic version of *Hollers,* and possibly beginning *The Third Generation.* The resort's owners, Frank and Elinor Bucino, visited on weekends. Frank, "a small dark Italian with a bad eye,"[13] Himes characterized as a Little Caesar type. Supposedly Frank Sinatra's godfather, he was accompanied everywhere by a tall, blond Swede who, Chester said, "looked almost exactly like a fictional bodyguard and killer called Sure in one of my *Esquire* short stories, 'Strictly Business.'"[14] Bucino had bought the resort, previously used as a training camp and parade ground for the German-American Bund, at government auction. Jean and Chester remained throughout the winter, until the resort crew arrived that spring, receiving a hundred and fifty dollars a month plus expenses. They took long walks in the snow, gathered watercress for salads from the woods by the lake, drove the ancient Mack firetruck that was their emergency transportation about the countryside as though it were a modern Jaguar sports car. That December, Horace and Ruby Cayton came for a weeklong visit.

From *The Primitive*:

It had been pleasant there among the empty houses, far from the hurts of modern city life. No condescensions and denunciations, no venomous intrigues and shattering infidelities, no Negro problem and bright shining world of race relations with all its attendant excitement and despair . . .

His duties had been light, raking leaves, a few minor repairs, and nothing after the snow came in late November . . . He and Becky had a car to use, a lovely cottage with central heating, a fireplace and plenty of wood. And there had been a little terrier, owned by one of the proprietors, that had stayed with them; and in the cellar a hogshead of homemade wine that tasted a little like muscatel but was dry and very strong, which they had drunk all winter. It was full of dead gnats and had to be strained, but on occasion, to show off his ruggedness, he drank it with the dead gnats floating about in the glass.

"Ah laks marinated gnats," he would say.[15]

While at the resort, Chester turned away from race literature in favor of books such as *Butterfield 8*, *What Makes Sammy Run?*, and *They Shoot Horses, Don't They?* He was pleased to have uninterrupted, undistracted time to write and seemed on the way to recovering his spirits. But the new year brought new disappointments. He learned that he'd been passed over for a Guggenheim. Van Vechten didn't like his play. Blanche Knopf turned down the latest rewrite of *Black Sheep*. Chester's writing, and Chester with it, foundered anew.

By March Chester and Jean were back in their furnished room in the Bronx. That summer Chester worked briefly as a bellhop at the New Prospects Hotel in the Catskills, leaving after a bout with ptomaine poisoning. He next found employment as warehouseman at the New York Museum of Science and Industry, and in October turned caretaker again at a summer camp in Ware, Massachusetts. He remained in Ware until February before returning to New York, where he stayed with friends in Brooklyn before signing on as caretaker again, this time at the Stamford, Connecticut, farm of a New York theatrical lawyer named Halperin.

The farm, once used to breed and train horses, was extraordinarily beautiful, with acres of rolling lawns and vivid green grass, well-appointed stables, and a huge red barn. Chester and Jean lived in the servant's house. They had a jeep at their disposal and often fished in the well-stocked lake. There were, again, dogs to care for—a pair of shepherds and their three offspring—as well as poultry. Chester's duties were minimal: mowing and minor repairs, and helping Jean serve dinner on weekends when the family came to the farm.

Chester's relation of one incident at the farm appears in *The Quality of Hurt* after earlier being appropriated for *The Primitive*. Halperin liked to sit around and talk over farm affairs—about which, Chester notes, neither of them knew anything. Halperin had recently installed two dozen pullets, whose eggs (because, as it turned out, the hens were being fed pig mash) came out soft-shelled and deformed.

When this attorney came back the following weekend he examined the soft-shelled eggs and stated authoritatively their deformity was due to the rooster fertilizing them. [They] sat around for two hours, drinking Canadian Club whiskey highballs, trying to decide what to do with the rooster . . . Jesse couldn't understand how the rooster who lived in the pigpen a half mile distant from the chicken coop could have fertilized the eggs, but of course he didn't say so, seeing as how he was drinking this attorney's good whiskey. Finally the solution burst on this attorney like a brain storm. He banged dramatically on the table with his open palm and said in the voice of a general giving an order to charge: "*Jesse! Kill the rooster!*"[16]

The Halperins met his departure with some bitterness, though Chester from the first had made it clear that his fealty was to his writing. Joe, now a sociology professor at the state Negro college in North Carolina, had arranged for Chester to give a seminar there in creative writing, and in June, Jean and Chester left for two weeks in Durham.

Chester had some concern over being back in the South, as well as over differences the brothers had in the past, but all went well. The couple stayed with Joe and wife Estelle in their pleasant, six-room house. Chester found himself a celebrity on campus; his seminar was well attended and written up in the Durham papers. (The newspapers' interest may have resulted in part, Chester held, from a wish to avoid the issues of the Korean War and a suit brought against the city by the NAACP demanding equal school facilities for blacks. Himes attended one of the hearings, at which future Supreme Court Justice Thurgood Marshall dropped by to advise the young Negro attorneys.) The brothers toured Duke University and local tobacco farms, visited North Carolina Mutual Insurance Company and other black-owned businesses in the area. Chester was impressed at the professional and personal courtesy extended Joe by librarians and researchers at the all-white University of North Carolina in Chapel Hill. Joe and he got on well but never again became intimate.

The latest version of *Black Sheep* had gone from Blanche Knopf to Rinehart, whose editor, Bill Smith, Himes met at a party given by Van Vechten's niece, and from there to Henry Holt when Smith moved on.

While in Durham, Himes received a telegram leading him to believe the novel had been accepted. He returned to New York, however, only to find the novel neatly wrapped in brown paper and waiting for him: Smith, his sole supporter at Holt, had backed down. On arrival Chester and Jean had thrown a party at the Theresa Hotel for everyone they knew; they were left with twelve dollars.

It's one of the recurring scenes, one of the touchstones, in Himes's life, this squandering. Years later Jean recalled how, again and again, sums of money came to Chester only to be burned away, in a matter of days, on alcohol, women, and parties. And if there was no money, then expectation of money might be good enough.[17]

Loosely modeled on that visit to Holt, Himes's portrait of a publisher's visit in *The Primitive* amounts to an illustrated version of his Chicago speech.

Pope's face resumed its customary expression of shame and guilt, like that of a man who's murdered his mother and thrown her body in the well, to be forever afterwards haunted by her sweet smiling face.

"I'm afraid I have bad news for you."

Jesse just looked at him, thinking, "Whatever bad news you got for me—as if I didn't know—you're going to have to say it without me helping you. I'm one of those ungracious niggers."

"We've given your book six readings and Mr. Hobson has decided to drop the option."

Jesse had been prepared for this from the moment he'd read Pope's letter and now, before the reaction had set in, he just felt argumentative. "I thought you were going to cut it."

Pope reddened slightly. "That was my opinion. I like the book. I fought for it all the way. I think all it needs is cutting. But Hobson thinks it reads like fictional autobiography. And he doesn't like the title."

"*I Was Looking for a Street*," Jesse quoted, turning it over in his mind. "I was looking for a street that I could understand," he thought, and for a moment he was lost in memory of the search.

"He said it sounds like a visiting fireman looking for a prostitute's address," Pope said with his apologetic smile.

Jesse laughed. "That ought to make it sell."

Pope again assumed his look of guilt and shame. "The truth is, fiction is doing very poorly. We're having our worst year for fiction."

"Why not publish it as an autobiography then?"

"It would be the same. Hobson thinks the public is fed up with protest novels. And I must say, on consideration, I agree with him."

"What's protest about this book?" Jesse argued. "If anything, it's tragedy. But no protest."

"The consensus of the readers was that it's too sordid. It's pretty strong—almost vulgar, some of it."

"Then what about Rabelais? The education of Gargantua? What's more vulgar than that?"

Pope blinked at him in disbelief. "But surely you realize that was satire? Rabelais was satirizing the humanist Renaissance—and certainly some of the best satire ever written . . . This"—tapping the manuscript neatly wrapped in brown paper on his desk—"is protest. It's vivid enough, but it's humorless. And there is too much bitterness and not enough just plain animal fun—"

"I wasn't writing about animals . . ."

"The reader is gripped in a vise of despair and bitterness from start to finish . . ."

"I thought some of it was funny."

"Funny!" Pope stared at him incredulously.

"That part where the parents wear evening clothes to the older son's funeral," Jesse said, watching Pope's expression and thinking, "What could be more funny than some niggers in evening clothes? I bet you laugh like hell at Amos and Andy on television."

Pope looked as if he had suddenly been confronted by a snake, but was too much of a gentleman to enquire of the snake if it were poisonous.

"All right, maybe you don't think that's funny . . ."

"That made me cry," Pope accused solemnly.

"I suppose you think I didn't cry when I wrote it," Jesse thought, but aloud he continued, "But how do you make out it's protest?"

Looking suddenly lost, Pope said, "You killed one son and destroyed the other, killed the father and ruined the mother . . ."

"I Don't Have That Much Imagination"   159

and Jesse thought, "So you find some streets too that you don't understand," and then, "Yes, that makes it protest, all right. Negroes must always live happily and never die."

Aloud he argued, "What about *Hamlet*? Shakespeare destroyed everybody and killed everybody in that one."

Pope shrugged, "Shakespeare."

Jesse shrugged. "Jesus Christ. It's a good thing he isn't living now. His friends would never get a book published about him."

Pope laughed. "You're a hell of a good writer, Jesse. Why don't you write a Negro success novel? An inspirational story? The public is tired of the plight of the poor downtrodden Negro."

"I don't have that much imagination."[18]

Jesse departs with his manuscript, singing his private dirge, *da-da-dee*:[19]

```
                                         di
             dee                         dee
       da    da-da-da              deeeeeee    da
    da-da              dee       dee-dee
                     da dee-dee                      do
          do                              da
                                     doooooo
```

Later, waking in his room at the tail end of a full-tilt binge, Jesse stands staring at the manuscript for several minutes before taking out his clasp knife and "with a cry of stricken rage, an animal sound, half howl, half scream,"[20] plunging it into the manuscript with all his force.

It's here, then, that the ever discontinuous life becomes ever more so. Outside, the world speeds by: traffic becomes a blur, trees bloom, grow tall, and expire in a single day, the sun sweeps across the sky in a sudden arc and is gone. Tuesday's TV show turns into Thursday's rerun. What of all this is real? imagined? dreamed? remembered?

After that everything was a hodgepodge. I am not certain of the truth of what I do remember. What I think are memories of actual events might in reality be memories of bad dreams and nightmares. All the time following, until I went to Europe, seems like a period of recurring blackouts. I wonder what you call that? Shock, perhaps.

We roomed somewhere in Harlem, but I don't remember where. We lived, but I don't remember how; I don't remember working, except for a week or so as doorman for an expensive Jewish hotel in Long Beach when the Jewish high holy days were being celebrated. But that wouldn't have kept us alive for a week.[21]

Chester and Jean again took refuge for a time with the Smiths in Vermont, and that fall Jean found work as recreational director at the State Women's Reformatory at Mount Kisco, New York. Required to live on the grounds, she was able to see Chester only on the two days a week she had off, spending a single night with him. Chester, after applying for editorial work with *Reader's Digest* and being turned down, worked a single day cutting stencils for the addressograph in its Pleasantville, New York, mailroom: "I must confess I ruined more of the metal plates than I got right and after I worked overtime on my first day the supervisor felt they could save money by keeping me away."[22] Chester used his day's earnings to buy Jean a cheap Christmas gift. He'd taken a room in the house of an elderly spinster in a black, staunchly middle-class neighborhood on the edge of White Plains. Following the *Reader's Digest* fiasco, he worked for three months as porter and janitor at the White Plains YMCA.

During this period, too, he bellhopped again in the Catskills' "borscht belt." He scratched away halfheartedly at his latest version of *Black Sheep*, at drafts of stories and the aborted *Immortal Mammy*, began working with autobiographical materials that would coalesce into *The Third Generation*, wrote to Van Vechten that he was contemplating (in the manner of "Da-Da-Dee"?) a first-person account of his stay at Yaddo, which he would call (and did, years later, in a much-transformed work) "The End of a Primitive." He and Jean spoke of returning to California, instead moved as caretakers to a luxurious country club on Lake Copake where in January a hurricane hit, then to Bridgeport, Connecticut, where each morning Chester drove to a park by the Sound and sat with the typewriter on his knees, "at peace with his work"[23] in the sound of lapping waves and the cry of gulls. But within months their money ran out and Chester was forced to sell the Plymouth he'd recently bought. On the day of sale he was involved in a minor traffic accident with the wife of a prominent white doctor and jailed overnight, with Jean out of touch in New York City looking for work and quarters. Absurdities proliferated: Jean returned from New York to find Chester gone and the buyer come to claim the car; the doctor's wife "had suffered from such severe shock"[24] that she was unable to appear at next morning's hearing; because he'd not made bail Chester was carted off to the county prison; bail money wired by Jean's brother was returned to the telegraph office, where Jean was unable to retrieve it.

By that time it was four o'clock in the afternoon and the telegraph office closed at five. In the meantime, I had been marched to the mess hall for my supper of stale bread, macaroni, and boiled cabbage, and marched back to my cell.

Luckily, the warden couldn't bear to see a woman cry. No doubt he thought she seemed to be a decent black woman and wondered how those decent black women always got mixed up with some no-good black man.

. . . .

When I went into the waiting room, I saw at once that she'd been crying. Her body was trembling all over and her eyes looked huge and dark with anguish in her small heart-shaped face.

"Let's get out of here," I said.

We went back to police headquarters, where I had parked my car, and found a traffic violation ticket on it for parking overnight. I put the ticket into my pocket, started the motor, and drove back to the house.

The young brother who wanted to buy the car was waiting for me on the porch. I knocked twenty-five dollars off the price because of the bent bumper and crumpled fender, and the brother was satisfied.

Jean fixed a makeshift dinner and we ate silently. Afterward I said, "Let's pack."[25]

This is another incident that Himes lops virtually whole from life to paste into *The Primitive*.

At three-thirty he drove down to the corner of Fairfield Boulevard to buy cigarettes. On his return, when pulling from the curb, his front bumper caught in the fender of a new Buick Roadmaster that was passing too close on his left, and jerked it off. The Buick was driven by a white-haired white lady, dressed immaculately in a mauve-colored tweed suit that looked as if it might have cost more than he had earned from his second book—on which he had worked for more than a year. She was a very important person, and despite the fact she had been driving on the wrong side of a one-way street, and that her breath smelled pleasantly of excellent cocktails, she sent for a policeman and had him arrested for reckless driving. This not because she hated Negroes or wished to humiliate or harm him in any manner; simply because her husband was continuously cautioning her to drive carefully and she intended to prove by the record that she had done so.

But he wasn't worried. He hadn't broken any laws. How could they arrest him?

He found out shortly that to arrest him required very little skill. The policeman said, "Follow me," and mounted his four-cylinder steed. "Shows what an ingenious people can do," Jesse thought sourly as he followed in his battered jalopy.

The desk sergeant set his bail at twenty-five dollars. "But I'm a well-known American writer," he said. "You can release me on my own recognizance."

The desk sergeant said the law didn't permit it.

"Should have told him you were a porter, son," Jesse reproached himself. "All Americans trust Negro porters and black mammies—even with their children."[26]

In its fictional avatar the incident occupies most of four pages, in its autobiographical about the same. Nowhere in Himes does the continuous dialogue being carried on among actual experience, recollected experience, and fictive reconstruction come closer to the surface. *The Primitive*, in particular—with its structural juxtapositions of what Jesse perceives or says and what he simultaneously thinks—calls into question this dialogue. And when the novel clicks to its end around just such a turnabout, rather like a couplet closing itself off—"'I'm a nigger and I've just killed a white woman,' Jesse said, giving the address, and hung up. 'That'll get the lead out of his seat,' he thought half-amused' "[27]—we've long been prepared for it.

At one point during this period Lurton Blassingame remained Chester's agent, selling his story "The Snake" to *Esquire*; at another, Margot Johnson began representing him, sending around *Black Sheep* and *The Third Generation*. Richard Wright and family returned from a year's stay in Paris. At some point, too, Chester and the Moons became terminally estranged. "Chester was really having a hard time," Joe explained years later, "and the Moons were not very nice to him, or at least he thought they were not. Chester thought they turned on him like a poor relation . . . He harbored a grudge."[28] Richard Wright and family reembarked for France. Chester moved again, alone, to a room on Convent Avenue in Harlem. There, avoiding old friends, he went to ground, playing cards, cadging meals, and watching mindless TV with brother Eddie. Again—a failure.

Where am I today? How did I get here? And tomorrow? (Never mind tomorrow.) Jean is there beside him when he turns his head, gone when he looks again. Then someone else, another woman. *Today he had planned to . . .* Sky outside, above, a blur. Street beneath also a blur. Feet moving along that street of their own volition, *they* know the way home. Still looking for a street he can understand. If only he could get that tune right. It's a blur, too, like his voice, like the whole of last week, like these five years.

Blur reigns.

February 1952. The manuscripts of both *The Third Generation* and *Black Sheep* were making rounds of publishers, but that had come to be of little import. Chester faced the worst failure of all: his marriage was over. By April the overnight visits had ceased; he and Jean were living apart. "We should have done it a long time ago," Chester wrote in a letter to Van Vechten late that year, ". . . Jean couldn't bear the things I wrote nor the processes of my thought which caused me to write them."[29]

> That summer I had convinced myself I was a failure as a writer, and poverty and loneliness and our enforced separation had convinced me I was a failure as a husband. After fourteen years of love and marriage we had lost each other. It was no one's fault, really. We had been together longer than anyone expected. One might say my sins had caught up with me—the sins of pride and arrogance. And I was beginning to pay. Jean stopped coming to visit me and to support me, and I was faced with the necessity of having to support myself.[30]

In his 1983 interview Joe likened Chester's parting with Jean to their mother's ultimate abandonment of Joseph Sandy. It was Estelle's self-orientation that Chester perceived there, Joe said, her attitude that if her husband couldn't take her where she wanted to go, then he was a liability and she'd just have to drop him and get there on her own.

> Well, I would guess—I am not sure about this, but I feel I have enough instinct to say—that Chester reached the point in the early 1950's where he had become totally disillusioned with the American society. This was after he had published *Lonely Crusade.* He had come to the conclusion that it was impossible for a black person to succeed as a writer in this country, and he needed to leave this country. I think Chester also perceived that a black wife would be a handicap in Europe.
>
> Now, Jean is a nice girl. I know Jean very well, and I am extremely fond of her. Jean couldn't help Chester do what he wanted to do in Europe, probably anywhere. So he said pragmatically, unemotionally, "Jean has to go. I'm going forward. She can't help me, so I leave her." And, he left her. I don't think it was because he didn't like Jean, or he didn't care for Jean. It was a simple calculation, and Chester is like that on

one level. Every thing that comes his way within sight is legitimate to be used to advance his goals.[31]

As for Chester's clamor over Jean's being the breadwinner, Joe said, that was another of the points Chester picked, rather cynically, to play up to his audience, like his supposed guilt over the accident that blinded Joe, or his insistence that their parents' discord centered on degrees of blackness. Jean indeed may have been the couple's sole support, but for a brief period only, and Joe could not imagine Chester's ever having been humiliated or bothered by this. "That does not strike me as consistent with his orientation to use people . . . There were so many times when he was using some woman to pay his bills and keep him while he wrote his books and lived the good life."[32] Chester could have been motivated simultaneously by shame at being kept and by gratitude to Jean, may have accepted her support as necessary in America while at the same time preparing to shed the skin of that support. Like the scientists in *Destination Moon*, he was lightening his load—dumping chairs and control panels and provisions overboard—in order to take off. People have many layers, Joe said. They have a layer that's pragmatic, utilitarian and exploitative, and they have another that's sensitive, "made of guilt material."[33] And with that observation Joe touched, again, what is at the heart of Chester's work, the very source of its amazing power: his ability to mine and shape into narrative, without losing any of their force, the many contradictions within himself.

Chester would book passage to Europe exactly one year later, in February 1953. His father would die in Cleveland that January.

Before her death in 1945, Chester's mother Estelle had spoken of writing the history of her ancestors both black and white and had in fact begun making notes, material which Chester saw while in Durham visiting Joe. Soon he was talking about a story to be called "The Cord," which would delve into the troubled relationship of parents closely resembling his own, the racial ambivalence that the mother had passed on to her sons, and her unnatural, investive attachment to one of the sons. This was the bare beginning of *The Third Generation*, of course, Himes's instincts and intuition hitting on all cylinders as he groped his way toward new work. Later he would say of this book: "[E]ven if many of the scenes in the novel are based on real occurrences, the things causing and linking them, as well as the dramatic climax, are completely imaginary."[34] There's scant record of the novel's composition, but by late 1951 it had joined Himes's prison novel on the great prowl, knocking at publishers' doors asking to be let in. Its dedication was "To Jean."

The prison novel, submitted under the title *Debt of Time*, briefly called *Solitary* and finally *Cast the First Stone*, sold that April to Coward McCann for an advance of twelve hundred dollars. In November Himes sent three versions of the novel to Van Vechten for archiving at Yale. One, he said, dated from the years 1936–37 when he was just out of prison, one from 1939–40 following his WPA internship up till the time he signed on at Bromfield's farm, and the *Black Sheep* version completed in 1949.

Chester had gone back to work as bellhop at the New Prospects Hotel in Sullivan County, where he'd once contracted ptomaine poisoning. One night while filling in at the switchboard he received a telegram that William Targ, vice president and editor-in-chief at World Publishers, wanted to buy *The Third Generation* and was offering a two-thousand-dollar advance. Targ's wife Roslyn would become Chester's longtime agent, and remains so today; Targ himself later brought out a beautiful limited edition of Chester's *A Case of Rape*, for many years the only available English-language edition.

> I had been saving my tips and had enough money for the fare back to New York. I went out to the kitchen and told the co-proprietor I was leaving, and went across the yard to my room and packed my bag. As I was standing by the gate trying to thumb a ride into town, he came out of the hotel and paid me what was due and had Joe, the other bellhop, drive me to the station in the old pickup.[35]

Chester knew a few things now.
He knew he couldn't make it as a writer here.

He knew that he'd been right when after publication of *Lonely Crusade* he'd made up his mind to leave for Europe.

He knew that with the two advances he was, at least temporarily and by his own standards, rich.

He knew he wanted to make love to a white woman.

10 Literature Will Not Save You

By December of 1952, the money was mostly gone.

In November, in the same letter to Van Vechten that discussed his and Jean's separation, Chester wrote: "I am quite interested in a woman, Vandi Haygood . . . If all goes well and I get my divorce we will probably marry some time next year."[1]

In truth the divorce was put off a few years—until 1978, when Chester petitioned for same through the French government. Jean at that time lived in Chicago, on South Shore Drive. Papers had been sent her on September 23, October 3, October 27, and November 27, all of which she ignored; finally, at the French government's request, a U.S. marshal was dispatched. Jean told the marshal that, yes, she had the papers, and that if Chester wanted a divorce, fine, but she was sixty-nine years old and *she* wasn't going to do anything about it. She also complained over the papers being in French. Divorce was granted, according to article 237 of the Civil Code, on May 2.

Neither did the anticipated (fanciful?) marriage to Vandi Haygood occur. In the wake of his windfall advance, Chester had grasped at the leavings of their old affair.

I still had my room on Convent Avenue, but the first thing I desired now that I had money was to sleep with a white woman, and the only white woman in the city I knew at the time who was likely to sleep with me was Vandi Haygood. I had spent a weekend with her in Chicago many years before, when Jean and I had been living in Los Angeles. Vandi had been acting director of fellowships for the Rosenwald Foundation during the war while her husband, the director William C. Haygood, had been in the Army; and I had been given a Rosenwald Fellowship to complete my first novel, *If He Hollers Let Him Go*. I had been to New York for some reason which I have forgotten, and on the way back to the coast I had stopped in Chicago and spent a wild, drunken week of sexual extravagance with Vandi, and for a time afterward she had genuinely loved me.[2]

Now that wild, drunken week of sexual extravagance became eighteen months, extravagances likewise mounting, sweeping the two of them relentlessly along in a flood of heightened sensation and displaced passions.

Blur still reigned.

Vandi had become an executive for the International Institute of Education (called the India Institute in the novel) at Fifth Avenue and Sixty-seventh Street in Manhattan, a screening center for government grants. Vandi always needed a man, "couldn't go to sleep without a man beside her, any man," and, divorced for five years, increasingly desperate, had just ended an affair with "a young Jew whom she had tried to get to marry her."[3] Neither Vandi nor Chester made much pretense that they were doing anything but using one another. Vandi was attractive, sexually uninhibited, terrified of being alone, self-destructive, white. Severely offtrack and balance, Chester grieved for his marriage as despair licked flames at his life and money burned holes in his pocket. His depiction of their affair in *The Primitive* on the one hand captures with clinical accuracy the animal-like, sexually obsessive, delirium-stained, and essentially heartless nature of their relationship while on the other, by means of superstructure and underpinning, elevating it to a kind of timeless myth: the particular and sordid become universal, tragic. Also at the heart of the book lies that identification of black man and white woman as damaged, perhaps irreparably, by American society which surfaces repeatedly in Himes.

My book *The Primitive* was about our affair, and although it doesn't tell the whole tedious story of my eighteen months with her, it gives the essence of the affair; in fact it is rather exact except that I didn't kill her. I left that for her own race to do; they had already mortally hurt her before I began to live with her, and it was no more than right that they should be the ones to finish her.[4]

Just such socially ordained destruction would become the central theme of *A Case of Rape,* but it was already in place in earlier work. Bob Jones's lust and loathing toward victim-vamp Madge Perkins in *If He Hollers* reflects the force of threats both real and imagined to his manhood. As Milliken writes, Bob's ambition is simply to live out the American myth of maleness as heroic fighter, leader of men, provider and protector of women—all things denied him by society. Lee Gordon in *Lonely Crusade* feels unmanned by his dependence on wife Ruth: "I like women who are women. I like to sleep with them and take care of them. I don't want any woman taking care of me or even competing with me."[5] But with women who appear to him helpless and lost, women like Jackie Forks, Lee is compelled by a need to take care of them. Only by pitying her, by turning her into a symbolic Negro, can Lee feel equal to Jackie. She in turn experiences a certain nobility in giving herself to a Negro, deriving from the union that complex equation of sexual fulfillment and social-sexual shame she requires.

With the intensity of her need and her responsible position, Vandi Haygood was the perfect embodiment of all these contradictory urges. Beleaguered by fear and self-doubt—round her barking the mad and hungry dogs—Vandi used sex both to validate herself, in a sense to assure herself that she was real, to keep from fading away, and to punish herself for the faults of her character, her essential valuelessness. For Himes, in turn, sex with Vandi at different times could be used as an interpersonal weapon, could channel his rage against white men (getting even with them—Vandi taunted him over that), and could give form to his longing to protect this vulnerable, deeply hurt, powerless woman, for in one part of his mind Chester always saw himself as the courtly protector of his women.

What we know of the affair, of those eighteen months, we know mostly from *The Primitive.* Himes had gone to ground for much of this time, avoiding old friends, drinking alone in his room or in cheap bars or wandering the city aimlessly. That *The Primitive* offers a symbolic depiction rather than a literal one, we take on faith. Still, given Himes's own assertion that it was "rather exact except that I didn't kill her,"[6] as well as the evidence of so many actual events incorporated virtually intact, we take it on *good* faith.

Here is Vandi's counterpart Kriss Cummings from the beginning of *The Primitive:*

The gold-plated Swiss clock on the nightstand whirred softly, curdling the silence of the small dark room. A woman stirred tentatively on the three-quarter-size bed, flung a heavy bare arm searchingly across the faded blue sheet. It encountered only emptiness. She became rigid, scarcely breathing, her nude body suddenly chilled beneath the two ample blankets, her emotions momentarily shattered by the blind panic she always experienced on awakening and finding herself alone.

. . . .

How many times during the five years since she had divorced Ronny had she awakened alone? She wondered vaguely. Too many! Too, too many! And not because she played hard to get. She was easy—too easy, she knew—but she couldn't help it; she hardly ever did it now for any other reason than to keep them near. God, what slobs some of them had turned out to be!

But at this moment of awakening, before her mind had restored its defenses, regained its equanimity, phrased its justifications, hardened its antagonisms, erected its rationalizations; at this moment of emotional helplessness . . . she could not blame it all on men. That was for a time later in the day. Night was the time for crying, and day for lying; but morning was the time of fear.[7]

Fumbling to piece together events of the night before (we're told she goes through six bottles of good Scotch a week), Kriss breakfasts, showers and dresses, fortifies herself with Dexamyl, and sets off to work.

And here, in the following chapter, is failed novelist Jesse Robinson waking from a dream in which, skating, he falls through the ice and no one saves him—or even sees him:

He awakened and went to the dresser and poured a water glass full of gin. The faint glow of the city night came through the two side windows, silhouetting his nude body in the dim mirror. His hand trembled and his teeth chattered against the rim of the glass as he forced the gin down his throat.[8]

Jesse falls back asleep and dreams in quick succession that he's at a banquet where no one will talk to him; in a chaotic parking lot watching cars lurch into one another in their desperate attempts to break the jam and get out, then witnessing a brutal fight; and sitting on a bed, seventeen years old, kissing the prettiest girl he's ever seen. "There's nothing lonelier than a double bed,"[9] he thinks upon waking again. The night before, he'd wandered from bar to bar looking for a woman. He'd come home and begun drinking gin and reading Gorky into the early hours, till the story he was reading started getting all tangled up with stories of his own imagining and "he'd become entombed in a completely new and frightening world,"[10] dreaming that he was dead with no record or evidence that he had ever lived.

> He got up and surveyed his nude body in the mirror. It was a trim, muscular body, the color of Manila paper, with the broad-shouldered proportions of a pugilist. From the neck down he could have been anywhere between twenty-five and thirty. Only his face ever showed his age; now it was swollen from heavy drinking and had the smooth, dead, dull-eyed look of a Harlem pimp.[11]

For the past five years, we're told, since publication of his latest novel met with universal condemnation, Jesse's brain has never let down but is always running with "futile rages, tearing frustrations, moods of black despair, fits of suicidal depressions,"[12] and no matter how much he drinks, no matter what he does to deaden his thoughts, there is no surcease.

From Kriss, Jesse has taken on the habit of stimulants. Day after day they stoke themselves with Dexamyl, then drink to level off or come back down: "Vandi and I had always drunk ourselves blind at night in order to get to sleep; and she took barbiturate sleeping tablets on top of that."[13]

Society's victimization of them perpetuated by their own demons, Jesse and Kriss circle one another in a ritual dance, a deadly pas de deux, backing and advancing, spinning past and sliding off one another, through collision to catastrophe to chaos.

Much of that dance, again, was taken from life, as when Chester discovered a supposed Washington business trip to be Vandi's alibi for a rendezvous with an old lover in Chicago.

> I began slapping her when she admitted the truth and all the hurts of all my life seemed to come up into me and I went into a trance and kept on slapping her compulsively until suddenly the sight of her swollen face jarred me back to sanity . . . For an instant I thought she was dead.[14]

Vandi, reeling about with her blackened face, couldn't leave the house for two weeks. Chester nursed her, bathed her, made excuses for her, cooked and cleaned, all the while overcome by guilt. Later, near the end of the affair, he returned from a movie to the apartment he'd vacated so that she could have a tryst with an elderly lover and, looking at the stack of bills beside her, felt his guilt drain from him. That misogyny one senses forever poised just behind Chester's chivalric manner—and in such seeming contradiction to the equation of suffering he asserts between blacks and women (though perhaps, finally, but another proof of it)—emerges when he writes of the incident in his memoirs, in a statement eloquently complex beneath its patent sheen.

> The final answer of any black to a white woman with whom he lives in a white society is violence. She knows as well as he, that no one, neither white nor black, will support his contentions. There may be many who will plead his cause, but if she is adamant, there are none who will take his side. Of course, like me, he might not give a damn if anyone takes his side or not as long as he thinks he's right. And the only way to make a white woman listen is to pop her in the eye, or any woman for that matter. But it is presumed only right and justifiable for a black man to beat his own black women when they need it. But how much more does a black man's white woman need it; maybe she needed it when she became his woman.[15]

Other times Himes's violent impulses were deflected from Vandi to visitors. The Caytons once watched in horror as Chester mocked Ralph Ellison for his success, verbal attacks stopping just short of physical. (Chester insisted in later years that Ellison had pulled a knife on him.) Much of all this, too, was layered into *The Primitive*. To Yves Malartic Himes wrote that American women, who in their hearts hate and envy writers, pursue them for the sole purpose of hurting them.

By December 1952 the affair was over. Himes departed for Vermont to stay with Bill Smith, lugging along the huge trunk that went everywhere with him, a horsehide suitcase given them by Jean's nephew back in L.A. days, and the clothes that proved almost his final word on Vandi.

> At least I had got some clothes while living with her. At that time, Kaskel's was a big pawnbroker on Columbus Circle with an outlet store on Fifty-seventh Street which sold new suits of good quality and seconds of those slightly damaged by window display, and I had bought two new suits from them at about half the customary retail price; a beautiful three-button suit in Oxford blue flannel the likes of which I've never seen since, and a two-button suit in beige wool gabardine. In addition I had bought a good suit of dark-gray herringbone tweed from Rogers Peet at Forty-second Street and Fifth Avenue and a gray Burberry overcoat from a shop on Fifth Avenue called Nica Rattner, as I remember. And some shirts and ties and good English-made shoes from Brooks Brothers, and some odds and ends, summer suits, shirts, pajamas and such, all seconds, from Klein's and Gimbel's.[16]

While Chester was in Vermont, helping Bill Smith with the rewrite of a novel, trying to walk off his daily Dexamyl buzz and adamantly doing little else, Joseph Sandy died of complications from a hip broken in a fall. Chester was prepared for his death, he said; his father had been in ill health for years. But he had no way to get to the funeral. Finally he called Vandi to borrow the money to fly to Cleveland.

> She did not like it at all. She felt that I was taking advantage of her, knowing that under the circumstances she couldn't refuse, and of course I was.[17]

Chester and Vandi would see one another again on April 22, 1953, when she arrived on a Paris visit within weeks of his own arrival. Chester's new friends were duly impressed by her, and the two old lovers passed such a riotous night together that the manager of their hotel was forced to relocate them to a back room. While in Paris Vandi learned that she was to be the subject of Himes's new novel. She pressed Ellen Wright, then serving as Chester's agent, to show her what he had written thus far, but Ellen refused. Two years later, in February 1955, Chester was back in the States on business, staying at the Albert Hotel in Greenwich Village, and tried to call Vandi. Told she had died of a drug overdose the night before, he hung up the phone and wept.

Scheduled for October 1952, *Cast the First Stone* was delayed until January. All through the affair with Vandi, Himes and editors at Coward McCann were in dispute; finally the novel reached publication in radically truncated form. That edition passed quickly out of sight, as did a 1972 Signet paperback. The novel didn't fare much better in Europe, going unpublished there until 1978. It became a difficult find in any edition, and not until 1998, when Old School Books and W. W. Norton, returning to the original manuscripts at Yale, reissued the novel under its original title *Yesterday Will Make You Cry*, did we see the novel Himes wrote. Himes's prison novel became his counterpart to Ellison's protagonist, Himes's invisible novel:

> I am invisible, understand, simply because people refuse to see me. Like the bodiless heads you sometimes see in circus sideshows, it is as though I have been surrounded by mirrors of hard, distorting glass. When they approach me they see only my surroundings, themselves, or figments of their imagination—indeed, everything and anything except me.[18]

Chester maintained that the publishers had pulled out the book's very heart. Van Vechten agreed, writing in a letter to John A. Williams that "*Yesterday Will Make You Cry* is probably his best but it was so cut for publication that in that form it is worthless."[19] The editors' changes, however, went much further than simply cutting. "They upset the whole structure of the book and reordered the chapters, even rewriting certain passages," restoring editors Marc Gerald and Samuel Blumenfeld assert. "The editors [at Coward McCann] deliberately and relentlessly erased the tenderer and more artistic aspects to turn Himes's manuscript into a hard-boiled prison novel,"[20] in effect turning an intensely personal

Photograph of Himes as dashing young man—note damage to teeth—inscribed "To my beloved sister-in-law 'Stell From my beloved me, Chester."
(From the papers of Joseph Himes. Reproduced with permission of The Amistad Collection)

Faculty of Lincoln University, 1912. Includes Chester's father, Joseph Sandy Himes (second row, far left).
(From the Lincoln University Yearbook. Reproduced by permission of the Ethnic Studies Center at Lincoln University)

Chester in teen years.
(Photograph from the collection of Lesley Himes. Reproduced by permission of Lesley Himes)

1946 Van Vechten sitting.
(Photograph by Carl Van Vechten. From the Carl Van Vechten Photograph Collection of the Library of Congress. Reproduced by permission of the Library of Congress and the Van Vechten Trust)

Above: Chester in 1954, shortly after arriving in Europe.
(Photograph from the collection of Lesley Himes. Reproduced by permission of Lesley Himes)

Right: Chester at work at La Ciotat, *circa* 1956.
(Photograph from the collection of Lesley Himes. Reproduced by permission of Lesley Himes)

Chester in Paris in 1958, at the time of publication of his first detective novel, *La Reine des pommes*.
(Photograph from the collection of Lesley Himes. Reproduced by permission of Lesley Himes)

Chester with the VW, Vence, 1957.
(Photograph from the collection of Lesley Himes. Reproduced by permission of Lesley Himes)

Chester and Mikey, Vence, 1957.
(Photograph from the collection of Lesley Himes. Reproduced by permission of Lesley Himes)

Chester, Marcel Duhamel, and Picasso at Picasso's château near Mougins, Cannes, 1961.
(Photograph from the collection of Lesley Himes. Reproduced by permission of Lesley Himes)

Chester with Mikey and pups, Paris, 1960.
(Photograph from the collection of Lesley Himes. Reproduced by permission of Lesley Himes)

1955 Van Vechten sitting.
(Photograph by Carl Van Vechten. From the Beinecke Rare Book and Manuscript Library, Yale University. Reproduced by permission of the Van Vechten Trust)

1962 Van Vechten sitting.
(Photograph by Carl Van Vechten. From the Beinecke Rare Book and Manuscript Library, Yale University. Reproduced by permission of the Van Vechten Trust)

Chester, Lesley, and Griot, *circa* 1965.
(Photograph from the collection of Lesley Himes. Reproduced by permission of Lesley Himes)

Chester and Lesley with Joe Himes and Arlone at Joe's house in North Carolina, Christmas 1973.
(Photograph from the collection of Lesley Himes. Reproduced by permission of Lesley Himes)

Chester with Joe Himes, North Carolina, 1973.
(Photograph from the collection of Lesley Himes. Reproduced by permission of Lesley Himes)

Chester and Lesley with Joe Himes and cousin, North Carolina, 1973.
(Photograph from the collection of Lesley Himes. Reproduced by permission of Lesley Himes)

Chester on his final visit to the States, 1980, taken while he and Lesley were staying at Ishmael Reed's home in Oakland.
(Photograph by Kaz Tsurata. Reproduced by permission of Kaz Tsurata)

statement into just another ready-to-wear, something instantly recognizable, a type.

Taking their cue from Himes's complaints, commentators have stated that reviews of *Cast the First Stone* were poor, as in the case of other early novels an exaggeration. While it's true that reviews were few, they were by no means altogether negative, and appeared in major publications.

Crime novelist W. R. Burnett (*Little Caesar, The Asphalt Jungle*) began his review for the *Saturday Review of Literature*: "This is a very odd book." Though troubled by the novel's preoccupation with homosexuality and apparent artlessness (two-thirds of the book, he said, had "none of the esthetic generalization of a novel, but instead the unrelieved particularity of factual writing"), he nonetheless pronounced it "highly original."[21]

Gilbert Millstein in the *New York Times* took the low road of damning with a sidelong gaze, noting that the novel

> reads exactly like the autobiography of one of those penitentiary lawyers very often thrown up by prison life. Such men are glib, reasonably literate, authoritative in a superficial way, full of self-pity and whining mannerisms.[22]

Frederic Morton in the *New York Herald Tribune* doubly praised the novel:

> Mr. Himes seems to have pounded his typewriter with brass knuckles without losing either accuracy or aim. He has succeeded twice: in recreating the inferno of a penitentiary; and in recording the ordeal of a convict's emotional growth.[23]

With that observation Morton urges into light the novel's chief structural problem: its bifurcate nature. For two novels coexist, not always peacefully, here. One documents the dreariness of prison life with its sadistic guards, horrible food, homicidal convicts, unrelieved boredom and petty hierarchies, the other is a novel of character, dramatizing Jim Monroe's coming of age as he moves toward a connection with humanity and eventual redemption, and the two narratives do prove at points immiscible. Himes's feet are one moment on this path, then on the next, some fields over.

Stephen Milliken, beginning chapter four of his Himes study with a brief essay on autobiography and fiction, points up the conflict that must always exist in the artist between the formal exigencies of art and "his sense of the unalterable reality of his own experience"[24]— compasses that may give quite different bearings. Unfortunately, Milliken says, Himes never chose to clarify in any detail the relation of fiction to fact in his three autobiographical novels of the early 1950s. Portions of his life explored exhaustively (one might say obsessively) in the novels are little more than sketches in *The Quality of Hurt*: six pages for his seven-and-a-half years in prison, a single chapter to cover all the events of his youth and his parents' doomed marriage, three pages devoted to his affair with Vandi Haygood.

> It is firmly established that almost all of the basic events that make up the plot structures of the three novels are factual, but no light at all is shed on the validity of the characterizations and patterns of motivation developed in the novels.[25]

To the language we use there is forever a kind of gravity that pulls narratives down into recognizable shapes, the shape of our own life, our preconceptions, shapes we know from other tales like the one we are relating, against which gravity the artist constantly must struggle if he is to say anything meaningful; the two streams of narrative in Himes's novel are discrete languages drawing his story toward different, perhaps irreconcilable ends. Still, we must remember that this is an early, in fact a first, novel, and one several times rewritten over a period of years, years in which the author was himself undergoing dramatic changes. That the novel is something of a patchwork should not surprise us. Nor, finally, is it at all unusual that Himes's text should be in conflict with itself; so many of them, so patently and so energetically, are.

Gone now, however, are the anachronisms that littered the previous edition's lawn with broken refrigerators and cracked fountains. Himes's prepublication updating of the novel had moved the period from just after World War 1 (1928–36, his own prison years) to just after World War 2 (1946–52) by altering a few dates and sprinkling in references to contemporary figures such as General Patton. But the time in which the prisoners exist remains adamantly the 1930s: they shave with straight razors, the prison band plays hot jazz, and the whistle of freight trains underlines their immobility.

Gone, too, is the first-person voice adopted for the book's initial publication, which had the effect, probably intended, of bringing the story in line with traditional hard-boiled fare and the circumstantial one of suppressing the reflectiveness so important to the novel's more personal aspect.

In addition to being his invisible novel, Himes's prison book proved a source of considerable confusion to early commentators. Assuming it to have been written after *If He Hollers* and *Lonely Crusade,* that is, in order of publication, epimethean readers perceived in the novel a shift in emphasis, a bending toward the brutalities and crime-laden atmosphere of the Harlem novels that followed five years later. There was confusion as well over Himes's choice of a white man as protagonist. Had Jimmy Monroe, they wondered, been written black and later changed, either at the author's discretion or at the behest of his editors, to white? and to what purpose if so? Was this a further attempt to reshape the stuff of a troubling book into something more mainstream, more identifiable—something *tamer?*

In an introduction written for its reissue, Himes's old friend Melvin Van Peebles relates, in a tone Himes would have admired, his rediscovery of the novel he thought he already knew.

> BLAM! By the second page, I realized what a chump I had been! I had accepted without question the swinging of the pendulum towards pulp in *Cast the First Stone* as Chester's unmitigated intention . . .
>
> What a fool I had been! Chester hadn't veered off toward the pulp genre, for which he later became famous, at least not of his own volition.
>
> Turns out *Yesterday Will Make You Cry* had made the rounds of the publishing houses with successive waves of editors and agents imposing "improvements" on the manuscript, forcing him to delete his more literary touches. They jammed Chester's head in their toilet of racist preconceptions and pulled the chain and kept pulling the chain, flushing away what they felt were his uppity literary pretensions, forcing him to dumb-down his masterpiece before agreeing to publish it.[26]

Reviews for Norton/Old School's reissue of *Yesterday Will Make You Cry* though not plentiful were on the whole intelligent and laudatory. Jabari Asim in *Book World* found Himes at his best in detailing the gray, grim realities of prison existence.

> Although maddeningly uneven, the book presents an illuminating sociological portrait of prison life—certainly one of the best available in fictional form . . . Himes spent his last days worrying about his posthumous reputation as a writer. He would be pleased to know that at least 18 of his books are now in print—and interest is high.[27]

Allen Cheuse, a reviewer with little sympathy for anything middlebrow or unambitious, contributed a fine, all but breathless appraisal for National Public Radio's *All Things Considered*. *Publishers Weekly* (bringing to mind that "indomitable quality within the human spirit that cannot be destroyed" from Himes's Chicago speech) capped its review:

> Himes . . . masterfully presents the arbitrary violence (from both inmates and guards), the corruption, the regularity of unlamented death, the uneasy relations of the races and the psychological elongation of prison time ("Each moment was absolute, like a still photograph"). Yet it is the depiction of Monroe's love affairs—their comic absurdity, obsessive intensity and transformative emotional depth . . . that mark the book as both a superior prison novel and a moving fictional record of the perseverance of humanity amidst unrelenting degradation.[28]

That, for all its horrors, lapses, and longueurs, is what the novel comes to represent to us. For *Yesterday Will Make You Cry* is at heart and uncharacteristically an upbeat, hopeful story. Its two major characters are engaged in a relentless struggle—Jimmy and the prison whose outstanding features are its dirtiness and its debasement, which would spread those qualities to each of the human spirits it houses—a struggle that Jimmy wins. "Big, ugly prison, but I've got it beat now."[29] Jimmy has won through, has managed to forge his identity in an environment conspiring on every side to negate identity and deny the human spirit itself.

H. Bruce Franklin argues that all Himes's achievements, even his existence as an author, came directly from his experience in prison; that this experience manifestly shaped both his creative imagination and outlook on American society. Pitching his elemental struggle in the closed environment of a prison that refused man's identity and threatened his very soul, Himes knew that he was writing about the plight of blacks in American society, recreating on personal ground the threads of a much older, an epic, struggle.

11 European Experience

Anything can save you, if you grab it hard enough and hold on.

On the ship across, two or three days out, Himes begins to convince himself that he is again in love of some sort, slipping into the state as into a fine, old shoe. He has earlier been introduced to Willa Thompson Trierweiler, Boston socialite, unhappily shanghaied wife to a Dutch dentist, novelist-in-progress; now, standing in a ship's corridor clutching at him, in a matter of minutes she tells Himes of her husband's sexual aggression and infidelities, of her four daughters, of her most recent nervous breakdown. She is returning home to obtain a divorce and is at work on an autobiographical novel, *The Silver Altar*. Flashes of intimacy and intimation are exchanged. They'll work on the book together, it's decided, meeting in Paris and proceeding to Majorca after her necessary return to Luxembourg. Willa is lively, "innocent"[1] and, very much like the Kriss we meet on *The Primitive*'s first page, beneath a facade of confidence and success emotionally bereft. Himes finds this combination of social status, bearing, and desperate insecurity irresistible. Another vulnerable, damaged woman to protect—with the added benefit of endless distraction from the work he's vowed to concentrate upon. Willa in turn sees in Himes, one supposes, or somehow manages to attach to him, a stability, balance, a leveling horizon; perhaps also, in his role as professional writer, in his dress and faultless manners, in his outward calm demeanor, a quality of wisdom.

Behind, America, a quiet, smiling man with darkness in his eyes, stood ashore watching Himes's departure with (as Joan Didion would write in quite another context) the look of a man who all his life has followed some imperceptibly but fatally askew rainbow. Always, here, this irresolvable mix: staid optimism and a sense of dread so acute that both national and personal life are driven to extreme commitments. To live on this shore, one had to split oneself into parts, hold contradictory notions. Forever half bright promise, half madness, America was. Always going on about the future, always on its *way* somewhere, never looking back. Excused all sorts of things.

Chester arrived in Paris on April 10, 1953, one week after departing New York. Wright, Yves Malartic, and old friend Dan Levin had come early to Gare Saint Lazare to meet the wrong train; speaking very little French and that badly, Himes took a cab to Wright's where, fuming, he was turned away by a monstrous concierge; he returned to the station, at length engaged a second cab, and made his way to Hotel Delavigne where, as it turns out, Wright had booked a room for him. The two finally met the next morning for breakfast at Wright's favorite haunt, Café Monaco.

> Dick expected a gathering of our soul brother compatriots, all of whom knew I was to arrive the night before, but not one of them appeared, an eccentricity which I was later to learn was the natural reaction of the envious and jealous American blacks who lived in Paris—or anywhere else in Europe, for that matter. They did not want any arriving brother to get the idea they thought he was important.[2]

Himes had been preparing himself for that breakfast for some time. There was nothing to keep him in the United States any longer. Mother and father were dead, wife Jean was on her own, the only supporter he had left in publishing was Bill Targ, who would do his best for *The Third Generation*. Himes had been bouncing back and forth rootlessly from boarding house to hotel room to Vandi's apartment or Bill Smith's home in Vermont. He'd been talking for some time in a wavery, aimless manner about going to Europe. And now the form of this talk began to take on substance as Himes convinced himself that random currents were a stream. If he were not chance's coconspirator, he was certainly its accomplice. Just as he wrote by intuition, he lived by it, finding his way into and sometimes through thickets, taking counsel from the entrails of circumstance.

Europe, then. Only lack of money held him back, and when Targ informed him that New American Library was buying reprint rights to *The Third Generation* for $10,000, half this sum being immediately available, that final door sprang open. Chester booked passage on the *Ile de France* and began putting his affairs in order. He exchanged a flurry of intelligence-gathering letters with Levin, Malartic, and Wright. He bought a Linguaphone French course, or borrowed one from Vandi, and sat in grim determination listening through his self-admitted tone-deafness and repeating phrases "with a parrotlike inaccuracy."[3]

Chester was to bring Wright two reams of 20-pound bond paper and six complimentary copies of his new Harper's novel, *The Outsider*. In his letters Wright praised Paris's quality of life and cheap living and suggested things Chester should bring along: American toilet articles, drip-dry clothing, an American can opener, an alcohol stove for cooking in his room. He also told Chester that he'd just written a preface for the French edition of *Lonely Crusade*. Dan Levin added tips of his own, telling Chester about the Hotel Delavigne, run by a retired U.S. army officer and his French wife, where he'd always be able to get a room.

When issuance of his passport took longer than expected, Himes grew fearful. Perhaps his prison record had come to light. Or, worse yet, his past association with Communists. The McCarran Internal Security Act had been in force since 1950, gathering momentum all the time, leaving muddy bootprints at the Constitution's door. Himes sent off a copy of the document restoring full citizenship to him following his prison term, along with copies of disparaging reviews of *Lonely Crusade* from the Communist press. Whether or not such concerns caused delay is moot; he received his passport.

A week before departure Himes moved into the Albert Hotel. He picked up his advance for *The Third Generation* from agent Margot Johnson, exchanged most of it for traveler's checks after paying his passage at the French Line offices on South Street, and took Vandi out to dinner. He bought the ugly nylon shirts Wright advised, a pair of wingtip Oxfords, and, from Abercrombie & Fitch (not knowing that in the Latin Quarter alcohol stoves sold for just a few francs), a fifty-dollar two-burner alcohol stove. He packed the big green wardrobe trunk full as a stuffed turkey and sent it ahead. His last night he planned to spend with Vandi, but a fight broke out, leaving Chester with a broken toe, a cold from sitting with his foot in a basin of water, and new bitterness.

It was no small thing to leave the United States at the age of forty-three, he wrote.[4] No small thing at all, even when this most important choice in Chester's life was made, like so many others, in— one cannot say impulsive fashion, for that would imply a certain passion, an engagement. In, then, an oddly distracted, offhand, *diffident* fashion.

In familiar contradictory manner Himes's impressions of Paris are difficult to hold on to, a sandwich thick with indignation, enormous changes that didn't take, a succession of affairs, the relief of new work, his unremitting sense of alienation, and bitterness recollected in quite unWordsworthian intranquility.

Written twenty years after the fact, Himes's comments regarding Paris in what James Campbell calls that "catalogue of misogyny, grievance and self-aggrandizement,"[5] *The Quality of Hurt*, are largely negative— *carping*, Michel Fabre says of them. Himes didn't like the bistros. The good restaurants were too expensive and the inexpensive ones were bad. He was overcharged everywhere. The naked women in Place Pigalle were just naked women, Montmartre's world-famous racy shows nothing more than tourist traps, the sexuality dull and unimpressive. He'd seen it all before. There were too many Cadillacs and too many hard, hurried American women along the Champs-Elysées, too many walls scribbled with U.S. GO HOME.

His evocations in an unpublished piece written for *Ebony* in 1954 are rather different in tone:

I found Paris very pleasant in April; the chestnut trees were in bloom, the weather was balmy, the cafés crowded along St. Germain, the students out in all their many-national glory on Saint Michel, the book stalls on the *quais*, fishermen on the Seine . . . I had brought an alcohol stove from America and I cooked my breakfast in my room, the good smell of Nescafé and *jambon* and *oeufs brouillés* permeating the waxed corridors, watering the mouths of hungry lovers and early-rising clerks.[6]

In correspondence with Michel Fabre near the end of his life, Himes turned a clearer eye toward understanding what Paris had represented for him.

For me France was the opportunity to write without the barriers imposed by race, politics, my state of health, finances, or my appearance . . .

In Paris, I found many ways to feed myself without disastrous effects. I gathered throwaway scraps in the markets, old bread, stale wine, and hotel proprietors let me live in rooms until I could afford to pay. Girls contributed love and sometimes encouragement, and I was permitted to use all public reference sources. France did not support me; it let me live and grow strong enough to concentrate on my work, which was writing . . . I became famous. My detective stories, along with other books published in France, sold to other countries. Eventually my books were picked up by the U.S.[7]

It's been said of Hemingway that for each book he required a new woman. In his first years abroad, before settling into life with Lesley, Chester became involved with several women one after another. (And we might question that preposition: sometimes the affairs overlapped or coincided.) Vandi visited him in Paris as anticipated, remaining for a week. He met a young German girl, Regine Fischer, at a party and, after a period of displaying her photo on his writing desk, took up housekeeping with her, even traveled to Germany to meet her family. One of the earliest mentions of an autobiography, in a letter to Van Vechten, considers structuring the narrative of his European experience around his relationships with Willa, Regine, and Lesley.

I would like very much to write this account of my years in Europe as a straight autobiography in three books; each book about my life with a woman, all three completely different; the first an American socialite (Boston-Smith college etc.), married, divorced, three daughters; the second an infantile, immature, very crazy German in her twenties; the third English, good family, in her thirties, a member of the right people.[8]

It's only in the relationships men manage that they live at all, Robert Creeley suggests. Chester's alienation had to do only in part and circumstantially with prison, with expatriation to alien cultures, even, finally, with being black; his estrangement was far more profound. And like many loners, many who feel they never belong *wherever* they find themselves, Himes needed a woman, that single, close, intense relationship, to help define and ground him.

Willa was the first of Himes's women in this new, European life—even before he reached Europe. In *The Quality of Hurt* he called her Alva, and the book ends, two hundred pages after their first meeting, with their final farewell. There's something of the feel here of Hemingway's lyrical ending to *For Whom the Bell Tolls*. Something, too, of Chandler's in *The Long Goodbye*: "On the way downtown I stopped at a bar and had a couple of double scotches. They didn't do me any good."

We stood very close on the platform and she kept turning to hide her face from the strangers all about us because she was crying. When the conductors blew their whistles for all aboard I took Alva in my arms and kissed her and it seemed to open the floodgates for I had to lift her onto the train. She stood in the open coach door, dangerously, perilously, waving frantically, desperately, until the train had turned the bend way up the track and passed from sight, although I doubted if she could have seen me through her tears.

I went across to a bar on rue Saint-Lazare and had a couple of Cognacs. Suddenly I found myself crying like a baby. Tears streamed down my cheeks. Frenchmen at the bar turned to stare at me.[9]

Willa's story, as she told it and as Himes (with asides by turns sympathetic and cynical) repeated it, was a timeless one of youth and innocence overcome by guile. Of good family, she had, aged eighteen, met at Bryn Mawr a Dutch exchange student who courted her mercilessly and, upon inviting her to his home, so preyed upon her naïveté as to force her into marriage, whereupon he demanded of her family her inheritance and over the following years, with the collaboration of his own family, held her virtual captive. Once when she got away, obtaining a divorce in the United States (which, alas, Holland did not recognize), he used the youngest of their daughters as hostage to persuade her to return. Her first breakdown had occurred during the war; now she was returning from the United States where she had fled following her third breakdown to keep him from institution-alizing her.

Willa's pain Chester perceived right away; it swept over him. She had been hurt terribly by life, just as he had. Hurt by her husband, hurt by his family and the "strange, cruel country where she had gone to live,"[10] hurt by her own family, whose busy lives had made them indifferent to hers. Hurt, too, by her own inabilities and inactions. Did Chester perceive the parallel here as well? Certainly he identified with her. And he sensed from the first—when she seized him in a corridor as he passed, crying "Don't leave me! Please don't leave me!"—that she was more than a little disturbed. Always "a sucker for the sentimental,"[11] he listened to the tale of her progressive degradation. But goodness does for the knight only so long.

> After two days I just wanted to lay her and have it done with. I had said all I had to say about her husband and I was sick and tired of hearing about him.
>
> . . . .
>
> My broken toe hurt, barring me from dancing, and I felt stuck with Alva when I could have found prettier and more amenable women.
>
> . . . .
>
> Emotions between black men and white women are erratic, like a brush fire in a high wind. For a time they burn brightly, burning everything in their path; but they are subject to skip over green patches or turn abruptly about and flicker out on the ashes of what they have previously burned.[12]

Nevertheless, the romantic shipboard *va-et-vient* continued. When they parted at Le Havre, Chester wasn't at all certain that he wanted to see her again. Self-knowledge is a bitter vegetable one doesn't plan on eating but can't leave alone, pushing it about on the plate. Filled with tenderness for Willa, Himes knows that he has been used, and that he has allowed it; he knows that only chance and despair have brought them together, and that, for all his loneliness and hers, this match is an impossible one.

I am completely blinded to my own welfare if there is a damsel in distress—and she doesn't really have to be a damsel, or even in real distress for that matter, just as long as I believe it.

. . . .

I must confess here that where women are concerned I have always been an ass.[13]

He thought he was leaving American white women behind, only to find one waiting for him there in the ship's corridor. His entire European experience would be of just such complexity. Fleeing the United States, he carried it everywhere with him, and finally found a way to confront it again in his books; running from his weaknesses, he learned to patch them together into a curious kind of strength. The decision to go to Europe had been as much an act of acquiescence as of volition, an acceptance of tides pulling at him, floodwaters bearing him up, sum of a hundred small cuts, pressures, guy lines. So it was with much else in Himes's life, including his affairs with women.

Himes's touchdown in Paris that first time was brief. He settled into an unassuming room in the Hotel Scandinavie on rue Tournon, made the acquaintance of Ollie Harrington, creator of the Bootsie cartoons and a central figure, perhaps *the* central figure, among expatriate American blacks, met young novelist William Gardner Smith, dined with Yves and Yvonne Malartic at the Deux Magots on St. Germain-des-Prés. It was mostly cold and rainy that April. When he could, he sat outside Café Monaco soaking up sunlight. And he spent time with Richard and Ellen Wright.

Always a champion of Wright, Himes nonetheless found himself dismayed at the couple's middle-class behavior: pretension, creature comforts, self-satisfaction, and self-absorption. Richard seemed too narrowly intent on status. He spent a fussy hour discussing with a bookshop owner how his new book might best be displayed, bridled at all criticism or any perceived slight, reigned like a ringmaster over the circus of literati and expatriate blacks at Café Monaco. Ellen chattered away about the bother and expense of having her hair dyed blond. Outspoken critic of the black middle class that Himes was, this rankled. It resounded, too, against his self-image as a writer. Himes knew that he, like all other black American writers, existed in, and largely because of, the shadow cast by Richard Wright. Wright was mentor and example to an entire generation of novelists—the father who had to be slain, as James Baldwin baldly put it. Another important point, one often overlooked, is that the years lost to prison and the disorders of his life had delayed Himes's debut as a novelist, making him something of a late bloomer, and delayed as well, in the manner of alcoholics, his emotional development, in effect protracting his adolescence so that, despite his chronological age, he was, effectively, a young writer.

At the tag end of one running defense of Wright in *The Quality of Hurt*, in documenting his first Paris leave-taking, Himes seems to be speaking as much of Wright and of himself as he is of the source of his negative impressions of Paris camaraderie. This comes, remember, from the man who all but single-handedly champions Wright's later return to *Native Son*-like material, and who had himself just written *The Third Generation*. As often the case, it's difficult to surmise the degree of Himes's self-awareness here.

> I wanted to get away and live a different life. At times my soul brothers embarrassed me, bragging about their scars, their poor upbringing, and their unhappy childhood, to get some sympathy and some white pussy and money, too, if they could. It was a new variety of Uncle-Toming, a modern version.[14]

Some element of this ritual stand against the father, and certainly Chester's innate contrariety, may help account for his attraction to William Gardner Smith. Seventeen years younger than Himes, Smith represents the expatriate urge in pure form: unlike most others, he *remained* abroad once there, dying in France in 1974, taking some pain all the while to become a part of his new society; and he seems to have found in expatriation the liberation that eluded others. Smith had been posted to Germany in 1945 while enlisted; following a stint at Temple University and a stay at Yaddo, he returned to Europe, this time to Paris, where he lived, with two years out as minister of information in Ghana and one brief trip to the States, until his death. Having worked as a journalist from age eighteen, upon relocation to Europe he continued such work, writing a column for the Pittsburgh *Courier*, the paper in which Ollie Harrington's Bootsie cartoons appeared, and serving as desk editor for a French news agency.

Smith's first novel, *Last of the Conquerors*, the story of the love between a black GI and a German girl, in which Smith suggested that the U.S. Army treated Nazis better than it did its own black infantrymen, came out when he was twenty years old. In 1950 he published the nonpolitical *Anger at Innocence*, another love story, this time between a middle-aged married man and a young pickpocket. *South Street* followed four years later and was a modest commercial success; set in the Philadelphia of Smith's youth, its themes are black militancy and, again, interracial love. Almost ten years passed before publication of *The Stone Face*. Telling of a black expatriate's gradual awakening to racial oppression in France after having fled such in his own country, the book evidences a mature, truthful and balanced view of racism. Smith, like Himes in his Chicago speech, makes the point that oppression dehumanizes the oppressor every bit as much as it does the oppressed; his expatriate blacks feel guilt at sidestepping the struggle; at book's end the protagonist is poised to return home, there best to fight the stone face of racism. Smith's last is a fine, completely unknown novel.

His second, affording considerable prestige and making him with Richard Wright the most visible of black American expatriates, had been selected by Club Français du Livre. None of Wright's novels at that time had been so lauded, though *Native Son* would be, and many suggest, Chester among them, that this gave rise to a certain tension between the two novelists. Smith had interviewed Wright in 1945 and upon planning the move to Paris had consulted with him at length. He had his own small court at Café Tournon, but made a point of attending Wright's at the Monaco. Chester remembered Smith as a "pleasant-looking, brown-skinned young man who talked very rapidly in choppy, broken sentences."[15]

Four years before his death, in 1970 (two years before publication of *The Quality of Hurt*), Smith's publication of *Return to Black America* consolidated his position abroad. A commercial failure in the States, the book attained celebrity in France as *L'Amérique noire*. It takes up again the themes of his fiction: rootlessness, urban poverty, interracial conflict, expatriate guilt. The expatriate, Smith writes therein, is "an eternal 'foreigner' among eternal strangers," words that

Chester well might have taken to heart. And yet, as Rimbaud writes: One does not escape.

Another important contact for Chester was Annie Brièrre, who not long after his arrival left a note at Chester's hotel asking if he might come to her house in Square du Roule to be interviewed for the newspaper *France-U.S.A.* When he complied, walking into the sort of apartment he'd always envisioned for the French aristocracy, he encountered "a big-boned woman in her fifties with the imposingly strong face and big nose of the old French."[16] She in turn perceived "a finely chiseled face, bright eyes, the manners of a gentleman."[17] Madame Brièrre became an occasional guide and dinner companion for Himes, later interceding as translator in a dispute with his publishers. In the published interview (December 1955) Brièrre cited *Lonely Crusade* as a powerful and gripping work while noting the directness of style, appealing structure, and human drama of *The Third Generation*. Addressing questions as to the novel's Freudian implications and autobiographical content, Himes remarked:

To me, that book is closer to *Sons and Lovers* by D.H. Lawrence. Our mother was fiercely ambitious for us. In order to make successes out of us, she made us study the violin for five years, which we thought was a complete waste of time. Any perceived weakness in us worried her. She wanted us to go out and conquer the world.

. . . even if many of the scenes in the novel are based on real occurrences, the things causing and linking them, as well as the dramatic climax, are completely imaginary.[18]

To Brièrre's question as to why his protagonists, intelligent people all, seem enslaved by their passions, Himes responded: "I think this is typically American. We're still a young nation and we seldom think before we act."[19] Not all white Americans hate blacks, he contends, but they do feel hostility toward people different from themselves: Catholics in the South, Asiatics in the West, elsewhere the Irish, or Jews.

One week in, Vandi arrived, cabling from the ship just before it docked that Chester should "COME QUICKLY: FOR YOU KNOW WHAT . . ."[20] Almost everyone she met was enchanted "by her fair complexion and magnificent shoulders and firm breasts which had always been unimpeded by bras, her light curly hair, but most of all perhaps by her knowing sensual grin."[21] She and Chester made the rounds, to the Monaco and Deux Magots, to the Dome with the Malartics for breakfast, "to good restaurants and to bed."[22] The highlight of Vandi's visit for Chester came when complaints from a neighbor over the noisiness of their lovemaking caused them to be relocated to a more isolated back room. Chester's stock, he wrote, rose exceedingly.

> By night the story was all over the American community in the Latin Quarter; no one had ever heard of a paying guest being put out of a hotel room in Paris for making love. In time it became something of a legend.[23]

Another encounter, one between Wright and James Baldwin that Himes witnessed, also became something of a legend, and throws the generational issue sharply into focus. Himes himself had little in common with the younger Baldwin. His unease around homosexuality was matched by Baldwin's toward left-wing activity; Baldwin, moreover, had reviewed *Lonely Crusade* unfavorably. But with Wright Baldwin had a long-standing relationship from which he had derived much support and inspiration, even if of late that relationship had begun to fall into disrepair. With publication of "Everybody's Protest Novel" in 1949, disrepair progressed to dismantling. Baldwin ended his discussion of *Uncle Tom's Cabin* in that essay with mention of *Native Son*'s Bigger Thomas as Uncle Tom's descendant, "flesh of his flesh, so exactly opposite a portrait that, when the books are placed together, it seems that the contemporary Negro novelist and the dead New England woman are locked together in a deadly, timeless battle; the one uttering merciless exhortations, the other shouting curses."[24] Wright took exception, on the day of publication calling Baldwin over to his table in the Brasserie Lipp.

> Richard accused me of having betrayed him, and not only him but all American Negroes by attacking the idea of protest literature . . . Richard thought that I was trying to destroy his

novel and his reputation; but it had not entered my mind that either of these *could* be destroyed, and certainly not by me.[25]

Nevertheless, just after that initial clash Baldwin began "Many Thousands Gone," an essay twice as long as that which provoked Wright's anger, this one a sustained assault on *Native Son* and, more deeply, on its author's integrity. The quote above, in turn, comes from another long essay written following Wright's death, "Alas, Poor Richard," in which Baldwin tried to parse the grammar of dissensions between Wright and himself. Here Baldwin offers up a haberdashery of complaints, some borrowed, some new: that Wright lives and behaves as if white, that he fails to comprehend jazz or to understand Africa, that he exaggerates his own importance, that he is hopelessly out of touch with current race problems back home, that he now bores the very younger writers who once revered him. (In "Many Thousands Gone" Baldwin had predicted with some accuracy that Wright would fall to repeating himself.) There's no doubt that personal elements had their place—both were proud, difficult, opinionated individuals—but the true quarrel, as James Campbell points out in his biography of Baldwin and again in *Interzone Paris*, strikes deeper, to the question of the writer's social and artistic responsibilities. Wright was a product of the proletarian thirties when being an intellectual meant being political, trailing behind him a lengthy history of engagement with social and left-wing causes, a history, too, of persecution for the same. Baldwin was by temperament far more the aesthete, Henry James to Wright's Dreiser, Chandler to his Hammett; his departure from the United States had been only in part to escape racial prejudice, in larger part to escape the grave necessity of being a "Negro novelist," to pursue the chance to become a free artist.

The incident that Himes witnessed, which took place in late April or early May 1953 at Deux Magots, became a fulcrum in dismantling the Wright-Baldwin relationship. In his last public appearance, a speech given at the American Church in Paris on November 8, 1960, shortly before his death at the end of that month, Wright gave his account of the incident, in which he slyly drafted Himes as accomplice.

I must tell you that there existed between Chester Himes and me, on the one hand, and Balwin [sic], on the other, a certain tension stemming from our view of race relations. To us, the work of

Balwin seemed to carry a certain burden of apology for being a Negro and we always felt that between his sensitive sentences there were echoes of a kind of unmanly weeping. Now Chester Himes and I are of a different stamp. Himes is a naturalist and I'm something, no matter how crudely, of a psychologist. This tension between Balwin and me and Himes, until that evening, had never been mentioned or directly written about.[26]

As they sit on the terrace sipping beers, Himes, Wright, and Baldwin in the company of a white woman, Baldwin asks what the older novelist thought of "that article I wrote about you." When Wright responds that he couldn't make much sense of it, Baldwin bristles.

He leaped to his feet, pointed his finger in my face and screamed:
"I'm going to destroy you! I'm going to destroy your reputation! You'll see!"[27]

Spurred on by the woman, Baldwin continues in such vein as Himes, excusing himself saying he can't take this, leaves, returning only after Baldwin is gone.

"That was horrible," Himes sighed.
"Well, I guess it's better for it to be said openly than just thought of in private," I said.
"But he said that in front of that white woman," Chester Himes voiced the heart of his and my objection.
"That was the point," I said.[28]

This is not, Campbell points out, a Baldwin that we easily recognize, not the Baldwin who wrote, referring to Wright, "For he and Chester were friends, they brought out the best in each other, and the atmosphere they created brought out the best in me."[29] Neither does one readily perceive Chester Himes walking away embarrassed from a good fight, or commenting afterward in such seeming naïveté on its racial aspect. Both accounts, Wright's and Himes's, were penned seven years or more after the fact, but it's most likely to the latter, Himes's, we should look for substance.

Then we hurried to the Deux Magots and found Baldwin waiting for us at a table on the terrace across from the Eglise Saint-Germain. I was somewhat surprised to find Baldwin a small, intense young man of great excitability. Dick sat down in lordly fashion and started right off needling Baldwin, who defended himself with such intensity that he stammered, his body trembled and his face quivered. I sat and looked from one to the other, Dick playing the fat cat and forcing Baldwin into the role of the quivering mouse. It wasn't particularly funny, but then Dick wasn't a funny man . . . Dick accused Baldwin of showing his gratitude for all he had done for him by his scurrilous attacks. Baldwin defended himself by saying that Dick had written his story and hadn't left him, or any other American black writer, anything to write about. I confess at this point they lost me.[30]

Quite an extraordinary conflict, that from which the ever quarrelsome Chester Himes emerges the calm, rational voice. Yet so universal are the precepts highlighted by this dispute—differing attitudes toward race relations, generational conflicts, questions of the artist's social positioning—and so well known the contretemps, that John A. Williams includes a fictionalized version of it in his chronicle-novel of this century's black literary and political life, *The Man Who Cried I Am*, a book of which Himes said: "Williams has written very accurately, I think, about the Wright who lived in Paris, grappling with complex problems and unethical people."[31] Williams's account gives us something of the feel of the encounter's mythic importance to the black intellectual as well perhaps as, through filters of time and fiction, something of its essence.

Young writer Dawes has called asking expatriate novelist Harry to meet him; he wants to borrow money. Another writer, Max, is having dinner with Harry and his wife and goes along. He's got his nerve, wife Charlotte says to Harry, after all the rotten things he's been writing about you. They meet at a café and, in addition to slipping him the requested money, Harry buys dinner for Dawes. Over coffee he asks Dawes why he's been attacking him.

Dawes's voice broke from him high-pitched and sharp. "It's the duty of a son to destroy his father." Max watched Harry recoil.

Harry then looked Max full in the face; his face, Max observed, was at once a puzzle, flooded with understanding and rejection of that understanding.

Gruffly Harry said, "What in the hell are you talking about? I'm not *your* father."

Dawes loosed an exasperated gasp that sounded like a hiss. "Harry, well, if you don't *know*—you're the father of all contemporary Negro writers. We can't go beyond you until you're *destroyed*."

Cautiously Harry said, "You're crazy, man. You've been hungry too long." But Max noticed a sudden gleam rise in his eyes and then slowly fall. Dawes finished his coffee in Harry's lingering silence. "Really," Dawes said. "As soon as I can, I'll pay you back. I've got a couple of pieces on desks in the States right now."

"I hope they're accepted," Harry said. "But aren't you working on a novel?"

"I've just finished it."[32]

Leaving, Harry asks Max if "these young guys" actually think of him as being the father of Negro writers.

"Yes," Max answered, remembering how eager he had been to meet and talk to Harry ten years ago at Wading River. "We've been thinking it a long time."

"We?" Harry laughed. "You trying to destroy me, too?"

Max laughed.

"No shuck?"

"No shuck," Max said. "You've been away too long or you'd know you're the father."[33]

Williams's indirect portrait of Wright and the Wright-Himes relationship is quite a fine one. Weary of France, Harry tells Max he is trapped. He can't return to the States because of his Communist past; England will not give him a permanent visa; and Spain, since he has written critically of what Franco wrought, turns him away at the border. Max notes that Harry remains the darling of French intellectuals, however, and, feeling always a certain distance, an exclusion, that "Harry's friends were very much like his books: they were not for lending; they were his. He had bought or written them, and he wasn't going to let them get out of his sight—or be shared."[34]

One conversation between Wright and Himes concerning European publishers Himes must have taken to heart and recalled often in later years, especially as he was at this time (with the assistance of Ellen Wright as agent) challenging the publishing firm Corêa over royalties for *La Croisade de Lee Gordon*, Corêa insisting that the novel, despite an estimable critical success, had not sold enough to earn its $250 advance.

> "Get all you can for an advance, boy," he said. "That's all you'll ever get." He went on to say that none of his books had ever earned more, according to the publishers' accounts, than the advance; and in the case of one, his Italian publisher, he'd had to go to Rome and sit in the publisher's waiting room until he was paid his advance. "I sat there for two days," he said, "and whenever anyone came in to see the editor I would ask, "Are you trying to get your money too?" They paid me to get me out of there."[35]

Himes's experiences would prove similar, even if, for many years of his life, books largely out of print in his homeland, it was upon those very European advances and royalties that he subsisted. His last act before leaving France for London in July would be to challenge publisher Albin Michel over royalties for *If He Hollers*; Annie Brièrre went along as translator.

From the first Himes was unusually clear-eyed about Wright, deeply respectful of him while at the same time freely acknowledging his humorlessness, his fussiness over small matters, his arrogance and affectations. Seeming instinctively to realize the importance of maintaining an emotional distance between them, Chester seemed also to be constantly aware of Wright's personal history and the ways in which it had shaped him; this was not a concession Himes vouchsafed many others in his life.

Himes's admiration for his senior emerges clearly in a 1963 interview with Michel Fabre. Wright, Himes insists, wrote exactly what he wanted to write. He never wrote for anyone but himself, spinning plots and characters out of his own emotions and inner life, wholly uninfluenced by others. Himes might have been speaking of himself, of course, and as though indeed aware of the self-reflective quality of his remarks, adds that what Wright liked most about him, Chester, was his inner toughness. His remarks on Wright's expatriation in that same interview reflect on Himes's own European expectations. Wright wanted, Himes held, to be a part of the bourgeoisie, wanted to achieve a place in French society consummate with his ambition and reputation, and when late in life he discovered this not to be possible, he became somewhat aimless and adrift. This was about the time of *The Long Dream*, Himes says, and occasioned Wright's return in that work to his Mississippi—American—past.[36]

Surely it requires a certain acrobatics of both expectation and thought to envision finding a place in foreign society when unable to possess or forge such a place in one's own. Initially Wright trusted that his work and presence would create, *ex nihilo*, such a place. Otherwise his approach was adaptive; he went native, became, in effect, a Frenchman, moving easily through every level of intellectual and daily life. Himes's approach by contrast, as in so much else, was headlong, combative. He always came to the ring expecting cheers, cheers he rightfully should have gotten, and when he didn't get them, began snarling and snapping contumaciously at the audience.

Then, suddenly, Willa was there. They had been writing one another daily throughout the three weeks spent apart, but somehow she'd not been real, not been truly *remembered* by Chester, until he spoke with her two days before her arrival, at which time he felt himself resoundingly in love with her. He sought and found somewhat better rooms, one for each of them, in a hotel near the Luxembourg Gardens. Wright, who had decided that Willa had to be little more than a tramp and made no effort to conceal his contempt, came along with Chester to meet her train. When eventually the couple got away from Wright, they went directly to bed.

> What mattered to her was she had lost herself in the darkness of my race. She had hid from all her hurts and humiliations. In a strange and curious way, by becoming my mistress, the mistress of a man who'd never been entirely free, she had freed herself. That is a curious thing about race relations. We can free the white man's women, and they can find freedom in us, but we cannot free ourselves.[37]

Unlike Wright, the Malartics took instantly to Willa, offering the use of their getaway villa in Arcachon. Himes gratefully accepted, receiving from Yves and Yvonne three pages of instructions, a *petite encyclopédie* Arcachon covering everything from keys and electric meters to where and when to put out trash, the best butcher shop, who might be loaned books from the villa's library. Lugging as always his oversize trunk (for which he routinely had to pay extra: "more for carrying that trunk around with me on European trains than I paid for house rent during my first two years abroad"[38]), Himes struck out one early morning by third-class carriage with Willa beside him. They arrived just after seven that evening. Chester was much relieved to be away from the contestations and boulevarderie of Paris. Here, he wrote, it was "peaceful and warm and friendly—the way one hopes the world would be."[39]

Arcachon is in southwest France, on the coast just west of Bordeaux in the Bay of Biscay. Originally a modest stucco building with bedroom, combination living-dining room and multifunction shedlike structure out back, the villa itself had been built up and onto until it now resembled "a typical summer camp in Sullivan County, New Jersey, except that the living room contained a roll top desk and several worn leather armchairs and the walls were lined with books in several languages."[40] Willa and Himes quickly and easily settled in. They swam, ate oysters and seafood, and drank quantities of the local wine, lounged in cafés and restaurants, painted the Malartic's boat, watched fishermen plod up and down the dirt streets, and tended the flea-ridden, pregnant cat Mrs. Moon, who came with the house, as well as her mate, a battle-scarred, scabby tom with missing teeth known as M. Berdoulas.

"When it was learned that I was a writer in addition to being a black American," Chester wrote, "I was treated with the awed deference accorded a zombie."[41] Children came to stare when he and Willa sat together on the beach, blushing and giggling when Willa spoke to them in her perfect French. Townspeople never spoke directly to Chester, addressing their remarks (Does Monsieur like seafood? Does Monsieur have money?) instead to Willa. They also vied for the couple's business. In one instance, to prove that her catch was the fresher, one of two competing fish merchants let loose an eel which bounded across the road, through the fence, and away.

Himes is often at his best when describing such Innisfrees: the desert ranchhouse he and Jean shared in California, the Newton, New Jersey, lakefront resort and Stamford, Connecticut, farm where he worked as caretaker. In such idylls words to the effect of "best [or happiest] time of my life" are likely to appear, and he writes movingly of the people, animals, the pace of life, seasons, nature itself. Fully nineteen pages of *The Quality of Hurt* are given over to Arcachon where, essentially, nothing happened.

> All in all, our two months there had been exquisitely happy and satisfying, and for a short time I had become completely free of my soul brothers' envy and jealousy and intrigues, and my fellow countrymen's obsession with the "Negro problem."[42]

While there, Chester received galleys for *The Third Generation* from Bill Targ and, at Targ's suggestion, trying to buck up dramatic impact, rewrote the final chapter. He and Willa began working together on her autobiographical novel *The Silver Altar*. (Himes also referred to the book as *The Silver Chalice* and *The Golden Chalice*.[43]) In early June Himes forwarded a portion of this novel to Targ, identifying Willa only as a writer staying temporarily in Arcachon; a larger portion followed, from London, that September. Willa and Himes, believing it to be very commercial, had high expectations for the book. They planned to publish under Willa's name, taking full advantage of that and of her social status, with every expectation of tapping the women's market and perhaps even selling movie rights. When Targ disliked the book and promptly returned it, they were shaken. Nevertheless, there in the secluded seaside villa, exposed continually to Willa's kind, adaptable manner, Chester conceived new respect and admiration for her.

On the first of July, they left Arcachon, initially intending to go to Daniel Guérin's writers' colony at La Ciotat, where the Wrights had sponsored Chester's stay for the months of July and August, considering for a time Majorca, where Vandi's ex-husband William Haygood then lived, at length deciding instead to resettle in London and turn their full attention to Willa's novel.

12 Story-Shaped Life

It is very difficult to say what Himes was looking for or what he hoped to find with his move to Europe. Certainly to some extent he believed that he might be fleeing racism and, like Baldwin, his frightening reactions to the same. Probably he believed that he could live more cheaply there. He may also have thought that, with Wright and his circle in place, he stood a chance of becoming part of a community of artists, something from which he seemed forever excluded in the States. There was, too, the possibility, if not of status, then at least of official validation for his work. Early interest in his novels suggested such a possibility; as with many other American writers abroad, it wasn't so much that Himes expected to be taken to be important as that he was gratified just to be noticed. Perhaps, finally, the move to Europe was Himes reverting to his gambling days: a simple roll of the dice. For years, whenever things became intolerable, his solution was to withdraw, to strike camp and move along. Italo Svevo has character Zeno say, "I honestly believe that I have always needed to be in the middle of an adventure, or of some complication that gives the illusion of one."[1] So it was, one suspects, with Himes. He seems to have needed adventure, craved complication; his solutions often worked only to create new and further difficulties. Was the move to Europe but the grandest of many self-deceptions? As Maugham wrote in *The Summing Up*, disparities between appearance and reality are the fount of all art; they become addictive, wonderfully diverting habits, those disparities, and one is apt when he cannot easily find them to create them.

Himes and Willa arrived in London on July 7, spending the first night in a hotel near the train station, where Willa was chased down the hall by an apparent madman, after losing their passports. The next day, seeking rooms, they made rounds of rental agencies (from the number of vacancies listed, Himes said, it seemed as though half of London were uninhabited) and were sent to interview with Mrs. Mather, "a tall, thin, impressively bony woman with hair and face of such indistinguishable whiteness as to create the effect of some nocturnal cereus blooming in the black-dark chair."[2]

The interview took place in an ice-cold, pitch-dark, musty-smelling parlor, securely curtained against the corrosive effects of the gray daylight and hermetically sealed against poisonous outside air, which the true Londoner breathes only when sleeping.[3]

Nonetheless, they took the four-room basement flat, even after Mrs. Mather stacked deposits, cleaning, laundry, and telephone fees atop the quoted rental. Presently they discovered her practice of tiptoeing down the stairs to close windows whenever, trying for a bit of breathable air, they opened them. She would descend "soundlessly, her garments billowing as though from an updraft, emerging from the perpetual gloom of the staircase like the last of the Shakespearean ghosts,"[4] and close windows to keep out the damp when it rained, to keep out cats in fair weather, and on bright days to keep out sunshine. While about it, she'd read their mail.

By the end of the first week Mrs. Mather, perhaps acting upon complaints from other tenants, had taken to trying to evict Himes and Willa, first with an appeal concerning relatives who required the rooms then with threats of legal action, but they held her to the contract she herself had insisted upon their signing. The couple left only after she capitulated and agreed to return deposits. Next they found lodging in a home owned by two ancient Polish sisters in Glenmore Road in Hampstead, a flat of two rooms with a separate attic kitchen, where they settled to work on the tale of Willa's love affair and nervous breakdown in Switzerland. Willa would turn out page after page in the sitting room of the flat proper while Chester reworked it into chapters in the little attic kitchen above, adding material on her background and sexual awakening with the apparent intent of transforming it from personal memoir to psychosexual history. Both still believed that the book had solid best-seller potential. For relaxation they walked to Hampstead Heath, Parliament Hill, Swiss Cottage, Jack

Straw's Castle. They often visited the Regent's Park Zoo, took cards at the local library on Finchley Road, sampled Soho nightlife and the occasional show in the West End, took in classic movies at Everyman's Theatre. Afterward, Willa remembered their time there in what Chester called "this big ugly and dismal city"[5] fondly.

They finished the book, 520 pages of manuscript, in mid-December, and though pleased at their accomplishment and happy to have it done with, were also completely out of money. Chester pawned his typewriter, Willa her wedding ring. She had assumed Chester from his outward style and manner to have plenty of money while he, characteristically, never broached the subject. They had both put their faith, though perhaps to different ends, in Willa's book. Rejected by Targ, the manuscript went next to an editor at Macmillan; it was finally published years later by Beacon Press, retitled *Garden Without Flowers*, in a shorter version with, apparently, all Himes's emendations excised.[6]

Increasingly desperate, striking out at every frustration, false exit, and blind alley, Himes resigned his membership in PEN when the organization declined to extend him an emergency loan, and withdrew cliency from New York agent Margot Johnson when she replied to his request for an advance with the observation that they were agents, not bankers. When in January Bill Targ wired $500, Himes and Willa promptly left for Majorca, bouncing restlessly from Palma, to Puerto de Pollensa a bit further along the coast, to Terreno in the southwest, Himes working all the while on *The End of a Primitive*.

I would get up at five, and by the time I had made coffee the first rays of the rising sun would strike our garden. I used the kitchen table for a desk and by the time the first peasants passed along the walk several feet below the embankment of our garden, humming the rising crescendo of the death song of the bullring, I would be typing happily . . . I wrote slowly, savoring each word, sometimes taking an hour to fashion one sentence to my liking. Sometimes leaning back in my seat and laughing hysterically at the sentence I had fashioned, getting as much satisfaction from the creation of this book as from an exquisite act of love. That was the first time in my life I enjoyed writing; before I had always written from compulsion . . . for once I was almost doing what I wanted to with a story, without being influenced by the imagined reactions of editors, publishers, critics, readers, or anyone. By then I had reduced myself to the fundamental writer, and nothing else mattered. I wonder if I could have written like that if I had been a successful writer, or even living in a more pleasant house.[7]

Reading this, one might well recall E. M. Forster's description of Greek poet Cavafy as "standing absolutely motionless at a slight right angle to the universe," or Cavafy's own lines:

> But we who serve Art,
> sometimes with the mind's intensity,
> can create—but of course only for a short time—
> pleasure that seems almost physical.[8]

In the early stages of writing *The End of a Primitive* Himes often strayed afield. He had reached a kind of abandon, lost in the emotional charge of his situation and language, an aura and a smell of sensuality emanating from him "like a miasma."[9] It was always Willa who brought him around, urging him to gear down, pull back—especially in those passages verging on the pornographic. While the essence of any relationship between a black man and a white woman in the United States was sex, Himes felt, to describe which—the blackness of his skin and shanks, the thickness of his lips, the texture of his hair alongside pink nipples, white thighs, silky pubic hair—tends necessarily toward the pornographic, this was not the point of his book. For, heir to all the vices, sophistries, and shams of their white enslavers, American blacks, far from being primitives, were, as he had said before in his Chicago speech,

> the most neurotic, complicated, schizophrenic, unanalyzed, anthropologically advanced specimen of mankind in the history of the world. The American black is a new race of man; the only new race of man to come into being in modern time.[10]

The financial crisis continued. World contracted for a book of stories to be titled *Black Boogie Woogie*, paying an $800 advance, but Himes grew disgusted with the stories when he read them and withdrew the book; grandly, he reported throwing the manuscript into the sea. Brother Eddie back in New York responded to his frantic appeal with $50 and a stern sermon on the necessity of Chester's becoming responsible. Backed, he felt, into a corner, Himes wrote a bad check for passage money. He and Willa made their way to the supposed refuge of Arcachon only to find that the Malartics had sold the villa, then settled into a cheap hotel in Paris on rue de Buci. There Chester lived off small sums borrowed from friends and made rounds of publishers, Corêa, Gallimard, Albin Michel, trying to stir up fresh interest in his books.

Willa seems at this point to have fallen to nervous prostration, barely functional and host to a variety of ills. For days she would lie abed weeping. Increasingly Himes felt her a burden, and felt that he could not help her in any significant way; she was wholly unsuited, he decided, by background and temperament, to the temporizing life he led. The rejection of their book, atop extended sieges of poverty and ongoing uncertainty, these last everyday facts of black life, had proved shattering to a woman of her class, background and race. Unable to sustain any longer her desperation, Himes made use of the $1,000 advance for *The End of a Primitive* from New American Library to pack Willa off to America. Following a brief return to London, by February 1955 Himes himself was back in New York, lodged again at the Albert Hotel, his and Willa's affair dissolving in a slurry of melodramatic letters, mutual mistrust and accusations, abortive meetings. It is in Paris, with Himes saying farewell to Willa, that the first volume of the autobiography ends; with him booking passage to New York that the second volume begins.

Meanwhile, on December 13, at about the time Himes and Willa were finishing their novel, just before they departed for Majorca, *The Third Generation* appeared from World.

One of the earliest reviews, from Edmund Fuller in the *Chicago Tribune Review of Books*, declared *The Third Generation* a strong addition to Himes's work, citing the novel for its tragic power while pointing out (an observation James Lundquist will echo twenty-two years later) that the book's structure and conception fail to bear up in strength to the general fine quality of its writing.[11] Both the *New York Herald Tribune Review of Books* and the *Library Journal* agreed. Frederic Morton in the first spoke of the novel as having "a strong if incoherent impact of its own," Milton S. Byam in the latter admired the quality of writing while remarking that, close upon a strong beginning, the novel degenerated into little more than a series of crises.[12]

The *Saturday Review of Literature* in the person of Martin Levin took to task the novel's excesses but held it to be nonetheless of great interest, as did an anonymous reviewer in the *San Francisco Chronicle* who spoke of the novel, despite its "dismal theme," as "sincere" and affecting, with "much food for thought."[13]

Like Edmund Fuller, Riley Hughes found the surety of Himes's writing unmatched by his sense of structure. In *Catholic World* Hughes fixed on the novel's major flaw.

> Through typing his story to a Freudian mother complex formula, ruthlessly applied, Mr. Himes removes his characters as far from the reader's sympathy as they are from convincing reality.[14]

One might, while admiring the verity of that adjectival *ruthlessly applied*, exempt only the final phrase. Or perhaps not. Himes's remark that *The Third Generation* was his most dishonest book could be taken, and has been, to call into question the novel's ultimate realism. (On the other hand, he may have been referring to the utilization of autobiographical over fictional material.) There *is* something breathless and melodramatic, something of the brandished cloak, about the relentless crises confronting the Taylor family.

In the *New York Times*, John Brooks wrote:

> Himes seems to have set out to grip the reader in a vise of despair by cumulative incident and detail. His searing book, with its terrible pathos of the oppressed set against each other, shows how increasingly firm a position he deserves among American novelists. But the impact is weakened by the introduction, in several cases, of chance misfortune unrelated to the characters or their ancestry, and the whole seems at times to lack a certain necessary measure of animal fun and human hope.[15]

That phrase *animal fun* Himes will appropriate for the satirical discussion between Jesse Robinson and his editor in *The End of a*

Primitive, just as he scooped up phrases from a review of *Lonely Crusade* to fine effect in his Chicago speech.

> "But surely you realize that that was satire—Rabelais was satirizing the humanist Renaissance—and certainly some of the best satire ever written . . . This—" tapping the manuscript neatly wrapped in brown paper on his desk—"is protest. It's vivid enough, but it's humorless. And there is too much bitterness and not enough just plain animal fun—"
>
> "I wasn't writing about animals—"[16]

In his Chicago speech Himes insisted that the American black lives always and inexorably with two forms of hate: he hates his oppressor and, living in constant fear of that hate being discovered, he "hates himself because of this fear."[17] It's a point that John A. Williams emphasizes as a cornerstone of *The Third Generation* in his introduction to the 1989 Thunder's Mouth edition, calling the novel "a chilling study of racism absorbed from whites and utilized by its black victims to victimize others of their own race." In this powerful, painful to read novel, he says, Himes "pulls aside the curtain—rips it down, in fact—on the class warfare within the black community."[18]

Still, despite the novel's considerable power, despite favorable reviews in important publications, and despite sale of paperback rights for an advance of $10,000 to NAL, who obviously believed *The Third Generation* capable of tapping into some ready market, sales were poor. By this time few expectations or illusions remained to Himes; he was aswim in quite different waters, thankful for whatever driftwood or flotsam he might grab hold of.

One forever wonders what might have happened had Himes's books been published with proper timeliness, *The Third Generation*, for instance, a decade later, in the midst of the civil rights movement; or *The Primitive* not in oblivious 1956 but in, say, 1986, when an audience, one responding to work by such as Maya Angelou, Alice Walker, and Toni Morrison, existed. But Chester was always there at the station too early, taking the train alone.

The Third Generation is, as the title might suggest, an historical novel rather in the manner that *If He Hollers* and *Lonely Crusade* are historical novels: exacting portraits of a lost time. Ostensibly it deals with the disintegration of one family, a disintegration deriving as much as anything from that internal racism indicated by Williams. As Edward Margolies notes in *Native Sons*,

> On the surface, rank bigotry seldom intrudes as the direct cause of their sufferings; they appear to be defeated by their own incapacities, weaknesses, blindness, and obsessions. But Himes makes clear that in order to understand them, one must understand the generations that preceded them, black and white: they are doomed not simply by their own psychic drives but by the history that created them and forced them into self-destructive channels. They are as much the victims of a value system they implicitly accept (and which indeed flows in their bloodstreams) as are men like Bigger Thomas who rebel against the social order.[19]

Joe Himes insisted that this racial aspect of his brother's novel was overplayed, blown out of proportion like the story of his, Joe's, blinding, because of the fascination it had for readers. Admitting that reading Chester "disturbs me too much," Joe recalled the family dynamics in more directly economic terms.

> I don't think there was any degree of love, passion and devotion between them ... They were married in the sense that there was a certain religious obligation about it. There were children. There was respectability. All this made for stability in the family.[20]

That stability disappears, in the novel as in life, with the father's loss of his professorship. Once he has stopped teaching, Fess's life becomes a long, sure glide downward. Mother Lillian's decline is little less catastrophic, the hysteria forever hovering about her blooming, with her husband's failure, into insanity.

Stephen Milliken suggests that *The Third Generation* be read as prequel to *Cast the First Stone (Yesterday Will Make You Cry)*, this novel in one sense completing the latter, presenting formative years that explain the protagonist's presence in prison. *The Third Generation*, Milliken writes, is Himes's least contrived, most fluid work, developing organically from characters who move "towards fates that they must both invent and discover."[21] He also elicits the parallel to *Sons and Lovers* in the manner in which its central conflict between plebeian father and aristocratic mother becomes displaced to a struggle between mother and son.

The novel is structured about a series of traumatic scenes much as Himes patterned *Lonely Crusade* around an aggregate of dialogues and *If He Hollers* around Bob Jones's nightly dreams. Here, though, the structure is much looser—disjunctive and associative rather than programmatic, in this respect prefiguring the vivid though often but marginally connected chains of imagery and incident that take the place of traditional narrative in the Harlem novels. Most of the novel's traumatic scenes result in one way or another from the elemental struggle at the novel's heart, that between the mother for domination and her son for freedom and personal identity. In the mother abstraction takes place, an arbitrary handful of traits gradually supplanting all others and calcifying into madness. Though greatly drawn to his mother's dreamy, unnatural way, her flights of fancy, her denials of reality, her escapes, the son does in the end avoid them and achieve a qualified redemption.

The elementality of that struggle translates to a kind of aggrandizement, so that for all their specificity, and for all the innate smallness of their lives, the characters take on a certain grandness, becoming as Milliken says "creatures of epic, of romance, of allegory."[22] Contributing to this is the very real presence in the novel of Lillian's righteous, chastising god, as well as a cosmic malevolence that "seems to stalk the Taylor family, inflicting crippling accidents upon them, blinding them to every possibility of tenderness, turning their loves to bitterness and hate."[23] Father Fess Taylor with his bitter pride also is presented in mythic aspect, as a man once afire, a man once illuminated from within. Hephaestus, limping after the fall.

> But unlike many proud men, who carry their pride in silence, he was boastful . . . Deep in his heart he wanted to be a rebel . . . But his wife and the circumstances of his life had put out much of the fire.[24]

Mr. Taylor has learned well the "Machiavellian cunning"[25] that lets him survive—survive both in the world and in his own self-estimations. He dissembles and postures with such accuracy, we are told, that no one can surmise anything of his innermost thoughts or feelings. This Mrs. Taylor despises as much as she does his dark skin, believing it manifest of his slave inheritance—and despises it ever more completely when she finds her son dragging behind him the selfsame sack and baggage. As for the son, as though the mix of his mother's irreality and brittle inflexibility in his blood were not acid-and-water enough, Charles must strive to reconcile there also his mother's absolutism with his father's utter temporizing. Nevertheless Charles, like *Lonely Crusade*'s Lee Gordon, by story's end does move toward acceptance of responsibility for his own actions and fate.

Surely in that Machiavellian cunning, as in Milliken's description of the character of Charles as "a study in excessive sensitivity and the harsh defiance that cloaks it" and of Charles's personality as "a deliberate construct of his will,"[26] we may be allowed to catch in passing the profile of Chester Himes, this man who could write so much of himself while leaving us with so many false impressions and so little knowledge of who he was.

In *The Third Generation*, Muller insists, we sense just how close Himes came to self-destruction.[27] He goes on to quote this passage regarding the family's time in St. Louis, one strongly prefiguring later disjunctures in Himes's life and work:

A curious phenomenon took place within his mind that winter. Whole periods of his past became lost to recollection. There was no pattern, no continuity, no rational deletions, as the editing of a text. Fragments of days, whole months, a chain of afternoons were drawn at random, a word would be missing from a sentence which he recalled with startling clarity, the intended meaning now gone . . . It was as if a madman had snatched pages from a treasured book, the story stopping eerily in the middle of a sentence, a gaping hole left in the lives of all the characters, the senses groping futilely to fill the missing parts, gone now, senselessly gone, now the meaning all distorted as if coming suddenly and unexpectedly into a street of funny mirrors.[28]

As early reviewers, chief among them Riley Hughes, rightfully noted, a principal problem with the novel lies with its relentless application of Freudianism. Not only does this at length prove distracting, even suffocating, to the reader, it creates an undertow constantly working at odds with the narrative, tending to reduce complex motive and action to mere schematic. Others such as Edmund Fuller have argued that the novel's overall structure fails to meet the challenge of its writing; that the novel's linearity, like its Freudian element, pulls it toward the programmatic. For some, the novel's unrelieved atmosphere of fear and anger have a similar deleterious effect. Further cavils have to do with the asymmetry of Himes's shift to foregrounding Charles in the novel's second half; with the false emphasis on racism as source of the mother's problems; and with the overdramatic ending, apparently worked up by Himes at the suggestion of Targ and of Van Vechten. Milliken summarizes the failure of this ending.

Lillian's bizarre racism, her morbid rejection of reality, somehow become part of the fabric of [Charles's] being. It is as though her spirit had invaded his, absorbed it completely. The paralyzing patterns of her neurosis gradually come to dominate his own thoughts. This sinister process is delineated with ruthless clarity in the last sections of the novel, as Charles's fatal weakness of will is demonstrated in incident after incident, then abruptly negated in the novel's bloody denouement. A tragic pattern is laboriously established then arbitrarily dissolved, a process that is all too frequent in life, but introduces an unfortunate note of confusion and indecision into a novel's structure.[29]

The third generation out of slavery, then. Yet now we know what came after this novel's ascensive conclusion: Charles Taylor wakes to find himself Jimmy Monroe, in prison. We should all fear those big words that make us so unhappy, *freedom* perhaps the biggest of them. And while of course we can never be truly free, free of heritage, fault, family, failings or self, we must always, as Tolstoy is said to have scrawled out with his finger on the sheets of his deathbed, *Keep . . . striving.* That's the measure of grace given us.

Did Himes achieve, with *The Third Generation*, as has been argued, some measure of freedom from what he perceived as a crippling past and, through new understanding of them, from his own self-destructive impulses? Does art truly work this way—or in claiming such, do we turn the conventions of fiction back on the life it issues from, pretending that life shapes itself in similar, conventional manner?

In "The Middle Years" Henry James has his dying novelist admit: "We work in the dark—we do what we can—we give what we have. Our doubt is our passion and our passion is our task. The rest is the madness of art."[30]

The patterns we discern as both reader and writer, in life as well as in fiction, may be those we bring with us to the task. We experience our lives forward while attempting to understand them backward; this is no less true of the lives of others toward which we turn attention, whether as novelist, as friend or family member, as biographer. We do change, we do find (like Charles Taylor) qualified redemptions, but quite probably never in any linear, quantifiable fashion.

Perhaps no one speaks better for personal and artistic change than did James Baldwin in "Nothing Personal."

It is perfectly possible to . . . walk through a door one has known all one's life, and discover, between inhaling and exhaling, that the self one has sewn together with such effort is all dirty rags, is unusable, is gone: and out of what material will one build a self again? The lives of men—and, therefore, of nations—to an extent literally unimaginable, depend on how vividly this question lives in the mind.[31]

Whether willfully or unwittingly, Chester Himes had begun a reconstruction of self. The "excessive sensitivity and the harsh defiance that cloaks it" were being reassembled, the personality that was "a deliberate construct of his will"[32] was being resewn of new rag, old bone. That the question Baldwin raised lived vividly in Himes's mind—out of what material will one build a self again—*The End of a Primitive* bears witness.

13 Doubt, Passion, the Madness of Art

In London, in the bed-sitting-room where often he was visited by the beautiful East Indian woman living downstairs and where his landlord's wife regarded him with "a look of infinite pity in her eyes,"[1] Himes sat reading Willa's letters and weeping.

She wrote to him of her family, of how much she missed him, of seeing *The Third Generation* alongside Wright's book occasioned by his trip to Ghana, *Black Power*, and William Gardner Smith's *South Street* on tables in New York bookstores. Persisting in her attempts to market their novel, soon she had obtained a job in a Boston dentist's office. For a time she lived with her aunt and uncle, whose conformist, unquestioning middle-class attitudes Himes perceived as a direct threat. He had said, to himself and to Willa, that he was sending her away only so that she could sell their book. He had said to himself, with sadness, that whatever life they had created together was over; to her, in consolation, that soon enough they would be together again. Now strong emotion swept in to fill her absence: he felt strongly his need for her, and at the same time the inevitability of ending things, of letting go. He knew, he said, that America would kill their love. Filled "with all manner of suspicions, doubts, antagonisms and resentments because she had returned into her white world," shortly before leaving for New York on December 14 he wrote to her:

> On re-reading your letters I see again the terrifying destructiveness of American life. Everything seems to go—integrity, self-confidence, honor, trust, gratitude, all human values—with awesome swiftness in the struggle for the dollar. And once gone what have you?[2]

What had he, for that matter? Sitting there in the cloister of his room with the smell of breakfast's streaky bacon and a half-drunk cup of tea strong enough to float an egg, with letters arriving for "Señor Chester Himes y Señora" or "Bien chères Amis" from friends in Majorca, with the yellow buzz of Dexamyl in his veins, down and out and at the end of his every rope, "sick and tired of all the shit that went along with a black man writing."[3]

Sometimes the sounds that broke from him were like those of his defeated novelist in "Da-Da-Dee," neither speech nor pain but something forever lost on the road between, a series of animal-like sounds; howls and moans; barely human. These sounds brought fellow tenants awake and upright in the dead of night. Once, as Himes sang over and over, compulsively, "I'll Get By," it grew so bad that the landlord was forced to call the police. Then as other times Himes's Indian friend Simi interceded, speaking with the police and with the landlord, calming Himes. Repeatedly, he says, he tried to "seduce" her ("Our landlord and his family could hear us scuffling in the kitchen below")[4] but, too strong physically, she rebuffed him—*seduce* chiming peculiarly against that *scuffling* and *too strong physically*, giving, one suspects, quite an accurate image of his desperation. "I suppose she felt sorry for me because I was unsuccessful and black and sick. I suppose all women had felt that way toward me for many years."[5]

Himes's predeparture letter to Willa was dismissive, cruel beneath a skim of kindness. He thought that she had regained some measure of confidence and faith in her time with him, he wrote, that she had moved toward more honest evaluations of life. But now he sees this to have been delusion; she has fallen back all too easily and naturally into a life of self-indulgence and the "cheap shabby sacrilegious forces of a greedy and intemperate society."[6] He feels, he says, as though he has opened the wrong door.

And now, of course, he must ease it shut.

Thus began a correspondence monstrous in every sense, a mutual battery not unlike the one between Himes and Vandi, that continued long after Himes had resettled in New York, at his accustomed Albert Hotel.

In this overflow of high-voltage words my mind was encompassed in a nightmare of fused impressions and blurred perceptions and days

Doubt, Passion, the Madness of Art | 215

running wildly together, here and there a lightning flash of clarity, a starkly glaring misunderstanding. We riddled each other with words, tore each other apart . . . We wrote things to each other which might normally have been spoken in the passion of anger, jealousy, suspicion . . . All this correspondence running into thousands of pages, hundreds of thousands of words, which if all put together would certainly have equaled six volumes of our five-hundred-page manuscript of *The Golden Chalice*.[7]

Everything lashed the couple's sense of pain and betrayal. America's strong currents and Willa's family bore her irresistibly away from him. Her weekend visits withered to bitter accusations and mechanical lovemaking. Chester's single visit to Boston guttered out in petty hostilities. He became impotent. Willa grew enraged when she learned that wife Jean had visited Chester at his hotel. And when he spoke of wanting to retrieve items left with Vandi, a scrapbook of press clippings for his first two books, a portion of his mother's silver, Willa became certain that he had resumed his relationship with her.

Himes had called Vandi about the items and been told to call back the following week, when her husband would be away. It would never occur to her, Himes wrote, that, given a chance to sleep with her, a man might choose not to. Monday he went round to collect his things from the maid and was handed only the silver and some blankets; Vandi, he decided, was holding the scrapbooks hostage. On Wednesday he called her office, met with a curious reaction from the switchboard operator and, passed along to Vandi's secretary, was told that Vandi had died the evening before while cleaning house. Dexamyl may have been a major factor; she had taken the drug, known to weaken the heart, regularly for years. Chester, who had picked up the habit from her, claims never to have used the drug again after that day.

> The taste of bile came up in my mouth in a tidal wave and I felt my scalp grow cold and prickly and my hair lifted from my skull. And the first thing I thought of was the line from *The End of a Primitive*: "*Forgive her, God, she was a good girl . . .*" And then, like Jesse, I was crying in the hotel telephone booth in great wracking sobs.[8]

How simply (as Wallace Stevens wrote) the fictive hero becomes the real.

Afterward Chester Himes must have hung up the phone, walked away, stood looking out on New York City thinking again about what this country was, what it claimed to be, and what it did to those who fell into the spaces and silences between. One gets the essentials of a culture, according to Alfred North Whitehead, not by looking at what is said but at what is not said, at the society's underlying assumptions, those too obvious and implicit to be stated. Truth, he said, resides in those silences. This was forever the text Himes saw when he looked upon America: things unsaid, silent truths—the speechless and unspeakable. It was the text Himes went on reading, the text he went on writing, all his life.

An unpublished autobiographical fragment now among Himes's papers in the Amistad collection at Tulane, reads:

> When I was forty-five years old, I made the biggest mistake of my life. It had taken me 44 years to get away from the U.S. And less than two years later I went back. And that was the mistake I had never gotten over.

With the return to America Himes felt he had estranged everyone, exhausted every career and personal resource, burned every bridge, closed it all down. No one wished him well now. Whatever respect he had gained with his early work was lost. He was a writer no longer, and something less than a man. Likening himself to a laboratory mouse in a letter that March to Van Vechten, Himes wrote: "those long walls have narrowed so quickly that I am in the last chamber already, and there in the corner stands the trap that I must run into."[9] And in *My Life of Absurdity*, in recollection: "I wished that I could make myself into nothing so I could pass through life unnoticed, unhated, irresponsible."[10] *Invisible*, in a word, an ironic inversion of future writer Brightlight's declaration in Himes's early story "Prison Mass": "I shall pass beneath this earth no common shade . . . I shall be no *forgotten man*."[11]

Himes was in New York for most of a year, from late January to mid-December 1955, a year filled with leave-takings of every sort; with endless self-laceration, isolation, and profoundly asocial behavior, with a scant handful of new stories, with odd jobs from "the slave markets on Chambers Street"[12] that could not have been other than degrading to a man of his age, accomplishment, and past ambition, and with seeing *The Primitive* through, traumatically, to publication.

From various pickup jobs Himes happened onto work as a substitute porter for Horn & Hardart, which at that time had over a hundred automats scattered about the city, then into a regular position as night porter at their location on Fifth Avenue and Thirty-seventh Street, not a bad compromise for someone needing employment but wanting to keep to himself. Predictably he failed to fit in or to get along with management there, boasting in his memoirs that he was the best porter and the most disagreeable employee they'd ever had. He railed about payroll deductions, about bookkeeping errors, about white waitresses and supervisors. But he ate extraordinarily well, three quarts of orange juice and two dozen raw eggs along with leftovers from the freezer and fried chicken or steaks in a single shift, and after a while the supervisors learned to leave him alone. When one night a drunken policeman staggered into the automat waving his gun at Chester and the other two night porters, many of the things Himes saw on the street and many of the things about which he was obsessively thinking began to come together; they'd coalesce almost a decade later in his novel *Run Man Run*.

Here is the automat from that novel. Detective Matt Walker, drunk, has forgotten where he parked his car and, stumbling into "Schmidt and Schindler" at five in the morning, accuses the Negro porters of stealing it, shooting two of them for no reason and for the remainder of the novel pursuing the third, younger porter, Jimmy.

> He pressed his face against the plate-glass window at front. Light from the Lord & Taylor Christmas tree was reflected by the stainless-steel equipment and plastic counters. His searching gaze probed among the shining coffee urns, steaming soup urns, grills, toasters, milk and fruit juice cisterns, refrigerated storage cabinets and along the linoleum floor on both sides of the counter. But there was no sign of life.[13]

Meanwhile, first in the company of Jamaican novelist George Lamming, whom he met at Van Vechten's, then on his own, Himes had taken to spending his leisure time in Harlem, becoming reacquainted with the rich street life, the pimps, gamblers, prostitutes, and other hustlers he had known so well from his younger years, discovering that

> I still liked black people and felt exceptionally good among them, warm and happy. I dug the brothers' gallows humor and was turned on by the black chicks. I felt at home and I could have stayed there forever if I didn't have to go out into the white world to earn my living.[14]

It's chiefly from this period that Himes takes those impressions of Harlem he'll use to such fine effect in the late novels. Just as references and asides in *Cast the First Stone* with its supposed contemporary setting betray a forties origin, so Himes's Harlem in these novels (published 1957 through 1969) seems patently to date from earlier years.

Some years back Chester's now-estranged cousin Henry Moon had written in a review for the *New Republic* that

> For nearly a quarter of a century, Harlem has been widely publicized as the world's most populous Negro community. At times it has been glamorized as a vast night club with gay and bizarre entertainment provided by the dancing feet and singing hearts of its carefree citizens.
>
> . . . .
>
> Color there is a plenty in Harlem. And joy and pathos, beauty and ugliness, triumph and defeat, indifference and revolt, hope and frustration. Yet out of this melange, there has come no novel of enduring quality, no story which has probed deep into the social and economic conditions and given a representative picture of the community.[15]

Little could Moon have suspected that it would be Himes who would provide that very picture, though if decidedly not in any manner one might easily have anticipated. There was with Himes, after all, and always, what Ishmael Reed calls his "cantankerous, irascible, feisty, brilliant self,"[16] the self that seemed forever to be snuffling after the most difficult means of conducting an affair, the most improbable way to go about writing a book, tree-strewn paths,

Doubt, Passion, the Madness of Art | 219

boulders. Coming to believe that straightforward social realism could never depict the truth of the American Negro's life, Himes called up parodic, folkloric elements common to African-American tradition to forge a new kind of narrative, one that might be able to get at the deeper, almost dreamlike realities: those things unsaid, those silent truths. Reviewing *Lonely Crusade* in 1947, James Baldwin had noted that it was "an ugly story but the story of American Negroes is a far uglier story and with more sinister implications than have yet found their way into print."[17] Himes would make damned sure they did.

Himes's story "The Snake," written some time before and triggered by an incident from Jean's and his stay at Hugo's ranch, sold to *Esquire*. In the story a woman kills her weak husband, who can't satisfy her, and buries him on their desolate South Dakota land, then tries to lure his father to her bed. Two other stories of the time, "Boomerang" and "A Little Seed," Himes based on Willa's marital strife; these apparently remained unpublished. "Spanish Gin" tracks the winding down of a party among expatriates at Puerto de Pollensa, Majorca. Its protagonist surfaces periodically through alcoholic blackouts, uncomprehending that his companion has died in a fall in the next room, or that, drunkenly priming his alcohol cookstove, he has set himself (and the villa cat) afire. A brief vignette, "One Night in New Jersey," follows a caretaker returning from a booze run to the summer camp where he and his wife work as caretakers; the sketch reads as though taken directly from life. "Daydream" with its shoot-'em-up fantasy of a strong black man wreaking vengeance on white Southern peckerwoods has been cited before, in Chapter 3. Fading to an insignificant black man sitting alone in his New York hotel room, the dream concludes:

> "You are sick, son," I said to my smiling reflection. After a moment I added, "But that isn't anything to worry about. We are all sick. Sicker than we know."[18]

After many rejections, Himes had finally sold *The End of a Primitive* to New American Library, receiving "a many-page contract that took all rights, hard-cover, paperback, domestic, and foreign,"[19] all of it for one thousand dollars. In an accompanying letter Victor Weybright extolled the virtues of the author's taking a small advance on "sizeable and continuing accruals."[20] He was still waiting for those accruals fifteen years later, Himes said. Difficulties with NAL's editors, adamant to delete anything controversial from the book, cropped up immediately. Himes responded that in that case they might as well throw the whole book away, because it was *all* controversial and damned well intended to be so. He must have recalled those days he sat in Majorca writing his novel, thinking the whole while that he was finally giving them "something to hate me for."[21] "I want these people just to take me seriously," he told John Williams years after. "I don't care if they think I'm a barbarian, a savage, or what they think; just think I'm a serious savage."[22]

Van Vechten's birthday came that June. Penniless, and believing Carlo close to the only American friend he had left, Himes handcrafted a present for him, an engraved copper plaque he spent hours fashioning from a roofing square and polishing to a high shine with steel wool. On July 27 Willa departed for Europe. She traveled first to visit her children in Belgium, then took work, again in a medical office, in Paris; for a time, at least, she stayed in touch. Two days after Willa's departure Himes celebrated his forty-sixth birthday by drinking both bottles of vodka Van Vechten sent him as a present.

The next day, he roused beneath the thunderhead of a massive hangover to receive galley proofs for *The Primitive*. It wasn't only that the title's tail had been bobbed; the whole thing looked like a different dog. Upon reading a few pages, Himes demanded to see his manuscript, getting it, he said, only after NAL became convinced that he wouldn't turn over the galleys until they acceded. Apparently everyone in the publisher's office had had a go at fixing up Himes's novel.

Five separate colors had been used to edit my manuscript and I supposed each color was employed by a different copy editor. Thousands of stupid, senseless, pointless, mean, petty, and spiteful changes had been made ...

It took days to restore my manuscript to its original form. Since the color green had not been used by any of the copy editors, I used green ink to restore all changes. When I had finished, my manuscript looked like a painting of a writer's nightmare by Dubuffet. Then I had to argue heatedly, vehemently, bitterly for each restoration. To get my manuscript published with even the slightest resemblance it now bears to the original required more effort than writing the damn thing.[23]

That year, 1955, the Supreme Court's 1954 decision on *Brown v. the Board of Education of Topeka* making segregation in schools illegal was reinforced by its *"Brown II"* ruling that integration must be accomplished with "all deliberate speed." In Montgomery, Alabama, Rosa Parks's arrest upon refusing to surrender her seat at the front of the bus triggered a yearlong bus boycott by blacks that put an end to segregation on public transportation; it was spearheaded by Parks's minister, the twenty-six-year-old Reverend Martin Luther King Jr. Countermeasures against blacks came quickly; further arrests, cancelations of automobile and home insurance policies, firebombings, KKK marches. In 1956 came "The Southern Manifesto":

This unwarranted exercise of power by the court, contrary to the Constitution, is creating chaos and confusion in the states principally affected. It is destroying the amicable relations between the white and Negro races that have been created through ninety years of patient effort by the good people of both races. It has planted hatred and suspicion where there has been heretofore friendship and understanding.[24]

And in 1957, in defiance of federal order, Governor Orville Faubus posted Arkansas National Guardsmen outside Little Rock schools to deny black children entry. Eisenhower pushed the issue, at last sending in over a thousand federal troops—the first time since Reconstruction that U.S. troops were in the South to protect the rights of blacks.

Also in 1955, the U.S. provided direct aid, military training, and more than $200 million to Cambodia, Laos, and Vietnam, much of it to the Saigon government. In October, following a rigged election organized by the United States, Prime Minister Diem proclaimed the Republic of Vietnam.

"The novels of Chester Himes," H. Bruce Franklin suggests,

together with the American critical responses to them, provide a kind of miniature social history of the United States from World War II through the days of the Black urban rebellions of the

1960s. Himes has been not only one of the most neglected of major modern American authors, but also one of the most misunderstood. In fact, it took those Black rebellions to make any significant number of critics realize that Himes *is* a major writer.[25]

Cotton Comes to Harlem, Franklin points out, was published in 1964, on the very eve of those Black urban rebellions of 1964–68. Five years then passed without new publication—as though Himes were waiting to see how they would turn out, Franklin says. In 1965, two weeks before his assassination, Himes met Malcolm X. In 1968 Martin Luther King was assassinated; the following year *Blind Man with a Pistol* appeared, its subject patently "the Black rebellions, the political and religious leadership of the Black community . . . and the beginnings of an apocalypse."[26] Himes couldn't carry through on the apocalypse; he tried in *Plan B* and bogged down hopelessly. But with the urban riots and stand-offs of the sixties, some had their first intimations that it was Himes's world we had been living in all along.

There in New York in 1955 Himes peered into newspapers and watched the streets to see what might come of all this. Driven by newly aroused social expectations as much as by personal failure, he grew furious at the invidious racism about him: white cab drivers who refused to take black citizens to Harlem or to pick them up at all, restaurants denying service to black customers by simply refusing to see them, publishers turning away books by black writers. This confirmed everything Himes felt pacing across the bare floors of his heart. He sought out argument, confrontation, wrung dissembling's neck. Sat in his "solitary room at the top of the Hotel Albert, where, except for the occasional sounds of revelry from my neighbors, I felt as remote from civilization as though I lived atop the Himalayas"[27] and went into the streets like some anchorite down from his mountain, amazed at what he saw and forever apart from it. Ascetic? Scourged, rather. And if nothing human was alien to him, neither was it, now, a part of him. Chester Himes had seceded.

He had been trying for some time to obtain an overdue advance from Berkley Books for its reprint of *If He Hollers*. Finally he appealed to the Authors' Guild, who straightened it out with a phone call. Himes went directly from the Berkley offices to a bank where he exchanged the publisher's thousand-dollar check for traveler's checks, and from there to the Holland America Line to book second-class passage for France. A week before departing, he had dropped by Van Vechten's to have his photograph, the one that eventually appeared on the cover of *The Quality of Hurt*, taken. "How I could appear so young and happy I will never know," Chester said.[28]

The S.S. *Ryndam* sailed at midnight on December 14. In Himes's luggage were a new tweed overcoat for windy, raw Paris days, a brown and black tweed jacket, and charcoal brown slacks that would be a "second skin" for him, and newly printed copies of *The Primitive*.[29]

The book's back cover read: "This is a powerful novel about a white woman and an embittered Negro man, each a misfit in his own world, whose desperate effort to find love ended in a nightmare of drink and debauchery." Three brief lines were quoted from a longish blurb Van Vechten had provided: ". . . immense flow of intensity and passion; it must have been written at white heat." Inside were ads for a Herbert Gold book, for Ann Petry's interracial novel *The Narrows*, for *Invisible Man* and *The Outsider*, and for Hubert Creekmore's saga of three generations of a Southern Negro family, *The Chain in the Heart*. It was Signet book #1264, and sold for thirty-five cents.

14 Beautiful White Ruins of America

"The more perfect the artist, the more completely separate in him will be the man who suffers and the mind which creates; the more perfectly will the mind digest and translate the passions which are its material."[1]

T. S. Eliot in "Tradition and Individual Talent"—and by Eliot's standards, Chester Himes might have been the very image of the imperfect artist.

But Eliot, for all the modernist trappings of his work, emerged from essentially late-Romantic notions wherein that conjunction of "perfect" and "artist" went unquestioned, a conjunction more likely, in our skeptical era, to bring knowing smiles. We might also suggest at this remove, apprised of the facts of his life, that Mr. Eliot plays hide-and-seek here, expressing in terms of general criticism something of the mask of propriety, of the life, he so carefully constructed for himself.

Deep underground rivers connect the pools of fiction and auto-biography. The writer uses what he can retrieve from the physical world around him, bits of string and cloth, twigs, straw, plastic, to build his nest. As capital he has his own life, what he has read and thought, the people he has known—and whatever accrues from his investments of same. The rub comes with how this contiguity is to be interpreted and according to what bias, whether, indeed, it should be of serious critical interest at all. There's little doubt, however, that at some level this opportunity to re-create oneself and one's world proves a major drive toward creative work. And one major attraction for the thematically minded reader may be those glimpses he catches of the author peeking out from behind the pillars and lean-to porches of his work.

Himes's work invites, insists upon, such speculation, even if, as Michel Fabre said of *A Case of Rape*, the reader attempting to construe what he reads as autobiographical repeatedly gets shunted back from actual events into the world of fiction.[2] But this is what the artist always does: with select strokes taken from life, a figure, light on broken glass, the sounds of a street, he builds a facsimile of one small corner of life, a facsimile which is clearly not a model *of*, but modeled *from*; an abstraction, a recombining and reclothing, a representation.

David Lodge stands among those believing that just such transformation and investiture are at the heart of being a novelist.

Faced with two versions of the same story, one historical and one fictional, most people in our culture will tend to regard the former as more "real," hence more meaningful; but the novelist is someone who believes the opposite—otherwise he wouldn't go to the trouble of writing fiction. These fictions, however, have the superficial appearance of the historical, and the novelist works his effect partly by concealing the seams that join what he has experienced to what he has researched or invented.[3]

Thinking of the early novels and most especially of *The Primitive*, a novel he greatly admires, John A. Williams with some justification calls Chester Himes our single greatest naturalist writer. Few others approach the acuity of structure and focus he reaches in *If He Hollers* and *The Primitive*. And Himes continues well into the Harlem cycle, even as his tales become increasingly fabulist, to shadow actualities of the world alongside co-opted elements of his own biography on the screen. Yet he is from the first an artist forever trying for, reaching for, grappling his way toward *more*, a writer beating at whatever walls would contain him—if not upon every occasion to satisfyingly aesthetic ends, then always to interesting ones.

Himes is preeminently a writer who is fully aware of the gap that separates art from life, of the permanent incapacity of art to capture fully the complexity of life itself. His style can veer sharply from soberly conventional naturalism to the most radical extremes of surrealism. He is forever seeking the form that will fit, and he never denies to his characters the full range of contradictions that he finds in himself.[4]

Seeking the form that will fit. Fit the historical facts of his life and the realer "fictional" ones, fit his ever-stronger vision of the American Negro's absurd life, a life in which horror and comedy blend so completely it becomes difficult to know where one ends and the other begins. The American Negro is something that has not existed before, a new man, Himes insisted, and the old forms to express his life would no longer do—these must be new as well. So by sheer force of will and intuition Himes pushes forward into unmapped territory, grapples his way hand over hand from paragraph to paragraph, page to page, toward those new forms. For the journey he has set himself there are no guides, no trails, no markers. And for this very reason, Milliken holds, for the very boldness of his ambition, this variety, this wildness, few writers resist classification as persistently as Himes:

> Chester Himes has always been above all else a man who does not take advice. His work is totally innocent of the smooth, professional polish of the writer who has been told ad nauseum, to the point of final belief . . . that you simply cannot do everything at once, that art involves choice, that final solutions have been found to many writing problems, that models that work do exist, and that in the end every writer must submit himself to the exigencies and expectancies of the typical cultivated reader. Chester Himes never even entertained the notion that his writing could be more effective if it were motivated by anything other than pure Himesian impulse and instinct. His work is ferociously idiosyncratic.[5]

In the most engaged and forceful contemporary writing, Maurice Blanchot perceives a shift from the genre dominating the European novel, that of the novel of formation or *Bildungsroman,* to the *récit.* Sequential, autobiographical, moored in time, this historical genre has as its concern verisimilitude and "the world of the usual sort of truth." The *récit* by contrast is unmindful of verisimilitude, antigeneric, ahistorical. It is not, Blanchot maintains, the narration of an event but the event itself, ever changing, ever in the process of becoming—

the process of thought rather than thought's reiteration—marked by the violence of its own internal transformations and, because it takes place at borderlines, as a voice for all that is excluded from the static worlds to either side where papers are always in order, forever contestatory in stance.[6]

Such a reading follows close upon George Lukács's definition of the genre of the traditional novel as one of accommodation in which, by accumulation of experience, exposure to received wisdom and a generalized process of acculturation, the problematic individual becomes reconciled to society at large.[7]

Or as Himes puts it in *The Primitive*:

No more worrying about what's right and what's wrong. Just what's expedient. You're human now. Went in the back door of the Alchemy Company of America a primitive, filled with things called principles, integrity, honor, conscience, faith, love, hope, charity and such, and came out the front door a human being, completely purged. End of a primitive; beginning of a human. Good title for a book but won't sell in America.[8]

This genre of the traditional novel as described by Blanchot and Lukács, of course, presupposes commonalities of belief and lifestyle that may no longer apply. And the movement of modern literature itself, in its break with or extension of tradition, has been away from an assumption that the world is transparent and thus available to lucid thought and language, to assuming that the world is opaque.

Himes's development is consonant with all this. *The Primitive* begins in earnest Himes's abandonment of the logical, sequential world that culminates in the Harlem cycle with what H. Bruce Franklin has described as an unraveling of the mystery genre. Classic genre figurations, along with its basis in accepted social forms and the application of reason, progressively give way to portraits of nightmarish characters and strings of incidents related more by resonance and rude poetics than causally, concluding on an image of absurdist impotence as Himes's detectives stand helplessly by in the midst of a citywide riot shooting rats.

Structuralists like Tzvetan Todorov would insist that any story is adumbrated in its first sentences, exfoliating from some central impulse; and that the mystery, a species of grail quest narrative, unlike adventure tales that proceed horizontally along lines of plot, action, and sequence, proceeds vertically through repeated events, echoes, aspects. Each fictive motion encompasses also the attempt to penetrate to the material's secret, its hidden truth, so that finally the story that is being told and the story that is telling become images of one another.

Just so is Himes's development as a writer adumbrated in his earliest work, in the dream sequences that structure *If He Hollers*, in the rage and murderous madness of *Lonely Crusade*'s Luther McGregor and Lester McKinley, and so does it continue exfoliating in *A Case of Rape*'s relativism, in the gravitational pull of history therein, in the farce and fantasy (no longer earthbound) of *Pinktoes*, in the city as stage for violence and transformation emerging through the early detective novels. *The Primitive*, this neglected masterpiece, one of American literature's great novels, is where the road forks.

The Primitive is, as Lundquist notes, the novel in which Himes pushes to the limit two obsessive themes: his rage at being rejected as a writer, and the black man's fascination with white women. Lundquist perceives the novel, in fact, as a culmination or stopping point, an end to the confessional period; more generally, as a summa after which Himes was done with settling old scores and with which he exhausted his autobiographical impulse.

Certainly interracial themes pervade Himes's work, as does his identification of black men with women in regard to the disempowerment and lasting psychological damage reserved for them jointly by society. In jacket copy written for *The Quality of Hurt* Himes described himself as "a black man who pitied white women." In *A Case of Rape* and in his collaboration with Willa on what is after all a quintessential woman's story, he gave that sympathy form. Very early on in *The Primitive*, struggling to formulate her father's defeat, Kriss also finds its image in self-identification: "Not defeated like a man in battle, but like a woman who is defeated by her sex, by the outraged indignity of childbearing, menstrual periods, long hair and skirts."[9]

There's little doubt that *The Primitive* was landmark work for Himes, or that he recognized it as such at the time. In *The Quality of Hurt* he describes writing the novel while living with Willa in Majorca:

I would get up at five, and by the time I had made coffee the first rays of the rising sun would strike our garden. I used the kitchen table for a desk and by the time the first peasants passed along the walk several feet below the embankment of our garden, humming the rising crescendo of the death song of the bullring, I would be typing happily, writing *The End of a Primitive*. I still had a good supply of Dexamyl. In fact, my tranquilizers sealed me inside of my thoughts so that I was almost completely unaware of the peasants and the flies and the movement in the distant street and could only experience the sweet, sensual, almost overwhelming scent of the lemon blossoms and the nearly unbearable beauty of the blossoming day far in the back of my mind. I wrote slowly, savoring each word, sometimes taking an hour to fashion one sentence to my liking. Sometimes leaning back in my seat and laughing hysterically at the sentence I had fashioned, getting as much satisfaction from the creation of this book as from an exquisite act of love. That was the first time in my life I enjoyed writing; before I had always written from compulsion. But I enjoyed writing *The End of a Primitive* . . . for once I was almost doing what I wanted to with a story, without being influenced by the imagined reactions of editors, publishers, critics, readers, or anyone. By then I had reduced myself to the fundamental writer, and nothing else mattered. I wonder if I could have written like that if I had been a successful writer, or even living in a more pleasant house.[10]

This is something of a new Himes for us, a man who seems at times, despite living in rank poverty and dejection, almost on the verge of weightlessness. Such was his concentration while writing that "Neither the pink mountains nor the swarms of flies in the dusty city could possibly be real, I thought. Only my book was real."[11] Distanced from America if not from the lands and grooves it had left on his soul, delivered by failure from further pretense of success in his writing, past the recall of censors internal or external, Himes wrote just what and as he wished, producing out of the bounds of this freedom the most carefully structured, closely controlled novel he would write. Milliken also avers to this transformation within Himes: "In his racist homeland he had been a borderline alcoholic, compulsively embracing the degradation of menial jobs to eke out a precarious living; abroad, he was a completely functional, generally dead broke, moderately happy, working writer."[12] In an introduction for the novel's reissue written not long before his death, Himes again emphasized the novel's liberating qualities.

> I was cleansed of envy and hate by writing about white Americans with satire and scorn . . . Writing this book not only purged me but made me strong. Forever afterwards, I have been shocked by the absurdity of racism. How more absurd could two people be than me and my white woman? My mind became free and highly creative and in the following eight years I wrote twelve books on the absurdity of racism and its effects on both black and white people . . . the only thing that stopped me from writing more about the innumerable instances of racism was a series of strokes.[13]

Naming *The Primitive* his favorite book, Himes told John Williams that he'd been able to achieve what he did with it only because in Majorca there were no distractions, physical, financial or otherwise, not even the distraction of expectations. He had written the book, he said, out of a completely free state of mind from beginning to end.[14] Jesse Robinson, too, was his favorite character. To Michel Fabre in 1983 Himes admitted: "I put a lot of myself into him. I probably said everything I wanted to say in that novel,"[15] and much of what he said was about the repressive influences of his time, about moral conceptions that fail to fit the actual circumstances of lives, about national (and often willful) blindnesses.

> In *The Primitive* I put a sexually-frustrated American woman and a racially-frustrated black American male together for a weekend in a New York apartment, and allowed them to soak in American bourbon. I got the result I was looking for: a nightmare of drunkenness, unbridled sexuality, and in the end, tragedy.
>
> What I wanted to show is that American society has produced two radically new human types. One is the black American male.[16]

And the other was the white American woman, who, Himes held, has more freedom, better education, and far greater financial wherewithal than at any time in the past, yet is desperately unhappy, shunted aside in society's relentless pursuit of its goals, incomplete sexually, unloved and uncared for. Often she turns to the black man, who will care for her, without realizing that he too has been fatally wounded by society —that he is in fact dangerous, both to himself and others.

The Primitive comes out of a particular time. Those visions of equality that drove American blacks in the forties, which Himes mirrored in *If He Hollers* and *Lonely Crusade* (and which he would pillage again for the satire of *Pinktoes*), had passed, with little enough if any true gain; the civil-rights era had yet to begin. America's sense of omnipotence, of its manifest destiny and diehard *rightness*, had attained plaguelike proportions. Having single-handedly delivered the world from ruin, America could now go on about its simple, wholesome life as that world's curator, wizard, and watchdog. Anything that failed to fit the template of *rightness* was to be shoved under the rug, into the far corner of the closet, onto back lots. Hey, everyone lived like Ozzie and Harriet, right? America's full-time job became trying to live up to the misbegotten image it had of itself. Like Aristophanes' Socrates, America walked along so lost in its thoughts that it stumbled on every pothole. Because America was its ultimate product, that which all history had gathered toward, there was no longer any need for the past. And what else could the future be but a string of perfect, democratic, *simple* days like this one—here at home in America?

It was, in short, the beginning of the time we would live, as we do now, without allusion, without depth or history, paddling about on the surface of our lives and desires like water spiders, marooned in an eternal present.

Irving Howe characterized this rearrangement of the social furniture in "Mass Society and Post-modern Fiction":

By mass society we mean a relatively comfortable, half welfare and half garrison society in which the population grows passive, indifferent, and atomized; in which traditional loyalties, ties, and associations become lax and dissolve entirely; in which coherent publics based on definitive interests and opinions gradually fall apart; and in which man becomes a consumer, himself mass-produced like the products, diversions, and values that he absorbs.[17]

As often as not, that eternal present came to us, as did "the products, diversions and values" of our society, by way of the TVs that had so suddenly become a part of our families. These were windows from our furnished cells onto the public reality, windows through which we perceived those lives we did not, could not, have; and in their endless chatter, like babbling old aunts desperate to keep our attention, increasingly they would say anything, just *anything*, wearing down the line between the actual and presumed, the real and imagined, news and entertainment.

"The Life of Riley" premiered in 1949, "Ozzie and Harriet" in 1952. Both offered up the day-to-day small crises and triumphs of families clearly intended to be just like ours. Our own life was being re-created, recast, reformed, on that screen—and somehow validated.

The life, that is, of a new white middle class whose father went off to work regularly, whose mother in starched dresses cooked hams and baked cookies, whose children dreamed of acceptance by peers, high-school dances, and having their own cars.

TV was the ultimate funhouse mirror. In it, the ordinary could become huge, overwhelming, monstrous. The misshapen dwarf, looking in, saw himself become tall and straight.

So does TV become an integral part of *The Primitive*, character, chorus and oracle all in one, underlining the characters' loneliness and utter isolation. The TV Jesse and Kriss watch obsessively (it is always on) is their window to the world. Its stream of comedy, chatter and "current events" comprises their knowledge of what takes place in the world beyond their tightly circumscribed lives, this room, the absurd tragedy whose downward spiral they are riding out. When Jesse's trial and conviction for the murder of Kriss is announced on TV, *before it takes place*, by the morning news show host's sidekick chimpanzee, this not only perfectly complements the novel's structure, in which perception and delirium have inter-penetrated to such extent that one can no longer be picked out from the other, it brilliantly illuminates the novel's themes of isolation and divestment.

"Saw it start to, saw it had to, saw it happen," Archibald MacLeish wrote in *JB* of the witness of a traffic accident standing helplessly by. The reader of *The Primitive* has much the same experience. Starting off with the daily waking of Kristina Cummings, then of Jesse Robinson, the novel initially moves back and forth between them, its tempo increasing as they approach one another, come together and together begin circling ever closer, downward, towards their fate. As Kriss and Jesse submerge themselves in nonstop drinking and desperate, increasingly violent sex, barriers between the internal and external, the real and imagined, give way. They grow more and more confused as to the sequence of events, what they have dreamed or remembered and what has actually occurred, whether it is day or night, how much time has passed. Himes's careful writing bears the reader directly and fully into that confusion, culminating in a blackout for the reader much like Jesse's own. We are deeply confused as to what has gone on, what is real. Like Jesse we come into the clearing of the novel's final pages unable to remember, unaware almost until that final phone call what has happened.

Milliken points up the novel's dramatic structure, arguing quite convincingly that its structure in fact mirrors that of a play in three acts with four scenes to each act. Like the text itself, with which Himes plunges the reader into the bleak and bleary physicality of his characters' lives, this structure gives the novel an immediacy of effect, a sense of lives being lived or directly witnessed, while at the same time underlining its affinity to classic tragedy: tragedy here, though, of a demotic, diminished, denatured sort.

In Chapter 1, in her downtown apartment on Twenty-first Street near Gramercy Park, Kriss wakes to an empty bed, the alarm of her gold-plated Swiss clock "curdling the silence."[18] She is terrified, as she is each morning, at finding herself again alone. Thirty-seven years old, married for years to a homosexual (one of many efforts to bridge that aloneness), she has slept, by latest count, with 187 men.

> In her apartment, situated as it was on the first floor rear, entombed by the concrete cliffs of other buildings, as remote from the sounds of voices and traffic on the street as the crown of Everest, a veritable dungeon where the light of day penetrated only for a few brief hours in the late afternoon when she was

seldom there, this sense of being alone was almost complete; not only shut off from people, from others of the species, but shut off from time, from seasons, from distance, from life—all life, dog life, cat life, cockroach life—shut off from eternity. It was like waking in a grave.[19]

Or in a cave, in which, following her daily ritual of Dexamyl, barbiturates, and alcohol, she sits allowing the TV's flickering firelight to fill the empty spaces, watching a talk show featuring a host named Gloucester and a chimpanzee who predicts the news. Cassandra, Greek chorus, Lear's Fool, newscaster, comic sidekick, image of the primitive within us all, the chimpanzee predicts, along with Jesse's murder of Kriss, such news as Eisenhower's 1952 election as president ("thereby giving Senator McCarthy a mandate to rid the nation of its mentality"), Nixon's 1952 speech justifying the source of his campaign contributions, and the Supreme Court's 1954 decision for desegregation.[20]

In Chapter 2, Jesse Robinson wakes, like Bob Jones of *If He Hollers*, from dreams that provide a nightmarish mirror image of his waking life: he was falling through the ice while skating, none of those around him taking notice. Jesse is separated from his wife, rapidly running through the $500 a publisher has advanced as option on his novel *I Was Looking for a Street*. Jesse drinks a water glass full of gin and goes back to sleep. New dreams suggest the degree of his isolation and a plenty from which he is excluded (he is sitting at a banquet table between two empty spaces), violence (on the parking lot outside the banquet hall two men are beating one another horribly), lost youth and love (he is seventeen years old and kissing for the first time).

Jesse lives on the borderland between the real and unreal, life and the imagined, the civilized and savage. This failed writer is a portrait, Milliken says,

not so much of Himes himself, the man he believed he had really been, but rather of the man he believed he might easily have become had the sequence of misfortunes that overwhelmed him been just a little bit worse, if the screws had been tightened, ever so slightly, just a few notches more.[21]

* * *

Many details of Jesse's background, his stints as caretaker and arrest for sideswiping a white lady's car, his apartment on Convent Avenue, his separation from wife Becky, are taken directly from Himes's own life; several of these recountings reappear almost verbatim in the memoirs.

Jesse is a man who wants, more than anything else, and desperately, to *understand*, a man who is coming to believe that he never will, that those principles of and around which he has formed his life—reason, independence, self-realization, the arts, faith in social progress—are but illusions. He will never see or know Vanzetti's "serene white light of a reasonable world."

> No matter how much he drank, whatever he did to deaden his thoughts, there was this part of his mind that never became numb, never relaxed. It was always tense, hypersensitive, un-certain, probing—*there must be some goddamned reason for this, for that.* It had started with the publication of his second book, five years before . . . *Some goddamned reason for all the hate, the animosity, the gratuitous ill will*—for all the processed American idiocy, ripened artificially like canned cheese.

> . . . .

> "Jesse Robinson," he said in a voice of utter futility. "Jesse Robinson. There must be some simple thing in this goddamn life that you don't know. Some little thing. Something every other bastard born knows but you." After a moment, without being aware that he had moved, he found himself in the window looking down across the flats of Harlem . . . like sharp-angled waves of dirt water in the early sun, moving just enough to form a blurred distortion. "Every other nigger in this whole town but you."[22]

As Chapter 2 ends, Jesse, having had several drinks, steps outdoors and, not knowing where to go once there, with no particular des-tination or purpose in mind or in life, heads for the cheap movie houses on Forty-second Street. Chapter 3 picks up Kriss at work, in Chapter 4 Jesse calls for the date that makes up Chapter 5, and in Chapter 6 (its opening sentence the same as the first of the book: "The gold-plated Swiss clock on the nightstand whirred softly, curdling the silence of the small dark room")[23] Jesse and Kriss wake together in her bed.

Both are at the end of a chain of personal defeats, turned out of their dreams, their faith, their trust in others and in society, "both now ostracized from the only exciting life they had ever known, both starved for sexual fulfillment, lost and lonely, outcasts drifting together long after the passion had passed."[24] They become, in fact, mirrors for one another. Answering the door, Kriss sees:

> This man before her, in the old trench coat she recognized immediately, was dead; hurt had settled so deep inside of him it had become a part of his metabolism. Not that he had changed so greatly in outward appearance . . . It was inside of him the light had gone out.[25]

Jesse sees in turn "no hint of the daredevil girl"[26] he once knew but a woman grown dull, humorless, and respectable, illusions and youthful vigor long gone. It is their very despair, the sight of their own emptiness in the other's face, that draws them inexorably together. That first night they drink until they pass out. Much of the rest of the novel will be a stagger from binge to blackout to eruptions of violence.

Mirrors figure prominently. In the novel's early pages Jesse, after waking, surveys in the mirror his "trim, muscular body, the color of Manila paper, with the broad-shouldered proportions of a pugilist"[27]; near book's end he attacks Kriss as much from rage at his own image and hers in mirrors as from any other incentive. Kriss can hardly pass a mirror without looking into it, as though to reassure herself of her existence. In one key passage Jesse dreams of being lost in a house of mirrors from which he escapes in horror only to find that the outside world's supposed normalcy appears to him even more grotesque and distorted.[28]

Kriss's self-destructive impulses spring out everywhere: in her abuse of alcohol and drugs, her promiscuity and continual playing off of people against one another, her verbal attacks on Jesse, her provocations of dangerous incidents. At one point she actually attempts suicide by swallowing sleeping pills but is too drunk to succeed or even to remember the attempt afterward.[29]

Jesse, of course, has his own self-destructive drive; and when the two of them meet again, it is as though each recognizes in the other, instantly, the instrument of his destruction. Night after night, Jesse lashes out in his sleep, shouting "I'll kill you!" At one point it comes to him in a flash: "This bitch wants me to kill her."

Jesse and Kriss in a sense are social leftovers, ghosts who have lived past periods of idealism and hope into a world of everyday realities to which they can't accommodate themselves. Himes's many references to grand old days at Maud's emphasize this aspect, as does his inclusion of portraits of threadbare civil-rights leaders like Kriss's old lover Harold and magazine editor Walter Martin, loosely modeled on Horace Cayton and Ralph Ellison. His depictions of Harlem here, too—as a place full to bursting with life and all kinds of pleasures, some to be had cheaply, others at great price—are penned with a new, almost romantic wistfulness.

> The Harlem of *The Primitive*, evoked with bittersweet nostalgia and a marvelous, completely original, laughter-filled lyricism, was to be Himes's major subject throughout the European phase of his writing career, carried through the long series of detective novels and on into *Pinktoes*. In his enchanted garden in Majorca Himes found within himself the gifts of a great humorous prose poet, whose destined and unique subject was to be Harlem, the great, crowded black metropolis, more a continuing explosion of human energy than a city. He was soon to win a whole new circle of readers, as the chronicler, the poet, of Harlem, Harlem seen as only Chester Himes could describe it.[30]

In her apartment far from that Harlem, Kriss sits watching the chimpanzee on the morning news show and *Zoo Parade* as Jesse dreams of a farm where pigs have the secret of producing sausage without being slaughtered but one pig rebels, refuses, and is led away, all the others shouting *Traitor!* behind him. At the breakfast table one morning, his publisher having turned down his latest for being just another protest novel and for its lack of "just plain animal fun," Kriss having said when he first called her that she hoped this book was "nothing like the last thing you wrote . . . I'm tired of listening to you Negroes whining," Jesse makes an announcement.[31]

"That's what I'll do!" Jesse said. "I'll write a book about chimpanzees." Then hastened to ask, "There isn't any chimpanzee problem, is there?"

"Not that I know of," Kriss said. "All of those I've seen—most at the zoo—seem well satisfied."

"I guess you're right at that," Jesse said. "I've never heard of a chimpanzee being lynched for raping a white woman and so far none have been cited as communists."[32]

In a pivotal scene, suave uptown editor Walter Martin at the end of a long course of drinking and dispute over "the Negro problem" pulls a knife on Jesse after telling him that he has to join the human race. Jesse's response is that he's been an ape too long.[33]

Any synopsis or other reductive discourse, turned on a book as complex and multilayered as *The Primitive*, can but hint, finally, at the novel's richness of character and reference, its essential textures, its suspensions of argument, metaphor, and image—in short, its rewards for the casual and the careful reader. Pointing out that each, according to personal taste and predilection, might just as easily be construed as strength, Milliken runs down what he believes to be the novel's weaknesses: its constant shifts in tone, its cloying density, that the narrator intrudes, often gratuitously, with philosophizing, that the structure is too worked over, too symmetrical, stylized to the point of obtrusive artificiality. Yet Himes, Milliken believes, here succeeds, as he failed to do with Charles Taylor in *The Third Generation* or Jimmy Monroe in *Cast the First Stone*, in transforming Jesse Robinson from self-reflection to novelistic creation. This, the least dependent of the early novels on external, autobiographical interest, nonetheless has been forged into an effective vehicle for Himes's deepest, most personal insights into the human condition.

The Primitive is, finally, a novel of great humor, of comedy both high and low and of considerable horror, strands of comedy and horror so interwoven as often to be indistinguishable one from another, and thereby profoundly unsettling. Here is Jesse chasing the tiny dog that has terrorized him from the novel's early pages.

He pursued, and got in another good lick before he slipped again and knocked over the white marble statue of a nude, that blocked the passage. He made a desperate lunge and caught the statue before it hit the floor, breaking its fall, then fell on top of it. He got up bruised and shaken and restored it to the table. "Good thing you're not in Georgia, son," he told himself. "Open and shut case of rape."[34]

From which slapstick, Himes can veer in a breath to such as the novel's concluding death scene.

He dreamed horribly of running naked across endless glaciers and awakened seven minutes later, deathly chilled, without being aware he had dreamed. "Damn, Kriss, aren't you cold, baby?" he asked. She didn't reply. He got up and slammed the window shut with a bang, then sat on the edge of the bed and poured a glass of wine. His teeth chattered against the rim of the glass . . . "You know, Kriss baby, you can be a very unpleasant bitch," he said angrily, and as his rage began to ride added, "You're going to get yourself good and fucked up someday." Then, prodded by her continued silence, he turned on her furiously, saying, "And whether you like it or not I'm—" His voice stopped short when he clutched her naked white shoulders. Her ice-cold flesh burned his hands.

His next action of which he was aware occurred two and a half minutes later. He was kneeling on the bed, astride her naked body, trying to make her breathe by means of artificial respiration; and seeing his tears dripping on the purple-lipped knife wound over her heart, thought she was beginning to bleed again. He felt such a fury of frustration he began beating her senselessly about the face and shoulders, cursing in a sobbing voice, "Breathe, Goddamit, breathe!"[35]

It is only in the relationships we manage that we exist at all. Excluded from many common human relationships, self-exiled from others, Jesse and Kriss form a relationship that both know instinctively is the only relationship that remains possible to them, a relationship that leaves one dead and the other just as effectively destroyed, but a relationship —an existence, however desperate, however brief—nonetheless.

15 A Serious Savage

In Paris anew, lugging his old self heavily along on his back like that oversize trunk, wearing it like his "second skin"of brown and black tweed jacket and charcoal brown slacks, Himes continued his underground life, "weird, grotesque, a drunken Walpurgisnacht."[1] Barrels of drink went down him. Obsessively he picked up any woman he could find who would consent to go along with him, students, prostitutes; it was only necessary that they come within earshot, sit at the next table, meet his eyes. His temper flared at the slightest provocation or none at all: at some imagined slight or mere glance. In isolation he grew paranoid, certain that others intended him physical harm, and took to carrying both a knife and a crescent wrench wrapped with machinist's tape everywhere he went. He was purging America from his mind, he said, but destroying himself in the bargain.

> I needed women desperately, not just for sex but safety, to help me control my temper. And I needed women to help restore my ego, which had taken such a beating in New York. I needed women to comfort me, to wait on me, to cook for me, to keep house for me, to talk to me, to assure me that I was not alone. And I needed English-speaking women to translate for me as much as to make love to me for I couldn't speak the language.[2]

Need so acute and all-embracing, of course, might better be called by some other name.

He was staying at the Hotel Royer-Collard in the Latin Quarter. At first Willa, infrequently, visited, but both had come to realize soon upon Himes's return that the bond once so strong between them had dissolved. Only passion, their sexual craving for one another, trailed on. And over time, as Himes began making bitter accusations, Willa withdrew, further underscoring his isolation. Here, as in so many aspects of Himes's life, the biographer, sorting his notecards, attributing motive and design in retrospect, proceeds at peril. Just why did Himes commit this great mistake of returning to the States? Much as, looking back, one educes a line of development from the protest and autobiographical novels through the farce of *Pinktoes* to the freewheeling parodic comedy of the Harlem novels, as though the author at some level had thought all this through, one imposes patterns a posteriori on the eventual materials of life. Surely the sole reason Himes had for returning was to discover what had become of the bond between Willa and himself, to salvage what he could of the relationship or else put it to rest. Yet one knows that for Himes decisions were often impulsive, made in acquiescence to influences buffeting him along in some particular direction, or taken in sudden, existential leaps. Fighter pilots are taught when caught up in complex, potentially paralyzing situations just to do *something, anything,* that might trigger a new chain of events. It's a tactic Himes understood.

Still, all was hardly unadulterated blight and despair. Ollie Harrington's Café Tournon circle had supplanted Wright's at the Monaco as expatriate central. Locals and tourists alike flocked to watch Ollie, looking "like Spencer Tracy in *Cannery Row,* painted brown,"[3] reign over his pickup band of social comics, storytellers, and hardscrabble intellectuals, men without countries all. These included the painters Herb Gentry, Berthel and Larry Potter, journalist Frank Van Bracken, who was Paris correspondent for *Ebony,* mathematician Josh Leslie, Ish Kelley (model for Fishbelly in Wright's *The Long Dream*), and William Gardner Smith's old friend and fellow Philadelphian novelist/newsman Richard Gibson. Wright often dropped by after lunch to play pinball. Himes quickly became with Bill Smith and Walter Coleman a central figure. After spending mornings writing in the Café au Départ or one of many others along Boulevard Saint-Michel, Chester would have lunch in his room—sharing both lunch and bed with a woman, if one could be found—then settle in for afternoons at the Tournon, he and Bill Smith and Ollie swapping eights and casting off dirty dozens as they vied to outdo one another in improvisations that straggled on long into the evening.

Wright's stock had declined appreciably among younger black writers. He was, for one thing, secure both financially and in reputation, long past struggles they still faced daily, all of which aroused jealousies and animosity. He seemed, moreover, blind to the Algerian problem that had divided all Paris along intellectual faultlines. And he was in fact, both by virtue of having lived abroad so long and of his middle-class aspirations, out of touch with contemporary black life, a fact underscored with publication of *The Long Dream* and subsequent attacks on both book and author. "He writes as if nothing had changed since he grew up in Mississippi," *Time* reported [4], echoing wife Ellen's reservations about the novel's recidivist nature. As James Baldwin described these years:

> He had managed to estrange himself from all the younger American Negro writers in Paris . . . Gone were the days when he had only to enter a café to be greeted with the American Negro equivalent of "*cher maître*" ("Hey, Richard, how you making it, my man? Sit down and tell me something."), to be seated at a table, while all the bright faces turned toward him. The brightest faces were now turned from him.[5]

Wright would die two years after publication of *The Long Dream*. Few besides Himes and Ollie Harrington realized how profoundly he was wrestling with depression and self-doubt in those final years. Always protective of Wright's stature when it was called into question and forever deferential to the older writer, Himes nonetheless during this time maintained his distance; or perhaps it was that both men did so, impelled in different directions by pride, temperament, and circumstance.

Himes's own confidence was assuaged by sale of *The Third Generation* to Librairie Plon's prestigious Feux Croisés, Chester politely asking for and receiving twice the advance ($150) first offered. Publication of *The Primitive* pended with Gallimard that February.

Nor were coffee-fueled mornings of work at the café unavailing. Having passed through multiple incarnations, his Majorca story "Spanish Gin" reached toward novel length as *The Lunatic Fringe*. The story would undergo further transformations before being abandoned. Himes was still working on it, under the title *It Rained*

Five Days, in mid-July after his return from the writers' colony at La Ciotat. He took it up again in October [1957], after signing with Gallimard for two further Harlem novels and fleeing again to Majorca. This time he tried to incorporate it, along with a story titled "The Pink Dress," into a novel about his affair with Willa on which he'd been working off and on since 1954.

Those mornings at cafés were also given over to something radically different, though having clear antecedents in previous work. "From here the 'Negro problem' in America seems very strange," Himes wrote to Van Vechten, "and I don't think I'll ever be able to write about it seriously. It doesn't make sense any more on either side."[6] Noting that the "old tired forms" for the black American writer did not fit any longer, and wanting perhaps more than anything else to avoid being typecast again in the Wrightlike role of protest writer,[7] Himes went for full-throated satire and sexual farce, equivalent in its way to those outrageous sessions of badinage held with Harrington and Company at Café Tournon.

From *The Primitive* he retrieved the figure of Harlem hostess Mamie, extracting also the comic voice that surfaced so strongly in that novel. (An early version of Mamie appeared in *Lonely Crusade*.) Again, as with *The Primitive*, he must have laughed aloud at the crazy, wild story he was telling. Just such freewheeling, wildly comic scenes, often but loosely strung together, will make up the Harlem novels; here it is almost as though the startling, stark images from Bob Jones's dreams in *If He Hollers* have been drained of their terror, bleached to pure comedy.

By April Himes, writing steadily, had over 120 pages completed even if, as he wrote Van Vechten, he still didn't know exactly what he was writing.[8] The book would be published both as *Mamie Mason* and as *Pinktoes*, and would become Himes's sole best-seller. First, though, like so many other Himes books, it staggered bewildered from publisher's office to publisher's office. Walter Freeman at NAL in turning it down nonetheless passed it along to James Silberman at Dial, who felt the portion he read too sketchy and undeveloped. Eventually the novel lodged at Maurice Girodias's Paris-based Olympia Press, brought out there, in English, in 1961, then by Plon, in French, in 1962. The question of rights became such a snarl of appeals and counterappeals and threats of litigation that at one point Himes asked the Authors'

Guild to assist him in figuring out just who truly controlled what rights. Eventually the novel was copublished in the States by Putnam and Stein & Day, each of whom had purchased rights independently.

In his letter to Van Vechten, Himes wrote:

At this time I feel as if there are billions of protons of intelligence (a new intelligence) floating about in the world and that some-time soon they are going to come together and form one great mass intelligence and from it everybody is going to be able to see at last what profound idiots we've always been. Because mankind can't keep on hating and fighting forever without knowing what they're hating and why they're fighting. [9]

As Himes himself pointed out, this doesn't sound much like a man trying to write a funny book. But in fact it's in fair part a key to the new direction his work is taking, to the farce of *Pinktoes*, celebrating what profound idiots we've always been, and to the detective novels in which he would limn so exactly the absurdity of urban Negro life. One of the new tools Himes was perfecting was what magicians call misdirection, channeling the reader's attention away from the real activity: dissembling become art.

The first of those detective novels lay just around the corner. Meanwhile, seeking relief from the strain of keeping *Mamie Mason* lighthearted, Himes had undertaken another project, drafting a story of American blacks in the Latin Quarter on trial for the supposed rape of a white woman who had been one of the men's lovers. This was blatantly a *roman à clef*, with representations of himself, Ollie Harrington, William Gardner Smith, Baldwin, and Wright. And it would sum up the story of his affair with Willa in much the same way he had codified his affair with Vandi in *The Primitive*. Passing through various avatars, at one point conceived as "a long, Dostoevskian work, possibly consisting of several volumes,"[10] this was eventually published as *Une Affaire de viol*, or *A Case of Rape*.

To Himes's many distractions that spring—the disillusion he had brought with him from America, his all but constant lack of funds, seeming disinterest among publishers in new books, thoughts of Vandi's death, the emotional aftermath of the end of his three years with Willa—was added the fact that he had fallen in love again, with, this time, a young German girl, Regine Fischer. Looking up drunkenly one day in Café Tournon to see her longish nose and widish mouth, dark blond hair pulled so severely into a ponytail that she had "a sweaty, surprised look," he had impulsively asked her to attend a party with him the following night, little suspecting that she was one of Ollie Harrington's many women.[11]

Regine was a drama student who, while pretending to be much more worldly than she in fact was, nonetheless by his own admission taught the much older, much experienced Himes a great deal about mutuality in sex. She introduced him to other things as well, escorting Himes to movies and plays in an attempt to introduce him to the French culture he largely ignored, even encouraging him to enroll in daily classes at the Alliance Française. When he had doubts about the detective novel he was writing, she rushed to reassure him of the book's validity.

How it is, it is no great book, but it isn't bad or cheap. Why should it be cheap? Just because these people don't have great social ambitions? Jackson certainly takes his Imabelle for as important as Lee Gordon his place in the world. The world is full of people and they are different. Your job is to make them convincing and true. In one of your letters you wrote that you would cut throats, eat spit, and live in sewers for the one you love. Make it the same for Jackson.[12]

From the first Himes was touched by her silly childlike grin, by the dress she had borrowed, three sizes too large, to wear to that first party, by her curious mix of forthrightness and shyness. Though in *My Life of Absurdity* his portrayal of Regine (whom he calls therein Marlene) verges sometimes on caricature, other times on the perverse, obviously he felt great tenderness for her. He also gave serious thought to marrying her, making his first inquiries about the possibility of a divorce, first directly to Jean, then to an attorney, at this time. What is perhaps of greatest interest is that the pages concerning Regine are saturated with sex. Himes writes of sex here as nowhere else in the memoirs with great frankness and physicality: his powerful attraction to her, the germ of violence always in their sex, the smell and sharp ache of bodies overused.

In early June Himes set his world in order, as was his wont, by organizing his wardrobe.

I packed my three suits—gray herringbone tweed suit from Brooks Brothers, blue nylon from Klein's and beige gabardine from Kolmar Marcus—along with my gray Burberry overcoat into my black horsehide suitcase, slipped my fourteen-carat gold tie clasp—which had cost me thirty dollars in a pawnshop on Columbus Avenue—into my side coat pocket [13]

and deposited it at the state-run pawnshop on rue des Francs-Bourgeois, adding the nine thousand francs he received to five thousand Ellen Wright had given him, and struck out for Daniel Guérin's writers' colony at La Ciotat. The gargantuan trunk he left for safekeeping in Yves Malartic's basement. The fabulous alcohol stove, kitchen and dining utensils went into storage at Ollie Harrington's. Regine saw him off at the Gare de Lyon.

Himes passed his stay at La Ciotat largely in seclusion working on *Mamie Mason,* and by mid-July was back in Paris. He and Regine settled first into her apartment on rue Mazarine, then in September moved to the Hotel Rachou on Rue Gît-le-Coeur. This haven for impoverished international travelers, later known as "the Beat hotel" for putting up in fair succession a straggle of writers such as Ginsberg, Corso, Burroughs, and Brion Gysin, was tucked onto a Left Bank side street just around the corner from the Place Saint-Michel. Christopher Sawyer-Lauçanno describes it evocatively in his study of American writers in Paris, *The Continual Pilgrimage.*

Of the thirteen categories assigned French hotels, the Rachou establishment, with its forty-two rooms, was at the bottom. The paint peeled from gray walls, the windows were perpetually glazed with a brownish sheen inside and out, the room furnishings were minimal—a sagging bed, a table, a single wooden chair; a small, often stained cold-water sink . . . Because of the ancient wiring, only a single forty-watt bulb was allowed for illumination in each room; if another appliance such as a tape recorder or radio was used, the light had to be turned out. On each stair landing was a Turkish toilet, with torn newspaper hanging from a hook for use as toilet paper.[14]

There Himes and Regine kept house of a sort, shepherding his last few thousand francs, preparing meals on his alcohol stove (cabbage and potatoes, or dog meat cooked with leeks to kill the odor when things got really bad), making love for recreation and reassurance more than from passion, Regine primping at the "vomit-colored hair" she had dyed while Himes was at La Ciotat.[15] Regine went off to her acting classes, "or wherever she was," four nights a week and often remained out till dawn.[16] Chester typed away at the final manuscript for *Mamie Mason*, wrote letters of panicked appeal to American and French publishers to request return of partial manuscripts, beg further advances, or demand new royalty statements, passed time with friends such as William Gardner Smith or Walter Coleman and his beautiful new Swedish lover Torun on the terrace at the Tournon. Living "with a little German tramp"[17] who he realized would bring disapproval from older, more conventional friends like the Malartics and Wrights or Annie Brièrre, he avoided them all. Nor were such misgivings expressed only reflectively, in terms of others. Again and again Himes told himself that Regine looked with her dyed hair like "a whore in Les Halles," remarked the ungainliness of her greasy face, silly smile, and pimples, said that he had taken from a brother a woman he didn't really want and was just "waiting for a chance to get away from her," wondered "What kind of girl have I got myself tied up with?"[18] In one abandoned passage from a draft of the memoirs he wrote that this "unripe Fräulein" had for him the advantage of being young and available and the best he could do, elsewhere remarking how exciting the affair was, how it boosted his confidence and made him feel important.[19] Before meeting her, Himes wrote, he had been "running around and drinking so much I was becoming impotent again and headed for a nervous breakdown."[20]

Often, as Fabre and Margolies point out, when Himes focused on Regine he perceived her only as a reflection or aspect of himself, what she could do for him, what she represented to him, while failing utterly to see what a troubled young woman she was. He wrote at some length of her courage, her brave affairs, her exercise of will in adopting a country not her own, overlooking blatant patterns of self-destructive behavior, her emotional lability, or just what those contradictions in her character he found so fetching might signify. And in fact Regine emerges from all Himes's passages and pages about her as curiously faceless, a catalog of tics and emotional stammers indicating to us little more than the impress of her instability, her youth and youthful bravado. Slight evidence exists that in daily life Himes understood her any less superficially, or made much of an attempt to do so.

There were happier moments, or moments at least less grim. Joe and Estelle, in Paris for a conference, joined Chester for dinner; he saw Ralph Ellison (Himes looked, Ellison said, as tortured as ever) at Wright's; he attended a conference of Negro writers and intellectuals at the Sorbonne. But by September finances had declined to such point that Regine sold the collection of beautifully bound books her father had given her and Himes pawned the only thing of real value he possessed, his typewriter. Things had gone shakily between them of late, with many violently verbal confrontations, when to further burden the situation Regine failed her final exams at the Vieux Colombier drama school. The day after she learned this, following yet another confrontation in which Himes ordered her out of the apartment, Regine swallowed his bottleful of Nembutal. Himes took her to the American Hospital where after an hour's wait he was approached by the night supervisor and told "with the irate disapproval and extreme outrage which only a slavery-minded old-fashioned American white woman could feel" that Regine would recover.[21] The suicide attempt, Himes decided, expressed Regine's terror at the thought of losing him, and now, "for good or bad," he was hers. [22]

So much hers in fact that in the wake of that suicide attempt he agreed to accompany Regine on a visit to her home in Germany, one of the strangest decisions he ever made, and precipitating one of the strangest scenes. "There were many reasons why I went with her," he wrote, "but the chief reason was to prove to myself that I was not afraid to go."[23]

At the family home in Bielefeld, Westphalia, Himes was cordially if guardedly received by Regine's father and mother in a fourth-floor sitting room complete with grand piano and overstuffed furniture. Dr.

Fischer, a small man with a snow-white goatee and equally white ring of hair around a shiny bald head, owned a bookstore and art gallery; he met them attired in black coat, striped trousers, and vest. Regine's mother, handsome and full-bodied, looked to Chester "like a voluptuous woman tightly bound in expensive clothes for propriety's sake."[24] Since neither parent spoke English, all conversation had to be routed through Regine, a situation creating, along with considerable embarrassment, not a little suspicion as each side began to wonder just what was being translated. This terrible comedy culminated with Himes and Dr. Fischer sitting facing one another on sofa and armchair as Regine, seated beside Chester, translated "in a dogged monotone, face without expression like a robot" her father's ponderous remarks about her neglected childhood, her poor education, lack of experience and shameful paucity of morals, her general unsuitability to life.[25] He did not doubt that his daughter loved Himes, Herr Fischer said, but there were such obstacles. Himes was twice her age, he was of another country and background, even another race. Herr Fischer asked only that they remain apart for one year. Meanwhile Regine could finish her secretarial studies.

Shortly thereafter Chester walked out, at Regine's insistence paying the family a final visit for dinner that night before returning the following day, alone, to Paris. Regine had told him that hers was one of the most bourgeois cities in Germany; he in turn, interpreting the family's stiff, old-world civility by his own measure, believed that he had never seen such hypocrisy. He professed surprise and shock at the trip's outcome, never intimating any realization (such realization as he must have had) that it could not possibly have gone otherwise.

For her part, Regine felt forsaken, believing that Himes should have taken a stand against her father. Daily she wrote pleading for Chester to send for her, to rescue her. Sometime before Christmas she briefly visited Paris, returning to her family for the holidays. When things began to fall into place with Gallimard, Himes wrote asking her to join him, but by the time he had completed his first novel for the firm, *The Five-Cornered Square*, in January, she still had not done so. Having pled for so long to come back, now she seemed to find excuse after excuse to delay doing so. Himes later came to believe that her father held her virtual captive; in the memoirs he reports her arriving at his door, having made her escape, half-starved and shabbily dressed. As the couple subsequently visited the Fischers on a regular basis, this seems doubtful. With completion of the novel, at any rate, he had sent a registered, special delivery letter: *I've done it. Come back now or never.*

Meanwhile, having received the remainder of his advance from Gallimard, Himes hit the streets feeling flush and thinking to himself: "Now I was a French writer and the United States could kiss my ass."[26] He celebrated in typical fashion by updating his wardrobe.

> I wrote a new ending the same day, and the next I went down to Old England men's store on Boulevard des Capucines to buy a shirt. After I had bought a shirt to please me, a tan and black checked woolen shirt to go with my brown and black sports jacket and charcoal brown slacks, I stopped in the shoe department and bought an outrageously expensive pair of English-made yellow brogues

and, after getting blind drunk, took comfort from a fat Swedish woman with "repellent, unkempt, greasy dark hair hanging over her fat repulsive shoulders like snakes from Medusa's head."[27] A few days later, Regine walked into his room. Himes bought her new clothes and a cheap imitation-silver ring; they worked their way through a major confrontation in which Himes hit her in the face and kicked her in the stomach in "a blind insensate fury," then went on to a party at Walter Coleman's and Torun's; they settled back into life together.[28] This was the period in which at Regine's urging Himes attended classes daily at the Alliance Française. The classes took up his mornings and, as he made little progress, after a month he dropped them, insisting that they interfered with his writing.

All those years, and all the years to come, the French language and Chester Himes were to stand staring one another down across an impassable river. He tells how the first time he tried out his new language, on the boat across, a waiter rather imperiously corrected him; he had used the incorrect auxiliary verb. Elsewhere he writes how, meeting translator Yves Malartic and wife Yvonne for the first time, he rushed toward them to enunciate the greeting he had memorized and practiced over and over: "Yves! Yves! Je suis très content de vous avoir."[29] Malartic, looking puzzled and not a little embarrassed, responded, "I'm so sorry, Himes, you must forgive me, but I don't understand American very well." It had been like that all along, Chester said. He shouted and screamed and threatened and cursed and these people just refused to understand him.

Just as they did in his own language—and in his books?

16 A New Intelligence

Jesse Robinson in *The Primitive*, walking New York streets and reminiscing about 1944 when all the liberals, black and white, were lining up behind Roosevelt and there was nothing like politics for getting love black *or* white, thinks of Harlem hostess Maud:

> "What a bitch!" he thought. "A great woman, really. Greater than anybody'll ever know!" Many times he'd considered writing a novel about her. But he'd never been able to get the handle to the story. "Great Madame, actually. Worked with her tools. That whore did everything. Besides which she was a cheat, liar, thief, master of intrigue, without conscience or scruples, and respectable too. That was the lick—the respectability." He felt a cynical amusement. "Son, that's the trick. Here's a whore who's friend of the mighty, lunches with the mayor's wife, entertains the rich, the very rich, on all kinds of interracial committees, a great Negro social leader."[1]

Maud had made an earlier appearance, as Mamie, in *Lonely Crusade*. There, she is a "fat, light-complexioned woman with black hair and sleepy eyes, clad in flaming red lounging pajamas"[2] who at her St. Nicholas Avenue apartment hosts a more or less continuous party in which important blacks and inconsequential whites mingle. On a trip to New York, Lee Gordon attends with an old friend he's run into at the Theresa Hotel.

> But he had listened in vain for anyone, white or Negro, to make a single statement that had any meaning whatsoever. The Negroes were being niggers in a very sophisticated manner as tribute to

their white liberal friends. And the whites were enjoying the Negroes' tribute as only white liberals can.

It would have had some meaning to Lee if the purpose of the party had been sex. A prelude for adultery, or even suicide. But there at Mamie's, sex had been but a vulgar joke.[3]

If Jesse Robinson never had been able to get the handle to the story, Chester Himes did. The result was *Mamie Mason*, published in the U.S. as *Pinktoes*, where, unlike that of *Lonely Crusade*, the purpose of the party, the purpose of everything, it seems, is sex. Himes's only extended satire, *Pinktoes* proves more successful by far than such earlier satiric forays as the scenes with Alice's family in *If He Hollers* or Kriss's drink-riddled black guests in *The Primitive*. Its sexual farce leapfrogs in part off a novel virtually unknown to whites but one which would have been familiar to black readers of the time, George Schuyler's *Black No More* (1931), in which Negroes pay to be by "the strange and wonderful workings of science in the land of the free" turned white, gaining "the open sesame of a pork-colored skin."[4]

Here, Mamie becomes "Harlem's most famous hostess . . . of a color termed 'yellow' by other Negroes and 'tan' by white people . . . a thirty-nine-year-old, big-boned, hard-drinking, ambitious, energetic woman with the instincts of a lecherous glutton."[5] Given to periodic consumption of entire turkeys and hams and eternal dieting in order to fit into her fashionable size-twelve sheath dresses, Mamie is always seen smiling or laughing, "both of which she could perform convincingly while in a state of raging fury."[6] With husband Joe, a consultant on interracial relations for the national committee of a major political party, she aspires by way of her freewheeling parties to be recognized as the undisputed social leader of Harlem and simultaneously to solve the Negro problem, or "if not solve it, at least tire it out."[7] Here, from a chapter entitled "Wrestling and Pole Vaulting," is one interracial summit conference.

So what happened to the unidentified distinguished-looking white lady and the young dark Negro poet who looked like Jackson? They left Mamie's to go somewhere and make some poetry, and, oh, brother, they are making it, white and black poetry, that is.

This poetry is not only being made but it is being said, between pants and grunts and groans, that is.

HE: Birmingham.

SHE: Oh, you poor lamb.

HE: Ku-Klux-Klan.

SHE: Oh, you poor black man.

HE: Lynch mob.

SHE: Oh, you make me sob.

HE: Little Rock.

SHE: Oh, what an awful shock.

HE: Jim Crow.

SHE: Oh, you suffering Negro.

HE: Denied my rights.

SHE: Oh, take my delights.

HE: Segregation.

SHE: Oh, but integration.

HE: They killed my pappy.

SHE: Oh, let me make you happy.

HE: They call me low.

SHE: Oh, you beautiful Negro.

Finally the verses ceased as the rhythm increased to a crashing crescendo with a long wailing finale:

HE: Oooooooooooo!

SHE: Negroooooooooooo![8]

Much of the inspiration for *Pinktoes* seems to derive from several months Chester spent as guest at the Moons' Harlem apartment in 1944 after returning to New York from California. Henry was then public relations director for the NAACP, Molly volunteer president of the National Urban League Guild she had founded two years previously; both, as part of the President's "Black cabinet," were staunch campaigners for FDR. Henry and Chester had corresponded on and off since Chester's prison days. Henry, passing copies of his cousin's stories on to Sterling Brown, then its director, had been instrumental in getting Himes work with the WPA; the Moons' support also helped secure the Rosenwald Fellowship that allowed Chester to complete *If He Hollers*. (The "Rosenberg" Foundation and its fellowships become a comedic element in *Pinktoes*.)

I went to New York to live with Henry and Mollie Moon in their fabulous apartment at 940 St. Nicholas. It was during the time Roosevelt was running for his last term. The communists, the negroes, the negrophiles and friends were getting together to elect Roosevelt. Henry Lee was working for the CIO Political Action Committee . . . and Mollie was giving parties sponsored and paid for by the various groups, including the Democratic National Committee . . . There is hardly a prominent middle class negro of today I did not meet at that time—Walter White & Co., Lester Granger, Ralph Bunche—oh hell, all of them. It was from this time and from these people I have taken the scenes and characters for my book.[9]

Relations grew strained even while Chester was there, especially over a woman with whom he had an affair and of whom the Moons roundly disapproved. Shortly after that 1944 visit, the relationship would decay. The Moons failed to praise unreservedly *If He Hollers* when published the following year and, with most liberals black and white, no doubt harbored still more fervid reservations toward Himes's portrayal of interracial relations and leftist movements in 1947's *Lonely Crusade*. On Himes's part there seems to have been a curious if altogether Himeslike anthology of emotions: envy of the Moons' central position in Negro and New York intellectual life, disdain of their middle-class lifestyle and disgust at their hypocrisy, disappointment that they'd not done more to help him and grudging resentment at what they *had* done. Either because he felt he had license to such use or because he had made them so imaginatively his own, so recast them, in the work, Chester always expressed surprise when those in his life from whom he had modeled characters—Jean, Vandi— disapproved, and it was no different with the Moons. How could anyone possibly be upset by this? It was all in the cause of good literature, or of good fun, was it not? And (this thought, too, must have crossed his mind) had he ever in his fiction been harsher on anyone, used anyone else harder or more unsparingly than he had himself?

For Silberman at Dial, Himes summarized his novel as the story of how Mamie Mason tries to force the wife of great race leader Wallace Wright to come to one of her parties, how in so doing she all but ruins the lives of a number of people and then must go about setting them right again. In a later note for one of his publishers Himes expanded rather grandiloquently on this synopsis, describing the novel as

> a Rabelaisian treatment of the sex motivation of New York City's interracial set by a member of long standing. The author reveals some of the backstage and bedroom scenes in the great struggle of Negro equality in a graphic detail seldom found outside psychiatric case histories. Underlining the depiction of the Negro people's illimitable faith in a just solution of their dilemma is a hilarious account of the aphrodisiacal compulsions of the "Negro problem" in which the dedicated crusaders against racial bias are shown more often falling in bed than in battle. The story is authentic and many of the scenes and characters are drawn so closely to life as to be recognizable.[10]

Like *The Primitive*, then, *Pinktoes* is a *roman à clef*, if a confusing one. Himes portrays himself as ever-broke and -hopeful outsider Julius Mason, brother to Mamie's husband Joe. He's something of a country-bumpkin figure, "a five-cornered square" who has left his wife behind in California and is staying with the Masons. Other life studies, though rarely direct given the nature of the novel, include Horace Cayton, Walter White, Himes's old editor Bucklin Moon, Richard Wright, Ollie Harrington, Paul Robeson, Adam Clayton Powell, and Ralph Bunche.

Pinktoes was quite a departure from Himes's prior novels, and finally may have had more in common with his freewheeling conversation, which we understand from friends teemed with jokes, stories, and exaggerations, and with the goings-on among Ollie, himself, and others at Café Tournon, than with his fiction up to that point. It brought Himes's flair for outrageous comedy, so much a part of the Harlem cycle, into the foreground, as well as the associative, anecdotal style that increasingly occupied those novels. Most important, the freedom of invention that he found or allowed himself in this book seems to have worked to liberate him both from the earnestness of writing "proper" protest novels and from the burden of autobiography. Retrospectively at least, Himes agreed, remarking in *My Life of Absurdity* that

> I had the creative urge, but the old, used forms for the black American writer did not fit my creations. I wanted to break

through the barrier that labelled me as a "protest writer." I knew the life of an American black needed another image than just the victim of racism.[11]

A June 1956 letter to Van Vechten from La Ciotat, where Himes completed the novel, reaffirms this. The novel's conclusion, he writes, is terrific, much of it funny, none of it bitter. Curiously he calls the book an experiment in good will (the French title in full is *Mamie Mason, ou un exercice de la bonne volonté*), adding: "I have a great feeling now that I am going to be free forever."[12]

Pinktoes came twelve years after Chester's extended stay with the Moons at their Harlem apartment. Much of it he wrote during long days at the heated Café au Départ, where he sat wrapped in his gray Burberry overcoat trying to stay warm, too impoverished to buy cigarettes or even stamps, cadging tiny sums from friends and watching the steady parade of interracial sex everywhere about him on the boulevards. He began the book in early 1956, in March sent two completed chapters to Walter Freeman at NAL, who in declining nonetheless passed it on to Dial Press's James Silberman. By April Himes had 120 pages in final draft. There, temporarily, feeling the strain of keeping up the novel's pace and comedy, he stalled, taking time out to write the synopsis of a long-contemplated novel about black American expatriates in Paris. Though he had conceived or at any rate spoken of the book as a major project, Himes went no further than this synopsis, eventually published as *A Case of Rape. Pinktoes*, however, he completed in two weeks at La Ciotat.

The new book went begging as Chester moved on to write the first of his detective novels. Finally in 1958 Plon, publishers of *The Third Generation*, offered an advance of 50,000 francs, then promptly lost the manuscript, necessitating Chester's appeal to Yale's James Weldon Johnson Collection for a copy of the manuscript he'd given over, per his agreement with Van Vechten, to their archives. Himes meanwhile sold the book to Maurice Girodias's Olympia Press, so that, when Plon in due course offered a contract, he signed it in violation of his prior contract with Girodias. Olympia published the book in English in 1961, Plon in its French translation in 1962; after much negotiation the two publishers agreed that, in exchange for making no claim against French rights, Girodias would retain all foreign rights.

Maurice Girodias heard I was in Paris and knew exactly where I was and I was surprised one morning when I got a telephone call from him asking me to bring in the manuscript for him to read. I told him the manuscript was owned by Plon but he said he would take good care of it and read it overnight and we'd talk about it tomorrow. When I talked to him the next day he said if I put in six good sex scenes he'd give me a contract and a thousand dollars advance. I had Marlene [Regine] type the original manuscript, the one Plon had bought, and I went to work putting in six sex scenes; but I put in so many sex scenes I had to take two thirds of them out. Girodias wanted to call it *Zebra Stripes*, but I came up with *Pinktoes*, which he liked better.[13]

Despite Himes's claim of juicing up the novel for Girodias, few significant variances between texts exist. Sex scenes there are, in abundance—"Bessie Shirley was hanging head down from a walking stick stuck through the chandelier with her long hair hanging to the floor, and embracing Mr. Tucker, who stood confronting her,"[14] for instance—but none appear to have been cobbled up to meet editorial demands or better suit Olympia's perceived image.

Mamie Mason as published by Plon, Himes wrote in his memoirs, made quite a stir. Copies were on display all about the Left Bank, the book was well reviewed in the newspapers and magazines (one, *Paris-Presse*, ran a front-page story headed "Do You Want to Look Like an Overcooked Frankfurter, Madame"), strangers greeted him on the street: "I felt like a real author."[15]

But the thickets kept getting deeper. In 1964, claiming afterward that he didn't understand the rights were not his, Himes sold *Pinktoes* to Putnam, only to learn that rights had already been sold, by Girodias, to Stein & Day. Eventually, after much sawing back and forth, the two U.S. publishers worked out a unique agreement for copublication. *Pinktoes* appeared in hardback in 1965, and, the following year, in a paperback from Dell. Both editions sold extraordinarily well, providing Himes his highest advance to date ($10,000) as well as his sole best-seller.

Walter Minton was buying up Girodias' books. He had been successful with *Lolita* and *Candy* and he was anxious to get *Pinktoes*. Stein & Day had offered me seventy-five hundred, so Minton upped it twenty-five hundred. And then Stein & Day and Putnam started a lawsuit against one another, and that's why they published it jointly. They figured it'd be more expensive to go to court so they just decided that they would work out a system, a very elaborate one, so elaborate that I ran into difficulties with Stein & Day because—Putnam kept the trade book edition, they were responsible for that and for collecting my royalties—Stein & Day were responsible for the subsidiary rights and the reprint and foreign rights and so forth. And finally Stein & Day began rejecting various offers from foreign countries. The last one—the one that really made me angry—was that they had an offer from a German publisher to bring out a German edition of *Pinktoes* and Stein & Day rejected that, and I went to the Authors Guild and to the lawyers to see what I could do. And they said that that was the most complicated contract they had ever seen.[16]

Himes's account, finding such fault with Stein & Day while failing to acknowledge at all his own culpability, is skewed in a fashion that, reading Chester, one soon comes to find familiar. He did, as cited, in mid-1968 address his misgivings to the Authors Guild. In a four-page letter of August 12 a Guild representative responded. In the usual one-author, one-publisher relationship, he wrote, there would be a number of fairly common and common-sense steps to take, though none seemed applicable in this case. He suggested several possible courses of action: putting the rights by mutual consent of all involved into the hands of an agent; arbitration; referral to a lawyer who would serve simultaneously as author's representative and as arbitrator between publishers. Ultimately, however, he had more or less to throw up his hands and quit the field: "I'm not King Solomon, and I don't have the wisdom to solve one of the most tangled contractual arrangements that I can recall hearing about."[17]

Pinktoes's plot, meanwhile, gets about on as many confusing legs as does its commercial history. Himes's most atypical novel, it is yet a part of his broken-field run toward what Lundquist calls an "extension of humanity," an opening outward on its author's part, an embrasure of compassion.[18] *Pinktoes*'s characters may exist to be targets of satire and of the choreographed pratfalls their author prepares for them (which, indeed, none escape), but they are, for all that, for all the funny hats they must wear and all the contrived mugging, people linked inextricably and intimately to others, people forever struggling to be better, to be more, than they are, people who *need* and who *feel* with an intensity almost childlike.

Himes here takes up again his old jeremiad against the middle-class Negro, satirizes the pretensions of all liberals, white or black, parodies his own obsession with interracial sex. But he fires in passing and scattershot at many other targets as well: the New York publishing scene (the authors of *Dreamland*, a book on drug addiction, have cribbed it from a forgotten WPA project); charitable foundations (the "Rosenberg," under direction of Dr. Oliver Wendell Garrett); fringe groups (D. Stetson Kissock and his Southern Committee for the Preservation of Justice); and the arts in general (white producer Will Robbins's latest film *Read and Run Nigger* has the subtitle *If You Can't Read Run Anyhow*).

The plot gathers, inasmuch as it coheres at all, chiefly about two figures. Wallace Wright is a much-acclaimed race leader and Executive Chairman of the National Negro Political Society (NNPS), one-sixty-fourth Negro, who looks "so much like a white man that his white friends found it extremely difficult, in fact downright irritating, to have to remember he was colored."[19] Art Wills is an editor, soon to take up those duties for a new Negro picture magazine, himself white, a philanderer, and generally so drunk that people have trouble getting his attention.

Harlem hostess Mamie Mason, angry at Wright for attending her parties without his wife, trumpets word of Wright's affair with a white woman. This leads to the rumor that he has left his wife of twenty years for a white woman half his age, and soon there's a run on hair straightener and bleaching cream, while black women's organizations champion slogans such as Be Happy That You Are Nappy and poets write poems with titles like "The Whiter the Face the Blacker the Disgrace."

Mamie is also angry at Wills because he won't agree to feature her in the first issue of his magazine—and because, too drunk to take notice, he wouldn't be party to her subversion of Wright. When she informs

Wills's wife, Debbie, that he has proposed to a young black woman named Brown Sugar he met at a drunken party, Debbie goes home to her mother. This leads to the rumor that white liberals all over are abandoning their wives for young black women, and there's a run on suntan lotions, ultraviolet lamps, and cosmetics as white women rush to kink their hair, dye their gums blue, redden their eyes. The cosmetic firm making "Black No More" now brings out a companion product, "Blackamoor," for whites.

The transformed white ladies quickly discover the advantages of being black, among them that sharks, not liking dark meat, will not eat them; that they needn't bathe, since dirt doesn't show on their skin; that they can now do the housework and pocket the maid's money; that they are able to wear all the loud colors they wish without friends laughing behind their back; that now they can forget the Negro problem and hate all the Negroes they wish without feeling guilty.

There is, too, a profusion of side stories. Panama Paul dreams of being in a heaven filled with white angels, unable to fly because his testicles are weighed down by anvils. Moe Miller in his Brooklyn home carries on a battle to the death with the rat who has taken it over. The nymphomaniacal Merto knits replicas of the genitals of all the black men she sleeps with, taking care to get size and color just right, and has to relate the story of each conquest, in precise detail, to gay husband Maurice; she turns up at the concluding costume ball as Eve, wearing a fig leaf and a necklace made of her knittings. Then there is Reverend Reddick, sent to Peggy, Wright's white mistress, by Mamie. He spends three days and nights there buck naked, wrestling with the demons inside Peggy, until the two of them, the Reverend and Peggy, decide to get married.

News of Peggy and the Reverend's marriage not only sends Art Wills over to Hoboken to fetch his wife home, it serves also to reunite Wallace Wright and wife Juanita.

And all along, you see, what Mamie Mason has *really* been worried about is her big masked ball at the Savoy Ballroom. Worrying about who would and who wouldn't come. About looking good for it. About having enough food. And "if no white people were there? There was no telling what might happen to the Negro Problem."[20] But the ball comes off magnificently, all the novel's characters reemerging for one final turn about the floor as a chorus line of Lots, Jobs, Sojourner Truths, Circes, Missing Links, Neros, Nanas, Toms and Topsys, Buddhas, Lucretia Borgias, Catherine the Greats, Simon Legrees, Moseses, and Aunt Jemimas—one "Rosenberg" applicant even comes as White Man's Burden, "no doubt intended as a gentle hint."[21]

From Himes's ten-page introduction to *Pinktoes*, "Excursion in Paradox":

> The inhabitants of Harlem have faith. They believe in the Lord and they believe in the Jew and they believe in the dollar. The Lord and the Jews they have, but the dollar they have not.[22]

Faith is a word upon which Himes rings changes throughout the novel, his code here for a peculiarly black version of the American dream, really a kind of structured hopelessness. The black American cannot afford to acknowledge futility, Himes suggests, for that is all he has. So, instead, he laughs at it. And that's what white visitors to Harlem see, all these black fellow citizens standing about, "not only laughing at what is considered funny, but laughing at all the things considered unfunny, laughing at the white people and laughing at themselves, laughing at the strange forms injustice takes and at the ofttimes ridiculousness of righteousness."[23]

Never has anyone been promised so much and given so little as the American black, Milliken remarks, providing in his general remarks a virtual gloss on Himes's Harlem novels:

> Citizen of a nation that offered unprecedentedly rich ideological and material opportunities, the black American found himself, at the same time, confronted by impassable barriers that existed for him alone, barriers maintained by violence, and by law . . . The black man's greatest pride is in what he believes to be his total freedom from comforting illusions, the special toughness he possesses that enables him to gaze without flinching on the grim realities of his life.[24]

It is just this commingling of horror and sorrow in black humor that makes it, for some at least, difficult, even deeply offensive.

Certainly critics have never been quite sure what to do with *Pinktoes*. Well, it's not quite what we'd call serious literature, after all—is it? And written for money, no doubt about that. Very popular in its time, I hear. What ever became of that fine, talented, *serious* young black man who wrote *If He Hollers Let Him Go?*

Some, both reviewers at the time of publication and later critics alike, have found *Pinktoes* prurient, disrespectful, silly, sophomoric, even insulting. Others find fault with its overabundance of characters, complain that transitions are too abrupt, that the author throws in far too many asides and secondary episodes.

One fair criticism concerns the ambiguity of its period. Certain of the book's references, such as allusions to war and "our fighting men," or the fact that books are being publicized on radio rather than on TV, suggest that the story is set in the forties, while references to reformed Communists and to the WPA as being "twenty years previous" imply the fifties. Perhaps the novel does lose some measure of potential authority or immediacy to this ambivalence, but the story is, after all, a farce, a type of folk tale, neither of which genre has any call to conform to novelistic standards.

Even Stephen Milliken, generally so clear-sighted, takes the novel to task for failing to give fair representation or assessment of the civil-rights movement, an intent clearly outside the book's purview. "It is," Milliken writes, "a cry of rage and disgust, the cry of a disillusioned zealot, an outraged and intransigent purist . . ."[25] It's none of those. It's a sport, a frolic, a rollicking, extraliterary raspberry. It's the sound of Chester Himes, that sound all those who knew him well heard often and talk about still, Chester Himes laughing at what fools we all, himself included, oh yes, are.

We are all guilty, it ends.

A Case of Rape, Himes's only novel set in Europe, with that concluding echo of Dostoyevsky ringing in our ears long after we have put the book down, stands among the strongest indictments ever penned of the racism endemic to Western civilization. Yet it was never intended, at least in its current form, for publication. Written in 1956–57, the book waited until 1963 for its initial publication in French, until 1980 for its first English-language edition (in a special edition of 350 copies by Bill Targ), until 1984 for general publication (by Howard University

Press), and appeared in a trade edition only with Carroll & Graf's 1994 reissue. As early as December of 1957, Himes mentioned the book in a letter to Van Vechten.

> A couple of years back I was still trying to write some good things, but the New American Library headed me off at every turn. The hard-cover publishers wanted NAL's approval before signing me to a contract, and NAL rejected all the ideas and manuscripts I submitted. I had (still have) a 72-page synopsis of a book in which I had great hopes. It was to be called *A Case of Rape*. It was a story about six U.S. Negroes in Paris and a U.S. white woman of good family. One of the Negroes had had an affair with this woman.[26]

Himes goes on to summarize the plot, remarking in conclusion that "The story is essentially the biographies of these people and the inner compulsions that have brought all their varying lives to this common focal point." If Himes ever wrote beyond those seventy-two pages, there's no evidence of it. Some years later, however, he made a decision to publish the synopsis itself.

> Originally it had been intended as a synopsis of sections of the "great novel" I was working on in 1956 when I first returned to Paris. But I got sidetracked by *Mamie Mason*. I dug up the manuscript and had it published by a little publisher who sympathized with the Algerians, in his collection Editions Les Yeux Ouverts. It was translated by André Mathieu, whom I had known at the Café Tournon, and a postface had been written by Christiane Rochfort, who was famous as a writer for women's lib, and also was the secretary for the Cannes Film Festival.[27]

Himes would always claim with typical hyperbole that his "little book" made quite an impression; it did receive some attention from the radical press, but this was occasioned more by the Algerian question (Les Yeux Ouverts being active in this debate) and by Rochfort's afterword, by the book's associations, that is, than by its intrinsic appeal.[28]

A Case of Rape offers, in its tale of young black expatriate writer Scott Hamilton and American-born neo-European Elizabeth Hancock, an analog of the Himes-Willa affair, one complementing intriguingly that offered years later in the memoirs. Scott's and Elizabeth's international interracial love affair, their collaboration on a novel, and their forcible separation from the United States all come directly from life, as does much of the couple's background: his white ancestry, her nervous breakdown, her abortive refuge among family in Boston. Central to the story, too, are recognizable portraits of Ollie Harrington, William Gardner Smith, James Baldwin, and Richard Wright. It is, then, another of those hybrid *romans à clef* Himes originated in *The Third Generation* and *The Primitive*. In these novels, Michel Fabre observes, the reader, attempting to construe what he is reading as auto-biographical, repeatedly gets shunted back from actual events into the world of fiction.[29]

Structured around a series of documents suggestive both in form and language of legal depositions, the novel reflects Gertrude Stein's observation that participation in the present is forever diluted by memory (the past) and anticipation (the future).

In April 1953 Scott Hamilton met the aristocratic Elizabeth Hancock, who subsequently left her sadistic European husband and their daughter to live with Scott in the south of France, London, and Majorca. Elizabeth's marriage had damaged her emotionally; Scott set himself "to cure her sick mind, heal her hurt soul."[30] Financial insecurity, however, destroys their relationship. Scott scrapes together enough money to send Elizabeth back to the United States, where eventually he follows, their affair starting up again only to collapse for good in America's racially charged atmosphere. Scott returns to Paris. A novel about their affair is accepted under Elizabeth's name, but the publisher, acting on an anonymous tip from someone in Paris that the novel was in fact ghosted by a black man, threatens to suspend publication. Elizabeth comes to Scott asking that he authenticate her sole authorship of the novel; she also suspects he may be the source of the rumor.

This is the back story.

Because of the retrospective form in which Himes casts the narrative, the actual plot, though in a sense the "present" of that narrative, also occurs in the past, recounted only in summary, in brief sections given over to précis of the events of the case and biographical sketches of the principals. This perspective, in concert with the flattened language, serves to give the narrative always a curious remove and impersonality, as though its events transpire not within individual lives and a circumscriptive society, but directly beneath history's indifferent gaze. As in *Rashomon*, we look back on the story from varying viewpoints, part of its message clearly that we can never know the truth of our past, never understand the full consequence of our actions.

The events around which the book accrues take place in 1956, three years after Scott's and Elizabeth's meeting. She comes to accuse him of the rumor that has given her publisher second thoughts and he, denying this, asks her to join an impromptu party of friends, who will vouch for him, in his room. The friends are all, like himself, expatriate black Americans: Caesar Gee, Theodore Elkins, and Sheldon Russell, modeled in turn after Ollie Harrington, William Gardner Smith, and James Baldwin. Elkins, feeling slighted because Elizabeth hasn't engaged him in conversation, hands her a bottle of sherry he knows to be spiked with Spanish fly, whereupon she convulses and dies. Across the courtyard a neighbor sees the men standing over Elizabeth trying to help, and calls the police. All four are arrested on charges of rape and murder, tried for same, and sentenced to life imprisonment. Only Scott knows that Elizabeth's death resulted not from the drug but from her husband's sadistic attentions the night before; Scott's sense of honor and of racial pride forbids his disclosing this knowledge.

Into this melee, after the fact, comes riding Himes's Richard Wright figure, famous expatriate writer Roger Garrison. Roger—who, we learn, is himself responsible for the letter to Elizabeth's publisher— sees the case as another platform from which to denounce racism. Blinded by his assumption that the verdict (like his own recent literary setbacks) must have had racist and conspiratorial origins, he goes about collecting evidence to reverse the conviction. Garrison has grown so accustomed to condemning the dominant white group for crimes committed by oppressed black minorities, Himes writes, that he is able blithely to ignore "the fundamental principle in the moral fabric of a democratic society, the assumption of innocence," and his pitiable efforts come to nothing.[31]

A Case of Rape is a powerful little book. The issues it raises are complex ones, issues that for the most part (perhaps because this *was* a synopsis) Himes remains content to put out on the table and leave there; never, unlike Garrison, does he insist upon the easy explanation, cleave to the foregone conclusion. His themes are as complicated, self-contradictory, and in the end as deeply mysterious, as his characters.

For all the diversity of their backgrounds, their differences in motivations and their complex, individual psychologies, all five black expatriate writers are fugitives of a sort, self-exiled and dragging along as baggage not only those guilts and confusions that were their birthrights but also the guilt and confusion of having fled the field of struggle—artists who, with their portable, recreative worlds are engaged in the continuous attempt to understand, exorcise, or at least gain some control over those guilts and confusions. Finally they prove incapable of defending themselves on the charges brought against them, believing from the first that, whatever they do, they are certain to be found guilty.

Nor are they blameless, for, marked by hate, they have learned to hate in return. It is "just pure, spontaneous, unpremeditated, racially-inspired *spite*"[32] that causes Elkins to hand Elizabeth the sherry he knows to be spiked with cantharides. Garrison's reverse racism emerges in his insulting, dismissive attitude toward Elizabeth, exactly paralleling Wright's treatment of Willa:

He had assumed from his brutal attitude toward such cases that Mrs. Hancock was like all other American white women lusting after Negro men. That she, like the others, had come to Paris to be loved by them. That she had deserted her husband and children for the sole purpose of sharing Scott Hamilton's bed.[33]

Himes, who always insisted upon the identification of black men and all women as fellow outcasts, barred from participation in society and crippled from the first by frustration, denial, perhaps most of all by the ever-widening gap between what they are told and what they perceive, here offers a profoundly sympathetic portrait of a woman.

Mrs. Hancock was a casualty of white Christian society which fails to enforce the moral laws it has ordained . . . one of those unfortunate victims of a code of ethics promulgated by the white race as its own private doctrine for the elevation of whites only.[34]

Here as elsewhere Himes holds that black men, and all women, live permanently excluded from, yet surrounded by, enclosed and defined by—bound by—that culture. That if they are misshapen, monstrous, or pitiful, it is only because they've grown to fit the mold they were formed in.

On the one hand, as Christopher Sawyer-Lauçanno points out in *The Continual Pilgrimage*, *A Case of Rape* shares its dominant theme of love overcome by society's strictures and taboos with that of the memoirs; on the other, in its relentlessness, in its exploration of the roots of violence and self-despite and its tragic outline, it provides an addendum, one powerful far beyond its slight proportion, to *The Primitive*.

In the end, *A Case of Rape*, like so much of Himes' work, must be read as a record of the destructive force of racism. At the same time, the book is not a protest novel in the sense of *Native Son*. Rather, it is a cry from the soul, an indictment of society from the inside out. Rarely did Himes write more convincingly, with such mastery over his narrative, than in *A Case of Rape*. It is a brilliant, multi-layered examination of the intricacies of race, sex, and power, but what ultimately makes the novel so compelling is that it is a chronicle of doomed love. Neither Hamilton nor Hancock can live in a world fully of their own making; instead they inhabit a vicious, absurd universe, which insists on cutting up everything literally into black and white.[35]

One might recall the ending of Nabokov's *The Defense* in which Luzhin, driven mad by his obsession with chess, looks down from the window from which he is about to throw himself only to see "the whole chasm" divide into dark and pale squares. Even in death he cannot escape his obsessions, cannot escape the way in which he has come to perceive the world, cannot escape his history or himself.

We are all guilty.

17 Gone So Long

Himes had been talking to Marcel Duhamel at least since January, upon his return from New York, about the possibility of writing a detective story. Duhamel had translated *If He Hollers* for its French edition and now was editor of Gallimard's La Série Noire, which published novels in the American hard-boiled mode. He thought Himes's writing with its stark prose and strong images would fit right in. But Himes demurred, saying that he didn't know anything about detective stories; that he was a serious writer.

By October, with Himes back in Paris alone from that initial visit to Regine's home, the situation was desperate enough to cause him to reconsider. Plon owed him $300 for *The Third Generation* but the book had yet to be published. And while Gallimard had published *The End of a Primitive*, Chester, since NAL retained all rights, received no payment for it. Retrieving a portion of his *Mamie Mason* manuscript from the typist he'd left it with, he took it around to Plon, telling them he needed a decision in two days. When they insisted on more time, he carted it on to Gallimard, and there ran into Duhamel, who again broached the subject of Chester's writing for him.

"Get an idea," Marcel said. "Start with action, somebody does something—a man reaches out a hand and opens a door, light shines in his eyes, a body lies on the floor, he turns, looks up and down the hall . . . Always action in detail. Make pictures. Like motion pictures. Always the scenes are visible. No stream of consciousness at all. We don't give a damn who's thinking what— only what they're doing. Always doing something. From one scene to another. Don't worry about it making sense. That's for the end. Give me 220 typed pages."[1]

Recalling that he had in fact started out to write *If He Hollers* as a detective story, Himes said he'd give it a try. Duhamel advanced him 50,000 francs out of pocket: "When you get about a hundred pages let me see it."[2]

Himes took him at his word regarding that 220 typed pages. In an interview five or six years later he told Melvin Van Peebles that before he started a new novel he'd count out 220 pieces of carbon paper and 440 pieces of typing paper. Then he would place a carbon sheet between two sheets of paper. The pile went on the right side of his typewriter. When he finished a page he'd take it out of the typewriter and put on his left. And when the pile on the right got low he'd know it was time to start winding the story up.[3]

With other of Duhamel's advice he had greater difficulty. When he had pushed his way through to sixty pages and took the portion in, Duhamel for the most part approved but counseled him to use more dialogue; there was still too much of the author in it. Keep the suspense going, he said. Don't have your people talk too much. Use the dialogue for narration, like Hammett. Himes revamped what he had, then went back to Duhamel, who said: "Just add another hundred and twenty pages and you've got it."[4] He wrote Himes a chit for 150,000 francs: half the advance of 400,000 francs, minus the 50,000 advanced earlier. To Chester's question "You think I should have some police?" Duhamel responded, "You can't have a *policier* without police"[5]—which is why Grave Digger and Coffin Ed appear almost as afterthoughts in the first book.

But first it was blank-paper time.

Chester recalled a con Walter Coleman had told him about, The Blow, that revolved around a machine purported to make large bills out of small ones. He began writing, chiefly about the square who becomes a mark for three hustlers. The title at that time was *Trouble Wears a Skirt*. He stalled out more than once, struggling all the while with the material, with his doubts that he could do this, and with himself. He was a serious writer, and this was anything but serious. How could he, writing it, be other than a cheap hustler himself, with Gallimard and readers as his marks? He consoled himself with the thought that he was writing only for the French:

I would sit in my room and become hysterical thinking about the wild, incredible story I was writing. But it was only for the French, I thought, and they would believe anything about Americans, black or white, if it was bad enough. And I thought I was writing realism . . . Realism and absurdity are so similar in the lives of American blacks one can not tell the difference.[6]

Shortly thereafter, the story "came unstuck,"[7] and Himes, working through Christmas Day and on into the new year fueled by boiled chicken and rice and quarts of rum, was able to complete it by January 18. The thought stayed with him the whole time he was writing, he said, that what he was writing was not a detective story but an action story, and that it was really a kind of protest against the idea of racism being behind all the brothers' sad faults. Black victims might be foolish, gullible, even childlike (they often were, in Himes), but the black criminals were grazing sharks, predatory, vicious, constant. The whole setup was absurd. And it wasn't *Mamie Mason*, as he'd thought, but *The Five-Cornered Square* (Himes's new title for the book) that came as the logical follow-up to *The Primitive*.[8]

In such musings we hear distinctly the clockwork of rationalization whirring and clicking, though finally there's considerable truth to them. Himes went on for some time convincing himself of the worth of his enterprise. By April, as he was finishing the second detective novel, he was, he said in correspondence, not at all ashamed of the work he was doing. He recognized at some level the freedom these stories gave him to write outrageously, to keep the game going without bogging down in protest, without having to overburden his tale with superficial meaning or follow through on any line of programmed argument. He could juggle balls, Indian clubs, knives, and a plate or two all at the same time. He began drawing attention, his own as much as others', to the books' singularities: their humor, the absurdly overdone bloodiness of them, their simple, jagged story lines. Yet he still spoke of Wright's novels as something apart, legitimate literature, even after himself gaining similar validation with publication of *La Troisième génération* by Plon in March, and that December wrote to Van Vechten from Majorca that should his present books become sufficiently popular he'll return to writing a different sort of novel. As late as 1965, in Cannes working on *Blind Man with a Pistol*, he was still wrestling with feelings—feelings any working artist knows well—that the books might be inferior, mere potboilers, uncommitted exercises. He had, at any rate, as of February 1957, a contract for eight Série Noire books to be delivered one every two months. "At the end of 1956," Christopher Sawyer-Lauçanno writes in *The Continual Pilgrimage*, "he was nearly destitute; six months later, thanks to three advances from Duhamel, he had nearly $4000 in his pocket, two books finished, and a third well underway."[9]

In *My Life of Absurdity* Himes wrote: "Making up stories was my business. Not only my business but my salvation. No one ever believed me when I told the truth, neither the blacks nor the whites, for different reasons of course."[10] He was writing here of a personal lie, as opposed to fiction, but his statement rings with much the same belltone of self-justification. If no one believed the truth when he tried his best to tell it, then why not just go ahead and tell lies? But he'd make them outrageous lies, lies that couldn't be avoided or ignored, lies that grabbed your attention and held it while they were slipping around behind to sink their teeth in. He would give them something (as he said of *The Primitive*) to hate him for.

By the time he completed the second book, Himes claimed that "the only time I was happy was while writing these strange, violent, unreal stories. I accepted them to myself as true; I believed them to be true as soon as they sprang from my thoughts"[11]—perhaps recognizing that he had tapped into some reservoir of expression beyond the personal, beyond the naturalistic and mimetic, something that had little to do with typical European models. He goes on (this is written, remember, some years later, circa 1970) to describe the Harlem books, both their character and their significance to him, as well as anyone has done.

> I was writing some strange shit. Some time before, I didn't know when, my mind had rejected all reality as I had known it and I had begun to see the world as a cesspool of buffoonery. Even the violence was funny. A man gets his throat cut. He shakes his head to say you missed me and it falls off. Damn reality, I thought. All of reality was absurd, contradictory, violent and hurting. It was funny really. If I could just get the handle to [the] joke. And I had got the handle, by some miracle.[12]

Himes also spoke here, in retrospect, with mixed bitterness and pride, of the way in which America, while rejecting the writing from which they derived, and by which he lived, increasingly over the years took up his thoughts.

Under the working title *A Jealous Man Can't Win*, Himes finished the second detective story, published as *The Crazy Kill* and as *Couché dans le pain*, "a simple domestic story which involved a couple of killings,"[13] in late April. The French title and opening scene came from a story Ollie Harrington had told him about a man falling unhurt from an upper-story window into a bread truck. Himes wrote that while working on it he went back to Faulkner again and again to sustain himself on that writer's ripe violence and absurdist view of life.

By the middle of September he'd finished a third, *If Trouble Was Money*, published as *The Real Cool Killers* and as *Il pleut des coups durs*. The following month, October 1958, the first of the series, *La Reine des pommes* (which had come out in the States the year before as *For Love of Imabelle*), was finally published.

Himes had gotten the handle. He'd started off writing for the French, giving his new public what he thought they wanted, peopling his Harlem with exotics, with figures so exaggerated and actions so unreal as to be cartoonlike. But he was a serious savage, and the material, as often before, changed in his hand, changed almost without his knowing it. The supposed lightness of what he was writing relieved him of what had become to him burdens—protest, high seriousness, autobiography—and offered in their stead a new freedom of imagination. Himes had found his way to a fresh language, to that "new intelligence' of which he had spoken, in which Harlem became, and remains, an enduring metaphor for America's many wars upon itself.

It was due to the detective novels, specifically Himes's receipt of the Grand Prix, that he met not only future wife Lesley Packard but longtime friend Melvin Van Peebles as well. Van Peebles, then working for the Paris-based weekly *France Observateur*, found himself on "a slow week in the mayhem department" assigned to interview "this guy who had just won some big French crime writing prize," a guy about whom he knew nothing at all:

A significant, insidious fact, striking to the core of the African American artist's dilemmas. Despite the fact that Chester, this literary giant, had been publishing essays, short stories and novels for over a quarter of a century, despite the fact that I, a black American, had grown up, gone to college and never once heard his name mentioned in the myriad literature courses I had taken spoke volumes about the walls of prejudice and the barriers of racism.[14]

The door was opened by "a not quite medium-built man with European features and caramel-colored skin, a dashing figure, in a matinée idol sort of way, his rakish features made even more handsome by several wicked scars lining his face."[15] He'd caught Himes working, with the remains of a breakfast of caviar and toast nearby. Van Peebles thought him "a mind-boggling mixture of frail and ferocious."[16] Each surprised to find the other black, the two men immediately got on, and were soon laughing so hard that Lesley called out from the next room to be sure all was well. In 1964 Van Peebles wrote the text for the Georges Wolinski comic of *La Reine des pommes* published first in the avant-garde magazine *Hari-Kiri* and later, by Editions du Square, as a stand-alone. Van Peebles also began a film scenario for *A Case of Rape* that went uncompleted. The following year, he won a prize from the French government allowing him to shoot his first feature-length film, *La Permission*. Earlier efforts had included *La Fête à Harlem*, about a raucous Harlem rent party attended by the Devil, who then can't find his way out. Van Peebles's *Sweet Sweetback Baaadass Song* was a commercial success in the U.S., though, believing it un-American, the selection committee refused to send it to Cannes; its maker was by this time a counterculture hero. Writing of Chester in 1996 to introduce the first of Payback Press's three-volume *The Harlem Cycle*, Van Peebles observed:

Chester was like that Flemish painter out of the dark ages, Brueghel the Elder. Brueghel called it like he saw it too. So unflinchingly in fact that doctors today, 400 years later, have been able to identify medieval maladies from studying the characters that he painted, diseases of which people weren't then aware. Chester saw America unflinchingly too—hilarious, violent, absurd and unequal, especially unequal. All of the so-called "new" racial antagonism bursting to the surface in the streets of these United States (diseases people claim weren't even there) lay festering just below the pavement of Harlem in Chester's work years ago.[17]

Writer and future TV producer Joe Hunter also met Himes about this time.

> I first met Chester in Paris in '59. I had read *If He Hollers* and *Lonely Crusade* in Philadelphia. Bill Smith and I were close. He, Bill, had not gone to Paris yet. He was truly pissed off with me for telling him that Himes was writing the way Blacks were supposed to write, and that he (Smith) was a pale imitation of Hemingway. He and Richard Gibson wanted to write like "white" writers.
>
> Smith went to Paris. While traveling in Europe, I stopped off in Paris to see him. He took me to the Café Tournon where I met Chester. When we looked at each other for the first time and shook hands, we both burst out laughing . . . as if we knew a secret about each other . . . I had never heard anyone laugh in that uproarious manner. It was as if we had known each other for years.
>
> Richard Wright then appeared and Chester introduced us. I was curious to see how those two reacted to each other. Wright was urbane, and Chester was his raucous self. I became just as raucous and Smith and Wright kind of looked at each other. When I looked at Chester we both burst out laughing. And I thought, how weird, we're both thinking the same damn thing which was: Smith and Wright must be saying to themselves— "what a couple of real Harlem niggers."[18]

Now, upon his connection with Duhamel, Himes had money and, having signed with Gallimard for further books, reasonable expectation, at least for a time, of more. One of his first purchases was a used VW that immediately demanded as disproportionate an amount of his time as it takes up disproportionate space in the memoirs. Page after page fills with breakdown adventures, convalescent stays in mechanic shops, letters to the VW factory, bills presented and paid, accounts of new pistons and engines and sheared lug bolts.

That June, Himes and Regine had barely cleared ownership of the auto (following a series of visits to government offices concerning import, licenses, taxes) and had barely cleared Paris on their way to Germany for a visit to Regine's family and Himes's literary agent in Stuttgart, when troubles began. They drove on, in literal stop motion, from garage to garage, at length making their way to Copenhagen for a visit with Timme Rosencrantz, a Danish jazz authority married to black singer Inez Cavanaugh, whom Himes had met in March back in Paris. Deciding that she liked Denmark, Regine prevailed on Himes to stay, which they did, taking a flat for the summer in Seeland, between Copenhagen and Helsingor. There Himes set himself the goal of ten pages a day and quickly completed his next detective novel, published second (as *The Real Cool Killers*) though written third. Ever the outsider and odd man out, outside of his work Himes found little to his satisfaction. Clean, ever civil Denmark displeased him fully as much as stern, regimented Germany; how far more tolerable he found Spain's many slow-moving, often maddening inefficiencies. He kept to himself and socialized with no one, complained bitterly of the continuous rain and wind, and became so furious at a Danish barber's miscutting of his hair that he shaved his head.

By October 1 the couple was back in Paris at the little hotel on rue Git-le-Coeur, where they learned of M. Rachou's death. Himes also learned that Duhamel was busily gathering testimonials for impending publication of *La Reine des pommes*, weaving into a tattersall such ringing phrases as "destined to become a classic" (*Mystère-Magazine*), "prodigious masterpiece" (Cocteau), and Jean Giono's declaration that he would "give all of Dos Passos and Fitzgerald for a few pages of Himes." Fall in Paris was the season of literary awards, and it was for this that Duhamel prepared. Already, the buzz among café literati was formidable.

Himes meanwhile had gone to Majorca with Regine, just as he once fled there with Willa, to write the new books he'd contracted with Gallimard. He failed to find the tranquility he recalled and sought anew, complaining of endless distractions, Regine, the VW, of the cold weather and uncertain electric supply, of "the sea boiling like dirty gray water striped with green"[19] and wind that howled and blew smoke back down the chimney. He worked erratically at a novel about his affair with Willa he'd begun in 1954, attempting at one point while there to incorporate "Spanish Gin" and a story he'd already written about Willa, "The Pink Dress," into it. "Spanish Gin" of its own right made a bid for noveldom in *It Rained Five Days*, soon to be *The Lunatic Fringe*, a "white thriller"[20] set in Spain for which Duhamel lacked enthusiasm when Himes pitched it to him and which he later rejected. Emotionally Himes was all over the place, as, apparently, was his writing.

In addition to Duhamel's rejection of *The Lunatic Fringe*, for which he had already drawn an advance, now Himes learned that NAL had rescinded its contract for the paperback of *Cast the First Stone*. He had received no income from the States that entire year. Nor could he place, anywhere, *A Case of Rape*. There were episodes of heavy drinking and of reckless driving. The whole of the dismal Spanish residence culminated in Regine's emergency appendectomy, Herr Fischer wiring money once Himes had exhausted what little he had left; following Regine's recuperation, the couple returned to Paris, moving into a hotel on rue Saint-André-des-Arts.

On the positive side, with publication of *La Reine des pommes*, Himes was on his way to becoming a celebrity. A publication party at Leroy Haynes's soul-food restaurant, with Himes and Regine, the Duhamels, Walter Coleman and Torun, and Ollie Harrington attending, momentarily darkened when a bristling Himes complained at everyone's speaking French, but Haynes finessed it. Himes learned in November, having resettled on the Côte d'Azur, that he was to receive the Grand Prix de la Littérature Policière, being the first American, and the first black, to do so. A month before, he had signed with Gallimard for two new novels under titles provided by the publisher, *Tout pour plaire* (which would become *The Big Gold Dream*) and *Il pleut des coups durs* (*The Real Cool Killers*). He had also spoken alongside Nikos Kazantzakis and Rebecca West at the thirtieth anniversary of Plon's Feux Croisés series. And he had bought a dog, an Irish setter pup named Mikey, soon a great comfort to him.

Himes, Regine, and Mikey didn't remain long in Paris. When Duhamel suggested that Himes write a thriller set in New York but without his detectives and offered an advance, and when within the week Plon bought *Mamie Mason* for 50,000 francs, the trio departed for the Côte d'Azur, in June renting a flat in a villa in Vence with a view sweeping from the suburbs of Nice to the lighthouse at Antibes. They remained there fifteen months. Chester loved the Riviera, its constant sunlight and beauty, the easy society of those who lived there, the energy and liveliness of both landscape and people. That old phrase "the happiest days of my life" returns in his memory of the time. Often this is Chester's code that writing went well, and indeed writing, too, went extraordinarily well there, with Chester completing *Run Man Run* in record time, writing it straight out. It was from Vence that Himes traveled back to Paris to receive his award and to be celebrated in such papers as *Paris-Match* and *L'Observateur*, the Brussels *Le Soir*, and *La Tribune de Genève*. Even *Time* magazine got in the act with a piece titled "Amid the Alien Corn," though this proved to be more about racism than it was about Himes. *Time* would feature him again in 1970 ("The Hard-Bitten Old Pro Who Wrote 'Cotton' Cashes In") after the success of the movie *Cotton Comes to Harlem*.

That January, having completed *Run Man Run*, Himes wrote most of a fourth detective novel *Imbroglio négro* (*All Shot Up*). He also continued to work sporadically on *The Lunatic Fringe*. He was famous. And he had turned out an enormous amount of new work in a few short months. But things were hardly as idyllic as they seemed. Are they ever? he must have wondered. Doubts could never be folded and put away like linen. He'd had his taste of success before, just enough to know what it was like and just enough to make it seem likely, only to have it torn from him by circumstance. His distrust of publishers, too, was profound. Again and again they had cheated him, robbed him of his royalties and subsidiary rights, done hatchet jobs on his books. (Even with Gallimard there were future uglinesses.) Now Gold Medal had published *For Love of Imabelle* in a version so severely cut and scrambled that he thought it all but unrecognizable. To Malartic he wrote, "As my fame increases, my fate remains the same—broke, desperate, urgent and trying to work beyond the capabilities of my poor brain."[21]

Uneasiness came to a head with a visit from Regine's mother during which she and Himes were often at odds. Frau Fischer adamantly urged her daughter to return and finish her secretarial studies in Hamburg and, while Himes avowed to having no objection, he strongly felt that he was being manipulated and said so. In one confrontation, perhaps fed by all his uncertainties, anxieties, and dissatisfactions, Himes's temper erupted, and he stalked from the house. Intending to discipline Mikey, he struck his own eye with a switch. Regine subsequently drove him, eye bandaged, to Guérin's La Ciotat, where he spent two weeks recovering (and where Mikey and the gardener's dog killed all Guérin's chickens) before returning, alone again, in April 1959, to Paris.

There Himes stayed at Hôtel Welcome, seeing a great deal now of Lesley Packard as together they strolled along the Seine, visited galleries and cafés, or motored into the French countryside with Mikey and Lesley's Siamese cat Griot. Chester stayed briefly in Ollie Harrington's apartment while Ollie was away in Berlin, then sublet an apartment in the 14th arrondissement on the southeast corner of the city belonging to a co-worker of Lesley's at the *Herald Tribune*. Not long after the move, the VW was totaled in a crash on Boulevard Saint-Germain, affording Himes another exasperating encounter with French bureaucracy. From another of Lesley's friends Himes bought a 1934 Fiat roadster he named Jemima, later still, from friends' friends, an old Hillman.

The thriller spawned by his Horn & Hardart days in New York, *Run Man Run*, was published by Gallimard as *Dare Dare*. By mid-October he was coming into the home stretch on his latest Harlem novel, *Imbroglio négro* (*All Shot Up*, working title *Don't Play with Death*), with its portrait of Harlem politician and closet homosexual Casper Holmes.

Himes first met Lesley on his return to Paris, and their relationship, for all his jealous nature and her own independence, for she was seeing others as well, developed rather quickly. She was, and remains, a remarkable woman, clear-sighted, practical, fiercely intelligent and capable, devoted. ("She would have had to be, to live with Chester all those years," one hears in interviews.) At the time, she lived in an apartment on rue Grégoire de Tours and worked five to midnight at the *Herald Tribune* as photo librarian. On the very day they met, as she sat in Café de Tournon with William Gardner Smith, a photo of Chester had appeared on her desk consequent to his winning the Grand Prix. They decided to celebrate, made a night of it, and thereafter were often together. It was wonderful, Lesley recalls:

Yet I did not see how there could be a future because I was young, attractive, had a good job, in fact two jobs, and was very independent. And while I had no hang-ups, probably due to the very secure environment in which I'd been brought up, Chester was so loaded with anger and complex emotions, all of which surface in his writing.[22]

Lesley learned quickly of his emotional lability, how a letter in the mail could ruin his day or fill it with light, how he could pass from blazing anger to laughter in the space of minutes. Humor, she says, was his last and greatest weapon. At a showing of the Harlem documentary he later made with Pierre Gaisseau, which he thought derisory and insulting, she "could feel him sitting next to me sizzling with fury."[23] And while she understood his mood swings, even understood something of the reasons for them, this did not necessarily make it any easier for her.

For his part, Himes persisted in his longing for things lost, in his compulsion to rescue and "protect" white women, and in his perennial attempt (just as progressively his mother had edited her life, cutting and pasting) to have one more go at "correcting" situations, at making them right in accordance with his preconceptions, ignoring realities. For better than two years he was to shuttle back and forth from Lesley to Regine, at one point adding a third woman, Marianne Greenwood, to his ever more complicated dance card.

That June Himes drove to Hamburg where he and Regine moved in as resident house- and dog-sitters for Dr. Ramseger, literary editor of *Die Welt*. Himes could not work, he drank heavily, drove wildly, finally had to be treated for ulcers: the rift between what seems and what is grew ever wider, ever more difficult to ignore. When Regine went in September to visit her family, Himes returned to Paris and to Lesley. In December, Regine joined him in Paris, where she had found a secretarial job. The reunion went poorly. Himes and Regine quarreled every day, and it was not long before Regine discovered that he was still seeing Lesley whenever he could slip away. Once Regine turned up screaming abuse at Lesley's door; another time she phoned to inform Lesley that she was about to kill herself, and was turning on the gas just as Chester arrived home. She and Himes fell to blows one day when she found Lesley and him together on the street. She returned to the apartment, where Himes came upon her later, and slashed her wrists.

Regine went from the local hospital to a psychiatric clinic at Vincennes, then on to clinics at Nogent-sur-Marne and Giesherslag. From there she posted an unbroken stream of "pitiful" letters to Chester. Correspondence from Herr Fischer meanwhile, to which Himes responded testily, begged him to assume moral responsibility and leave his daughter alone.[24]

Beginning work on a new detective novel he was calling *Be Calm* (*Ne nous énervons pas!*, *The Heat's On*, later filmed as *Come Back, Charleston Blue*), Himes's feelings toward Regine were deeply ambivalent. Her dependency, underlined by the suicide attempt and intensified by the hospitalizations, infuriated him. Yet he was drawn to his old caretaker role, and certainly, that given, could not in the present circumstances abandon her. And while her instability frightened him, he seemed unable or refused to see how he contributed to it. "What is the right thing?" he asked in a letter to Dr. Fischer.[25]

That March Himes and Lesley went off on holiday, driving to Italy in the Fiat Roadster to visit a prospective publisher before renting a house short-term at Cagnes-sur-Mer near Biot. One night while visiting Walter Coleman and Torun, who lived nearby, Chester grew jealous that Lesley was speaking to Walter's brother Emmett and struck her. They quarreled, Lesley insisting "I won't accept to be treated this way" and Chester that "You're my woman" before they came to some understanding or some impasse they could agree to let stand as one. Returning to Paris, they discovered that Regine was back in her old apartment and back at her old job. Lesley told her that she didn't know where Chester was when she phoned. Chester then fled back to Biot to stay with Walter and Torun, remaining with them all that spring.

By summer 1960, however, pity or latent guilt perhaps having got the upper hand, Himes was again living with Regine, this time in Austria, at Kitzbühel.

By September, he had left Regine and was back with Lesley, representing her as his fiancée in a letter to Van Vechten. In two months while at Kitzbühel he had finished *The Heat's On*, "about Sister Heavenly, Uncle Saint, Pinky (a giant Negro halfwit), a three-million-dollar bundle of dope . . . and my two hard shooting detectives."[26]

Shortly thereafter Lesley resigned her job at the *Herald Tribune* and she and Chester drove once again, in the Hillman, to Italy, touring Genoa, Naples, swinging in from the coast to visit Rome, before settling into a house at Acciaroli on the western shore below Salerno. Himes spoke vaguely of going from there to Africa. But the trip proved expensive and, winding up in Rome by the second week of November, Himes had to borrow money from Duhamel to settle debts. He and Lesley returned to the Riviera, to St. Tropez, where late that month they learned of Richard Wright's death. Back in Paris, Himes consoled Ellen and the children, helped with funeral arrangements, and afterward encouraged (perhaps even had a hand in) Ollie's writing of "The Last Days of Richard Wright" for *Ebony*.[27]

This period in Himes's life is the most unsettled of all, ceaseless hopscotch as he moves restlessly from Paris to Italy to the Côte d'Azur, from Lesley to Regine and back again. He and Lesley returned to the Riviera in early December following Wright's funeral. In March they were in Paris to attend the opening of an exhibition of Walter Coleman's jazz portraits. By April Chester appears to have been living alone in a small flat on the edge of Paris, across from the park at Les Buttes-Chaumont, as he put finishing touches on *Mamie Mason* for Olympia Press. The following month, it seems, he was again living with Regine, and in June the two of them returned to Hamburg, house- and dog-sitting again for Dr. Ramseger. From there they made their way to Darmstadt just south of Frankfurt, where they were guests of Chester's publisher, then on to Wiederstadt, where in early August Chester was arrested for drunken driving, held overnight, and, brought before the court the next morning, forbidden to drive again in Germany. Furious, Regine departed for her parents' home. Chester stayed with Walter and Torun before taking an apartment in Mougins-Village not far from Duhamel's splendid new home; at his editor's instigation he lunched and spent an afternoon with Picasso and family. Lesley, meanwhile, had returned to work, now with *Time-Life*.

Himes's emotional state, as one might surmise from the heavy drinking and arrest, was as inconstant as his address. He was heavily overdrawn on his account with Gallimard and months behind on the new book due them. External distractions abetted the internal: bad weather, visitors, the temptation of new work (journalism, scripts and treatments) that promised to bring in money but seldom did, the constant scramble for funds. He loved Lesley yet still felt bound, often infuriatingly so, to Regine, and at any rate "responsible" for her. He felt himself to be directionless, writing in a letter to Van Vechten that, now aged fifty-two, he has found neither country nor work nor destiny. "My brain was stale," he wrote of this period in *My Life of Absurdity*.[28] As for his work, he sensed little unity there either; in a manner, he believed, he had spent his time chasing after phantoms, skittering from one bare foothold to the next. All the old dissatisfactions with what he was doing reemerged. His detective stories had been fun at first, a pleasant change, full of new challenge and adventure and freedom, but now they'd become a grind. Even commercially, for all their popularity, the books remained on shaky ground. He couldn't count on U.S. publishers. They didn't know what to make of his thrillers, failing to realize, as the French did, that these novels were "violent and funny in a way never seen before,"[29] and proved hesitant to take the books on. When they did, they paid little, and brought them out in versions markedly cut, jumbled, or rearranged—*scrambled*, as Himes said. Even Gallimard, he suspected, constantly gave him short shrift, manipulating royalty statements, copies in print, and even actual sales to keep him in their debt and turning the books out.

He seems, in short, to have grown sick of the whole business, weary and exhausted from what he perceived as a continuous struggle. Quite the worst of it may have been that the drive to write, whatever it was that for all those years had impelled him past frustration and failure, was in decline: "I didn't like to write any more, but I knew there were several stories I had to write. I had to write until I found the definitive story or as long as I was able."[30] The passion was gone, or going, he suspected— and if not the passion, then certainly the energy. Yet at fifty-two, with absolutely nothing to fall back on, with no home—no country or other work, no destiny—what else could he do but go on writing?

A long letter to Lesley from this period serves both to reflect Himes's mood and as a rare document of self-analysis—a letter that, in its honesty, Lesley found deeply moving. He is, Himes says, hopelessly incomplete, wounded, alone and insecure; it is essential that Lesley understand this, that she not embrace some fantasy image of him. He is a liar, undependable, and for the most part despicable. He drinks to deaden his emotions and has lived in an agony of self-torture all his life.

I am in for it. The only thing that is going to let me out is death . . .
You should have known. Can you and I change this old and
terrible world?[31]

Yet he bid heartily for her love, and would continue to do so. He loved
her, he said, as he had loved only one other woman, Willa. Early the
next year (1962) they began living together. Three years later from the
Riviera, where he was working on the novel that would become *Blind
Man with a Pistol*, he wrote asking her again to marry him.

At the same time that he was writing his letter of confession to
Lesley, Himes initiated an affair with Marianne Greenwood, a
photographer and friend of Torun who lived in Antibes. Both Chester
and Marianne thought the affair time-limited, as she was soon to leave
for Guatemala to do a book on Latin America with writer Ernest Taube.
Taking her to Paris when the time came, on October 23, and starting
back home at 3 A.M., Himes fell asleep at the wheel and crashed the
Hillman. Lesley hurried to the hospital at Sens, having been called by
the police, and after Chester's discharge (Ollie Harrington paying the
bill) stayed with him at Hotel Aviatic, where shortly he collapsed. This
time they went to the American Hospital at Neuilly. Acute anemia and a
broken pelvis required weeks on crutches and bedrest.

Marianne, meanwhile, had delayed her departure until December,
and once released from the hospital at Neuilly, Chester flew to
Stockholm to spend a week with her. Returning to the Riviera, he rented
Marianne's apartment at Antibes. Himes spent the year's final weeks
courting Lesley, who had known of this affair almost from the first. In
March he moved into her new ground-floor, two-room apartment on
rue de la Harpe in the Latin Quarter near the Saint-Séverin church.

While at the American Hospital, Himes had been contacted by Pierre
Gaisseau, whose feature film *The Sky Above the Mud Below* had gained
much attention and who now with Arthur Cohn wanted to make a film
about Harlem life. Himes began drafting the script of what would
become *Baby Sister* while in hospital and completed it at Marianne's
apartment at Antibes. *Baby Sister* was never filmed, the project crippled
by failure to find support among American studios, conflicts between
Cohn and Gaisseau, and, at one point, a breakdown on Gaisseau's part;
Himes published the script in 1975's *Black on Black*.

That July, settled back in with Lesley, at the suggestion of Pierre Lazareff of *France-Soir*, and despite the unhappy collapse of an earlier collaboration with Lazareff, Himes traveled to New York to work with Gaisseau on a documentary of Harlem for French TV. Headquarters established at Lewis Micheaux's bookstore across from the Theresa Hotel, Himes, Gaisseau, and crew ranged far and wide: the Afro-American bank on 125th Street, Rosa Meta's beauty parlor, the upper fringe of Central Park, Adam Clayton Powell's Abyssinian Baptist Church. This was the film at a private showing of which Himes sat beside Lesley "sizzling with fury." Believing it filled with derisory, insulting clichés, not only did Himes withdraw his name from the project, he also wrote the article "Harlem, an American Cancer" in rebuttal. He had hoped to print it in Lazareff's own paper, such a piece being part of his and Lazareff's agreement, but *France-Soir* ignored it; eventually it appeared in *Présence Africaine* and *Die Welt*.

Back in Paris from New York and before the private showing, Chester had gone with Lesley, on vacation from her job, to Corsica, stopping off in Marseilles, where Chester was given royal treatment by the local Communist party paper, to visit Himes's old friend, physician and jazz drummer Roger Luccioni.

With Marianne, however, there was to be one further rendezvous. In January of the new year, 1963, using money advanced by Plon for a new detective novel, Himes flew to New York claiming business with agent Samuel French, and within the fortnight had touched down in the tiny fishing village of Sisal in the Yucatán. With little else to do, he turned out almost half of a new book, making no mention of Marianne in regular letters to Lesley, intimating to John A. Williams that he and Marianne had come to recognize irreconcilable differences both in their careers and their very personalities. Carl Brandt, meanwhile, whom Chester had approached to be his agent, wrote that upon asking around he had been told that Himes was "untrustworthy," and declined taking him on. Frequent letters from Lesley left Chester sodden with guilt.

One morning while in the Yucatán, February of 1963, Chester woke to find himself virtually unable to speak and paralyzed on one side. At the Merida Hospital it was believed that he had been stung by a scorpion. Lesley tried to get money to him and failed; finally he was able to return to the States on money wired to him by Van Vechten. There, while at New York's Presbyterian Hospital, he was looked after by Van Vechten and John A. Williams. Doctors diagnosed a stroke—the first of many that would eventually confine him to a wheelchair and make speech increasingly difficult. Ed and Constance Pearlstien remember his speech being slurred at this point. Discharged, Himes recuperated at the Albert Hotel before returning to Europe, and in March of 1963, one year after first moving in with Lesley, he again settled into the apartment at rue de la Harpe.

His old agent Samuel French refused to release him until he paid $500 they claimed he owed them. For all his labors, *The Lunatic Fringe* had failed either to develop into a viable novel or to attract publishers' interest. He proved unable to resell rights to *The Primitive* and *Cast the First Stone*, as he had felt certain of doing. Gallimard, having advanced money on two books still unwritten—and having learned in the bargain that Himes had contracted with Plon for a detective novel—was growing impatient, and now said that he owed the firm some 13,000 francs. Himes replied with complaints that Gallimard had billed him unfairly for costs incurred by them, while he often had spent his own funds for publicity on the publisher's behalf. To Duhamel he penned a bitter, spiteful letter that much upset the editor.

Still, while recuperating, Himes had finished his new detective novel, *Back to Africa*, which as *Cotton Comes to Harlem* became for him something of a breakthrough novel.

Through it all, even if sometimes patchily, work continued. Besides *Run Man Run*, *All Shot Up*, *The Heat's On*, and *Cotton Comes to Harlem*, Himes wrote the film treatment "Blow Gabriel Blow" for Louis Dolivet and the script of a documentary on Harlem (this is before the collaboration with Gaisseau) for Pierre Lazareff, neither of which was filmed. While living across from the park at Les Buttes-Chaumont, in two months he rewrote *Mamie Mason* for Olympia Press. He may have written in whole or in part another script, "An American Negro in Black Africa," that has been lost; in March of 1962, at any rate, he applied to the Association des Auteurs de Films for a copyright of that title. For some time, also, he was occupied in planning a multirecord history of jazz (which projected production costs prohibited taking any further) for Nicole Barclay, for whose company Richard Wright had begun writing liner notes late in life. And while in hospital, of course, Himes had begun, finishing soon thereafter, *Baby Sister*.

Whatever else he was, Chester Himes was visible:

1954:	*The Third Generation*	World
1955:	*The Primitive*	NAL
	If He Hollers Let Him Go	Berkley
1956:	*La fin d'un primitif*	Gallimard
	The Third Generation	Signet
1957:	*For Love of Imabelle*	Fawcett
	La Troisième génération	Plon
1958:	*La reine des pommes*	Gallimard
	Il pleut des coups durs	Gallimard
1959:	*The Real Cool Killers*	Avon
	Dare Dare	Gallimard
	Tout pour plaire	Gallimard
	Couché dans le pain	Gallimard
	The Crazy Kill	Avon
1960:	*The Big Gold Dream*	Avon
	Imbroglio Négro	Gallimard
	All Shot Up	Avon
1961:	*Ne nous énervons pas!*	Gallimard
	Pinktoes	Olympia Press
1962:	*Mamie Mason*	Plon
	The Real Cool Killers	Berkley
1963:	*Une affaire de viol*	Les Yeux Ouverts
1964:	*Retour en Afrique*	Plon

Did Himes exaggerate his renown? "My name had become a byword," he wrote. "I felt I had become more famous in Paris than any black American who had ever lived. Maybe I was right."[32] He was acclaimed, no doubt about it, and had been around the Latin Quarter long enough to have become a kind of sage to younger writers and artists, with Melvin Van Peebles, John A. Williams, poet Ted Joans, Cuban novelist Carlos Moore, Phil Lomax, and many others paying court. Still, Himes's manner is rarely less than hyperbolic; this is the man whose egocentricity allowed him to persuade himself, upon seeing Marcel Duhamel's new home, that it had been built with money swindled from Gallimard's authors—chiefly from his own detective novels, one senses that he wants to say, though he comes short of doing so.

In the arts, if you stay around long enough, if you survive, eventually you get acknowledged, even if but grudgingly so: reviewers, journalists, and the reading public can go on stepping over you only so long. Himes found himself becoming a sage, idolized not for the work itself (which was always in some measure cast away, as he said) but for the ideas and attitudes the work expressed. Interviews and articles became plentiful. *L'Arche* wrote of Himes and anti-Semitism in the United States. *Adam* wrote of Himes and poverty in the ghettoes, the black man's compulsion for white women. *Nouvel Observateur* wrote of Himes and of integration versus race nationalism. This was the dialectic around which black intellectual life had revolved since the days of W. E. B. Du Bois and Booker T. Washington. Now, though, the urgency had become such that speaking of it was like reading from a paper set on fire. (In New York in July of 1962 Himes saw for himself the early, non-combative manifestations of the burgeoning civil-rights movement, from which he would draw for the protestors of *Blind Man with a Pistol*.) Publication of *Une affaire de viol* in 1963 at the height of the Algerian War by a small leftist publisher famously sympathetic to the Algerian cause brought some notoriety, though much of this was secondary to the preface by novelist, feminist, and secretary of the Cannes Film Festival Christiane Rochfort, for the book was little read. Himes's account of the book's reception, Michel Fabre affirms, is grossly exaggerated: "To most French people who knew of him, he remained simply a writer of great detective stories."[33]

In his memoirs, typically, in a matter of pages Himes turns away from delight at his Parisian fame to complaints that he never made money from his books in France.

> The only French people who saw me were those who thought they could use me or get something out of me. I thought often of Duhamel; I have always thought he permitted French acquaintances to steal me blind but I do believe that every now and then he spoke up for me and said, "Enough's enough."[34]

This manifest of the victim mentality echoes Himes in his Chicago speech: "the effects of oppression on the human personality." Yet "It is not enough," remember, "to say we are victims of a stupid myth. We must know the reasons for this stupid myth and what it does to us."[35] Like Malcolm, Himes believed that one urgent revolution had to be against the misshapen black psyche itself. The other revolution believed necessary, that of a violent delivery from white society, he would try to describe, and finally abandon, in *Plan B*.

The hopscotch game, the movings-about, remained as frantic as ever. There were trips with Lesley to Biot and Cannes, to Antibes for summer holiday, Chester's retreat in December 1963 to Saint-Laurent-du-Var near Nice to work on *Back to Africa*. Chester and Lesley moved together in January of 1964 to a new flat at 3, rue Bourbon-le-Chateau near the Buci market, where their neighbor was painter Jean Miotte— truly a world away from the three-room shack where Chester wrote much of *Lonely Crusade*, or from rooms at the Theresa Hotel and Hotel Rachou.

> It was a fantastic location with the market at one end of the block and a clear view of St. Germain-des-Prés on the other side, with a small park just beneath the windows—Place de Fürstenburg. But the difficulty was one had to climb seven flights of stairs to get to it . . . It had a big, ornate bath with many mirrors inside the door, then a medium-size bar, behind which was the stove and sink for washing up and in front of which was a large expanse of living room with a window and a big dining-room table built around the central beam; beyond was the open chimney with a long settee in front, then stairs that climbed to a bedroom upstairs with large double doors opening onto a large railed balcony which held six or eight chairs with a clear view of the nearby park and St. Germain-des-Prés at the end of rue de l'Abbaye.[36]

Chester and Jean Miotte often came across one another in the St. Germain-des-Prés, and began spending time together at one another's apartments. They had first met the year before, 1962, at the Café Old Navy, when Chester and Lesley were living at the Hotel de Seine. Miotte's wife, like Lesley, worked at *Time-Life*; it was Miotte who found the apartment for them, having lived in the building since 1959.

These two artists of a different sort would go on visiting and corresponding over the years. On one of the visits, for which Chester met Miotte at the Harbor of Valencia in his Jaguar, they engaged in a series of conversations of which Miotte kept a record, later transcribing them into the dialogue *Miotte-Himes*, published by SMI/L'art se reconte in 1977. There was also talk of a proposed ballet, *Angels in Harlem*, for which Miotte would design sets, and for which Chester drew up a scenario. Miotte believes that both Chester's comedy and the sheer force of his personality shining through, his deep and abiding anger, tend to obscure the work's intense tragedy. He remembers going into the Doubleday bookstore on Fifth Avenue and asking for the newest Chester Himes book and no one there knowing who Chester was. He remembers Chester smiling and laughing with friends, not at all a difficult man, though he kept his reserve among people he didn't know. Of course he was upon occasion bitter at the reception of his books, Miotte says—how could he not be?—but for all that always charming, intelligent, spiritual and open-minded. Even in later years, after a number of strokes and through heavy pain, Chester went on producing strong work, Miotte says; we must admire that. Miotte last saw his old friend during one of the final visits to Paris when he pushed Chester in his wheelchair across the Luxembourg Gardens to Montparnasse to dine at La Coupole.

The lease on the rue Bourbon-le-Château apartment having expired, Lesley moved to another on rue d'Assas while Chester withdrew to the Palais Ravage in Cannes to work on *Blind Man with a Pistol*. From there he soon wrote to complain of pedestrian progress. The book was coming along but would not come alive. He had little notion where it was headed, worried that he had lost control. Whatever he did, the story refused to "swing" the way he wanted it to do.[37] There was no sense of style, his pacing was off.[38] Old doubts swarmed up, that eternal horror of the creative artist before bare canvas or page, the suspicion that, *this time*, he won't be able to bring it off, the magic won't return to him, he hasn't a clue. Autumn weather wore on Himes, underscoring his isolation, uncertainties and self-interrogations. To make matters worse, the Colemans' marriage was breaking up before his eyes.

Following a trip to New York to resolve problems with *Pinktoes*, to be published that year (1965), Chester moved in with Lesley at the apartment on rue d'Assas. In New York he learned that Bill Targ was about to marry literary agent Roslyn Seigel. In Paris he bought a Jaguar.

Chester and Lesley had vacationed that June in Greece. In October Lesley gave up her job at *Time-Life* and the couple drove in the new Jag to Denmark, where they lived for some months near Copenhagen. Chester first began writing about his early European experiences while here. By February he and Lesley had grown weary of the harsh winter and (to Chester's thinking) the equally harsh Danish character. Mid-March, before proceeding on to Aix-en-Provence, they were Daniel Guérin's guests at La Ciotat, no longer an artists' colony but again Guérin's private residence; here Chester began his autobiography in earnest.

They removed then, in July, to Aix-en-Provence, to a farmhouse near Saint-Hippolyte at Venelles, outside Aix on the route to Manosque where Jean Giono lived. Chester loved the seclusion, lack of distraction, and easygoing pace, loved even having visitors. He was increasingly troubled by arthritis, however, and lacking in energy. He puttered about the farm, retired early, worked sporadically at the autobiography and piecemeal at novels or other projects. From the congested manuscript of *Plan B* he worried out "Tang" and "Prediction" for publication as short stories.

Beset for years by dental problems, and mistrusting French dentists as he mistrusted Danish barbers, in May Chester flew to New York to have dentures made. While there, at the insistence of Samuel Goldwyn, who had bought the book the previous year, Himes wrote a treatment for *Cotton Comes to Harlem* that was nonetheless rejected. Lesley joined him in mid-June, after which they returned to Venelles, briefly since the farm had been sold, then sublet a friend's Paris flat in the 5th arrondissement at 21, rue de l'Estrapade, close to the market on rue Mouffetard and just off tourist-thronged Place de le Contrescarpe.

In October then, at the invitation of Chester's Dutch agent, Chester and Lesley relocated to Holland for several months. Later in the year they went to Spain, touring Madrid, Alicante, and Gibraltar, crossing to Tangiers for the holidays. In Alicante, overlooking the sea at Moraira-Teulada, they bought land upon which to have a house, Casa Griot, built. Remaining in Spain till the following May, they returned to Paris in time to witness the student riots, staying first in an apartment on rue Abel-Ferry in the 16th arrondissement belonging to

Nicole Toutain, longtime companion of Himes's old friend and Tournon compatriot Larry Potter. Upon return from a brief trip to London, however, they discovered that the rioting had broken out of the Latin Quarter and grown to dangerous levels, and they withdrew to quieter lodgings near Montparnasse.

That September, 1968, Chester and Lesley moved to Alicante, after which time visits to France were rare and of short duration: a stopover in May of the following year on the way to London, attendance at the Nice Book Fair from May 26 to June 2 of 1970, a trip then with the Targs to St. Tropez and Arles. Also in 1970 they returned to Paris to celebrate publication of *Blind Man with a Pistol* with parties at Gallimard, a TV program from ORTF and a private showing of *Cotton Comes to Harlem*. This was one of only three visits to Paris in the whole of the seventies, these generally for medical reasons. Chester's French decade, seven years in Paris, three mostly in the south of France, was over.

From Holland during that 1968 sojourn Himes had sent Bill Targ an early version of the autobiography. Targ divined in this early sample many of the project's ongoing problems. The whole thing was strangely off center, oddly displaced. There was far too much of Himes's emotional and romantic life, and far too little, finally, of the man himself, to engage the reader's sympathy. Page after page rushed past his writing, his first marriage, his literary friendships, the expatriate community, the development of his books, only to eulogize the white women he loved and expatiate yet again at the social taboos set against them.

From Holland also, Himes sent Roslyn Targ, on November 11, the manuscript of *Blind Man with a Pistol*.

18 Black Ruins of My Life

In the summer of 1901, Harvard's Charles Peabody arrived in the Mississippi Delta to excavate Indian mounds near the Stovall and Carson plantations. In time-honored safari tradition he stopped at the nearest civilized outpost, Clarksdale, to stock up on provisions and equipment, and to hire a band of local workmen. As they struck out together for the site, Peabody was astonished to hear the band break into song. A leader would holler out a line, improvising, Peabody slowly realized, on the life about him—scenes they passed, women or other community members everyone knew, the proclivities of certain men in the crew—and others would respond. Shortly, as work at the site began, Peabody found himself incorporated into the songs. "Mighty long half-day Captain," the crew sang at one point, on a Saturday when work failed to break off at noon as promised. On another, as Peabody and a white associate sat idly by, tossing a knife into the ground while workers labored deep in the excavation: "I'm so tired I'm most dead/ Sittin' up there playin' mumbley-peg." It was all remarkably impure: the workers sang (to Peabody's ear) badly out of tune, from time to time breaking into wild whooping sounds or contorting their voices as they commented on their surroundings, swapped insults, passed tall tales back and forth, or quoted from the Bible. But they were, Peabody perceived, and in ways he had never before encountered, all the while imaginatively, fluidly, vividly re-creating their world, even as it flowed about them.

Despite the excellence of much other work and *The End of a Primitive*'s deserved recognition as a classic, it is almost certainly for his Harlem detective novels that Chester Himes will be remembered. Even throughout Europe and in France, where *Lonely Crusade* upon publication was named one of the five best new novels from America,

Himes's greatest fame derived from the detective novels. These are the books that have kept him (if generally far back from the footlights) before the American public, attracting new generations of readers and conducting the more serious of them to earlier work. Much Himes criticism, circumventing or summarizing the rest of his output, goes directly to the detective novels; these, at least, have come to be regarded as extraordinary achievements, unique contributions in extending the reach of both the detective novel and the American social novel. Lundquist, Milliken, and Muller all devote fully a fifth of their studies to the Harlem novels. Dozens of scholarly and more general articles have addressed such aspects as the place of these novels in the history of the urban detective story or of protest literature, their affinities with the work of Hemingway and Faulkner and *Black Mask* writers, their satire or use of religious figures, relation to African-American storytelling traditions, possible origins in Himes's own background. Robert Skinner has written a fine, full-length study of the detective novels, *Two Guns from Harlem*. What Himes described almost thirty years ago in these novels and what people at the time thought flights of bitter fantasy, Skinner holds, has become routine front-page news:

> Himes chronicled a bitter decade during which Blacks stopped allowing whites to ignore their world and forced Black concerns and Black problems into the light . . . Like Raymond Chandler and a few others, he has written, in fictional blood and crime, a social history of a time and place . . . the mean streets of Black America at mid-century.[1]

Stephen Soitos in *The Blues Detective* considers at length Himes's central position in transforming the black mystery from such early work as Rudolph Fisher's to the metacultural investigations of Ishmael Reed and Clarence Major. Soitos tracks four tropes through the work of all these. The black detective persona, in contrast to that of the typical lone-wolf white detective, Soitos finds uniquely representative of a community with its own intrinsic values. "Double-consciousness detection" discovers its image in these works as an emphasis on masks, disguises, and false identities, embodying the figure of the trickster from African and African-American folklore. Black vernaculars, not only those of speech but also of cuisine, music, dance, and dress, are embraced. Finally, in what may be the most potent expression of alternative African-American worldviews, hoodoo traditions assert their presence. Hoodoo is itself a type of black vernacular, one with tacit, deep-rooted assumptions about the true (as opposed to visible) nature of the world.

"While the Negro lives and moves in the midst of white civilization, everything that he touches is re-interpreted for his own use," Zora Neale Hurston wrote.[2] Just as the black had initially to reinvent his life in this new land so utterly alien to him, so must he go on, in a land no longer new but one that still denies him much and remains in many ways alien, reimagining again and again a place for himself, a history and community, an identity, life. Himes in the Harlem novels directly occupied himself with depicting these reimaginings, those documented by the blues and by Professor Peabody on his expedition into deepest Mississippi as much as those signaled by Hurston and by Soitos's discussion of hoodoo. Himes's stories present themselves to us masked, borne up on floes of language, braggadocio, artful insult, irony, and circumlocution, spinning out tall and wild even as the tale-teller assures us all the while they are true—telling truths unavailable to mimetic European models. These stories document realities of African-American life as nothing before had done, give us 72-point headlines from a world that never existed: real toads in the most unrelenting imaginary gardens.

Until well into his forties, Chester Himes struggled to fit his individualist vision into accepted modes of the time. For all his brilliance and for all the force, sometimes raw, other times carefully marshaled, of his writing, his work was not all that different from contemporaries like Richard Wright. Whatever else he might be, though, he was a *serious* writer; his transition to writing detective novels, at least initially, surprised himself as much as it did his critics. *Surprise* may be the key word. Himes, like a jazzman taking up some old sow's ear of a song, looking to see what's *in there*, found a great deal in there, turning it to silk-purse music never heard before.

His remarkable combinations of humor, pathos, sex, horror, and just plain home truths are very similar to those of the bitter and beautiful blues lyrics and to the traditional black humor that is essentially laughter at black degradation, laughter curiously close to tears or to howling rage. He kept intact all the paraphernalia of the detective subgenre—complicated intrigues, heroes and villains, shaggy monsters and interesting victims, horrendous acts of violence. He managed at the same time, with the sense of lived reality he infuses throughout these novels, to suggest very clearly what the quality of life must be in a huge black urban ghetto, a vast area within a modern city that is literally a jungle filled with rapacious animals, thanks to the impenetrable indifference of established authority to everything that goes on there.[3]

The form of the detective novel freed Himes from autobiography and, one assumes, because of its presumed lack of seriousness, from inhibitions. Perhaps in giving him license to depict no-holds-barred his vision of our society as fundamentally racist and profoundly corrupt, the form also gave some release from his sense of the injustices America had done him. Certainly he discovered that the form's emphasis on suspicion, violence, and fear could prove a perfect vehicle for conveying his view of blacks in American society. And while their thrust was no longer autobiographical, Himes peopled the novels with intimates from his Ohio days and with protagonists modeled in part on himself. Sheik in *The Real Cool Killers* closely resembles Himes in appearance and mien;[4] Johnny Perry in *The Crazy Kill* seems almost an idealized self-portrait. With these books, Lundquist says, Himes reached "an objectified vision in which the pain he has known as a black man becomes externalized and even universalized,"[5] his detectives at once personifications of the racial problem in the United States and an inquiry into both its absurdities and possible outcomes. Most importantly, with creation of his larger-than-life detectives and overblown, hyperbolic style, Himes claimed for his work something of the power and authority of myth.

Grave Digger and Coffin Ed weren't crooked detectives, but they were tough. They had to be tough to work in Harlem. Colored folks didn't respect colored cops. But they respected big shiny pistols and sudden death. It was said in Harlem that Coffin Ed's pistol would kill a rock and that Grave Digger's would bury it.

They took their tribute, like all real cops, from the established underworld catering to the essential needs of the people—

gamekeepers, madams, street-walkers, numbers writers, numbers bankers. But they were rough on purse snatchers, muggers, burglars, con men, and all strangers working any racket. And they didn't like rough stuff from anybody else but themselves. "Keep it cool," they warned. "Don't make graves."[6]

Himes intended Grave Digger and Coffin Ed from the first to be heroes. They are, Milliken says, "just possibly the two toughest men alive."[7] Born around 1922, homeboys raised in Harlem and veterans of World War 2, probably as M.P.'s, they were promoted to the rank of detective in the early fifties, and are still awaiting, over a decade later, when the books end, any further promotion, steadily losing ground to inflation, ever-higher costs of living, debts they've contracted for cars and neighboring homes on Long Island. They are, and are increasingly aware of being, mediators, go-betweens, ambassadors between parallel cultures—interlocutors. But on the streets of Harlem they rule, as in their unforgettable first appearance.

> Grave Digger stood on the right side of the front end of the line, at the entrance to the Savoy. Coffin Ed stood on the left side of the line, at the rear end. Grave Digger had his pistol aimed south, in a straight line down the sidewalk. On the other side, Coffin Ed had his pistol aimed north, in a straight line. There was space enough between the two imaginary lines for two persons to stand side by side. Whenever anyone moved out of line, Grave Digger would shout, "Straighten up!" and Coffin Ed would echo, "Count off!" If the offender didn't straighten up the line immediately, one of the detectives would shoot into the air. The couples in the queue would close together as though pressed between two concrete walls. Folks in Harlem believed that Grave Digger Jones and Coffin Ed Johnson would shoot a man stone dead for not standing straight in a line.[8]

Physical descriptions of the detectives verge on the formulaic, "tall, loose-jointed, sloppily dressed, ordinary-looking dark-brown colored men"[9] in that first appearance, subsequent descriptions echoing it while adding *lanky, big-shouldered, flat-footed, big, rugged, rough,* and *dangerous* to the catalog of adjectives. At various times the pair is said to resemble "plowhands in Sunday suits at a Saturday night jamboree" and "two hog farmers on a weekend in the Big Town."[10] They are "dressed in black mohair suits that looked as though they'd been slept in," "wearing dark battered felt hats and wrinkled black alpaca suits."[11]As though to emphasize the universality of his detectives, Himes rarely carries descriptions of them much further than this, demonstrating that particular genius informing the Harlem novels: his ability simultaneously to locate his narrative in a realistic, seemingly "ordinary" world, and in one timeless, dreamlike, metaphorical. For this very reason, Milliken notes, despite over half a million words devoted to them, "the two detectives remain to the end, in many ways, shadowy and elusive figures, more adumbrated than defined."[12]

Repeatedly, as with the hog farmer and plowhand similes, Himes stresses—quite in contrast to their fierce reputation throughout Harlem—the unremarkable appearance of his pair, adding again and again, still further to emphasize this, that they are virtually indistinguishable one from another. Ed's face, scarred by acid thrown at him in *A Rage in Harlem*, represents the chief difference. For this, Ed has gained comparisons to and the occasional nickname Frankenstein. The grafted skin is a shade or so lighter than the old; in addition, a tic develops when he is tense and helps transform his face to a devil mask. Ed is ever the more pragmatic and quicker to act, and often must be restrained by Digger, who is himself more given, if but slightly more, to thoughtfulness, even to brooding. The two, however, are remarkably in accord, machines that, set in motion, continue on course, rolling through or over every obstacle, until the job gets done. This heroic stance makes all the more vivid their growing impotence, so that when in *Blind Man with a Pistol* we see them standing forlornly by, their car having been torched and themselves beaten, or told by young Black Muslim minister Michael X that the two of them "don't really count in the overall pattern,"[13] these are terrible moments.

Robert Skinner has suggested that Himes was taken by the romanticism of the heroic myth.[14] Not only Johnson and Jones but also characters such as Casper Holmes and Johnny Perry reflect this. Himes's heroes, though, are not the saintly heroes of Christian myth but ambiguous, deeply flawed ones common to such as Greek or Norse mythology, who use otherworldly strength and power to satisfy quite worldly instincts. Skinner points to the pistols, always lovingly described and brandished about like the magical weapons of sword-and-sorcery heroes—even, in the tracer bullets favored by the detectives in *Cotton Comes to Harlem*, taking on the gods' own element, fire.

Near the end of *Blind Man with a Pistol*, in pages riddled with the words *think, believe, know, ask*, Grave Digger and Coffin Ed look about them in the African-American bookstore where they meet Michael X. Stripped of their powers and of understanding, the detectives find that "In that room it was easy to believe in a Black World."[15] But outside, the streets of Harlem are boiling over, and one of the store's back rooms is filled with relics of the slave trade. Michael intimates that he knows who Mister Big is but won't say, telling the detectives repeatedly to ask their boss. We all know by this time who "Mister Big" is, of course: the whole corrupt society.

> "You keep on talking like that you won't live long," Grave Digger said.
>
> Michael X put on his polished spectacles and looked at the detectives with a sharp-eyed sardonicism. "You think someone is going to kill me?"
>
> "People been killed for less," Grave Digger said.[16]

Except for the fact of his black characters and Harlem setting, Himes began the series in *A Rage in Harlem* as more or less standard crime fare. The plot hinges on a scam, a machine that supposedly turns small-denomination bills to larger ones. There is an ongoing parade of Harlem lowlife, a treasure (in this case a trunk of "gold ore") that keeps changing hands, a good-hearted innocent suffering at the hand of sharpies, the ever-present imprint of religion (Jackson repeatedly prays for strength during his ordeals and twice visits a minister for counsel, half-brother Goldy works the streets disguised as a nun), and comedy of every mettle: slapstick, cartoonlike, bitter. Much of the text expounds Himes's own brand of outrageous street-level realism; the canvas is large.

> The Harlem of Chester Himes's detective stories is seen almost exclusively through the distorting lens of crime, but the spectrum of characters included is astonishingly full and varied. Almost all of these characters are representative types . . . but they

are all vigorously alive. They function as caricatures and symbols but also as viable literary characters. The axis about which they orient themselves is crime, either adherence to crime as a way of life or a passionate (though not exactly uncompromising) rejection of crime in all its forms. They are either innocent or guilty, in the terms of Grave Digger and Coffin Ed, but, more fundamentally, they are either "squares" or "sharpies," an equally absolute distinction.[17]

Skinner points out that Himes's work resembles not so much Hammett's or Chandler's as it does that of James M. Cain or W. R. Burnett, writers who dealt with life at the bottom, often writing from the transgressor's point of view. For Himes's detectives violence, greed, treachery, and deception of every sort are simple coin of the realm; they expect little else. The pair maintain a network of snitches among Harlem's petty thieves and hustlers, routinely use their influence to shield some wrongdoers in exchange for information on others, even keep a pusher on tap to supply drugs to their stoolies. In *The Real Cool Killers* Grave Digger slaps a barkeep after pulling him halfway across the bar; in *The Crazy Kill* the detectives torture young gambler Chink Charlie for information; in *A Rage in Harlem* Digger tells Imabelle "I'll pistol-whip your face until no man ever looks at you again"; in *The Heat's On* Ed strips a witness and cuts her, then, when she faints, slaps her back to consciousness.

Johnson and Jones take their attitude from the American national philosophy, pragmatism: damn the explanations and full speed ahead, go with what works. Their judgments are simplistic, rigid, self-righteous, authoritarian. Yet, as if from the first they recognize some deep divide in their souls, they spend considerable time rationalizing their actions to others and to themselves. They know that in their own manner they are as morally wrong, as misdirected in their efforts and as predatory, as are those they come up against. They belong to a simpler, less complex time—as they themselves come to realize. By *Blind Man with a Pistol* their world simply does not work anymore. Given a series of cases to solve, they beat at the heads of presumed witnesses and threaten half the populace of Harlem all to no avail. They cannot penetrate any of the mysteries presented them, they no longer understand the swirls of activity about them on the street. And they wonder aloud what has changed. *Their* generation never really believed that white America would give them equality, Grave Digger says. *This* generation does, and it makes them crazy.

"Hell, Ed, you got to realize times have changed since we were sprites. These youngsters were born just after we got through fighting a war to wipe out racism and make the world safe for the four freedoms. And you and me were born just after our pappys had got through fighting a war to make the world safe for democracy. But the difference is that by the time we'd fought in a jim crow army to whip the Nazis and had come home to our native racism, we didn't believe any of that shit. We knew better. We had grown up in the Depression and fought under hypocrites against hypocrites and we'd learned by then that whitey is a liar. Maybe our parents were just like our children and believed their lies but we had learned the only difference between the home-grown racist and the foreign racist was who had the nigger. Our side won so our white rulers were able to keep their niggers so they would yap to their heart's content about how they were going to give us equality as soon as we were ready."[18]

Coffin Ed and Grave Digger came into being at a critical time in the civil-rights struggle. From the first, born to accommodation's formal dress and living with more contemporary casual styles, they were anachronistic, brandishing icons of black pride and black culture while enforcing the white man's coercive laws. And in their lifetime the world has bootstrapped itself almost beyond recognition. As Lundquist notes: "Gamblers and opium-addict preachers are one thing to deal with; Brotherhood, Black Power, Black Jesus, and the Black Muslims are quite another."[19]

It's in part from the social changes swirling about the detectives, in larger part from the divide within their own souls, that the Harlem books evolve. The unwinding of Grave Digger and Coffin Ed as they move from earlier settings, in which crimes are actually solved, through increasing confusion to the cul de sacs of *Blind Man* is in itself a powerful statement on this period in our country's history, Lundquist points out, continuing: "But it is perhaps not so much what Himes says by way of protest as he extends the Grave Digger and Coffin Ed stories over the years that is important, but how he says it through the modification of the detective novel itself."[20] This modification, like any evolution, was gradual and progressive, following a logic of its own as Himes pushed ever deeper into the territory. Edward Margolies suggests that Himes never transcended the formula, as occasionally Hammett and Chandler did, but that instead he simply pushed the pulp-detective view to its logical conclusion. As he did so, his Harlem figures become ever more grotesque, moving from clownish innocents, fast-talking hustlers, and pimps to the Black Jesus, or Reverend Sam with his bevy of wives and flock of naked children feeding from troughs.

Margolies also points out that Himes's detective novels, six of the eight published within five years and three written in one twelve-month period in 1957–58, may appear at first glance artless. Momentum and surprise seem everything. The often bewildering plots accrue from chains of brief scenes which are themselves composed of runs of dialogue, like planks laid out across sawhorses of physical description. Narrated in omniscient third person, the stories move back and forth in time as well as space, hopscotching from one line of action or set of characters to another, from present-time scenes to scenes set hours, even days, earlier.

> The action unfolds in perpetual, and very elastic, present time. Whenever the narrative line shifts, and it shifts drastically every five or six pages, the move is always to the point of maximum contrast, without regard to chronology.[21]

No one had written like this before. Yet it was the perfect medium for capturing Himes's inner city, the fervid, feverish activity of it, its diversity and confusion of forces, the eternal present of its people. The technique, Milliken notes, is close to that of film, perhaps as close as writing can come. There is little discursiveness. We know Himes's characters solely by their appearance, their conversation, their actions. Passages such as this one from *The Crazy Kill* demonstrate how remarkably visual the style has become. While watching police chase a thief in the streets below, a man has leaned too far out an upper-story window and landed in a delivery truck.

Time passed.

Slowly the surface of the bread began to stir. A loaf rose and dropped over the side of the basket to the sidewalk as though the bread had begun to boil. Another squashed loaf followed.

Slowly, the man began erupting from the basket like a zombie rising from the grave. His head and shoulders came up first. He gripped the edges of the basket, and his torso straightened. He put a leg over the side and felt for the sidewalk with his foot. The sidewalk was still there. He put a little weight on his foot to test the sidewalk. The sidewalk was steady.[22]

Throughout the series, too—these quickly became a trademark—Himes introduced static, descriptive vignettes, brief set pieces that have a documentary feel, reading as though the camera were tracking soundlessly down Harlem streets and across rooftops.

Even at past two in the morning, "The Valley," that flat lowland of Harlem east of Seventh Avenue, was like the frying pan of hell. Heat was coming out of the pavement, bubbling from the asphalt; and the atmospheric pressure was pushing it back to earth like the lid on a pan.

Colored people were cooking in their overcrowded, overpriced tenements; cooking in the streets, in the after-hours joints, in the brothels; seasoned with vice, disease and crime.

An effluvium of hot stinks arose from the frying pan and hung in the hot motionless air, no higher than the rooftops—the smell of sizzling barbecue, fried hair, exhaust fumes, rotting garbage, cheap perfumes, unwashed bodies, decayed buildings, dog-rat-and-cat offal, whiskey and vomit, and all the old dried-up odors of poverty.

Half-nude people sat in open windows, crowded on the fire escapes, shuffled up and down the sidewalks, prowled up and down the streets in dilapidated cars.

It was too hot to sleep. Everyone was too evil to love. And it was too noisy to relax and dream of cool swimming holes and the shade of chinaberry trees. The night was filled with the blare of countless radios, the frenetic blasting of spasm cats playing in the streets, hysterical laughter, automobile horns, strident curses, loudmouthed arguments, the screams of knife fights.

The bars were closed so they were drinking out of bottles. That was all there was left to do, drink strong bad whiskey and get hotter; and after that steal and fight.[23]

. . . .

Blank-eyed whores stood on the street corner swapping obscenities with twitching junkies. Muggers and thieves slouched in the dark doorways waiting for someone to rob; but there wasn't anyone but each other. Children ran down the street, the dirty street littered with rotting vegetables, uncollected garbage, battered garbage cans, broken glass, dog offal—always running, ducking, and dodging. Listless mothers stood in the dark entrances of tenements and swapped talk about their men, their jobs, their poverty, their hunger, their debts, their Gods, their religions, their preachers, their children, their aches and pains, their bad luck with numbers and the evilness of white people.[24]

. . . .

Looking eastward from the towers of Riverside Church, perched among the university buildings on the high banks of the Hudson River, in a valley far below, waves of gray rooftops distort the perspective like the surface of a sea. Below the surface, in the murky waters of fetid tenements, a city of black people who are convulsed in desperate living, like the voracious churning of millions of hungry cannibal fish. Blind mouths eating their own guts. Stick in a hand and draw back a nub.

That is Harlem.

The farther east it goes, the blacker it gets.

East of Seventh Avenue to the Harlem River is called The Valley. Tenements thick with teeming life spread in dismal squalor. Rats and cockroaches compete with the mangy dogs and cats for the man-gnawed bones.[25]

Himes's Harlem is an imaginary place, owing as much to traditions of the folktale as to observation or attempts at verisimilitude. Out of this "big turbulent sea of black humanity"[26] surface a wide range of characters, some but for an instant, others for the duration of a book, all of them, for all their diversity, their bizarreness, and their cruelties, united by suffering. Forced to live in such circumstances, their lives have become warped and stunted to fit. Life is a continuous struggle just to stay afloat, so one must keep moving. Death—ugly, quick, real—peers out at them from every dark doorway, every alley mouth, every stopped car.

Deception, violence, and death are the very streets and stairways of Himes's Harlem. And because the comic voice springs up always to fill the crawlspaces between the presumed and the actual, between what we pretend life to be and what it is, comedy here becomes Harlem's native language. In *A Rage in Harlem* everyone plots to take possession of a trunk of what turns out to be only fool's gold. In *Cotton Comes to Harlem* it's a bale of cotton filled with $87,000 belonging to a fanatic white Alabaman colonel that keeps changing hands, in *The Heat's On* three million dollars' worth of heroin stuffed into a string of Hudson River eels. A motorcyclist chased by Grave Digger and Coffin Ed passes a truck carrying sheet metal and is decapitated, but his body carries on, the motorcycle at last crashing into a jewelry store whose sign reads *We Will Give Credit to the Dead*. A man walks about Harlem with a knife handle protruding from one side of his skull, two inches of blade from the other. A lady talking to her minister has the back of her dress cut away by a thief to get the purse strapped to her back and goes off down the street showing buttocks and rose-colored underwear to passersby, one of whom finally tells her "Lady . . . your ass is out." An old man sits on the marquee of a movie house fishing with his cane pole among pork ribs cooking on a makeshift grill below.

Interestingly, Himes's theme of violence and his most exacting depiction of Harlem, of an actual rather than metaphoric Harlem, reached its peak in his one nondetective thriller, *Run Man Run*, a small masterpiece of sustained narrative momentum and intense psychological terror. Himes took great pains to get everything right here, describing streets and settings in detail, freely appropriating elements of his own life, from alcoholic blackouts and the ignominy of an educated man relegated to unskilled labor, to actual circumstances of his employment at Horn & Hardart, to lend his story verisimilitude.

Jimmy Johnson, graduate of a black college in Durham, North Carolina, attends Columbia University, where he studies law, and works nights as porter in an automat. Six feet tall and powerfully built, he is intelligent, thoughtful, and articulate, but also upon occasion truculent, unwilling to yield when his rights are challenged by whites: "He just wanted to be treated like a man, was all."[27] One night Jimmy witnesses the murder of two other porters by white policeman Matt Walker who in thrall to an alcoholic blackout has misplaced his car and wildly surmised that the porters are responsible then thinks better of it but decides "to scare the Negroes anyway. It'd be good for them. If they were innocent, it'd help keep them that way."[28] Accidentally shooting the first man sobers Walker at a blow but he goes ahead and kills him, then kills the second porter and chases after Jimmy, who has just surfaced from the basement. The book is given over to Walker's inexorable pursuit of Jimmy Johnson.

Walker is boyish, attractive, and charming, protected by his position, by his very whiteness, and by his brother-in-law, Matt's direct superior on the force, who knows early on what has happened yet keeps hoping Walker will come to his senses. But with the shooting something has snapped, setting free within Walker a psychotic hatred of blacks.

Matt Walker may be the purest symbol of American racism Himes ever proposed. To all pretense and appearance one thing—a force for the good, a protector, a kindhearted man who takes an interest in those he meets (presenting himself in this manner to Jimmy's girlfriend before he seduces her)—he is quite another. In a closed loop reminiscent of the later *Blind Man*'s absurdism (recalling also Kenneth Fearing's classic use of this trope), Walker is set to investigate the very crime he committed. He is protected by society's own two-facedness, by the gaps between what it says and what it does—by, in fact, every force of society. And Jimmy cannot get away from him. "What menaces Jimmy, basically," Milliken states, "is not one sick young man in a privileged position, but the national psychosis of racism, fully exposed."[29]

Jimmy's constant attempts, as an intelligent man, to understand what is happening only serve to highlight the meaninglessness of Walker's violence.

"Maybe he was all right when he first went on the force. Maybe something happened to him since he's been a detective. Some of them can't take it. There are men who go crazy from the power it gives them to carry a gun. And he's on the vice squad too. There's no telling what might happen to a man's mind who constantly associates with criminals and prostitutes."[30]

All of Jimmy's intelligence and understanding are of no avail against Walker's hatred and society's indifference. Himes's choice of scenes and language, the very artfulness of this book, with *The Primitive* and *If He Hollers*, his most carefully constructed novel, lend an amazing impact to Jimmy's plight. On the novel's first page "an ice-cold razor-edged wind" whistles down Fifth Avenue. Jimmy first escapes Walker through a series of underground passages linking the basements of separate buildings, after which in effect the entire city becomes a maze, a labyrinth.

Rather like Himes's detective team by the time of *Blind Man*, Jimmy Johnson in many ways seems the product of earlier, simpler days. Girlfriend Linda calls him a fool and a baby, protected (she implies) by his privileged upbringing, his education, and his pretense of a rational world. Harlem here, too, sometimes seems more closely akin to the Harlem Renaissance's brief, bright headlights than to the surrounding darkness. Passing a bookstore, in a scene reminiscent of Grave Digger's and Coffin Ed's meeting with Michael X in another bookstore where they feel for a moment the possibilities of a secure black world before venturing again into the streets, Jimmy sees books by Richard Wright, Claude McKay, George Schuyler, James Weldon Johnson, Langston Hughes, and Rudolph Fisher on display.

> Suddenly he felt safe. There, in the heart of the Negro community, he was lulled into a sense of absolute security. He was surrounded by black people who talked his language and thought his thoughts; he was served by black people in businesses catering to black people; he was presented with the literature of black people. *Black* was a big word in Harlem. No wonder so many Negro people desired their own neighborhood, he thought. They felt safe; there was safety in numbers.[31]

But of course, as Jimmy finds, there *is* no safety in numbers, nor in Harlem, nor in American society, and his sense of same is little more than further manifestation of his self-deception.

Stephen Soitos believes that the detective story, conflated with the social background of Harlem, perfectly suited Himes's anecdotal style, race-consciousness, and flair for satire, allowing him in the Harlem cycle to fuse imagination and reality in fresh, exciting ways. Himes took the violence so integral to detective fiction to new planes of expression, Soitos holds, moving "from comic vision to a serious confrontation."[32] Gradually violence replaced religion, sex, and money as the means of unifying Himes's narrative and, ultimately, of describing his world.

> The violence in Himes's novels develops throughout the works as he portrays a community in turmoil, tilting towards chaos and then erupting into anarchy. Finally, in the last works, violence becomes a tool of revolt as well as an expression of despair.[33]

For Soitos, *Run Man Run*, with its portrayal of racial hatred in the pursuit of young Jimmy Johnson by psychotic white policeman Matt Walker, and *Blind Man with a Pistol*, with its condemnation of unorganized violence, are key texts in Himes's use of violence. *Plan B*'s apocalyptic vision of the futility of *all* violence took this theme to its last bitter end, but the apocalypse is there already at the halfway point of *Blind Man with a Pistol*. On Nat Turner Day, three marching groups, all of them led by messianic figures, converge from different directions towards a free-for-all at 135th Street and Seventh Avenue. Brotherly Love is shepherded by a well-intentioned, simple-minded black youth and his white female companion, Black Power by a man whose exceedingly comfortable life is supported by funds from disciples and from the troop of black prostitutes he manages, Black Jesus by Prophet Ham whose own hatred of whites whips his acolytes to a frenzy. While Himes presents the confrontation in broad comic strokes, clearly he despises the simplistic thinking and hypocrisies these groups represent, self-exploitations that can only add to the misery, impoverishment, and isolation of the black community. The clash, the cataclysm, is inevitable, however, and at book's end his detectives stand impotently by, shooting at rats as they swarm from a tenement under demolition. The novel's final words are:

"That don't make any sense."
"Sure don't."[34]

The investigation is over, abandoned. The self-interrogations—of the detective story, of Harlem, of American society—are done. We are all guilty, and Chester Himes has written our confession.

19 The Bad Mother

In the last years Lesley would shower and dress her husband and, because he refused to stay in all day, take him on long drives through the Spanish countryside where he would sit beside her, looking quite debonair, and soon fall fast asleep. One day they had a flat. Lesley, who knew nothing about changing a tire, got Chester into his wheelchair and positioned so that he could direct her, but proved too weak to loosen the lugs. As she crouched there struggling, two cars pulled up alongside, and, turning to look at Chester, Lesley found that he had moved his chair back and fallen into the ditch. Only his feet were visible, waving in the air above like pennants. Drivers and passengers exited cars angrily, certain that she had knocked this man into the ditch. Once she had convinced them that she was not trying to kill him, that he was her husband and both of them victims of misadventure, the tire got changed in no time.

It was a story the two of them often laughed over in later days, as they did so many other stories. People are forever recalling Chester's laughter: how it would spring up suddenly at the least provocation, how it would change his face and take over the room. Humor, Lesley says, was his last and greatest weapon. And it held out for him, as the strokes shut down compartment after compartment of his brain like rooms never to be come back to, as his speech slurred and became unintelligible and finally stopped, as gradually he lost control of body and of self, almost to the end.

They were by this time in their second home in Spain, a smaller one that Lesley had built without stairs and with doorways wide enough to accommodate Chester's wheelchair, Casa Deros, named after the cat Lesley had sent from England to replace their beloved Griot.

But a few years before, in June 1970, Chester and Lesley had sat with Bill and Roslyn Targ in the courtyard of Casa Griot, into which they had moved four months earlier, drinking Bloody Marys as Roslyn exclaimed "Chester, at last you've got your own house"—at age 61— and they all had a good cry.

Writing had become ever more difficult for Himes these past years. Distractions accounted in part for this: relocations and resettlings, the never-ending search for housing, inquiries from foreign publishers, visitors, joustings with filmmakers. Health problems contributed significantly, as did his boredom with what he'd been writing. He wondered if he had not by this time followed that road to its natural end, burrowed in like a hedgehog and snuffled out like a fox everything those detective novels had to tell him, so that the experience of writing yet another resembled more the filling-in of a crossword than it did true composition: mere pattern-making. In *My Life of Absurdity* he recalled 1966, when he and Lesley touched down in Aix-en-Provence.

I tried to write. Until then I had written the start of several detective stories. I stuck some paper into my typewriter and started another one. That made the sixth or seventh start. I had a standing contract with Duhamel. I didn't really want to write another detective story or even about Harlem any more or even about American blacks. But I didn't really know anyone else. I knew so little about the French I couldn't even talk about them, much less write about them. I didn't really think too much about them. That's why I became obsessed with a house, and not even my house. When it came right down to the facts, I didn't really know anyone but myself. I didn't go to see French movies or plays or read French books, newspapers, or about French wars, or politics. I had never really arrived in France, but the Americans didn't want me. I wrote quick, short vignettes about the way I saw blacks in their country, or even in other countries. I kept writing about myself, the life of my mind, hoping to put these vignettes together into a book. And it had become very boring.[1]

Among their many visitors during this time was Phil Lomax, who at one point presented himself to Lesley saying that he must speak to Chester in private, wishing to confess that he had plagiarized material of Chester's for an article published under his own name. Chester told him no harm done. During another visit Lomax related something that had happened back home in Brooklyn, when a blind man on the subway pulled out a pistol and shot at the man who had slapped him, killing an innocent bystander. Himes grew obsessed with this story.

> It signaled me but I didn't know how; it was telling me something but I didn't know what. I put my story of Marlene [Regine] aside and concentrated on the beginnings of detective stories I had written . . .
>
> In the meantime Samuel Goldwyn Jr. renewed his option for a year on *Cotton Comes to Harlem*. At the same time he wrote asking me to come to Hollywood to collaborate with him on the screen treatment, all of which he thought I had in my head. At the time my head was filled with the story of *Blind Man with a Pistol*, of which I had written the first three chapters up to the middle of Chapter 4, and I did not want to go to Hollywood.[2]

He finished the book not long after, disparate and seemingly discrete strands of narrative congealing around the image of Lomax's blind man. When the new novel came back from Bill Targ, who had brought out his last in the U.S., with a detailed letter of rejection, Chester wrapped it again and sent it to Roslyn, who in March of 1968 sold it to William Morrow. Chester and Lesley returned to Paris the following month, camping out at Nicole Toutain's apartment and witnessing the start of the student riots.

Back in the States, as well, 1968 was a fulcrum year. The first Kennedy had already gone down; the Watts riots were just around the corner. Memphis lay in wait for Martin Luther King Jr., L.A. for Robert Kennedy, a lectern in the Audubon Ballroom, Harlem, for Malcolm X. Three civil-rights workers were murdered down in Mississippi. During the summer Olympics in Mexico City two African-American athletes were suspended for giving a black-power salute. The Tet Offensive also started up that year—along with bloody racial riots on the unreported back lots of Vietnam.

Early September, the couple packed and debarked for Spain, proceeding directly to Alicante and lodging at the Palace Hotel until they found an apartment behind the city's market. There they stayed while having Casa Griot built.

In the building in which we lived we had a wood-burning furnace for central heating taken care of by the doorman, who started it up about three o'clock every afternoon and ran it until midnight. We bought a small gas burner for our bedroom, which was at the back of the apartment with windows opening onto the terrace. We would use the heater in a small bedroom beyond the tiny kitchen which I used as a study. Sun poured into the big front room through the glass panes heating it from nine o'clock in the morning until dark, bleaching all the furniture, reminding me of my landlady in London who used to draw the shades against the sun to protect the furniture.[3]

Following lines of thought pursued also in *Blind Man*, Himes had started a new detective novel, *Plan B*, about a black revolution in which ultimately his two detectives take opposite sides, Grave Digger killing Coffin Ed. There in the Alicante apartment he continued work on the book, though he recognized that it "was gradually heading for disaster."[4] Some years later in an interview with Michel Fabre he recalled the difficulties he'd set for himself:

I started another thriller, called *Plan B*, which is about a largescale black rebellion led by a black subversive organization, but I didn't quite finish it. In it, the man who secretly sends weapons to blacks finds his plan wrecked because black people don't have the political maturity needed to band together into an effective force. Instead of waiting for an organization to form, each one of them begins shooting white people for his own personal reasons . . . I became uncomfortable with it after a while, because the story became too exaggerated. I originally envisioned a general conflict between the races, but in the final scene Coffin Ed and Grave Digger shoot at each other. One of them takes the side of his race brothers, while the other one chooses to uphold law and order, not because he feels any loyalty to whites, but because the political and social implications of the rebellion are too much for him.[5]

Himes had by this time finished the first volume of the autobiography, for which shortly he would receive an advance of $10,000 from Doubleday, and begun, most likely working from the fictionalized version of his affair with Regine he had earlier sent Roslyn, on the second.

In September 1969, following a stay in Paris and a brief jaunt to London where Chester appeared on the BBC, he and Lesley summarily packed their belongings for the move to Spain but discovered upon arrival that their new house remained only half built. By turns exasperated, furious, and depressed, they found an apartment nearby and, five months later, at last took occupancy, though not without first coming to the verge of litigation over the contractor's malfeasance. Construction fell ever further behind schedule, walls and doorways were set askew, wiring and plumbing were slipshod throughout. Chester recalled watching from afar as unsupervised workers milled about ineffectually. In his letters Himes poured out an unbroken stream of invective against Spain: its roads had ruined his car, the entire country was as racist as the American South, workers were lazy, incompetent, and hopelessly ignorant, no one there was to be trusted, they couldn't even produce acceptable cat food. His railings against publishers continued as well, despite Gallimard's proud launch of *L'Aveugle au pistolet* (*Blind Man with a Pistol*) under its prestigious Du monde entier imprint, the decision of *Le Monde des Livres* to feature him in the center spread it reserved for only the most important writers and issues, interviews with the London magazine *Nova*, the *Sunday Times* and the BBC, and the stream of journalists, critics and students who increasingly wrote or in many cases made the trip to Spain to interview him.

It was a time, too, of strong if distant attachments as Himes sent out from Spain letter after letter, like grappling hooks seeking purchase. There were dozens to John Williams, a long series to Ishmael Reed, finally, even once most others had stopped, cascades of letters to Roslyn Targ. Those letters, the daily mail, were Chester's lifeline and anchor, Lesley said; by them were his days measured, his mood set. Disappointing mail left him distraught and unable to work. Good news, checks, and letters from friends cheered him, leveled him out, made him talkative: "He was so geared up that his mail was the most important thing to him. It was his means of keeping in contact with the world."[6]

Sometimes, as well, it became his means of breaking contact. Deciding that Melvin Van Peebles's hit play *Watermelon Man* had been stolen from an old short story of his, "The Ghost of Rufus Jones," Himes fell out of communication with Van Peebles. Later, he persuaded himself that John Williams had copyrighted anthologized material of his (his Chicago speech "The Dilemma of the Negro Novelist in the United States" in *Beyond the Angry Black*) in order to collect royalties. Williams heard of his complaints and confronted him, explaining that he had done this only to protect Chester's material, but Chester persisted in his belief; soon after, their correspondence fell off, not to be resumed.

Chester's anger, always close to the surface, broke through more and more often now in sudden fits of rage. While Lesley learned to turn these aside, she could never understand them. And while she maintains that Chester was never violent towards her, the question arises again and again in interviews. John Williams recalls a time when, failing to negotiate a step from one room into another at the Albert Hotel, Chester flew into a rage at Lesley, shouting that he *told* her not to wax the floors. There was the time at Walter Coleman's that he supposedly struck her in jealousy over the attention she gave Walter's brother. Ed Pearlstien recalls coming across Chester in the lobby of the Albert Hotel not long after first meeting him.

> He was sitting on a bench, and Lesley was standing in front of him. He was furious about something, and Lesley motioned to me not to stop . . . There had been a racist incident, I think when he went to get a haircut. What impressed me was the intensity of his anger—I could feel it as I passed.[7]

"There was only one time that I saw him lose his temper," Constance Pearlstien insists.

> He and Lesley came in from shopping when Edward and I were living at the Albert Hotel. Chester had one huge bag of oranges, much too full, and it split down the side. Oranges rolled all over our kitchen floor. He yelled at Lesley that it was her fault. She should have gotten a stronger bag or fewer oranges. Edward, Lesley, and I did not answer and we all, Chester included, began picking up the oranges. By the time we'd finished, Chester was laughing at the episode. That was another quality; he could laugh at himself and often did.[8]

Chester's emotional lability, the way in which he could be joking and laughing one moment, then suddenly sullen, closed in, not talking at all, or how he'd pass from fury to laughter in a beat, gets remarked universally. Still, for all the reported incidents of anger, fury, and rage, there remains little evidence of physical violence, and those closest to Himes adamantly deny it. That he often blazed with anger can't be questioned. Nor that sometimes he spoke of, even threatened, physical violence. Years back, in prison, he had learned that physical violence might be circumvented by his intelligence and command of language, a lesson he never quite forgot.

Joe Hunter, who remembers several incidents when, challenged, Himes flew into rages, and who is quick to add that the "violence" remained merely verbal, also suggests that Chester was a man you got to know only so well, to a certain depth, before he instinctively drew back and away.[9] You could see the eyes change, Hunter says; as though curtains had been pulled. Many report Himes's reluctance to talk about himself in person, even though in his writing he would broach the most intimate, cruel, personal things. One questions to what extent all these, the anger and remove as much as the laughter, were protective mechanisms, tools honed early on and kept in good repair for survival.

Only for brief periods had Himes ever felt he was securely in control of his life. Again and again decisions were being made, beyond his ken, by others: school officials, parents, judges, prison guards, editors, publishers, critics. Now, compromised physically by multiple strokes, advancing arthritis and severe back pain, stomach and dental problems, he knew that he was losing control on far more elemental levels. What else could he do but rage—rage, and try to fix in memory the forms of that life slipping away from him, try to make certain the work that had been so much of his life did not fade with him. Rage, and remember, and laugh.

Even if loss was the tonic from which the daily music departed and to which it always returned, still there were many grace notes and bridges.

In 1970 Chester and Lesley flew to New York for the opening of *Cotton Comes to Harlem*. A "Welcome Home, Himes" reception with entertainment by the Jackson Five was held, also a party for Chester at the UN Building, with Ruby Dee, Ossie Davis, and many others in attendance.[10] Among interviewers was *Life*'s Rudolph Chelminski, whose article "The Hard-Bitten Old Pro Who Wrote 'Cotton' Cashes In" began:

> Hollywood has finally cottoned on. The amazing success of the wild detective comedy *Cotton Comes to Harlem* has proved once and for all that movies do not have to be lily-white—or even "integrated"—to be big box office. They can be jet black. Directed entirely in Harlem by black actor-playwright Ossie Davis, *Cotton* has grossed over $6 million in three months.[11]

If Godfrey Cambridge and Raymond St. Jacques in their tailored suits failed to match Himes's own description of Grave Digger and Coffin Ed as "two hog farmers on a weekend in the Big Town,"[12] they nonetheless gave credible, strong performances, and they shared with the detective pair they were recreating at least one important trait, that of imposing presence. As Milliken remarks, the two actors

> had built their careers on their ability to dominate the films they appeared in with no dependence at all on strongly written parts. Both had developed stage presence that went far beyond charismatic, all the way to hypnotic, and they managed to upstage the film's heady combination of erotic nude scenes and noisy gunfights with little more than exchanges of sidelong glances.[13]

Himes's attitude toward the film seems to have shifted according to his audience. He told *Black News* that what he had seen was a minstrel show. In *My Life of Absurdity* he wrote: "On first sight of the film *Cotton* I thought it was badly acted and noisy, but time changed my opinion until I thought it was both reasonably acted and relatively quiet."[14] Elsewhere he criticized the producers for not following his story closely enough, complaining that they had dropped some of his best material; praised Davis's rewrite of the original script by Arnold Perls, which gave the whole a much stronger black orientation; and spoke out against the excessive violence of popular black films.

Among those soon to see *Cotton* was future community activist and crime writer Gary Phillips, then seventeen, and its influence on him was profound.

Up there on the Temple's screen was the tall and menacing Raymond St. Jacques as Coffin Ed Johnson, and a slimmed-down Godfrey Cambridge as the only slightly more reasonable Grave Digger Jones. They were razor sharp in their grey tailored suits, wide black ties offset by their slate-blue shirts, glinting gold cufflinks, and bad-ass felt fedoras shoved down on top of their skulls. Certainly not the lived-in suits and hog farmer builds Himes described his characters as possessing in the books, I'd later discover.

What hit me the second these two cats made the scene was just how cool and aware they were; how they inhabited a world called Harlem I'd only been to once because I had cousins who lived there; and how their Harlem was like my South Central Los Angeles, a place that was part of, yet very much removed from, the rest of America.

The film led Phillips, as it led others, to Chester Himes's books. To the Harlem novels, shot through with violence. To the amazing *Blind Man with a Pistol*. To *Lonely Crusade*, whose insights had Phillips, by then immersed in community work, nodding his head in agreement. Still today, he says, those books affect the very way he thinks and writes.

Himes wrote the Coffin Ed and Grave Digger stories because he was down and out in Paris. Like the ex-patriot African-American jazz men who populated Paris in that era of the Fifties, Himes was riffing and improvising on the typewriter his unique take on detective fiction. His plots were only the starting point as he set down his red hot licks, taking his two crusaders on errands that even they couldn't quite articulate. But in the doing, the being, they existed and blew through a life that promised nothing and delivered less. Coffin Ed and Grave Digger were the original gangstas who lived by their wits and ruthlessness, trying their damndest to keep shit from raining down on their stomping grounds.

Himes got the cosmic joke, and let us in on parts of it in each successive book. I keep trying to follow his lead.[15]

In February 1972 Chester and Lesley flew to New York for the launch of *The Quality of Hurt*, were again met with warm receptions everywhere, and spent several days in North Carolina with Joe and Edward, the first time all three brothers had been together since their mother's funeral. That Christmas Joe and wife Estelle visited them in Spain; the following December, Chester and Lesley flew to New York to visit Edward, then on to Greensboro to see Joe and Estelle. On the February 1972 American visit Chester was widely interviewed and gave a brief speech at a reception for black writers by the Carnegie Endowment for International Peace. One interviewer was Nikki Giovanni, for CBS's *Camera Three*. Another, for *The Village Voice*, was novelist Charles Wright, who found Himes in the Chelsea Hotel, "a place where a man might wait for the countdown or enjoy the spoils of victory," and sat with him admiring "the magnificent Edward Hopper window view" as seventeen-year-old Griot twined about their legs.

> Chester Himes looks like an elegant sportsman, a man of distinction, and—with his beard—bears an uncanny resemblance to Ernest Hemingway. However, Himes is black and basic. "You know there is only one black writer. Just as soon as he makes it, they tear him down. We black writers have got to stop fighting each other. Whitey has always pitted one black against the other. The field slaves and the house slaves. Their motto has always been divide and conquer."[16]

Publishers Weekly also ran a feature in connection with Himes's visit.

> Chester Himes, ex-convict, jewel thief, bedroom athlete, busboy, porter, expatriate, but above all writer, talks about himself— something he does with verve and brilliance—in the first volume of his autobiography, *The Quality of Hurt* (Doubleday), and in conversation with *PW*:
> "I was speaking to a black studies class at Hunter College," he told *PW*, "and the young professor, who was black, kept quoting

from an article in the *Sunday Times Book Review* (which I hadn't read) that said I wasn't a true spokesman for the black race, that the Harlem of my books was not the real Harlem . . .

"Well, I explained that I had created a Harlem of my mind; that I have never attempted to be the spokesman for any segment of the black community. I take my stories from the Black Experience as I have undergone it.

"Before long, the kids were on my side. Young people don't want to confuse stories in books with their own reality. They resent books that claim to show the interior of their minds. They aren't looking for any 'spokesmen.' They can speak for themselves. The best a black writer can do is to deal with subjects which are personal; so he can tell how it was for him."[17]

That is very much what Himes had tried to do, according to his own lights, in *The Quality of Hurt*: to tell how it was for him. A major essay-review from Ishmael Reed for *Black World* (running to twenty-three pages when reprinted in Reed's collection *Shrovetide in New Orleans*) held that Himes had met his charge head-on, deeming the first volume "a big book; big as the career and as the man."[18]

The Quality of Hurt . . . is a love story, sometimes amusing, sometimes sorrowful; it's a cops and robbers story as gory as Peckinpah; it's a story about the tragedies that shatter a proud, noble, and gifted family.[19]

. . .

Volume I . . . is told coolly and objectively, Himes utilizing his considerable novelistic gifts, one of the major qualities of which is a fantastic memory. His descriptions of Los Angeles, Cleveland, and New York geography read like street maps. He and writers like Albert Murray are scholars of Harlem's topography as well as its innards.[20]

. . .

Chester Himes is a great writer and a brave man. His life has shown that black writers are as heroic as the athletes, entertainers, scientists, cowboys, pimps, gangsters, and politicians they might write about.[21]

. . .

The achievement of Volume I is even more staggering when you realize that another volume is on the way. Surely that will be an additional monster destined to mind slam the reader.[22]

Time, meanwhile, was at the barricades of that "fantastic memory." Not long after the New York trip, in April, Chester suffered another stroke and briefly entered the British-American Hospital in Madrid. In August of that year, 1972, Griot died. Himes was devastated, missing him terribly, but Lesley ordered from England a six-month-old Siamese kitten, Deros Cantabile, which Chester received on January 12. While in London on business that September, Himes consulted a number of English specialists who agreed that, given his general condition, there was little more to be done for him regarding his complaints of worsening arthritis, hernia, and stomach pain. Early in the new year he received word that not only was the second Grave Digger/Coffin Ed movie *Come Back, Charleston Blue* failing to make the inroads *Cotton* had, it had lost close to two million dollars. That spring Himes was guest speaker at a Black Literature Week organized by the NAACP in Stuttgart. He read there a revised version of the introduction he had written for Ishmael Reed's anthology *Yardbird Reader* the year before, in which he claimed that the African American, summarily and for so long oppressed, ironically had attained as a result, in transcending his suffering, racial superiority.

His letters make clear Himes's gradual realization that his creative years were over. Hundreds of petty details (house, business correspondence, interviews) claimed his time and what energy he had left. He wrote that he had one more novel in him, and that would be it; that he hoped only to finish the second volume of his autobiography; that he would do whatever he could, travel anywhere, to promote his work and help keep it in print. He fiddled about with older material, assembling stories for a second collection, licensing reprints of the novels, but there was no new work. Loss of physical control—arthritis, severe back pain, increasingly slurred speech—heralded more urgent losses. He was prone to easy distraction and found it ever more difficult to concentrate. Things were getting away from him. He grew absentminded and feared that his memory, too, might be giving way, perhaps the only loss he felt he could not sustain.

He was also, in a sense, losing America, "the bad mother"[23] that had made him what he was and given him his eternal subject. On visits now he felt hopelessly out of touch, scarcely recognizing his erstwhile home, its society alien to him, the ways in which younger blacks thought and spoke all but impenetrable. He must have thought of old friend Richard Wright at the end of *his* career, gone so long from the homeland. And so Himes stood apart and at a hard angle to the new confrontations and accommodations building in America, gazing upon a world ever more surely taking on the shape of the one he had described in the Harlem cycle: bloody, unjust, absurd.

Some time in the sixties, like a hammerblow it had struck an entire circumscribed nation: *Things do not have to be this way.* Young people, blacks, women, and minorities everywhere struggled to break through the crust of the culture's dominant impulses and rediscover accountability, freedom, connection, spirituality. It was a gallant swim upstream against all currents, an attempt to bring on a revolution in values—and perhaps, as well, the last flare of our nation's romanticism. And while the impulse lasted but a few years, brought down by excess, impracticality, and a dilating economy, bringing out at the same time something of the worst and something of the best in us all, a bitter residue remained. Now America was back on track, headed down that long, lonesome road of consumerism and complacency, unable to recollect just why it had ever seen fit to swerve off the road in the first place. It all seemed so impossibly idealistic now—just as had the social dreams of Himes's young manhood. Cynicism and irony were the new hallmarks, as though, having rejected the possibilities of freedom along with its attendant responsibilities, like Caliban we could no longer bear to look straight on into the mirror.

Through it all Chester Himes stood, as always, outside, watching.

America's very permutability, Himes knew, makes sincere difference-taking or protest all but impossible. Protean, the American process absorbs and transforms everything. The larger, commercial culture co-opts transgressive impulses wherever they pop up, subverts them without ever seeming to do so, holds them down and tickles till they give in. In a 1963 article written for a Marseilles jazz magazine Himes contended that white society's talk of equality and justice was little more than bluff and misdirection. The white man, he wrote, believes that if he gives a sufficiently persuasive performance he will convince the world that he earnestly wishes to accede to the Negroes' demands for equality and justice—and perhaps convince the Negroes too. If, in the end, he can do no better, he will try to corrupt the Negroes by allowing them enough of the benefits of American life to divert their desire for equality and justice to the accumulation of wealth (like himself).[24]

Thereby dissipating, Himes continues, the very qualities of humanity that Negroes have earned in their generations of oppression. Often it seemed *all* bluff, misdirection and distraction. Here again is Ishmael Reed, the closest we have to a direct successor to Himes, looking back on Chester's visit:

> In 1972, when Chester Himes made his triumphant return to the United States on the occasion of the publication of the first volume of his autobiography, *The Quality of Hurt*, the establishment was just beginning to take revenge on black men for having caused much of the political ferment of the 1960s.
> Aware of this atmosphere, Himes said, prophetically, on the television show *Soul*, that the establishment was going to start a war between black men and black women. Himes was right. And so, unlike in the 1960s, when a vague entity known as the "white power structure" was blamed for the continuing problems of many African Americans, by the late 1980s, African Americans, or more specifically, black men, were blamed for these problems.[25]

Whether or not one accepts that observation, even the most cursory glimpse at recent work by Toni Morrison, Alice Walker, Terry McMillan, Gloria Naylor, and others (for it is—this, too, calling out for thought—black women who today among African-American novelists get *read*) has to give one pause. Atop the age-old hatred for the white, oppressor society, like a layer of sedimentary rock, is a secondary layer of rage against the shiftless, shirking, predatory black man, what Sven Birkerts has called "the story of the black matriarchy as written with a poisoned pen."[26]

Citing Himes's contention that black people in this country are the only new race in modern times, Reed elsewhere argues that "nothing in history quite happened like it happened here" and that it's for this reason that African-American fiction, while abjuring the weight of the white literary past, is forever historical in a way white fiction can never be. Addressing the confusion of white readers over loose-jointed, nonconformist African-American fiction, he might well be speaking of Himes; certainly he has him squarely in mind.

> So this is what we want: to sabotage history. They won't know whether we're serious or whether we are writing fiction. They made their own fiction, just like we make our own. But they can't tell whether our fictions are the real thing or whether they're merely fictional. Always keep them guessing. That'll bug them, probably drive them up the walls. What it comes down to is that you let the social realists go after the flatfoots out there on the beat and we'll go after the Pope and see which action causes a revolution. We are mystical detectives about to make an arrest.[27]

In sparsely populated auditoriums of the mind, Reed falls silent and out there in the darkness beyond the footlights we hear Chester Himes, a man who knew a great deal about confusing them and who took great pleasure in bugging them till they climbed the walls, a man who knew not a little, as well, about mystical detectives, begin to applaud.

20 "I Never Found a Place I Fit"

Toward the end Chester had grown so frail, his contractures so terrible, that, forcing his arms down to bathe or dress him, even to take his blood pressure, Lesley feared she might break his bones. Who would have thought I'd wind up like this, a cabbage? he asked her. When she read to him reviews of his work, letters or copies of essays written by young admirers, tears came to his eyes. He cried often, those last months. Finally he stopped speaking. One morning instead of following her with his eyes he turned his head toward her, and Lesley understood that he could no longer see.

Late in May of 1974, Chester had entered University College Hospital in London for prostate and hernia surgery. Arthritis had become so bad, deterioration of his spinal column had so progressed, that even the physical effort of typing seemed too much for him. Two strokes had swept through his brain like thunderstorms, leaving wreckage and devastation behind. Now, following surgery, another occurred and, left side of his brain deprived of blood supply and oxygen, Chester fell into a brief coma, waking to find that he had lost further motor control. A string of visits to medical facilities would follow: that June to a Spanish clinic for hemorrhages, in September a return there, the following month a trip to the American Hospital in Paris, then in January another to Madrid for a checkup; in November 1976, following publication of *My Life of Absurdity*, a visit to New York's Presbyterian Hospital for tests and consultations. Chester's movement had become so restricted that Lesley feared leaving him alone. Nor was his mind often clear. His irritability, his irascibility, flew at the many walls closing in on him. Lesley wrote to his brother Joe that Chester was losing his memory, breaking into rages over the least upset. Chester himself not long before had written to Roslyn that he could scarcely walk and that he feared his mind, like the use of his legs, was going. "I don't think I can continue,"[1] he told his new editor at Doubleday, Larry Jordan, after seeing Jordan's editing of the manuscript of *My Life of Absurdity*. Whether from introspection brought on by his work on the autobiography or from an inwardness ushered in by declining health, Chester found his way toward voicing regrets. In a September letter to Roslyn he begged forgiveness for his bad behavior and lack of thoughtfulness.[2] Three months later he wrote her that he had been "an unmitigated pig" toward most women: "I was such a detestable person it makes me sick to write about myself . . ."[3]

What concentration and resources of will he had left, Chester largely expended on finishing the second volume of the autobiography, stubbornly typing away at it with two fingers while Lesley, in another room, labored to make sense of and retype his pages. By spring of 1975 they had stitched together a first draft of the manuscript. That July, Chester and Lesley visited Chester's cousin Robert Thomas, who was working at the U.S. Embassy in Lisbon. Fall visitors to Spain included old friends Jean Miotte and Herb Gentry. A later visit, to Lesley's family in England (spring 1977) did not go well. Edgy and tense the whole time, Chester began ranting when Lesley's brother-in-law tousled her hair; on the third day he insisted they return to Spain.

Another project, Chester's proposed follow-up to 1971's collection *Black on Black*, finally saw light in 1982 when Lieu Commun published *Le Manteau de rêve*. *Black on Black* had brought together stories mostly from the thirties and forties, Chester's script for *Baby Sister* being the notable exception. This record of one soul's struggle against all the forces conspiring to cheapen and degrade it serves as a précis of Himes's eternal theme. In both form and theme, Milliken points out, *Baby Sister* is indeed quite close to Greek tragedy:

> It is, at least in part, an exercise in awe before the phenomenon of human greatness, the classic tragic formula. It offers a protagonist who is larger than life, heroically intense, crushed by forces that are inexorable and irrational but also predictable and consistent. It has the stark simplicity of myth and the precise symmetry of ritual.[4]

The scenario restricts itself to three days, each day culminating in an act of violence against Baby Sister. With this introduction to a familiar Himesland, the film's narrator sets the tone early on:

> Only the *will* of the community can save her from the wolves. But the inhabitants of this community, restricted, exploited, prostituted, violated and violent, timid and vicious, living in their rat-ridden, hotbox, stinking flats, are either the hungry wolves themselves, or are struggling desperately to save themselves from the hungry wolves.[5]

Le Manteau de rêve completed the summing up of Himes's early work begun with the initial volume. Originally to be titled *Black on White*, it collected such stories as "Crazy in the Stir," "The Ghost of Rufus Jones," "Spanish Gin," "The Snake," "One Night in New Jersey," "A Night of New Roses," and "In the Rain." The book was dedicated

> To Lesley, my wife,
> for her love, her patience,
> her good humor and her solicitude.
>
> To Mrs. Roslyn Targ,
> my dear friend and my literary agent
> who has believed in me all these years.
>
> To Professor Michel Fabre,
> for his friendship and assistance.

The book's cover (by Yves Besnier) depicts a white-bearded, pensive Himes sitting alone in a room of bare walls and tiled floor, cane in hand, overcoat draped across the back of the chair. He is well dressed in sweater and sharply creased slacks, good shoes, yet seems to be dissolving: part of the crosshatch of the wicker chair's back shows through his body.

In these last years Himes's spirits and temperament careened back and forth from bravado to lamentation. One moment he had become in his own mind a social force to be reckoned with, a prophet for young blacks back in America, a hero for the cause; in the next he and his books were forgotten, he said, beaten down by time's hammers or by disinterest, discarded, cast aside. He wrote to editor Larry Jordan that America was the "bad mother," that all his life he'd been America's whipping boy, that he'd tried again and again, and against all reason, to force America to "forgive" him.[6] "His self-absorption had made it hard for him to imagine that most Americans had not heard of him,"[7] Fabre and Margolies note, though at another level of mind, given that he knew the fate of his books in the United States, he must also have known (this knowledge held suspended in contradiction) the truth of his situation.

But anything can keep you afloat if you grab it hard enough and hold on, and that was Himes's lifeline: that sense of his work, that all this had been *for* something. Very little is needed to destroy a man, Artaud wrote; he needs only the conviction that his work is useless— against all intimations of which Chester now pitched his final struggle, wrestling the angels of history.

In his poem "In Memory of Joe Brainard" Frank Bidart speaks of

> *the remnant of a vast, oceanic*
> *bruise (wound delivered early and long ago)*

and goes on:

> In the end, the plague that full swift runs by
> took you, broke you;—
> > *in the end, could not*
> > *take you, did not break you—*[8]

That vast, oceanic bruise, Chester knew well. He spent his life trying to understand it, giving himself over to doubt, passion, the madness of art, and if, in the end, of the three it was doubt that surfaced most surely, that doubt was not directed toward the work itself, the worth and value of which Himes rarely doubted, but toward the question of whether the work, so contrary, so sideways, so long in contempt of the larger society, would be allowed to endure. To Lesley in the final days he said:

> Would you . . . keep my books alive? I don't want to feel that I have
> lived without having accomplished something that's going to be

remembered and I don't want to leave this world a common shade and I do so hope that my books will be read and that people will remember me.[9]

The world is taken from us, as it was given, by degrees. We learn to close doors knowing we'll not come back to these rooms again. People, faculties, memories go away from us, and only slowly, with time, do we realize they are gone; only then do we begin to miss them. However he presumes to do so, a man can never sum up his life, as Chester tried to do, at the end; rather, he is summed up by it. But if he is a thoughtful man, a writer, Reed's mystical detective, he has the privilege of being able to record the forces at work upon him both from within and without. In *My Life of Absurdity* Chester wrote:

> I travelled through Europe trying desperately to find a life into which I would fit; and my determination stemmed from my desire to succeed without America . . .
>
> I never found a place where I even began to fit[.][10]

The bruise would not fade, the bad mother would not be left. Yet Chester Himes had long ago determined, like his stand-in Brightlights in the story "Prison Mass," that he would pass through life no common shade. In one of his last works, "Island of Hallucinations," intended as a sequel to *The Long Dream*, Chester's friend Richard Wright addressed through an amanuensis the loss of racial history and the necessity of witnessing:

> "Fish," Ned said, "our race has no memory. Each generation lives as though no one has lived before it. What my father learned from his living died with him . . . You can't blame your father if he died and left you poor; maybe he had no chance to control the economic forces that shaped his destiny. But, dammit, we can blame our fathers for dying and leaving us ignorant of what they encountered in life, what they felt about it. Now, Fish, it is to try to establish that continuity of experience that makes me talk to you like this."[11]

Chester would not leave those who came after him ignorant. His life, his work, would be a record. *I am a man, Jupiter*, he said to his jailers—addressing himself as much as the others. He was, Milliken writes, "a man in the business of making verbal scale models of the world as he has known it, felt it, and lived it . . . a constructor of elaborate extended metaphors designed to guide readers into his own unique and private realm of experience."[12] And so he has left this amazing many-volumed record of what it was like, from his perspective, to live in his time, a record of encounters and collisions. He did not choose racism as his subject, but

he drove deeper into the subject than anyone ever had before. He recorded what happens to a man when his humanity is questioned, the rage that explodes within him, the doubts that follow, and the fears, and the awful temptation to yield, to embrace degradation.[13]

In April 1976, four months after a final version of *My Life of Absurdity* reached Doubleday, at Jean Miotte's suggestion Chester and he began a series of conversations intended to become a book but Chester, unable to concentrate and exhausted by the effort, soon gave up. He was fiddling about with the contents of *Black on White*, but even correspondence had become too much for him; at one point he began a letter to Larry Jordan only to apologize that he would have to let Lesley finish it for him. Stephen Milliken sent copies of his book on Himes's work, which appeared that year and of which Chester thought highly; James Lundquist's study also came out. Chatham Bookseller had begun republishing his older novels and planned an edition of *The End of a Primitive*, but in 1978 wrote that it was bankrupt. Chester was pleased with Yves Malartic's translation and editing of the autobiography into a single volume for publication by Gallimard. French editions of *Cast the First Stone* and of *A Case of Rape* in a new translation were due that fall. That fall as well, in October, a film crew came to Moraira to make a TV documentary on Himes. In November his divorce from Jean was final; later that month he and Lesley traveled to England to marry.

In May 1980 Chester and Lesley flew again to the United States. Tests at the Mason Clinic in Seattle confirmed what they had been told in Paris and Marseilles: the left side of Chester's brain was virtually destroyed and there would be further, inevitable decline; neither medication nor treatment of any sort could counteract this. While on this visit Chester was given a party by the staff of *The Black Scholar* and much fussed over by Bay Area writers. Ishmael Reed wrote of the visit:

> Though disabled by a series of strokes, Chester Himes and his devoted wife, Lesley, managed to visit the United States for the last time in the summer of 1980. Writer Floyd Salas and I greeted them at the airport with flowers. He was celebrated by the Northern California literary community. He didn't talk very much, but the wit and the mischief were still there. I remember the gleam in his eyes, that which Carl Van Vechten captured in one of his portraits of Himes, when Lesley recounted how he'd recently run into trouble with Spanish courts for engaging members of the police force in a gun battle. He'd mistaken them for burglars. "It was the kind of gun you'd shoot an elephant with," Lesley said. Bad contracts with publishers had left Himes in need of funds during his last years. As a nominator for a foundation with billions at its disposal, I tried to obtain a grant for Chester. Instead, the money went to members of the permanent graduate school that's done so much to turn American poetry into gibberish and alienate the average reader and student from verse. Unlike Himes's friend, the intellectually daring and political hot potato Richard Wright, who died under mysterious circumstances surrounded by enemies, Himes managed to survive his critics and to see the country that hurt him so honor him, however belatedly.[14]

During their stay Chester and Lesley were guests not only in Ishmael Reed's home but also in that of Maya Angelou. Lesley recalls Angelou setting the table with absolutely huge plates and glasses, explaining that *she* was such a big woman she had to have everything about her big: a reflection of the poet's appetite for life that Chester must have enjoyed. Another time she queried how he responded when asked what kind of books he wrote. That had always been a problem, Chester told her, but he thought that from now on he was just going to say he wrote best-sellers. On their next shopping trip Angelou did just that, Lesley laughing the whole time, when a shopgirl posed the question.

Sometimes visibly disoriented on the California visit, Chester, upon returning to Spain where he received copies of Bill Targ's fine limited edition of *A Case of Rape*, seemed to rally. Chester and Lesley moved from Casa Griot into Casa Deros; *Le Manteau de rêve* was published to good notices and sales; the same publisher, Lieu Commun, in 1983 brought out *Plan B*, reconstituted from drafts and a detailed summary that Michel Fabre discovered among Chester's papers.

One of the most important things any writer or other artist does is to try to make the world large again, to reinvest it, or our attentions to it, with something of the grandness, mystery, and wonder everywhere about us, to break through the crust of dailyness, of our habits and self-limitations. But Chester's world now was shrinking daily, receding into itself. He could no longer read. The correspondence that had meant so much to him, that had been for so long his connection to the world, was beyond him now, increasingly of little interest. He grew ever weaker. One morning he woke to find all use of his legs gone; by July he had become totally paralyzed. There were severe blockages in his arteries, an aneurysm near his heart. His esophagus had grown so contorted that he had great difficulty swallowing, eventually being put on a liquid diet when he refused to eat. Finally he gave up even speaking, though Lesley believed that he might still have had the capacity and heard him, hours before he died, murmur "Oh Lord, oh Lord."

Lesley tried to see to and to anticipate all his needs. On the morning of November 13, 1984, alarmed at Chester's appearance—he had become so pale, she thought, and somehow insubstantial, as though he were fading before her eyes—Lesley called the doctor, who came and told her that Chester would be dead within hours, then a priest, who failed to arrive in time. Wishing no pictures to be taken of Chester in his drained, emaciated state and this being the custom in Spain, Lesley prevailed upon the mortician, a fan of Chester's work, to help. He did so, taking the coffin to an older, little-used graveyard in Benissa to divert journalists there before returning it to the newer cemetery just in time for the graveside service. The plaque Lesley placed by her husband reads:

Chester Himes
Escritor
Missouri, USA, 1909
Moraira, 1984
Su esposa Lesley

What all art finally asks is this: How should we live, and how work against the self-destructive nature of ourselves and our history? If there are no final answers—and one suspects there are not—there is still great privilege and honor in forming the material of our individual lives and our times, as Chester Himes did again and again, into the very shape of the question.

A fellow Triestine who had known the great writer Italo Svevo for decades once wrote to Eugenio Montale about the danger of overanalyzing Svevo, of coming to see him as something more than just a man who wrote—a man like the rest of us, spilling over with faults, failures, fears, foibles—thereby turning his life into legend. What this correspondent said might well have gone on the marker of Chester Himes's final resting place: "All he had was genius, no more."

Selected Bibliography

Bailey, Frankie Y. *Out of the Woodpile: Black Characters in Crime and Detective Fiction*. New York, Westport, and London: Greenwood Press, 1991.

Baker, Houston A., Jr. *Blues, Ideology, and Afro-American Literature: A Vernacular Theory*. Chicago: University of Chicago Press, 1984.

Baldwin, James. *Collected Essays*. New York: Library of America, 1998.

————. *The Price of the Ticket: Collected Nonfiction 1948–1985*. New York: St. Martin's/Marek, 1985.

Bell, Bernard W. *The Afro-American Novel and Its Tradition*. Amherst: University of Massachusetts Press, 1987.

Berry, Faith. *Langston Hughes Before and Beyond Harlem*. Westport, Conn.: Lawrence Hill & Company, 1983.

Bone, Robert. *The Negro Novel in America*. New Haven and London: Yale University Press, 1965. (Revised edition of 1958 publication.)

Bontemps, Arna Wendell. *The Harlem Renaissance Remembered*. New York: Dodd, Mead, 1994.

Campbell, James. *Paris Interzone*. London: Secker & Warburg, 1994.

————. *Talking at the Gates: A Life of James Baldwin*. New York: Viking Penguin, 1992.

Cooke, Michael. *Afro-American Literature in the Twentieth Century: The Achievement of Intimacy*. New Haven: Yale University Press, 1984.

Ellison, Ralph. *Going to the Territory*. New York: Random House, 1986.

————. *Invisible Man*. New York: The Modern Library, 1994.

————. *Shadow and Act*. New York: Random House, 1964.

Fabre, Michel. *From Harlem to Paris: Black American Writers in France, 1840–1980*. Urbana and Chicago: University of Illinois Press, 1991.

———— and Skinner, Robert, eds. *Conversations with Chester Himes*. Jackson: University Press of Mississippi, 1995.

Franklin, H. Bruce. *Prison Literature in America*. New York: Oxford University Press, 1989. (Expanded edition of *The Victim as Criminal and Artist*, Oxford 1978.)

Gates, Henry Louis, Jr. *The Signifying Monkey: A Theory of Afro-American Literary Criticism*. New York: Oxford University Press, 1988.

Harrington, Oliver W. *Why I Left America and Other Essays*. Jackson: University Press of Mississippi, 1993.

Hughes, Carl Milton. *The Negro Novelist.* New York: Carol Publishing Group, 1990. (Originally published 1953.)

Kostelanetz, Richard, ed. *On Contemporary Literature.* New York: Avon Books, 1964, 1969.

Lundquist, James. *Chester Himes.* New York: Frederick Ungar, 1976.

Margolies, Edward. *Native Sons.* Philadelphia and New York: J.B. Lippincott, 1968.

——. *Which Way Did He Go?* New York: Holmes & Meier Publishers, Inc., 1982.

—— and Fabre, Michel. *The Several Lives of Chester Himes.* Jackson: University Press of Mississippi, 1997.

Martin, Roger, ed. *Hard-Boiled Dicks #8–9.* Paris: L'Introuvable, December 1983. (Special Himes issue.)

Milliken, Stephen F. *Chester Himes: A Critical Appraisal.* Columbia: University of Missouri Press, 1976.

Muller, Gilbert H. *Chester Himes.* Boston: Twayne Publishers, 1989.

O'Brien, Geoffrey. *Hardboiled America: Lurid Paperbacks and the Masters of Noir.* New York: Da Capo Press, 1997.

Palmer, Robert. *Deep Blues.* New York: Viking Penguin, 1981.

Peplow, Michael W. *George Schuyler.* Boston: Twayne Publishers, 1980.

Rampersand, Arnold. *The Life of Langston Hughes.* New York and Oxford: Oxford University Press, 1986 and 1988.

Reed, Ishmael. *Shrovetide in Old New Orleans.* New York: Atheneum, 1989.

——. *Writin' Is Fightin'.* New York: Atheneum, 1988.

Sawyer-Lauçanno, Christopher. *The Continual Pilgrimage: American Writers in Paris, 1944–1960.* San Francisco: City Lights Books, 1992.

Schuyler, George S. *Black No More.* New York: The Macmillan Company, 1971.

Silet, Charles L.P., ed. *The Critical Response to Chester Himes.* Westport and London: Greenwood Press, 1999.

Skinner, Robert. *Two Guns from Harlem: The Detective Fiction of Chester Himes.* Bowling Green: Bowling Green State University Press, 1989.

Soitos, Stephen F. *The Blues Detective: A Study of African American Detective Fiction.* Amherst: University of Massachusetts Press, 1996.

Walker, Margaret. *Richard Wright: Daemonic Genius.* New York: Warner Books, 1988.

Williams, John A. *Flashbacks: A Twenty-Year Diary of Article Writing.* Garden City, NY: Anchor Press, 1973.

——. *The Man Who Cried I Am.* New York: Quality Paperback Book Club, 1994. (Originally published 1967.)

——. *The Most Native of Sons.* New York: Doubleday, 1970.

Wright, Richard. *Richard Wright Reader.* Ellen Wright and Michel Fabre, eds. New York: Da Capo Press, 1997.

Works by Chester Himes

Black on Black. Garden City: Doubleday, 1973.

A Case of Rape. New York: Carroll & Graf, 1994.

Cast the First Stone. New York: Signet, 1952.

The Collected Stories. New York: Thunder's Mouth Press, 1990.

The End of a Primitive. New York and London: W. W. Norton & Company, 1997.

The Harlem Cycle. Edinburgh: Payback Press, 1996–97.

  Vol. 1: *A Rage in Harlem*
       The Real Cool Killers
       The Crazy Kill
  Vol. 2: *The Big Gold Dream*
       All Shot Up
       The Heat's On
  Vol. 3: *Cotton Comes to Harlem*
       Blind Man with a Pistol
       Plan B

 (Also published individually by New York: Vintage Crime, 1988–89.)

If He Hollers Let Him Go. New York: Thunder's Mouth Press, 1986.

Lonely Crusade. New York: Thunder's Mouth Press, 1986.

My Life of Absurdity. New York: Paragon House, 1990.

Pinktoes. New York: Dell, 1966.

The Primitive. New York: Signet, 1955.

The Quality of Hurt. New York: Paragon House, 1990.

Run Man Run. New York: Dell, 1966.

The Third Generation. New York: Thunder's Mouth Press, 1989. New York: Signet, 1956.

Yesterday Will Make You Cry. New York and London: W. W. Norton & Company, 1998.

Notes

1. Unnatural Histories

1. *My Life of Absurdity*, p. 391.
2. *The Harlem Cycle*, Vol. 2, p. xv.
3. *Writin' Is Fightin'*, p. 123.
4. *My Life of Absurdity*, p. 391.
5. *The Quality of Hurt*, pp. 65–66.
6. Muller, p. ix.
7. *Conversations with Chester Himes*, p. 68.
8. Lundquist, p. 117.
9. *The Harlem Cycle*, Vol. 3, p. 379;Vintage, p. 191.
10. *My Life of Absurdity*, p. 106.
11. *Cakes and Ale* (New York and London: Penguin Books, 1988), pp. 201–202.
12. *The Quality of Hurt*, p. 4.
13. Ibid., p. 5.
14. *The Third Generation* (Signet), p. 26.
15. *The Quality of Hurt*, p. 22.
16. *The Third Generation*, p. 26.
17. Ibid., p. 38.
18. Ibid., p. 37.
19. Ibid., p. 32.
20. *The Quality of Hurt*, p. 4.
21. Chester Himes to Carl Van Vechten, Feb. 18, 1947, Yale.
22. *The Quality of Hurt*, p. 5.
23. "The Dilemma of the Negro Writer in America," *The Harlem Cycle*, Vol. 2, p. xii.
24. *The Souls of Black Folk*, p. 215.
25. From diploma, quoted in Fabre/Margolies, p. 5.
26. "The Atlanta Compromise," 1895.
27. "East St. Louis Riots", *Report of the Special Committee Document No. 1231*, 65th Congress, 2nd Session.
28. Ibid.
29. Claude McKay, "If We Must Die," *Selected Poems of Claude McKay* (New York: Bookman Associates, 1953), p. 36.

30. *The Quality of Hurt,* p. 8.
31. *The Third Generation,* p. 117.
32. *The Quality of Hurt,* p. 13.
33. *The Third Generation,* p. 142.
34. *The Quality of Hurt,* p. 14.
35. Ibid., p. 13.
36. *The Third Generation,* p. 143.
37. Ibid., p. 153.
38. Ibid., p. 155.
39. Ibid., pp. 155–56.
40. *The Quality of Hurt,* p. 16.
41. *The Third Generation,* p. 184.
42. *The Quality of Hurt,* p. 16.
43. *Which Way Did He Go?,* p. 55.
44. *The Quality of Hurt,* p. 47.
45. *The Third Generation,* p. 200.
46. Ibid., p. 201.
47. *The Quality of Hurt,* p. 18.
48. Ibid., p. 20.
49. *The Third Generation,* p. 221.
50. *The Quality of Hurt,* p. 24.
51. Ibid., p. 25.
52. Ibid., p. 27.
53. *The Third Generation,* p. 235.
54. *The Quality of Hurt,* p. 28.
55. Ibid., p. 29.
56. *The Third Generation,* p. 245.
57. *The Quality of Hurt,* p. 31.
58. Ibid., p. 36.
59. Ibid., pp. 37–38.
60. Ibid., p. 38.
61. Ibid., p. 39.
62. Ibid., p. 42.
63. Ibid., p. 47.
64. Ibid.
65. Ibid.
66. Ibid.
67. Ibid., p. 51.
68. *Collected Stories,* p. 173 ("Prison Mass").
69. *The Quality of Hurt,* p. 52.
70. Ibid., p. 56.
71. Milliken, p. 22.
72. *Cast the First Stone,* p. 19.

2. 59623

1. *Crisis*, May 1919, "Returning Soldiers" (editorial).
2. *The Quality of Hurt*, p. 60.
3. Ibid., p. 60.
4. *Prison Literature in America*, p. 210.
5. *The Quality of Hurt*, p. 61.
6. Ibid., pp. 65–66.
7. Ibid., p. 3.
8. *Cast the First Stone*, p. 20.
9. *The Quality of Hurt*, p. 61.
10. Ibid., p. 117.
11. *My Life of Absurdity*, p. 125.
12. *Cast the First Stone*, p. 19.
13. Milliken, p. 136.
14. *The Quality of Hurt*, p. 62.
15. Ibid., p. 62.
16. Ibid., p. 65.
17. *Collected Stories*, p. 191.
18. *The Quality of Hurt*, p. 64.
19. *Cast the First Stone*, p. 124.
20. Introduction to *The Harlem Cycle*, Vol. 1, p. x.
21. Joe Himes to Bob Skinner, quoted in *Two Guns from Harlem*, p. 10.
22. *The Quality of Hurt*, p. 64.
23. Ibid., p. 64.
24. Milliken, p. 40.
25. Skinner p. 11.
26. Milliken, p. 32.
27. *Stories*, p. 148.
28. *Esquire*, Aug. 1934, p. 28.
29. Ibid., Oct. 1934, p. 10. A different version appears in *Stories*, pp. 283–84.
30. *Cast the First Stone*, p. 137.
31. *Blind Man with a Pistol*, Vintage p. 73; *The Harlem Cycle*, Vol. 3, p. 261.
32. *Pinktoes*, p. 109.
33. *Conversations*, p. 77.
34. *Black on Black*, p. 132.
35. *Conversations*, p. 59.
36. *Abbott's Weekly and Illustrated News*, December 1933, quoted in Milliken.
37. *Cast the First Stone*, p. 112.
38. Ibid., p. 126.
39. Ibid., p. 302.
40. Ms. version of novel, Yale, p. 382.
41. Ibid.
42. Chester Himes to Carl Van Vechten, Feb. 18, 1947, Yale/Amistad.
43. Milliken, p. 1.

44. *Cast the First Stone*, p. 303.
45. *Conversations*, p. 23.

3. "One Way to Be a Nigger"

1. "A Nigger," *Black on Black*. p. 132.
2. *Stories*, p. 213 ("The Meanest Cop in the World").
3. Ibid., p. 55 ("With Malice Toward None").
4. Ibid., p. 24 ("All God's Chillun Got Pride").
5. Ibid.
6. *If He Hollers*, p. 2.
7. *Stories*, p. 364 ("Daydream").
8. Ibid, pp. 370–71 ("Da-Da-Dee").
9. *The Quality of Hurt*, p. 66.
10. Ibid., p. 67.
11. Ibid., p. 66.
12. Ibid.
13. Fabre and Margolies, p. 40.
14. Chester Himes to Carl Van Vechten, Sept. 13, 1946, Yale.
15. "The Negro Artist and the Racial Mountain," *Nation* 122, summer 1926, pp. 692–94.
16. "It's About Time," Langston Hughes papers at Beinecke Library, James Weldon Johnson Collection, Yale University; quoted in Rampersand, *The Life of Langston Hughes*, Vol. 2, p. 119.
17. *The Life of Langston Hughes*, p. 134.
18. *The Quality of Hurt*, p. 71; Chester Himes to John A. Williams, Oct. 31, 1962, quoted in Skinner, p. 12.
19. Ibid., p. 71.
20. Quoted in Milliken, p. 31, from telephone conversation with Moody.
21. Seid to Fabre, 1988, quoted in Fabre and Margolies, p. 43.
22. Levin to Margolies, 1998, quoted in Fabre and Margolies, p. 44.
23. *Stories*, p. 55.
24. *The Quality of Hurt*, p. 72.
25. Ibid., p. 133.

4. The Things a Writing Man Will Do

1. E. B. White, "Book Review," *The Second Tree from the Corner* (New York: Harper & Row, 1948).
2. *Conversations*, p. 53.
3. *The Quality of Hurt*, p. 74.
4. Ibid., p. 73.
5. *Conversations*, pp. 55–56.
6. Ibid., p. 56.
7. Ibid., p. 14.

8. *Black on Black,* p. 224 ("Zoot Riots Are Race Riots")
9. Milliken, p. 61.
10. *Conversations,* pp. 53–54.
11. Chester Himes to John A. Williams, Oct. 31, 1962, Rochester, quoted in Fabre and Margolies, p. 48.
12. *Conversations,* pp. 53–54.
13. Milliken, p. 60.
14. Ibid., p. 65.
15. *A Fan's Notes* (New York: Vintage, 1998), p. 359.
16. *Stories,* p. xi.
17. *Shrovetide in Old New Orleans,* p. 95.
18. *Conversations,* pp. 33–34.
19. Ibid., pp. 33–34.
20. *The Quality of Hurt,* p. 75.
21. Ibid., pp. 75–76.

5. Round Us Bark the Mad and Hungry Dogs

1. *The Quality of Hurt,* p. 76.
2. *Invisible Man,* p. 3.
3. *The Quality of Hurt,* p. 76.
4. Constance Webb Pearlstien to James Sallis, Dec. 10, 1998.
5. Milliken, p. 74.
6. *Conversations,* p. 14.
7. Skinner, p. 15.
8. *The Quality of Hurt,* p. 77.
9. Milliken, p. 71.
10. *The Quality of Hurt,* pp. 76–77.
11. Ibid., p. 93.
12. Ibid.
13. Ibid., p. 13.
14. *Conversations,* p. 37.
15. Chester Himes to Carl Van Vechten, June 10, 1946, Amistad.
16. *The Most Native of Sons,* p. 81.
17. Ibid., p. 93.
18. Ibid., pp. 94-95.
19. Richard Wright, *The Long Dream* (New York: Harper & Row, 1958/1987), p. 290.
20. Margaret Walker, *Richard Wright: Daemonic Genius* (New York: Warner Books, 1988), p. 307.
21. *The Quality of Hurt,* p. 77.

6. "I'm Still Here"

1. *If He Hollers,* p. 1.

2. Ibid., p. 153.
3. Ibid., p. 2.
4. Introduction to *If He Hollers*, p. ix.
5. *Prison Literature in America*, pp. 206–207.
6. Ibid., p. 227.
7. *Conversations*, p. 15.
8. *The Negro Novel in America*, p. 174.
9. Lundquist, p. 46.
10. *If He Hollers*, p. 124.
11. Ibid., p. 4.
12. Lundquist, pp. 29–30.
13. *If He Hollers*, pp. 120–21.
14. Ibid., pp. 3–4.
15. *The Negro Novel in America*, p. 174.
16. Muller, p. 28.
17. *If He Hollers*, pp. 35–36.
18. Ibid., p. 38.
19. Ibid., p. 74.
20. Ibid., pp. 84–89.
21. Ibid., p. 101.
22. Ibid., pp. 127–28.
23. Ibid., pp. 150–51.
24. Ibid., p. 152.
25. *Conversations*, p. 86.
26. New York *Herald Tribune Book Review*, Nov. 4, 1945.
27. *Common Ground*, Summer 1946.
28. *Crisis*, Dec. 1945.
29. *American Mercury*, Feb. 1946.
30. Earl Conrad, *Chicago Defender*, Dec. 22, 1945, "The Blues School of Literature."
31. *The Negro Novel in America*, p. 173.
32. Gerald Houghton to James Sallis, March 17, 1999.
33. Chester Himes to Richard Wright, Oct. 19, 1952, Yale.
34. *Conversations*, p. 144.
35. *Richard Wright Reader*, p. 425.
36. *If He Hollers*, p. 88.
37. "The Dilemma of the Negro Novelist in America," *The Harlem Cycle*, Vol. 2, p. xiv.

7. A Street He Could Understand

1. *Hardboiled America*, p. 16.
2. *The Quality of Hurt*, p. 93.
3. *Stories*, pp. 365, 370–71.
4. Ibid., p. 369.

5. *The Quality of Hurt,* p. 78.
6. Ibid., p. 84.
7. Ibid., p. 92.
8. Ibid., p. 93.
9. "Chester Himes—The Ethics of Ambiguity: An Interview with Joseph Sandy Himes, Jr." in *Xavier Review,* Vol. 14, No. 1, Spring 1994.
10. *The Quality of Hurt,* p. 93.
11. Ibid., p. 95.
12. Ibid.
13. "The Average," *W. H. Auden: Selected Poems*, ed. Edward Mendelson (New York: Vintage Books, 1979), p. 105.
14. Chester Himes to Carl Van Vechten, Feb. 28, 1947, Yale.
15. Ibid., Feb. 18, 1947, Yale.
16. Ibid., May 23, 1947, Yale.
17. Robert Frost, "The Fear of God," *Selected Poems* (San Francisco: Rinehart Press, 1963), p. 258.
18. *The Quality of Hurt,* p. 99.
19. Lundquist, p. 13.
20. *New Masses,* Sept. 9, 1947.
21. *Atlantic Monthly,* Oct. 1947.
22. *New York Times Book Review,* Sept. 14, 1947.
23. *The New Yorker,* Sept. 13, 1947.
24. *The New Republic,* Oct. 6, 1947.
25. *Saturday Review of Literature,* Oct. 25, 1947.
26. *New York Herald Tribune,* Sept. 7, 1947.
27. *The Life of Langston Hughes,* p. 134.
28. *The Quality of Hurt,* p. 101.
29. Fabre and Margolies, p. 66.
30. *Conversations,* pp. 39–40.
31. *The Quality of Hurt,* pp. 101–102.
32. Ibid., p. 101.
33. Ibid., p. 103.

8. Going Too Far and Too Far Gone

1. *Lonely Crusade,* p. 207.
2. Fabre and Margolies, p. 65.
3. Muller, pp. 37–38.
4. Milliken, p. 97.
5. Ibid., p. 108.
6. Ibid., p. 112.
7. *The Afro-American Novel and Its Tradition,* p. 177.
8. Muller, p. 36.
9. *Lonely Crusade,* p. 129.
10. Ibid., p. 3.

11. Ibid., p. 354.
12. Milliken, p. 99.
13. "The Well Dressed Man with a Beard," *The Palm at the End of the Mind* (New York: Vintage, 1990), p. 190.
14. *Lonely Crusade,* p. 328.
15. Muller, p. 30.
16. "I Tried to Be a Communist," *Atlantic Monthly,* August 1944.
17. *Lonely Crusade,* p. 85.
18. Ibid., p. 32.
19. Ibid., p. 39.
20. Ibid., p. 40.
21. Ibid., p. 39.
22. Ibid., p. 4.
23. Ibid., p. 7.
24. Ibid., p. 187.
25. Ibid., pp. 7, 8, 122.
26. Ibid., p. 279.
27. Ibid., p. 28.
28. Ibid., p. 133.
29. Ibid., p. 149.
30. Ibid., p. 60.
31. Ibid., p. 61.
32. Ibid., p. 33.
33. Ibid., pp. 33–34.
34. Ibid., p. 14.
35. Ibid., pp. 48–49.
36. *Invisible Man,* p. 244.
37. *Lonely Crusade,* p. 361.
38. *Invisible Man,* p. 347.
39. *Lonely Crusade, p. 75.*
40. Ibid., p. 70.
41. Ibid., p. 328.
42. Ibid., p. 327.
43. Milliken, p. 5.

9. "I Don't Have That Much Imagination"

1. *The End of a Primitive,* p. 36.
2. *The Quality of Hurt,* p. 117.
3. Ibid., p. 103.
4. Ibid.
5. "The City," *Collected Poems* (New Jersey: Princeton University Press), 1992; paraphrased.
6. *Stories,* p. 367 ("Da-Da-Dee").
7. Ibid., p. 365.

8. Ibid., p. 370.
9. *The Quality of Hurt,* p. 104.
10. Ibid., p. 104.
11. *Conversations,* p. 73.
12. *The Quality of Hurt,* p. 104.
13. Ibid., p. 105.
14. Ibid.
15. *The Primitive,* pp. 72–73.
16. Ibid., pp. 142–143.
17. Conversation with Norlisha Crawford.
18. *The Primitive,* pp. 93–94.
19. Reproduced from *The End of a Primitive,* p. 126.
20. *The Primitive,* p. 102.
21. *The Quality of Hurt,* p. 115.
22. Ibid., p. 131.
23. Ibid., p. 74.
24. Ibid., p. 112.
25. Ibid., p. 114.
26. *The Primitive,* pp. 74–75.
27. Ibid., p. 160.
28. *Xavier Review* interview.
29. Chester Himes to Carl Van Vechten, Nov. 23, 1952, Yale.
30. *The Quality of Hurt,* p. 133.
31. *Xavier Review* interview.
32. Ibid., pp. 13–14.
33. Ibid., p. 13.
34. *Conversations,* p. 3.
35. *The Quality of Hurt,* p. 135.

10. Literature Will Not Save You

1. Chester Himes to Carl Van Vechten, Nov. 23, 1952, Yale.
2. *The Quality of Hurt,* p. 135.
3. Ibid., pp. 136, 135.
4. Ibid., p. 136.
5. *Lonely Crusade,* p. 91.
6. *The Quality of Hurt,* p. 136.
7. *The Primitive,* p. 6.
8. Ibid., p. 19.
9. Ibid., p. 22.
10. Ibid., p. 23.
11. Ibid., p. 25.
12. Ibid., p. 22.
13. *The Quality of Hurt,* p. 139.
14. Ibid., p. 136.

15. Ibid., p. 137.
16. Ibid., pp. 137–38.
17. Ibid., p. 139.
18. *Invisible Man*, p. 3.
19. Carl Van Vechten to John A. Williams, Nov. 6, 1962, Yale.
20. Editors' Note, *Yesterday Will Make You Cry*, p. 8.
21. *Saturday Review of Literature*, Jan. 17, 1953.
22. *The New York Times*, Jan. 18, 1953.
23. *New York Herald Tribune*, Jan. 18, 1953.
24. Milliken, p. 137.
25. Ibid., p. 136.
26. Introduction to *Yesterday Will Make You Cry*, p. 19.
27. *Book World*, Feb. 20, 1998.
28. *Publishers Weekly*, Nov. 24, 1997.
29. *Yesterday Will Make You Cry*, p. 363.

11. European Experience

1. *The Quality of Hurt*, p. 161.
2. Ibid., p. 179.
3. Ibid., p. 140.
4. Ibid., p. 144.
5. *Paris Interzone*, p. 120; *From Harlem to Paris*, p. 216.
6. Unpublished manuscript, quoted in *From Harlem to Paris*, p. 218.
7. *From Harlem to Paris*, p. 216.
8. Chester Himes to Carl Van Vechten, Nov. 29, 1962, quoted in *My Life of Absurdity*, p. 252.
9. *The Quality of Hurt*, p. 351.
10. Ibid., p. 162.
11. Ibid., p. 170.
12. Ibid., pp. 165, 166.
13. Ibid., pp. 169, 168.
14. Ibid., p. 224.
15. Interview with Fabre, quoted in *From Harlem to Paris*, p. 243.
16. *The Quality of Hurt*, p. 185.
17. *Conversations*, p. 1.
18. Ibid., p. 3.
19. Ibid.
20. *The Quality of Hurt*, p. 190.
21. Ibid., p. 191.
22. Ibid., p. 192.
23. Ibid., pp. 196–97.
24. "Everybody's Protest Novel," *The Price of the Ticket*, p. 33.
25. Ibid., p. 276 ("Alas, Poor Richard").
26. "The Position of the Negro Artist and Intellectual in American Society," Yale.

27. Ibid.
28. Ibid.
29. *The Price of the Ticket,* p. 278.
30. *The Quality of Hurt,* p. 200.
31. *Conversations,* p. 139.
32. *The Man Who Cried I Am,* p. 217.
33. Ibid., p. 218.
34. Ibid., p. 219.
35. *The Quality of Hurt,* p. 208.
36. *Conversations,* pp. 6–7.
37. *The Quality of Hurt,* p. 219.
38. Ibid., p. 224.
39. Chester Himes to Carl Van Vechten, June 1, 1953, Yale.
40. *The Quality of Hurt,* p. 226.
41. Ibid., p. 233.
42. Ibid., p. 243.
43. *My Life of Absurdity,* p. 14; *The Quality of Hurt,* p. 265.

12. Story-Shaped Life

1. *Confessions of Zeno* (New York: Vintage Books, 1958), p. 332.
2. *The Quality of Hurt,* p. 257.
3. Ibid., p. 256.
4. Ibid., p. 260.
5. Chester Himes to Yves Malartic, Oct. 21, 1953, quoted in Fabre and Margolies, p. 82.
6. Conversation with Lesley Himes.
7. *The Quality of Hurt,* p. 302.
8. *Pharos and Pharillon* (New York: Knopf, 1962), p. 96; "Half an Hour" from *Collected Poems* (New Jersey: Princeton University Press, 1992).
9. *The Quality of Hurt,* p. 286.
10. Ibid., p. 285.
11. *Chicago Tribune Review of Books,* Jan. 10, 1954.
12. *New York Herald Tribune Review of Books,* Jan. 10, 1954; *Library Journal,* Jan. 15, 1954.
13. *Saturday Review of Literature,* March 13, 1954; *San Francisco Chronicle,* Feb. 7, 1954.
14. *Catholic World,* April 1954.
15. *The New York Times,* Jan. 10, 1954.
16. *The End of a Primitive,* p. 123.
17. *The Harlem Cycle,* Vol. 2, p. xiv.
18. Introduction to *The Third Generation* (unpaginated).
19. *Native Sons,* p. 88.
20. *Xavier Review* interview.
21. Milliken, p. 139.

22. Ibid., p. 140.
23. Ibid., p. 145.
24. *The Third Generation*, p. 11.
25. Milliken, p. 147.
26. Ibid., pp. 151, 154.
27. Muller, p. 61.
28. *The Third Generation*, pp. 162–63.
29. Milliken, p. 157.
30. "The Middle Years," *Complete Stories 1892–1898*, The Library of America, 1996.
31. "Nothing Personal," *The Price of the Ticket*, p. 384.
32. Milliken, pp. 151, 154.

13. Doubt, Passion, the Madness of Art

1. *My Life of Absurdity*, p. 7.
2. Ibid., pp. 9–10.
3. Ibid., p. 9.
4. Ibid., p. 6.
5. Ibid., p. 5.
6. Ibid., p. 10.
7. Ibid., p. 15.
8. Ibid., p. 18.
9. Chester Himes to Carl Van Vechten, March 28, 1955.
10. *My Life of Absurdity*, p. 25.
11. *Stories*, p. 191.
12. *My Life of Absurdity*, p. 28.
13. *Run Man Run*, p. 7.
14. *My Life of Absurdity*, p. 23.
15. *New Republic*, May 31, 1943.
16. *Shrovetide in New Orleans*, p. 96.
17. Baldwin, *Collected Essays* (New York: Library of America, 1996).
18. *Stories*, p. 364.
19. *The Quality of Hurt*, p. 349.
20. Ibid., p. 349.
21. Ibid., p. 301.
22. *Conversations*, p. 47.
23. *My Life of Absurdity*, pp. 24–25.
24. *The Southern Manifesto*, 1956.
25. *Prison Literature in America*, pp. 206–207.
26. Ibid., p. 227.
27. *My Life of Absurdity*, p. 25.
28. Ibid., p. 30.
29. Ibid.

14. Beautiful White Ruins of America

1. T. S. Eliot, *Selected Essays* (San Diego, New York, and London: Harcourt Brace Jovanovich, 1988), pp. 7-8.
2. Michel Fabre, "A Case of Rape," *Black World*, March 1972.
3. *The Practice of Writing*, p. 143.
4. Milliken, p. 5.
5. Ibid., pp. 1–2.
6. "Le Chant des sirènes."
7. Lukács, *Theory of the Novel.*
8. *The Primitive*, p. 159.
9. Ibid., p. 6.
10. *The Quality of Hurt*, p. 302.
11. Ibid., p. 305.
12. Milliken, p. 184.
13. Introduction to *The End of a Primitive*, pp. 11–12.
14. *Conversations*, p. 67.
15. Ibid., p. 132.
16. Ibid., p. 133.
17. Irving Howe, "Mass Society and Post-modern Fiction," in *The American Novel Since World War II*, ed. Marcus Klein (New York: Fawcett, 1970).
18. *The End of a Primitive*, p. 13.
19. Ibid., p. 15.
20. Ibid., p. 24.
21. Milliken, p. 195.
22. *The End of a Primitive*, pp. 33, 94–95.
23. Ibid., p. 13.
24. Ibid., p. 75.
25. Ibid., p. 73.
26. Ibid., p. 72.
27. Ibid., pp. 37, 178.
28. Ibid., p. 132.
29. Ibid., p. 148.
30. Milliken, p. 198.
31. The End of a Primitive, pp. 123, 70.
32. Ibid., p. 92.
33. Ibid., p. 190.
34. Ibid., p. 134.
35. Ibid., pp. 203–204.

15. A Serious Savage

1. *My Life of Absurdity*, p. 36.
2. Ibid., pp. 31–32.
3. Ibid., p. 58.

4. *Time,* Oct. 27, 1958.

5. *The Price of the Ticket,* p. 285 ("Alas, Poor Richard").

6. Chester Himes to Carl Van Vechten, April 26, 1956, Yale.

7. *My Life of Absurdity,* p. 36.

8. Ibid., p. 39.

9. Ibid., p. 26.

10. Michel Fabre, "A Case of Rape," *Black World,* March 1972.

11. *My Life of Absurdity,* p. 43.

12. Regine Fischer to Chester Himes, Dec. 1956, Amistad.

13. *My Life of Absurdity,* p. 61.

14. *The Continual Pilgrimage,* pp. 261–62.

15. *My Life of Absurdity,* p. 73.

16. Ibid., p. 74.

17. Ibid., p. 71.

18. Ibid., pp. 69, 72, 73.

19. Ibid., pp. 96–97.

20. Unpublished fragment, Amistad, quoted in Fabre and Margolies, p. 97.

21. *My Life of Absurdity,* p. 79.

22. Ibid., p. 79.

23. Ibid., p. 81.

24. Ibid., p. 88.

25. Ibid., p. 96.

26. Ibid., p. 113.

27. Ibid., pp. 113, 107.

28. Ibid., p. 118.

29. Ibid., p. 121.

16. A New Intelligence

1. *The Primitive,* p. 46.

2. *Lonely Crusade,* p. 95.

3. Ibid., pp. 95–96.

4. Dedication, *Black No More,* p. 35.

5. *Pinktoes,* pp. 24–25.

6. Ibid., p. 24.

7. Ibid., p. 23.

8. Ibid., pp. 95–96.

9. Chester Himes to John A. Williams, Oct. 31, 1962, Yale.

10. Amistad Collection.

11. *My Life of Absurdity,* p. 36.

12. Chester Himes to Carl Van Vechten, June 16, 1956, Yale.

13. *My Life of Absurdity,* p. 221.

14. *Pinktoes,* p. 92.

15. *My Life of Absurdity,* p. 244.

16. *Conversations,* p. 35.

17. The Authors Guild to Chester Himes, Aug. 12, 1968, Amistad.
18. Lundquist, p. 134.
19. *Pinktoes,* p. 82.
20. Ibid., p. 189.
21. Ibid., p. 216.
22. Ibid., pp. 19–20.
23. Ibid., p. 21.
24. Milliken, pp. 10–11.
25. Ibid., p. 269.
26. Quoted in *My Life of Absurdity,* p. 170–71.
27. *My Life of Absurdity,* p. 268.
28. Ibid., p. 268.
29. Michel Fabre, "A Case of Rape," *Black World,* March 1972.
30. *A Case of Rape,* p. 83.
31. Ibid., p. 68.
32. Ibid., p. 98.
33. Ibid., p. 70.
34. Ibid., p. 72.
35. *The Continual Pilgrimage,* p. 204.

17. Gone So Long

1. *My Life of Absurdity,* p. 102.
2. Ibid., p. 102.
3. Introduction, *The Harlem Cycle,* Vol. 1, pp. ix-x.
4. *My Life of Absurdity,* p. 105.
5. Ibid.
6. Ibid., p. 109.
7. Ibid.
8. Ibid., p. 111.
9. *The Continual Pilgrimage,* p. 206.
10. *My Life of Absurdity,* pp. 109–110.
11. Ibid., p. 126.
12. Ibid.
13. Ibid., p. 120.
14. Introduction, *The Harlem Cycle,* Vol. 1, p. xi.
15. Ibid., p. viii.
16. Ibid.
17. Ibid., p. xiii.
18. Joe Himes to James Sallis, Aug. 10, 1998.
19. *My Life of Absurdity,* p. 171–72.
20. Chester Himes to Marcel Duhamel, quoted in Fabre and Margolies, p. 106.
21. Chester Himes to Yves Malartic, December 1958, quoted in Fabre and Margolies, p. 110.
22. Introduction, *The Harlem Cycle,* Vol. 3, p. xii.

23. Ibid., p. xiv.
24. *My Life of Absurdity,* p. 198.
25. Ibid., p. 200.
26. Chester Himes to Carl Van Vechten, Sept. 8, 1960, Yale.
27. Harrington, p. 25.
28. *My Life of Absurdity,* p. 218.
29. Ibid., p. 201.
30. Ibid., p. 213.
31. Chester Himes to Lesley Packard, partially quoted in Fabre and Margolies, p. 121, and in Introduction, *The Harlem Cycle* ,Vol. 3, pp. xv-xvi.
32. *My Life of Absurdity,* p. 270.
33. *From Harlem to Paris,* p. 231.
34. *My Life of Absurdity,* p. 281.
35. "The Dilemma of the Negro Writer in America," *The Harlem Cycle,* Vol. 2, p. xiv.
36. *My Life of Absurdity,* p. 276.
37. Ibid., p. 295.
38. Conversation with Margolies, reported in Fabre and Margolies, p. 137.

18. Black Ruins of My Life

1. Skinner, p. 49.
2. *The Sanctified Church* (New York: Marlowe & Company, 1981), p. 58.
3. Milliken, p. 251.
4. Conversation with Robert Skinner.
5. Lundquist, pp. 24–25.
6. *A Rage in Harlem,* Vintage pp. 49–50; *The Harlem Cycle,* Vol. 1, p. 53.
7. Milliken, p. 226.
8. *A Rage in Harlem,* Vintage p. 44; *The Harlem Cycle* Vol. 1, p. 47.
9. Ibid.
10. *The Real Cool Killers,* Vintage p. 15; *The Harlem Cycle,* Vol. 1, p. 191; *Cotton Comes to Harlem,* Vintage p. 13, *The Harlem Cycle,* Vol. 3, p. 13.
11. *The Crazy Kill,* Vintage p. 28, *The Harlem Cycle,* Vol. 1, p. 356; *The Heat's On,* Vintage p. 9, *The Harlem Cycle,* Vol. 2, p. 329.
12. Milliken, p. 227.
13. *Blind Man with a Pistol,* Vintage p. 175, *The Harlem Cycle* ,Vol. 3, p. 363.
14. Conversations with Robert Skinner.
15. *Blind Man with a Pistol,* Vintage p. 173; *The Harlem Cycle,* Vol. 3, p. 361.
16. Ibid., Vintage p. 175; Ibid., p. 363.
17. Milliken, pp. 241–42.
18. *Blind Man with a Pistol,* Vintage p. 170; *The Harlem Cycle,* Vol. 3, p. 358.
19. Lundquist, p. 125.
20. Ibid., p. 130.
21. Milliken, p. 220.
22. *The Crazy Kill,* Vintage p. 7; *The Harlem Cycle,* Vol. 1, p. 335.

23. *The Heat's On*, Vintage p. 23; *The Harlem Cycle*, Vol. 2, p. 343.
24. *Cotton Comes to Harlem*, Vintage p. 35; *The Harlem Cycle*, Vol. 3, p. 39.
25. *A Rage in Harlem*, Vintage p. 93; *The Harlem Cycle*, Vol. 1, pp. 102–103.
26. *Cotton Comes to Harlem*, Vintage p. 81; *The Harlem Cycle*, Vol. 3, p. 95.
27. *Run Man Run*, p. 28.
28. Ibid., p. 12.
29. Milliken, p. 257.
30. *Run Man Run*, p. 134.
31. Ibid., p. 152.
32. *The Blues Detective*, p. 163.
33. Ibid., p. 126.
34. *Blind Man with a Pistol*, Vintage p. 191; *The Harlem Cycle*, Vol. 3, p. 379.

19. The Bad Mother

1. *My Life of Absurdity*, p. 333.
2. Ibid., p. 347.
3. Ibid., p. 363.
4. Ibid.
5. *Conversations*, p. 135–36.
6. Introduction to *The Harlem Cycle*, Vol. 3, p. xiv.
7. Ed Pearlstien to James Sallis, Nov. 4, 1999.
8. Constance Webb Pearlstien to James Sallis, Dec. 10, 1999.
9. Conversation with Joe Hunter.
10. Lesley Himes to James Sallis, Oct. 22, 1998.
11. *Conversations*, p. 23.
12. *Cotton Comes to Harlem*, Vintage p. 13; *The Harlem Cycle*, Vol. 3, p. 13.
13. Milliken, p. 227.
14. *My Life of Absurdity*, p. 382.
15. Gary Phillips to James Sallis, Jan. 24, 1999.
16. *Conversations*, pp. 112–13.
17. *Conversations*, p. 105.
18. *Shrovetide in Old New Orleans*, p. 98.
19. Ibid., p. 91.
20. Ibid.
21. Ibid., p. 99.
22. Ibid.
23. Chester Himes to Larry Jordan, Feb. 1976, Amistad.
24. "What One Must Know," manuscript at Xavier University Special Collections.
25. "Chester Himes' Last Visit Home," *The Black Scholar*, Vol. 28, No. 1.
26. "A Postscript on Black American Fiction," *American Energies* (New York: William Morrow, 1992), p. 334.
27. Quoted in *The Contemporary Afro-American Novel*, p. 337, note 83.

20. "I Never Found a Place I Fit"

1. Chester Himes to Larry Jordan, Jan. 21, 1976, Amistad.
2. Chester Himes to Roslyn Targ, Sept. 27, 1974, Amistad.
3. Ibid., Dec. 24, 1974, Amistad.
4. Milliken, p. 288.
5. *Black on Black,* p. 11.
6. Chester Himes to Larry Jordan, Feb. 1976, Amistad.
7. Fabre and Margolies, p. 169.
8. Frank Bidart, *Desire* (New York: Farrar, Straus and Giroux, 1997), p. 13.
9. Introduction to *The Harlem Cycle*, Vol. 3, pp. xii–xiii.
10. *My Life of Absurdity,* p. 155.
11. Quoted by Julia Wright, foreword to Harrington, p. xiii.
12. Milliken, p. 305.
13. Ibid., p. 306.
14. *Writin' is Fightin',* pp. 130–31.

Index